This book provides the first full account of legislative recruitment in Britain for twenty-five years. The central concern is why some politicians succeed in moving through the 'eye of the needle' into the highest offices of state. The study explores the dearth of women, black and working-class Members of Parliament, and whether the social bias in the British political elite matters for political representation.

Evidence is drawn from the first systematic surveys of parliamentary candidates, Members of Parliament and party selectors in Britain, as well as detailed personal interviews. This study explores how and why people become politicians, and the consequences for parties, legislatures and representative government.

The book will be of interest to politicians, party activists and journalists, as well providing material for courses in political behaviour, sociology, elections and voting behaviour, political parties, gender politics, racial and ethnic politics, and British politics.

POLITICAL RECRUITMENT

POLITICAL RECRUITMENT

Gender, race and class in the British parliament

Pippa Norris

Harvard University

Joni Lovenduski

Southampton University

CAMBRIDGE
UNIVERSITY PRESS

Published by the Press Syndicate of the University of Cambridge
The Pitt Buildings, Trumpington Street, Cambridge CB2 1RP
40 West 20th Street, New York, NY 10011–4211, USA
10 Stamford Road, Oakleigh, Melbourne 3166, Australia

First published 1995

Printed in Great Britain at the University Press, Cambridge

A calalogue record for this book is available from the British Library

Library of Congress cataloguing in publication data

Norris, Pippa.
Political representation and recruitment : gender, race, and class
in the British parliament / Pippa Norris, Joni Lovenduski.
    p.   cm.
Includes bibliographical references.
ISBN 0 521 46558 3 (hardback)
1. Great Britain. Parliament – Elections.
2. Legislators – Recruiting – Great Britain.
3. Nominations for office – Great Britain.
4. Women legislators – Great Britain.
5. Minorities – Great Britain – Political activity.
6. Representative government and representation – Great Britain.
I. Lovenduski, Joni. II. Title.
JN558.N67 1995
324.6'3'094109045–dc20 94–14115 CIP

ISBN 0 521 46558 3 hardback
ISBN 0 521 46961 9 paperback

CE

Contents

Figures

Tables

Preface

Many debts have been incurred in the course of writing this book. We are most grateful to all party officers, particularly Joyce Gould, Peter Coleman and Vicky Phillips at Labour Party headquarters, and Sir Tom Arnold, Andrew Mitchell and Victoria Braxton at Conservative Central Office, for patiently answering our many queries and providing access to certain records. Conservative agents who helped provide information included Rachel Dyche, Martin Perry, and Donald Stringer. Labour agents and regional officers who helped included Paul Wheeler and Eileen Murfin. The surveys depended upon the constituencies which welcomed us to their meetings, and all MPs, candidates, applicants and party members who took time from busy schedules to complete the questionnaire, or to be interviewed during the course of the project.

We greatly appreciate the support of the Economic and Social Research Council who financed the study (Research grant 0000–23–1991). We would also like to thank Anthony Heath, Roger Jowell and John Curtice who collaborated to establish comparable data between the BCS and the British Election Study, 1992, and Pat Seyd and Paul Whiteley who provided data from the Labour Party Membership survey. The research assistants who helped administer the survey at Edinburgh and Loughborough universities included Andrew Geddes, Jackie Goode, Denise McKnight, Ian Ross, and Catriona Burness. We are most grateful to everyone who took time to read and comment on all or part of the draft typescript, or of publications emerging from the project, including Malcolm Anderson, Hugh Berrington, Alice Brown, Ivor Crewe, David Denver, Janet Ford, Michael Gallagher, Sarah Perrigo, Michael Rush, Elizabeth Vallance, and Alan Ware, as well as party officers already mentioned. Joni Lovenduski would like to thank the Department of European Studies, Loughborough University where the research was completed and the Institute of Governmental Studies, University of California, Berkeley, for academic hospitality during completion of the typescript. Lastly, Pippa Norris would like to thank Marvin Kalb and colleagues at the Joan Shorenstein Barone Center for Press, Politics and Public Policy at the Kennedy School of Government, Harvard University and Chris Allen and colleagues at Edinburgh University for facilitating completion of this book.

1 PUZZLES IN POLITICAL RECRUITMENT

This book aims to provide the first full account of legislative recruitment in Britain for twenty-five years. The central concern is why some politicians succeed in moving through the 'eye of the needle' into the highest offices of state. In democracies, many participate as grassroots party members, community activists, and campaign donors. Some become local or regional elected officers, party leaders, or lobbyists. From this pool of eligibles, some run for parliament, a few are elected, and even fewer rise into government office. Recruitment operates for offices at all levels. *Legislative* recruitment refers specifically to the critical step as individuals move from lower levels into parliamentary careers. In practice, given the accidents of political life, many careers are far from linear. During their lifetime, politicians may transfer laterally, skip a step or two along the way, or move up and down offices, like a game of snakes and ladders. This study of legislative recruitment explores how and why people become politicians, and the consequences for parties, legislatures and representative government.

Many different perspectives within political science provide insights into this common concern.[1] Among the most traditional approaches, a rich biographical and historical literature documents the careers of political leaders based on memoirs, letters and public records. Early sociological theorists such as Mosca, Pareto and Michels, and neo-marxists, were concerned about the outcome of the recruitment process, the way legislative elites restricted access, and their privileged class origins.[2] More recently, increased concern has been expressed about the barriers to entry facing women and ethnic minority candidates.[3] Institutionalists interested in party organisations have studied the decision making process over candidate selection, for the insights this provides into the distribution and centralisation of power within parties. Following Lasswell, political psychologists concerned with political motivation sought to identify a distinctive personality among lawmakers, which drew them into public life.[4] Psephologists have concentrated on the electoral consequences of candidacies, notably the 'personal vote' incumbents may attract.[5] Rational choice theorists have sought to model the decision to run, based on the perceived costs

1

and benefits of different levels of office.[6] Legislative specialists have studied how the background and careers of politicians relate to their activities and roles, and the consequences of candidate selection for parliaments.[7]

Recruitment studies stand at the intersection of research on mass political participation, elections and voting behaviour, political elites, legislatures, party organisations, and interest groups, as well as, more recently, gender and racial politics. This intellectual diversity exerts centrifugal pressures which tend to fragment recruitment studies, as each perspective emphasises different theoretical frameworks, key questions and methodological approaches.[8] But the potential ability to draw on many subfields can also be a source of considerable intellectual strength.

To understand recruitment, this study seeks to reintegrate the literature from two primary subfields in political science. Studies of political elites have been concerned with the social composition of parliament. Studies of party organisations have focused on how the process operates and what the selection process tells us about the distribution of power within parties. This book seeks to build on this literature, developing a more comprehensive theoretical model and analysing new evidence – the British Candidate study (BCS). The aim is to link our understanding of the process of Candidate recruitment with the outcome for the social composition of parliamentary elites. This study provides a fresh exploration of three major questions:

(i)   Who selects, and how?
(ii) Who gets selected, and why?
(iii) Does the social bias of the outcome matter?

Studies of party organisations: who selects and how?

Parties serve vital functions linking citizens with government: they structure electoral choice, provide a legislative agenda for government, and recruit legislative candidates. Candidate selection may seem at first sight like a routine and obscure function of political parties, conducted behind closed doors in small meetings long before the public drama and excitement of the election campaign. In marginal seats, who gets into parliament is determined by voters. But in safe seats with a predictable outcome the selectorate have *de facto* power to choose the MP. And in Britain, about three quarters of all seats are 'safe', with majorities greater than 10 per cent.[9] In choosing candidates the selectorate therefore determines the overall composition of parliament, and ultimately the pool of those eligible for government. In federal systems such as in Canada or the United States, there are multiple routes into government. But in Britain there is a single ladder into the highest offices of state; the first hurdle is adoption as a prospective parliamentary candidate in a local constituency.[10]

The main approach to studying recruitment in Britain has focused on identifying who controls selection decisions within parties, whether national leaders, local officers, or grassroots party members, and how this power has evolved over time. Studies have documented the basic steps in the selection process, and what this tells us about the distribution of power within party organisations. The recruitment process has commonly been evaluated according to whether the process is 'democratic' in the sense of involving local activists and grassroots members; 'fair' in treating all applicants equally; 'efficient' as a decision making process; and 'effective' in producing 'good' candidates. The appropriate weight given to these criteria, and whether the system meets these objectives, have been subject to heated debate.

The question of internal party democracy, particularly the appropriate role for national and local organisations, has been one of the most controversial issues. Ever since publication of Ostrogorski's classic work at the turn of the century,[11] studies have been interested in *who* has, and who should have, control over selection, comparing the role of the national party leadership, local constituency officers, party factions, and grassroots party members. Struggles to control the process have always been one of the prime areas of intra-party conflict, as Schattschneider notes, because gatekeepers who select ultimately control the composition of the party leadership:

The nominating [i.e. candidate selecting] process ... has become the crucial process of the party. The nature of the nominating procedure determines the nature of the party; he who can make nominations is the owner of the party.[12]

In Ranney's words, factional struggles to control the nominating procedure are contests for 'nothing less than control of the core of what the party stands for and does'.[13] Placing candidates in safe seats, possibly for a lifetime political career, has more significant consequences than getting conference resolutions adopted, or supporters nominated to internal party bodies. In the Conservative party, disputes over nominations have usually, but not always, been resolved behind closed doors. In the Labour party, factions have struggled more publicly to control the selection process. In 1993 this was vividly illustrated by the heated Labour party debate about the appropriate powers of trade unions versus grassroots party members, with the conference argument over 'one member – one vote' which almost brought down the leadership.

The locus of control over candidate selection varies substantially cross-nationally. In most countries the recruitment process is governed primarily by internal party rules, rather than by law.[14] A comparative approach indicates that decision making in the recruitment process varies along two dimensions. First, there is the question of the dispersion of power. Is the process centralised with the main decisions taken by the national party leadership, is it left to regional party officers, or is it dispersed with grassroots local party members exerting most influence? Secondly, there is the question of the formalisation of decision making. Is the process informal, a matter of tacit norms with few binding rules and constitutional regulations, or it is formalised so that the procedures at each step are standardised, rule-governed and explicit. These distinctions suggest six main types of selection process (see figure 1.1).

In *informal-centralised* systems (such as the French Union pour la Démocratie Française – UDF) there may be democratic constitutional mechanisms, but in practice the process is characterised by leadership patronage. Rules serve a largely symbolic function. Without any established tradition of internal party democracy, and with loose organisations, party members play little role in the process. In *informal-regional* systems (such as the Italian Christian Democrats) faction leaders bargain with each other to place their favoured candidates in good positions.[15]

In *informal-localised* systems (such as in the Canadian Progressive Conservatives), local ridings decide on the general procedures used for selection, as well as the choice of individual candidate. Without established guidelines, practices vary widely; some constituencies may nominate at large-scale meetings open to all 'members', while patronage by a few local leaders may be significant in others. Reflecting weak organisations, this system may be open to manipulation by small groups.

Alternatively, in *formal-centralised* and *formal-regional* systems (such as in the Liberal party in the Netherlands, the old Italian Communist Party (PCI), or the old Japanese Liberal Democrats), party executives or factional leaders at national and regional level have the constitutional authority to decide which candidates are placed on the party ticket. Lastly the most common pattern in European parties is one of *formal-localised* recruitment. Here constitutional rules and national guidelines are established to standardise the process throughout the party. The fairness of the system, ensuring all applicants are treated alike, rests on the implementation of

	Central	Regional	Local
Informal process			
Formal process			

Figure 1.1   Decision making agencies

clear, transparent and equitable rules. Within this framework the selection of individual candidates takes place largely by local agencies at constituency level.

Based on this classification, it becomes apparent that in the long term the main change in recruitment within British parties has been in process rather than power. There has been a gradual evolution from an 'informal-localised' system based on patronage in the nineteenth century towards a more 'formal-localised' system today based on more meritocratic standards. This change has gone further in some parties than others. At the turn of the century Ostrogorski provided one of the earliest accounts of the transformation of this system.[16] In mid-Victorian Britain, local patronage predominated; a few local notables would throw their weight behind candidates with sufficient independent resources and social connections for an effective campaign. The 1832 Reform Act led to the development of more formal Registration Societies. At local level the first Conservative associations developed during the mid-1830s to bring in regular subscriptions, organise electoral registration, and rally electoral supporters.[17] At national level the great political clubs – the Carlton and the Reform – provided a rudimentary party organisation, functioning as a social base bringing together politicians, party agents, local associations and influential supporters from the provinces. Formal party labels meant little, after the split over the Corn Laws, when there were shifting parliamentary factions based around political leaders.[18] Ostrogorski was concerned with the development of modern parties from small, informal factions into structured mass-branch organisations following expansion of the franchise, the introduction of the secret ballot, and reform of corrupt practices.[19]

The 1867 Reform Act provided the major catalyst for the organisation of mass parties. The Liberal party was transformed by Joseph Chamberlain's creation of the 'Birmingham Caucus' in 1867, and the subsequent development of the National Liberal Federation in 1877. The Conservatives were similarly transfigured by the creation of the National Union in 1867 to bring together the constituency associations, the creation of Central Office in 1870 to coordinate the professional services, and Lord Randolph Churchill's reorganisation of the National Union in 1886. From its earliest beginning, the organisation of the Conservative party outside of parliament was conceived as a servant of the party within parliament. Local branches were established as election machines, to mobilise the newly enfranchised voters who became too numerous to reach by traditional means.[20] Reflecting their stronger organisation, constituency associations were given two new functions: to enable supporters to influence the party programme, and to provide a more popular body for selecting candidates.[21] Ostrogorski's central anxiety was the effect of 'caucus control'; if MPs became accountable to rank-and-file party members, he feared this would undermine the independence of members of parliament.

Following in his footsteps, McKenzie's authoritative study of British parties in the mid-fifties established that Ostrogorski's fears of caucus control were groundless.[22] McKenzie found that Conservative and Labour constituency associations had considerable autonomy over whom they adopted, within certain agreed rules. Nevertheless, once elected legislators were rarely accountable to local members. So long as they remained 'en rapport' with their constituency party, McKenzie concluded that British MPs could act as Burkean trustees, able to exercise independent judgement over issues. Due to the deference of party members, MPs rarely functioned as delegates mandated by local activists.[23] There were few cases of constituency de-selection of elected members. Nevertheless, the growth of organised parties did undermine the independence of MPs. Party discipline was applied directly through party whips and national officers, who could threaten the ultimate punishment; official withdrawal of the party label.[24] In short, McKenzie concluded that constituency powers over the selection process did not lead, as some had feared, to direct local control over MPs, although national party control increased.

This established the textbook wisdom for many years. Following in this tradition, the major books on the recruitment process in Britain, published in the 1960s by Austin Ranney and Michael Rush, were concerned with documenting the main steps in the selection process.[25] The focus was on identifying the influence of key actors and analysing sources of potential conflict between central party headquarters and local activists. The studies outlined the rules, examined the social characteristics of candidates on the basis of aggregate data, and compared case studies in some constituencies. The selection of candidates, the authors confirmed, remained the prerogative of local parties, with the main decisions in the hands of constituency officers. Indeed, this was one of the few areas where local parties remained largely autonomous. The outcome of the process – why some candidates were selected over others – was treated as an issue with few conclusive answers.

At the same time, Peter Paterson produced a strong case for reform, arguing that undue power rested with secretive and unrepresentative party cliques.[26] Influenced by the movement against caucuses in the United States, Paterson felt that small selection committees in Britain needed to be replaced by democratic party primaries, open to all members. This proposal was supported in the mid-1970s by the Hansard Society.[27] Subsequent work has focused on the causes and consequences of bitter internal splits over selection battles within the Labour party,[28] and left wing moves to introduce mandatory reselection, in an attempt to make the parliamentary party accountable to Labour activists.[29] The debate about the appropriate influence of trade union affiliates over the choice of Labour candidates follows this tradition,[30] and proposals for greater internal democracy with 'one-member–one-vote' echo back to Paterson.

Previous studies established the characteristic 'formal-localised' nature of the recruitment process as it operated in British parties during the 1950s and 1960s. During this period constituency associations – mainly core activists and affiliated factions – made the major decisions about the choice of individual candidates. At the same time the national leadership determined the general rules, supervised the process, and exercised formal veto powers, to ensure that the process was fair and efficient.

It was commonly assumed that a formal-localised system was functional for British party organisations. Without some central management the process might become factionalised and divisive, since in moribund constituency associations small groups might 'capture' the party label for their preferred candidate. Standard procedures for selection and appeal help ensure that the rules are seen as uniform and legitimate by all participants. All British parties, except the Greens, have national guidelines, and formal vetting of all proposed candidates by national officers. On the other hand it is usually assumed that too much control by the national party leadership might cause resentment at the grassroots level. The constituency association has to work closely with their candidate on a day-to-day basis for an effective grassroots campaign. Local members are most in touch with the needs of their area. Therefore, many believe that local associations should exercise most power over the choice of individual applicants, working within nationally standardised selection rules.

Changes in the Selection Process

Given this literature there are several reasons for a fresh look at the recruitment process. First, there is a need to establish how the process has operated in recent years, taking account of changes over time. Observers of selection meetings today, reading accounts of the 1950s and 1960s, would recognise much that is strikingly familiar.[31] In time-honoured fashion candidates continue to apply for particular constituencies, undergo a process of interview and short-listing by local party bodies, until one becomes the official party standard-bearer. Nevertheless, during the last decades many aspects of the Labour and Conservative selection process have changed significantly. Reforms have usually been initiated during periods in opposition, when parties have sought to regain electoral popularity by improving the quality of their candidates. The selection process has altered in accordance with the dominant ethos and traditional practices in each party. In the major parties the main impact of these changes has been two-fold: to increase the formality of the process; and to shift power slightly away from the core constituency activists, simultaneously upwards towards the central leadership and downwards towards grassroots members.

As described in chapter 3, the Conservatives revised the 'model' rules guiding procedures following the Chelmer report in 1972, slightly strengthening the role of party members at the expense of the constituency executive committee. In 1980, Conservative Central Office introduced managerialist selection boards to scrutinise the pool of eligibles on the Approved List before they could apply to particular constituencies. These boards were designed to produce better quality candidates and a meritocratic, open and fair system. This legitimised and thereby strengthened control over the pool of eligibles by Central Office. At the same time the Conservatives tried to make sure grassroots members in general meetings had a genuine choice of finalists.

Labour changed its rules during the 1980s, as part of the general process of party modernisation, described in detail in chapter 4. Driven by conflicting internal pressures, Labour implemented mandatory reselection for incumbent MPs, formalised the selection procedure, shifted power downwards from the constituency General Management Committee to an electoral college of all members, and allowed greater NEC intervention in the choice of by-election candidates. To encourage more women candidates, Labour altered the shortlisting rules, expanded training programmes, and has recommended the use of all women shortlists in half the seats where Labour MPs retire and half the Labour target marginals, although it remains to be seen whether there will be legal challenges, and if and how this will be implemented. The role of trade union sponsorship, and the power of union affiliates over selection, became subject to increased criticism in the 1980s. In October 1993 Labour decided to move towards a one-member–one-vote selection system, with trade unionists participating as individual members.

During the last decade, innovations have also been introduced in the minor parties. The SDP/Liberal Alliance, subsequently the Liberal Democrats, developed training programmes for candidates, introduced postal ballots for members, and initiated shortlisting quotas for women. The decentralised Greens adopted more informal procedures; local parties largely determine their own procedures, and all applicants stand for constituency hustings, unlike other parties there being no prior process of shortlisting. The Scottish National party uses a fairly rigorous series of exercises to establish whether applicants can be placed on their approved list.

The attitudes of party selectors

The second reason for a fresh study lies in the need to move beyond the formal process to analyse the attitudes, values, and priorities of party selectors. The continuing puzzle is to understand *why* some are chosen over others. Bochel and Denver produced a path-breaking survey of the attitudes of party selectors in the Labour party in Scotland and the north.[32] This survey was innovative but limited in scope, and has not been replicated. Recent surveys of party members allow the first systematic analysis of the political behaviour of grassroots activists.[33] But, somewhat surprisingly, these studies did not gather information about the experience of party members in the candidate selection process, or members' attitudes towards their elected representatives. These surveys have been limited to comparing members and voters. Without a broader theoretical model of representative democracy they have not envisaged activists as a middle stratum linking electors and MPs. The institutional focus of organisational studies means we know more about the main steps in the process than the experience and attitudes of the key actors. What are selectors looking for in candidates, when they make their decisions? Do participants feel that selection procedures are fair, democratic and efficient? Are party members and candidates satisfied with the process? What do members feel about the relative influence of national and local party agencies? To understand the experience and perceptions of the main actors we need to go beyond the formal steps in the process.

The sociology of political elites: who gets selected, and why?

The study of party organisations focuses on how the process operates and who has power over recruitment. This perspective can be understood as one half of the equation. It is supplemented by the extensive literature on political elites, concentrating on the outcome of the process. The traditional sociological study of political elites sought to explain how those in power reinforced and consolidated their position.[34] Robert Michels provided the richest theoretical account of how party leaders exercised control over grassroots members through the 'iron law of oligarchy', even in parties like the German Social Democrats which officially subscribed to notions of intraparty democracy.

Most of the empirical work on political elites in Britain has been concerned with documenting trends rather than with explaining the composition of parliament in terms of the process of recruitment. That is, studies have focused on *who* got into positions of power rather than *how* they got there. The empirical study of British parliamentary elites was pioneered in 1939 by J. A. Thomas, who examined the composition of the Commons during the Victorian period.[35] J. F. S. Ross described the social background of MPs in the inter-war period, documenting trends in age, education and occupation.[36] This was followed in 1963 by W. L. Guttsman's modern classic in this field, along with work by Tom Bottomore, Anthony Sampson and Jean Blondel.[37] In a richly detailed study, Guttsman traced the changing social structure of the British political elite from the expansion of the franchise in 1868 to the mid-1950s. Drawing on historical and biographical sources, Guttsman analysed the social class and educational bias of MPs and cabinet members, including the decline of the traditional aristocracy and the rise of the 'new men'. Yet, as a product of its time, the study focuses on socio-economic class; there was little recognition that the dearth of women in parliament required explanation, or that racial representation would become an issue.[38]

Guttsman's path-breaking work set the elite research agenda in Britain for two decades. Building on this foundation Colin Mellors constructed a detailed record of the social and economic background of the Member of Parliament from 1945 to 1974, documenting trends over time without seeking to explain the pattern.[39] This work, based on public sources, has been updated by many authors including Anthony King, Martin Burch and Mike Moran, Anthony Sampson, Andrew Gamble, John Scott, and Dennis Kavanagh, as well as in regular accounts of candidates in every election by Byron Criddle.[40]

What may be concluded from this research? Studies of legislative elites in many countries have established that legislators tend to be drawn from a privileged social background compared with the electorate.[41] The British parliament fits this pattern. Far from representing a microcosm of the nation, the 'chattering classes' with professional occupations fill benches on both sides of the aisle.[42] Although the number of old Etonians and Harrovians has gradually decreased, many new members continue to follow the traditional path of attending public school and Oxford or Cambridge.[43] Over time the Labour and Conservative parties have become more middle class, with a decline in members from the traditional aristocracy and the manual working class, although there remains an important public–private sector split by party. In other regards the Commons has become slightly more diverse; after the 1992 election the Commons included sixty women (9.2 per cent) and six Asian and black MPs (1 per cent).[44] Concern about the gender and racial composition of parliament has risen during the last decade although the general social bias has been familiar for years. As W. L. Guttsman noted,

If we ascend the political hierarchy, from the voters upwards, we find that at each level – the membership of political parties, party activists, local political leaders,

MP's, National Leaders – the social character of the group is slightly less 'representative' and slightly more tilted in favour of those who belong to the middle and upper reaches of our society.[45]

The decline of the traditional aristocracy, and the slight fall in public school products, mitigated concern about the socio-economic bias of parliament. But at the same time work on political elites was reinvigorated during the 1970s and 1980s by the new politics of gender and race. The development of the second-wave women's movement stimulated concern about gender under-representation in political elites. Despite rising expectations, from 1945 to the mid-1970s there were no substantial gains for women in parliament. The number of women MPs rose significantly in the 1987 and 1992 elections, but in this regard the British parliament continued to lag behind most other European countries. Issues of black representation were raised by the growing ethnic minority population from the mid-1920s onwards. Those concerned to understand the reasons for this social bias took up the old issues of elite studies, with alternative explanatory frameworks. Despite numerous studies documenting the social characteristics of members of parliament, our understanding of the biases in social composition remains limited. It remains a long-standing puzzle which prompts the question: why the social imbalance? A fresh approach to the research design is required to overcome several common limitations in past studies.

The Experience of Applicants

Most previous work has relied upon aggregate trends in the composition of the elite over time, for example their age or education, since this information is easily available from public records. Studies have too frequently counted what can be counted, without a broader theoretical framework. Individual-level survey evidence needs to be considered to understand how applicants experience the process, their perceptions of the selectorate, and their strategy in securing seats. What do they see to be the main obstacles in running for parliament? What are the most rewarding aspects? If elected, what are their primary goals? Unless we understand micro-level data – lifetime career patterns of individuals to see how some politicians move into elite positions while others fail – we will be limited to describing rather than explaining this phenomenon. We need to understand *who* are members of the legislative elite, but, more importantly, *why* and *how* they got there. Just as studies of party organisation tended to neglect the outcome, so studies of the outcome have tended to neglect the process.

The Experience of Losers

Another reason for a new approach is that the winners – MPs – are only the tip of the iceberg. The elite literature describes the social background of MPs, and sometimes parliamentary candidates, but studies are usually silent about those in the wider pool who aspire to a political career but fail. As a result, it is well known that parliament contains many public school and Oxbridge trained barristers, journalists and company directors. Many assume this pattern must reflect the preferences of selectors. But the outcome might reflect the characteristics of those who pursue a political career. Studies have compared the social background of MPs with parliamentary candidates, the next strata down. But again this tells us little about the reasons for the social bias. We would expect significant differences in social background and political experience because MPs represent an older generation than candidates. The only research which has looked at the 'losers' who never get past the interview stage are Martin Holland's study of candidates in the first, direct elections for the European parliament,[46] and Jenny Chapman's work on elections for Scottish local government.[47] This approach has not been used for other elected offices although to understand the outcome, the social background of the winners (MPs) needs to be compared with that of the total pool of eligibles.

Legislative behaviour: does the social bias matter?

Despite all the studies of trends in occupational class and education, previous research has not clearly established that the social background of politicians has a significant influence on their attitudes, values and behaviour. Does the social bias matter? There are reasons to be sceptical since we can identify MPs from an impeccably patrician background who are radical left wingers on the Labour benches, just as there are working-class Conservatives who are among the most enthusiastic 'hangers and floggers'. Some women members, such as Margaret Thatcher, acknowledged no sympathy with feminist concerns while others were ardent defenders of abortion rights, child care provision and equal opportunities policy. Anecdotal evidence suggests a complex relationship between background and attitudes.

In the 1950s pioneering work on legislative behaviour in the British parliament, by Finer, Berrington and Bartholomew, sought to replicate roll call analysis in the United States.[48] The authors found a significant association between support for Early Day Motions on issues such as pacifism, welfare and capital punishment and the occupational and educational background of MPs. Unfortunately this approach was limited by the strength of party discipline in voting for all major legislation in Britain, and this avenue was not developed further by other authors. Since then the most detailed work on parliamentary votes, by Philip Norton, concentrated on other concerns, namely backbench dissent, party cohesion and the growth of more independent MPs.[49] In the United States a body of work has found that the gender of elected representatives influences their legislative priorities and roll call votes.[50] But there is no reason to assume that the same relationship holds in Britain, where party discipline and ideology are much stronger influences on parliamentary votes.

Further, there are significant differences in the roles MPs adopt, and the priorities they give to different sorts of activities, such as individual case-work, committee work, and attending debates. Studies have tried to explain these differences by party affiliation, type of constituency, and political generation.[51] But they have not examined the relationship between behaviour and the social background of legislators. There are a range of plausible hypotheses to be tested, for example do 'local' MPs who grew up in their constituency spend more time on constituency surgeries than 'carpet-baggers'? Do women members give a higher priority to social policy than men? Does the social class of members relate to their political values? We do not know. In the absence of good evidence, as a thorough review of the literature by Czudnowski suggests, a connection between the social background and attitudes of elites is frequently assumed, but rarely demonstrated.[52] Matthew echoes this conclusion:

Does it make any difference whether legislators are better educated, enjoy higher status, or are far more often male than the people they represent? The research literature has yet to answer that question ... These scattered and inconclusive research results certainly do not add up to a finding that the social, economic or gender biases in legislative recruitment results in a consistent policy bias of legislative institutions.[53]

We need to explore whether the social bias of the British parliament, which is so extensively documented, has any impact on legislative attitudes, policy priorities or behaviour.

Research design, data and methods

Recruitment studies draw on many other subfields in political science, incorporated at later stages in this book, including theories of representative government which shape the underlying premises for this study, theories of socialisation which help explain political activism, theories of progressive ambition which provide insights into legislative careers, and theories of voting behaviour which help model the relationship between elected representatives and their constituents. But the main intellectual foundations for this study lies in the work on party organisations and political elites as outlined. The primary aim of this book is to reintegrate this work, to bring together an understanding of the process and outcome in legislative recruitment. To achieve these aims the research design reconceptualises the candidate recruitment process. Based on a 'supply and demand' model, the study distinguishes between the factors influencing the 'supply' of candidates willing to come forward and the factors influencing the 'demand' of party selectors in making their decisions.

The supply and demand model

Demand　The supply and demand model, discussed in detail in chapter 6, provides an analytical framework to understand factors influencing the selection process. The most common explanations of the outcome usually assume demand by selectors is critical. On the *demand-side* the model assumes selectors choose candidates depending upon their perceptions of the applicants' abilities, qualifications, and experience. Since candidates are rarely well known to most selectors, these perceptions may be coloured by direct and imputed discrimination towards certain types of applicant. The term 'discrimination' is used here in a neutral sense. Discrimination can be for or against certain groups, whether lawyers, farmers, trade unionists, southerners, women or Asians.

Direct discrimination means the positive or negative judgement of people on the basis of characteristics seen as common to their group, rather than as individuals. Party selectors, faced with non-local candidates, often have minimal information on which to make their decisions. The curriculum vitae gives the bare bones. There may be hundreds of application forms. The interview process is relatively short and formal. Members may therefore rely upon background characteristics as a proxy measure of abilities and character; prejudice functions as an information short-cut. As a result, individuals are judged by their group characteristics.

Imputed discrimination is different. Here party members may personally favour a certain category of candidate ('I'd like to vote for a woman', 'We need more blacks in parliament') or an individual applicant ('The Asian was the best-prepared speaker'). But members may be unwilling to choose such a candidate because they expect they would lose votes among the electorate ('But she'd never get in', 'There aren't enough black voters in Cheltenham'). Demand-side explanations therefore suggest that the social bias in parliament reflects the direct and imputed discrimination of party selectors. These explanations are pervasive in popular thinking, and often reflected in the academic literature, although rarely substantiated. Evidence for direct and imputed discrimination by selectors is reexamined in chapters 6 and 7.

Supply The obvious cause of the social bias in parliament – discrimination by party members – is not necessarily the most significant one. Discrimination may be a popular explanation, but this might be based on inferences from the outcome, rather than any good evidence. In a plea of mitigation party members frequently claim their hands were tied: they would like to short-list more well-qualified woman, Asians from the local community or experienced working-class candidates, they say, but few come forward.

Supply-side explanations suggest that the outcome reflects the supply of applicants wishing to pursue a political career. Constraints on resources (such as time, money and experience) and motivational factors (such as drive, ambition and interest) determine who aspires to Westminster. Most citizens, other than a few categories such as lunatics, traitors and peers, are legally qualified to stand. Few do so given the risks and demands of life at Westminster. Supply-side explanations of the social bias in parliament, – examined in chapters 6, 8 and 9 – suggest that the outcome reflects the resources and motivation of the pool of applicants seeking a political career.

Supply-side and demand-side factors interact. Potential applicants may be discouraged from coming forward by the perception of prejudice among party activists, complex application procedures, or anticipated failure. The concept of hidden unemployment ('Why apply? I won't get the job') is a perfect analogy for the 'discouraged political aspirant'. If seen as a 'systems model', this produces a feedback loop from the outcome back to the pool of those who aspire to a political career. The assumptions in this model suffer from certain limitations, explored in chapter 6. Nevertheless despite these qualifications there remains an important distinction between the *supply* factors holding individuals back from applying for a position, ('I'm not interested', 'I don't have the right experience', 'I can't afford to move', 'I couldn't win') and the *demand* factors which mean that, if they apply, they are not accepted by selectors ('He's not locally known', 'She's not got the right speaking skills', 'He would not prove popular with voters'). The supply-side and demand-side distinction therefore provides a useful analytical framework to explore alternative explanations in subsequent chapters.

To operationalise this model, the process of getting into parliament can be conceptualised as a multi-step ladder of recruitment, illustrated in simplified form in figure 1.2. *Party strata* are groups at different levels on the ladder. *Party voters* are those who supported the party in the 1992 general election. *Party members* are the grassroots card-carrying activists at

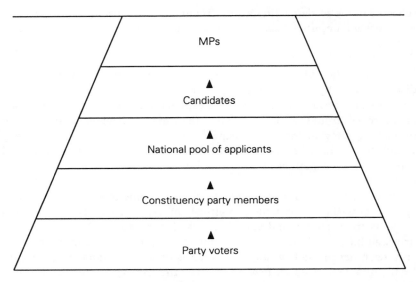

Figure 1.2   The ladder of recruitment

selection meetings.[54] In the next step up the ladder, *applicants* are those on the party list, the 'pool of talent' who failed to be selected by a constituency in the 1992 election.[55] Next are parliamentary *candidates* (PPCs) adopted for a constituency in the 1992 election, who can be further classified by type of seat, as discussed later. At the top of the ladder are incumbent *Members of Parliament* (MPs) who were returned in the 1987 election. The term *party elite* refers to the combined group of applicants, candidates and MPs.

To explain the outcome of the process we need to know the total pool involved at every level: MPs, candidates, list applicants, party members and voters. By comparing strata we can see whether the outcome of the selection process reflects the *supply* of those willing to stand for parliament or the *demands* of party activists when adopting candidates for local constituencies. This simple method, in brief, is the heart of our research design.

To compare party strata this book uses evidence drawn from the British Candidate Study (BCS) in the 1992 election. The BCS collected data at different stages of the process for almost a three-year period, from January 1990 to October 1992. The research design includes eight main components, documented in detail in appendix A.

(i) *Party members*: This included a survey of Labour and Conservative members (N = 1,634) who attended selection meetings in twenty-six constituencies throughout Britain.

(ii) *MPs and candidates*: This included a survey of MPs and parliamentary candidates (N = 1,320) adopted by all parties for the April 1992 general election.

(iii) *Applicants*: This included a survey of Conservative and Labour applicants from party lists (N = 361) who failed to be adopted.

(iv) *Personal interviews*: This included detailed personal interviews with MPs, candidates and applicants (N = 39) as well as briefer background interviews with constituency activists, party agents and national party officers.

(v) *Official documents*: This included a review of official documents outlining party constitutions, selection rules and procedures.

(vi) *Meetings*: This included participant observation of a range of Labour and Conservative selection meetings at different stages of the process.

(vii) *Voters*: Survey items were designed to be identical across different levels of party strata, as well as to be comparable with the British Election Study 1992, conducted by Anthony Heath et al.[56]

(viii) *Constituency data*: Aggregate information on constituencies, including their electoral history and demographic characteristics, was merged with the data.[57]

The research focused most attention on the Labour and Conservative parties, given their dominance in parliament, although the study compares the process in all British parties for a comprehensive overview. The surveys measured the social background, political experience and attitudes of the main actors involved in the process. Personal interviews allowed the opportunity to explore some of the findings of the survey data in greater depth. The constituency meetings to which we had access were selected as broadly representative in terms of party, region and marginality. Throughout party officials gave us the fullest cooperation, and it would not have been possible without their assistance and support.

The first section focuses on the political system and party processes. Chapter 2 outlines the context for candidate recruitment and the opportunity structure in Britain, shaped by the legal system, electoral system, and party system. Chapters 3, 4, and 5 describe respectively the selection process within the Conservative, Labour and minor parties, analysing the influence of the main players and the key stages in the process. The second section of the book considers how we explain the outcome of the process. Chapter 6 describes trends in the social composition of parliament in the post-war period, then analyses the effects of supply and demand on social group representation. In subsequent chapters separate parts of the supply and demand model are examined in depth, including the role of discrimination by party selectors (chapter 7), candidate resources (chapter 8), and candidate motivation (chapter 9). The selection process in Britain is then set in comparative perspective to understand the impact of the political system (chapter 10). The last section considers whether the social bias has significant consequences for the attitudes, values and roles of legislators (chapter 11) and for electoral support (chapter 12). The final chapter summarises the overall conclusions and considers possible reforms to the system (chapter 13).

I   Who selects, and how?

2   The structure of political recruitment

In understanding political recruitment we can draw a distinction between three levels of analysis. First there are systematic factors which set the broad context for recruitment within any country – the legal system, electoral system, and party system. Second, there are factors which set the context within any particular political party – notably the party organisation, rules and ideology. Lastly, there are factors which most directly influence the recruitment of individual candidates within the selection process – notably the resources and motivation of aspirants and the attitudes of gatekeepers. This book therefore proceeds from the general political system, through party organisations, down to the specific factors influencing particular decisions to run for office. This chapter aims to clarify the structure of opportunities for different types of candidacies, then to see how the legal, electoral and party system, and the rate of incumbency turnover, influences the recruitment process in Britain.

Opportunity structures

In recent years the dominant framework for understanding legislative recruitment in the United States has focused on rational choice theories of office-seeking.[1] Much of this approach derives from Joseph Schlesinger's influential work,[2] which suggests potential ambition only becomes manifest within a particular opportunity structure. That is, candidates choose to run for office in response to the possibilities which are available. Opportunities are determined by the institutional and political environment, notably the structure of elected offices and the rules which define the way to achieve these offices. This includes, in the American political system, the strength of party organisation, the number of elected offices at different levels, the rate of personnel turnover, and the level of party competition within each state. Hence, opportunities to move from local-to-state, from state-to-House, from House-to-Senate, or from Governor-to-Presidency are different between New York and Vermont, or between California and Montana. On this basis studies have attempted to predict – with some success – which

House members would try to move into the Senate by taking account of constituency factors such as competitiveness and size, as well as personal factors such as seniority, age, and party.[3]

Rational choice models explain the decision to run in terms of the costs and benefits of pursuing office. It is assumed that all politicians are rational goal seekers who desire higher office. The simple utility model assumes that individuals will run if they believe the probability of success is high, when the perceived benefits of office are great, and/or when the cost of losing is low. This rational actor model does not seek to explain *why* some people are ambitious for office. It simply takes this as a given, and tests certain deductive predictions about how politicians will react to the structure of opportunities. Indeed, for this reason, Hibbing has correctly suggested that the so-called theory of ambition is in fact a theory of office-seeking.[4]

This approach has become popular in the United States, because American politicians running for elected office can be seen as strategic political entrepreneurs, developing their own resources and support networks, managing their own primary and general election campaigns, balancing the estimated costs against the potential rewards of office.[5] In most states parties have lost their gatekeeping role: the rise of primaries in the last two decades means party bosses no longer pick candidates in the traditional smoke-filled rooms. The function of candidate selection has been transferred to primary voters. Politicians are self-nominating; they offer themselves as candidates, raise money, create publicity and make the key decisions about how to generate votes. Since parties no longer play a major role on the 'demand-side', the literature has shifted to focusing on the supply-side of the equation: why candidates choose to campaign within a particular local context.

This model seems particularly suitable for the United States for three reasons: due to residency requirements candidates run for elected office within a local context; due to federalism and the division of powers, there are diverse routes into higher office; due to the growth of primaries and weak parties, candidates are self-nominating. Under these conditions it makes sense to regard American politicians as strategic calculators estimating the costs and benefits of running for the House, Senate, Gubernatorial or Presidential office in different contexts.

Can this model be used to analyse other political systems, as Schlesinger claims?[6] To some extent. There are some parallels in Britain because the opportunity structure is one plausible explanation for candidate competition. When the MP in a safe Conservative seat retires, for example, the Conservative leader of the local council, who may never have expressed any interest before, may decide to apply for the vacancy. The specific opportunity, which may be the first time there has been a selection in the constituency in twenty or thirty years, triggers the application. On the other hand an ambitious young trade unionist living in Sussex, whose father had been active on the Labour backbenches, may be keen to follow the family tradition but may never apply, as there are few winnable Labour seats in the area. The importance of the opportunity structure was recognised by our respondents. As one Labour MP remarked, the emphasis on a local candidate may exclude many high calibre applicants:

It is difficult now on a geographical basis, because if you are someone who has the makings of a good parliamentarian, and you live somewhere, or your roots are in an area – say all your political experience was in Bournemouth and you applied to be a Member of Parliament for Bristol, you'd have a hard time.[7]

There are good people who don't get selected because they've not got access to a constituency.[8]

One reason, for example, why there were more gains for black MPs in 1987 than 1992 was the pattern of seat vacancies which became available in inner London and Midland constituencies with a high ethnic minority population.[9] In the British system the decision for individuals to move up the ladder of recruitment may be triggered by the opportunities provided by their situation, in particular the number of good seats available in a particular area.

Nevertheless, there are important differences between the American and British political systems which, on balance, limit the use of this theory. In Britain there is a fairly uniform vertical ladder of recruitment: from party to local government office, to Westminster backbenches, and finally into ministerial office. Most politicians tread the same pathway: in the last election three quarters of all parliamentary candidates had stood for local government, and half had been elected. The more centralised nature of power in the British political system means ambitious politicians cannot by-pass the House of Commons. Only a few transfer from the European to Westminster parliaments, or vice versa. Civil servants, judges and most policy makers in public office are disqualified from running unless they first resign their post. The strategic calculation for British aspirants is therefore restricted; they can try to move up the vertical ladder within their party or they can stay put, there are almost no lateral options. In the words of Shirley Williams:

In the British parliamentary system, political career paths offer only a limited number of choices. Because politics is more subject than most callings to chance and circumstances, the career path of any politician will twist and turn, rise and fall. But for a British politician the goals are limited, and the direction is plain. Once elected to the House of Commons, the possible career paths are few, and one dominates all others. Most members of Parliament aspire to become ministers or shadow ministers.[10]

Although localism is an important tradition in British constituencies there is no legal residency requirement. Most Labour candidates come from their area but, as discussed in the next chapter, Conservative applicants chase seats around the country. Therefore, the local context may be important but it does not determine the opportunity structure.

Moreover, although this theory may account for the behaviour of ambitious Labour and Conservative applicants, it is implausible to start from the premise that most candidates are office-seekers. They are not. Candidates in the minor parties, as well as major party contestants fighting low prospect seats, run for many different reasons, usually to help their party. Most of these do not stand to gain office, since they recognise they will not win. Lastly, the critical role of the selectorate in British recruitment, and lack of certain information about their priorities, mean applicants can rarely calculate their chances of being selected (rather than elected) with any degree of accuracy. For all these reasons the opportunity structure provides an important but limited part of the explanation of British political recruitment.

Types of candidacies

The opportunity structure in Britain can be conceptualised as a tiered, hierarchical pyramid. At the bottom tier, there are few legal barriers to becoming a parliamentary candidate. If they want to, most British citizens can stand as independents. Almost 3,000 contestants fought the 1992 general election campaign. Nevertheless, there are few opportunities to become a candidate for the major parties, and still fewer to become a Labour or Conservative candidate with a realistic chance of winning. There are certain main types of candidacies which will be analysed throughout the book:

Incumbents are MPs elected in the previous general election who are standing for the same seat, and for the same party, in the subsequent general election.

Inheritors are candidates selected for an open seat previously held by their own party, where the previous MP retired.

Challengers are candidates fighting a seat held by another party. This group can be further sub-divided:

High prospect challengers are in second place in marginal seats (with a majority of less than 10 per cent).

Low prospect challengers, in contrast, have poor chances of winning, since they are fighting non-marginals, and/or their party was in third or fourth place in the constituency in the previous general election.

In the 1992 general election the candidate pool included 565 incumbents, 84 inheritors, and 2,297 challengers (see table 2.1, figure 2.1).[11] Each faces different prospects of winning. Incumbents who choose to stand again will probably be returned; 92 per cent were reelected in 1992 (see table 2.2). Inheritors stand an equally good chance, 93 per cent became new backbenchers. In contrast out of the total pool of challengers, only sixty new members (2.6 per cent), entered parliament by defeating their rival in the last general election.[12] Nearly all the winners were high-prospect Labour challengers; only two other challengers succeeded against the odds. A stronger two-party swing would produce greater seat change, but the number of MPs defeated in the last election was fairly typical of the post-war average. Combining all routes to Westminster – by-elections, inheritance and general election defeats – in the post-war period each parliament has seen the influx of about 140 new MPs. The process of recruitment is one where many run, but few succeed. For almost all, the route to Westminster requires standing for Labour or the Conservative party as an inheritor or high prospect challenger. Other candidates may gain many benefits from the campaign, by helping their party or increasing their experience, but essentially their role is one of cannon-fodder in the wider electoral battle.

At the apex of the pyramid, opportunities in the British system are further narrowed by the constitution. In a federal system such as the United States there are multiple routes to power, and politicians can move laterally, from the House to the Senate, from the Senate to state Governor, from the state house to mayoral office, from the cabinet to the courts, from elected office into the lobbying and advocacy think tanks. Politicians make strategic horizontal and vertical moves in a complex pattern of opportunities. In

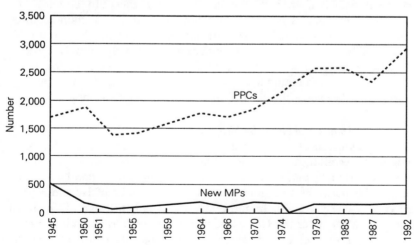

Figure 2.1   Trends in parliamentary candidates, 1945–92

Table 2.1 *Types of candidates in the 1992 general election*

	Con	Lab	Lib. Dem.	SDP	SNP	PC	Green	Other	Total	%
Incumbents	311	208	21	2	4	2	0	17	565	19.2
Inheritors	58	24	1	0	0	1	0	0	84	2.9
Challengers	276	402	611	0	68	23	250	667	2,297	78.0
Total Candidates	645	634	633	2	72	26	250	684	2,946	100.0

Note: including the Speaker.

Table 2.2 *Election rate of candidates in parliamentary parties (percentage)*

	Con.	Lab.	Lib. Dem.	Nat.	All
Incumbents	88	100	71	100	92
Inheritors	90	100	100	100	93
High-prospect challengers	4	41	3	4	14
Low-prospect challengers	0	2	0	0	1

contrast, in Britain the system provides a narrow ladder for the ambitious politician, usually from party activism into local government, from councils into Westminster, and from the backbenches into government office. All members of the cabinet and the opposition frontbenches are drawn from parliament, usually from the Commons. Therefore, except for appointed or hereditary peers, access to the highest offices of state in Britain requires being adopted for a winnable constituency as an unavoidable step up the political ladder. The most talented and ambitious British politician, if they fail to be adopted in successive elections for a winnable seat, lose their constituency through boundary changes, or get swept out of a marginal by an electoral tide against their party, may never get another opportunity.

The legal system and eligibility criteria
In common with most democracies, the British system provides few legal barriers to becoming a candidate. The law establishes certain minimal eligibility criteria by nationality and age: those who want to stand have to be citizens of Britain, the Commonwealth, or the Republic of Ireland, and at least twenty-one years old. In addition, certain categories are disqualified from being MPs under the *House of Commons Disqualifications Act, 1975:*[13]

Lunatics: members detained for more than six months under the Mental Health Act 1959 have to vacate their seat.

Undischarged bankrupts: members who continue to be bankrupt after six months lose their seat.

Corrupt or illegal election practices: persons convicted may be disqualified from standing in any constituency for five years, and for the constituency where the practice was committed for ten years.[14]

Other convicted persons: a person sentenced or imprisoned for more than one year is disqualified from membership of the Commons and, if elected, the result is declared void.[15]

Treason: persons convicted of treason are disqualified from either House.

Peers of England, Scotland, Great Britain and the United Kingdom, (but not Ireland) and peeresses in their own right, are disqualified from the Commons unless they have renounced their title during their lifetime.[16]

Clergy: ministers of the established church in England, Scotland and Ireland, and Roman Catholic priests, are disqualified. In contrast, holders of ecclesiastical office in the Church of Wales and non-conformist churches may stand.

Office-Holders: to avoid conflict of interest, a range of office-holders is excluded from membership of the Commons including civil servants, members of the armed forces, the police, holders of many judicial offices, ambassadors and high commissioners, election and boundary commissioners, and members of many public bodies such as the boards of nationalised industries.

To stand, candidates pay a £500 deposit, which is returnable if they get over one twentieth of the total votes cast, exclusive of spoilt papers. In 1985 the deposit was increased from £150 to £500 in an attempt to deter frivolous candidates from fringe groups (like the Monster Raving Loony party) without producing an undue deterrent for others like the Greens.[17] The number of candidates fell slightly in 1987, but subsequently rebounded. In the 1992 election the average number of candidates per seat increased from 3.6 to 4.5, partly due to the number of constituencies contested by the Greens, the (old) Liberals, and the Natural Law Party (see figure 2.2). In a few seats there were only Labour, Conservative and Liberal Democrat contenders although some had as many as ten contestants. In by-elections, the increased deposit has similarly failed to deter minor party and fringe candidates especially in well-publicised campaigns.[18]

Although recourse to the courts is occasionally sought by disgruntled contestants, in recent decades only a handful of candidates have been legally disqualified due to bribery, corrupt practices, felony, bankruptcy, or

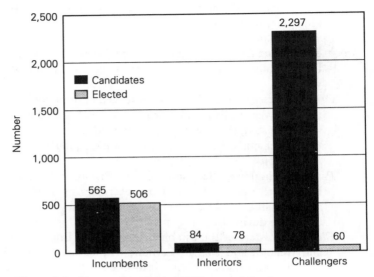

Figure 2.2   Types of candidate, 1992 general election

membership of the Lords.[19] Most citizens are eligible to stand for parliament, should they so choose. In this sense the British system is similar to most other liberal democracies. Recruitment processes are usually governed by party constitutions, rules, and informal practices, with little outside interference. The selection process is only regulated in detail by law in the United States, Germany, Norway, Turkey and Finland (see chapter 10).[20]

The electoral system   The British electoral system is usually believed to influence opportunities to stand. Britain's first-past-the-post system is based on 651 plurality, single-member districts. Opportunities are determined by the number of seats, which are subject to periodic revisions by the Boundary Commission. The redistribution of seats following the 1991 Census, due to come into effect in time for the next general election, will expand the number of rural and suburban seats in the south at the expense of some inner-city Labour seats with falling populations in such areas as Liverpool, Glasgow and Tyneside.

The British electoral system is commonly seen as contributing towards the localism of the selection process, by strengthening the links between individual MPs and their constituency.[21] Nevertheless, a wider comparison of liberal democracies found a weak relationship between the centralisation of candidate selection within parties and the type of electoral system.[22] Parties in some countries which have used first-past-the-post, like New

Zealand and India, have fairly centralised selection processes.[23] On the other hand, some proportional systems using national or regional party lists, such as Belgium, Norway, Germany, Finland and Austria, have constituency-level selections in most parties.

There is another way in which the electoral system constrains voters. There is least choice in closed party lists where the electorate can vote only to accept or reject the whole ticket. Who gets into parliament is determined by the party's share of the vote/seats and the order of names on the list. There is greater choice in countries with open party lists, where voters are able to prioritise certain names within the list, and thereby influence the selection of MPs. The British parliamentary system based on first-past-the-post elections, with no primaries, offers a constrained choice. The electorate can vote for or against individual candidates. But a loyal party voter has no say over their party's candidate. Through casting their ballot British voters face a bundled option combining candidate, party and government. As explored further in chapter 10, the relationship between electoral and selectoral systems is therefore complex and mediated by party organisations and political culture.

Incumbency Turnover

One of the most significant factors constraining opportunities to enter the British parliament is the rate of incumbency turnover. Incumbency turnover (that is, total change in membership of the House between one general election and the next) can be calculated as the product of three factors: the number of members leaving (for whatever reason) at *by-elections*; those *retiring* at general elections; and those *defeated* at general elections.

By-elections in the post-war period have most commonly been caused by the death of the sitting member, accounting for half of all contests. Another third of by-elections resulted from resignations, usually for non-political reasons such as ill-health or a career transfer, although occasionally members resigned to seek an electoral mandate under a new party banner. The number of by-elections has declined significantly over the years; there were sixty-one British by-elections during the 1959–64 Conservative administration but only twenty-three in the 1987–92 parliament. This trend is partly due to fewer by-elections caused by the acceptance of an office of profit under the Crown, or legal grounds for membership disqualification.[24]

These developments did not have a major impact on the overall rate of turnover, however, as the fall in the number of by-elections has been counterbalanced by the increased number of voluntary retirements. As King has pointed out, due to the rise of 'careerism' members have been

Table 2.3 *Turnover in the House of Commons 1945–92*

	Total MPs in House of Commons	MPs leave at by-election	MPs retire at general election	MPs seeking re-election	MPs defeated at general election	Total re-elected MPs	% of these seeking re-election	Re-elected MPs as % House members	Total new MPs	% new MPs	Months of parliament	Standard annual turnover
1945–50	640	52	60	580	70	510	87.9	71.6	182	28.4	52	42
1950–51	625	16	29	596	25	571	95.8	88.8	70	11.2	19	44
1951–55	630	48	42	588	19	569	96.8	82.7	109	17.3	42	31
1955–59	630	52	66	564	33	531	94.1	76.0	151	24.0	51	36
1959–64	630	62	60	570	61	509	89.3	71.0	183	29.0	59	37
1964–66	630	13	38	592	51	541	91.4	83.8	102	16.2	17	72
1966–70	630	38	78	552	77	475	86.1	69.4	193	30.6	49	47
1970–74F	635	30	70	565	53	512	90.6	75.9	153	24.1	43	43
1974–74O	635	1	14	621	30	591	95.2	92.9	45	7.1	6	90
1974–79	635	30	61	574	65	509	88.7	75.4	156	24.6	53	35
1979–83	650	20	77	573	63	510	89.0	75.4	160	24.6	48	40
1983–87	650	16	87	563	41	522	92.7	77.8	144	22.2	47	37
1987–92	651	23	85	566	60	506	89.4	74.2	168	25.8	57	35
Mean	636	31	59	546	50	497	91.4	76.2	140	23.8	42	45

Sources: calculated from *The Times Guide to the House of Commons 1945–87*

elected slightly earlier in life. Today there are fewer Labour backbenchers entering after a long career devoted to the union movement, or landed baronets from the Shires in the Conservative ranks.[25] Since they enter earlier, members are more likely to retire at the conventional pensionable age. During the last decade this tendency has been reinforced by party managers. In order to avoid potentially embarrassing by-election defeats for the government, Conservative Central Office has encouraged older members to stand down voluntarily at general elections.

The number of MPs defeated in general elections depends largely upon the size and direction of the two-party swing, the number of marginal seats, and geographical variations in the swing. The number of two-party marginals has fallen since the early 1950s, but a comparison of multi-party marginals shows no significant decline over time. An analysis of trends in general elections since the war suggests no clear-cut change in the rate of party seat losses or gains, instead the pattern is one of trendless fluctuations over time.[26]

What is the net effect on turnover of all these factors? As shown in table 2.3, turnover varies substantially from one general election to the next. The rate was relatively high in the 1959–64 and 1987–92 parliaments, and, as might be expected, far lower during the brief parliaments from February to October 1974, or from 1950–51. The greatest turnover occurred during the 1935–45 parliament, due to the record post-war Labour landslide and the exceptional duration of the war parliament. For consistent comparisons of trends over time the rate of turnover needs to be standardised to take account of the length of parliaments. When this is done, the annual rate of turnover from 1950–92 shows a fairly stable pattern from one parliament to the next, with about forty-five new MPs on average per annum. Over time the standardised data suggest trendless fluctuations, rather than increased safety or vulnerability for MPs. In the post-war period, from one general election to the next, on average about thirty-one MPs usually leave at by-elections, another fifty-nine retire at general elections, while fifty are defeated in general elections. This means from one parliament to the next about three-quarters (76.2) of all MPs are reelected to office. As shown later, turnover in the British House of Commons is fairly similar to the rate in other legislatures.

The party system and candidate competition

The party system is the last factor constraining the structure of opportunities. The term 'party system' refers to the structure of party competition which occurs in the electorate and in parliament. Party competition has two principal dimensions: the strength of parties, conventionally measured by votes in the electorate and seats in parliament, and the position of parties across the ideological spectrum. In the post-war period, the dominant two-party system has gradually weakened. This shift became evident at the electoral level from the mid-1960s, and at the parliamentary level from the February 1974 general election onwards. Change is apparent but it is more difficult to characterise the nature of the current system. It can be seen as a declining two-party system, or perhaps as an emerging 'predominant one-party' system.[27]

From 1945–66 Britain was usually seen as the exemplar of a stable, responsible, balanced two-party democracy. The Labour and Conservative parties regularly rotated between government and opposition, with fairly even balance in electoral support at national and regional level. In general elections during this period support for the major parties never fell below 39 per cent, or rose above 50 per cent. In UK general elections from 1945 to 1966, Labour and the Conservatives dominated the political landscape: contesting 98 per cent of all seats, nominating 77 per cent of all candidates, gaining 92 per cent of the vote, and winning 98 per cent of all parliamentary seats. During the post-war period most constituencies offered voters the choice of a 'straight fight' between Labour and Conservative candidates. Minor parties were politically and electorally marginalised. In general elections during the 1950s, Liberal candidates contested about one in three seats, but the electoral results were miserable: over half lost their deposits. In 1951 and 1955, Liberals gained less than 3 per cent of the UK vote. From 1945 to 1950, Liberals increased the number of seats they contested, from 306 to 475, but their share of the vote only rose from 9.0 to 9.1 per cent, and 319 candidates lost their deposit. The Liberals were almost extinguished in the early 1950s.[28] Nationalist parties were equally quiescent. From 1945 to 1966, voters faced a Conservative–Labour choice in half the seats.

The British party system changed significantly from the mid-1960s onwards. This was evident from the roller-coaster fortunes of the minor parties; increased intra-electoral volatility as measured by opinion polls and by-elections; and the decline in the proportion of 'strong' Labour and Conservative party identifiers. The share of the UK vote won by Labour and the Conservatives fell from 94 per cent during the 1950s to only 75 per cent during the 1980s. There was a significant rise in candidate competition. From 1966–92 almost all seats (94 per cent) had three candidates, often more and the total number of candidates more than doubled (see figure 2.1). The two-party share of parliamentary candidates fell from 77 per cent in the period 1945–66 to 55 per cent from 1974 to 1992.

Despite these dramatic developments, change at the parliamentary level has been far slower, largely due to the impact of the first-past-the-post electoral system and the regional distribution of Liberal Democrat support.

The share of parliamentary seats held by Labour and the Conservatives fell marginally, from 98 to 95 per cent in the period 1974–1992. Largely due to the fragmentation of Northern Ireland politics after February 1974, more parties gained parliamentary representation: there were four to eight parties in the Commons in the period 1945–70, compared with nine to eleven in the period 1974–92. Minor parties could be marginalised during the Thatcher administrations, when the Conservatives enjoyed comfortable majorities. They had more 'blackmail' potential following the 1992 election, when the Major administration depended on a slim majority of twenty-one, which was further eroded through by-election defeats and internal party splits over Europe.

Conclusions

Changes in the British party system have had a significant impact on the total number of contestants fighting general and by-elections. This has expanded the structure of opportunity to be selected, but not elected. The British legal system means that almost all citizens can stand, but in practice the key to a parliamentary career, often for life, is selection by the local Labour or Conservative party to inherit an open seat held by their own party or, far riskier, to become a high-prospect challenger. Who gets these seats, and why? We now turn to the operation of the selection process in the main parties in Britain in the post-war period.

3 Conservative recruitment

One of the most remarkable features of the Conservative party is the way it has usually managed to maintain unity, with little public discord between the leadership and local associations. This is particularly evident in the Conservative selection process where disagreements have usually been resolved discreetly behind closed doors, by a process of informal discussions between leaders, MPs and local associations. This is in marked contrast to Labour, where factional disputes over the adoption of candidates have been far more common, and there have been heated conference battles over the selection rules.

The aims of this chapter are threefold. The first is to describe the main steps in the Conservative selection process as it operated during the 1987–92 parliament, to understand how it works from the perspective of participants. The second is to summarise how the process has gradually evolved over time from a 'patronage' towards a more 'meritocratic' process today. Lastly, the chapter concludes by analysing how the Conservative process has functioned effectively to maintain party unity. Broader issues, including explanations of the *outcome* of the selection process, will be left until they can be explored in depth in later chapters.

The main steps in Conservative selection

The role of Central Office

The Conservative party has three components: the parliamentary party consisting of the party leader, MPs and Conservative peers; the National Union of Conservative Associations which links constituency parties in England and Wales, and is primarily responsible for organising the annual conference; and Central Office.[1] Based in Smith Square, Westminster, Central Office is the party's organisational hub in England and Wales.[2] It was founded in 1870 to provide the party with professional support. This office comes under the direct control of the party leader who appoints the Party Chairman. This post was held by Chris Patten until he was replaced after the 1992 general election by Sir Norman Fowler. Smith Square supervises all central functions: publicity, research, finance, campaigning, coordination, and candidate selection.[3] The vice-chairman with day-to-day responsibility for candidate selection, traditionally an MP, was Sir Tom Arnold from 1983 until 1992, when he was replaced after the election by Andrew Mitchell. The vice-chairman reports to the formal body supervising this process, the Standing Advisory Committee on Candidates (SACC).[4]

Application to Central Office
The first step for any applicant involves getting onto the Approved List maintained by Conservative Central Office (see figure 3.1). This list defines the 'pool of eligibles' who may apply to vacancies as they arise in individual constituencies. During the 1987–92 parliament about 900 applications were

Figure 3.1   The Conservative selection process, 1987–92. *Note:* the numbers in parentheses indicate the approximate number of potential candidates at each stage of the process.

received by Central Office. Those seeking to get on the Approved List start by completing a detailed form, similar to any job application. The form requests information about their personal background, educational qualifications, employment history, political experience, the sort of constituency they are seeking. Central Office requests three references, preferably including an MP and constituency chairman. Each applicant is interviewed by their area agent, who produces a written report. The party vice-chairman with responsibility for candidates reviews the application and references, particularly the agent's report, and decides whether to proceed with a Central Office interview.

Central Office interview

In the past this interview was the main hurdle to being on the Approved List; the vice-chairman, helped by two or three MPs, evaluated the applicant's personal qualities, party service, speaking ability, political experience and educational qualifications.[5] Today the interview remains important but has been supplemented by weekend selection boards. The initial vetting process by Central Office seeks to eliminate applicants with an obvious legal disqualification, such as undischarged bankrupts.[6] The interview may also reject those who might prove an embarrassment, for example if they have a criminal record, or have been members of extremist parties such as the National Front. Politically an unsuitable applicant, in the words of one party manager, is someone 'wearing a Union Jack under his shirt'.[7] Applicants need to be in the appropriate age range: some in their early twenties were told they should reapply after gaining more experience in local government or party office.[8] A woman in her mid-forties was warned she was almost on the political shelf, 'another few months and you'll be what we would consider past it'.[9] Applicants are also warned to consider the financial implications of nursing a constituency.[10] Most applicants said they found the formal interview fairly straightforward and fair. The interview process remains a significant hurdle; out of 900 applicants about one quarter are rejected at this stage.

Weekend selection boards: 'Sandhurst selection'

About 700 go on to the next step, attending a residential selection board. These were first introduced in 1980, designed by Brigadier Sir Nicholas Somerville, based on his experience of reorganising the officer recruitment process for the British army.[11] The old system of vetting, which relied solely on the Central Office interview, was open to the criticism of informal patronage since the process was closed, the criteria for evaluation highly subjective, and only a few people were involved. There was some concern that Central Office might be biased towards favouring the 'old boy' network. Rejected applicants, without any system of appeal, might feel decisions were unfair. In contrast, in line with personnel management practices common in private companies, the selection boards have been designed to produce a more thorough and meritocratic process.[12] The effect of 'Sandhurst selection' has been to legitimate the role of Central Office, to make participants feel they have been given a fair hearing, to evaluate carefully applicants by a wide range of criteria, and to broaden the pool of judges by involving members of the National Union and the parliamentary party. Since they were first introduced, about 1,500 applicants have gone through the process in about thirty-four boards.

During a selection weekend, applicants are subject to a series of exercises to evaluate their intellectual, personal, and political skills. It is assumed that good candidates require a range of different qualities; formal educational qualifications may be useful but a degree will not necessarily guarantee political awareness or breadth of interest. Speaking skills are an obvious advantage for public meetings but equally planning and organisational abilities count in an effective campaign. Ambition may be necessary for success but it is also important that candidates demonstrate traditional virtues such as a sense of responsibility, the ability to mix socially, and the qualities of initiative and determination. The job of being a Member of Parliament is therefore broadly defined. On the other hand political, ideological and policy positions, whether applicants can be classified as 'wets' or 'dries', does not seem to count. Passing the residential selection board is necessary for inclusion on the party's Approved List, which is a virtual requirement for candidacy.[13]

Boards evaluating about forty to fifty applicants are held at regular intervals, about every four months. Applicants are divided into small groups of about eight, assessed by an MP and group leader. To ensure consistent standards two other assessors divide their attention between two groups. To make sure that the assessment standards reflect the views of different sections of the party, scrutiny is by a mix of MPs, senior party activists, outside representatives of business and industry, and full-time party agents. The aim is to subject the applicant to the sort of pressures an MP might experience. The exercises are designed to test character, leadership, intelligence, practical skills, and confidence, and to be sufficiently diverse so that an applicant who fails in one exercise can perform well in another. Standard one-to-one interviews are mixed with small group discussions about how to deal with a problem in their constituency, a parliamentary debate with participants taking both sides on a topical issue, written exercises, a mock media interview including non-political questions, and social events. An MP provides a vivid description of the process as participants see it:

No activity lasts for more than half an hour, forty five minutes, and then you immediately trot into something quite different ... They were looking for general political skills, speaking skills, writing skills; you had to write an essay ... You were given a number. Mine was 21, I remember it vividly. You're given a group to work within, and I was told you were very much spotted for leadership and teamwork and all the rest. You had observers all round you. They crept around you in the room. You sit in a circle and you have these observers creeping around you to see how you relate with yourself, with the others, and all the rest. Whether you've got humour, whether you're courteous, whether you're rattled.

Many applicants felt the pressure to perform was high:

It was gruelling. It was on a par with what I understand army officer selection to be like. It really was gruelling.[14]

Mum said to me when I got back, 'How do you think you've done'. And I said, 'I honestly haven't a clue'. But I was utterly drained, it took me about a week to recover. I think if you can get through that (the weekend board) without falling apart, then you're *en route*. Clearly that is why it's held, it's held to see how you react under pressure, and to see if you can in fact cope[15].

It was very stressful, I didn't realise how stressful it was until I had finished it.[16]

I didn't feel very comfortable, and I was always conscious that whatever you were, and whatever you were doing, somebody was watching you, somebody was assessing you.[17]

Overall most applicants were fairly positive towards the weekend selection boards, reporting that they were very fair:

It is absolutely meritocratic in the sense that everyone goes through the board. I think the board is very good because it is a very testing experience for people's abilities and it's got the right sort of things, and if you're very bad, you fail, and if you're all right, you pass.[18]

You were put through various hoops, because there are all sorts of facets to being an MP. Public speaking is just the obvious one, but there is also getting on with Mrs Bloggs who wants to complain ... there is relations with the press and issuing the press release, and just general mixing and all the rest of it, so many different facets. I felt that over a weekend you could test out that. . .you could get a much better idea of how people were likely to perform.[19]

Others were more critical about the process, believing that it was lengthy and produced a 'standardised' product.[20]

I would discard the week-end [boards] if I were Central Office, myself. I think it's been a mistake. Its enormously expensive, slow, difficult. I think it's outdated management process, and I don't think it produces the best result.[21]

At the end of the weekend, applicants are assessed by a selection board of about nine observers. The criteria for assessment are explicitly defined and measured, allowing members of the board to compare notes, and to judge each applicant by the same standards. A balanced range of abilities are sought so that, for example, poor speaking skills or limited educational qualifications will not automatically disqualify applicants. Evaluators compare the performance of each applicant, across twenty criteria, assessed on a five-point scale (ranging from strong to weak). The pass rate varies according to the group, from 50 to 90 per cent. Applicants are put into four categories: a general pass suitable for all seats; a restricted pass suitable for certain types of seat such as an urban or a farming constituency; a deferred pass, that is, an applicant who should reapply in a few years with more experience; and an outright fail. As a result of the selection boards about half (51 per cent) receive a general pass, 9 per cent get a restricted pass, 14 per cent are deferred, while the remaining quarter (26 per cent) fail outright. Out of the 900 who applied in the 1987–92 period, 700 attended residential boards, and about 500 got through to the final Approved List. They joined those who were included from previous years, so in 1987–92 the Approved List contained the names of 800 applicants.[22]

The role of constituency associations

The local unit of the Conservative party is the constituency association. The size of associations varies widely, and there are difficulties establishing accurate figures given loose criteria for formal membership and imprecise membership records. In the mid-1970s the Houghton Committee estimated that the average membership in each constituency association was about 2,400.[23] The most recent study estimates that the average membership has been halved, to about 1,200 in 1992.[24] Another study found that membership ranged from about 1,853 in safe seats to 277 in unwinnable seats.[25] Associations operate primarily as election machines and support organisations for the parliamentary party. Their main objective is the return of a Conservative Member of Parliament and this determines their range of activities including campaigning, social fund-raising, propaganda, and recruitment. Political functions, such as the discussion and formulation of policy, does occur, particularly in constituency Conservative Political Centre meetings, but policy debate normally takes a back-seat to campaigning.[26] At local level the selection process involves four basic steps: application, shortlisting by Selection Committee, further elimination by the Executive Committee, before final approval by the Special General Meeting.

Table 3.1   *Conservative candidates in the 1992 election*

	Prior to Dissolution	New Parliament	Lost	% Lost
Incumbents	311	273	38	12.2
Inheritors	57	51	6	10.5
Challengers	277	10	266	96.0

Application to a constituency

Once on the Approved List, individuals may apply for specific constituencies, and they are automatically notified about vacancies as they arise. Most seats are filled one or two years before the general election, in a normal election cycle. It is assumed that candidates might become discouraged if they have to nurse a constituency for too long, although obviously they need sufficient time to become known in the area. The timetable is designed to fill the best seats first. In choosing seats applicants face a narrow opportunity structure. As discussed in chapter 2, there are three main types of candidates. 'Incumbents' are MPs restanding. 'Inheritors' are selected for an open seat previously held by their own party, where the previous MP retired. 'Challengers' are fighting a seat held by another party.

The pool of Conservative candidates at the time of dissolution (March 1992) included 311 incumbents, 57 inheritors and 277 challengers. Conservatives returned to Westminster included 273 incumbents, 51 inheritors, and 10 Conservative challengers. In other words, only 61 new Conservative MPs were elected out of the 800 on the Approved List, or just 8 per cent. Most of the new Conservative members entered parliament by inheriting a seat from a retiring MP. Almost all (96 per cent) Conservative challengers lost (see table 3.1). Of course the prospects for new Conservative MPs depends on the size and direction of the overall party swing, and there was a far greater intake in the 1979 and 1983 elections. Nevertheless, as discussed in earlier chapters, the range of opportunities for new candidates is usually relatively limited. Applicants on the Approved List must engage in a fierce rivalry for the most desirable seats. Compared with other parties the Conservative process is more competitive because the dominant party ethos does not discourage carpet-baggers.

What strategies do applicants follow when deciding which seats to contact? As discussed below in chapter 9, some applicants, thinking about the costs of nursing the constituency over a long period, adopt a regional strategy, while others are prepared to search anywhere around the country. Applicants may be willing to try any difficult seat for their first general election, to gain experience, but they may only consider better prospects the second time around:

The first week you tick everything. The second week you think a little bit more sensibly and then you start and decide where your relations live and where you could have accommodation and help and assistance.[27]

Normally you're just a carpet bagger, you go round and pray that a seat with a decent majority selects you.[28]

Basically I always intended to apply for Yorkshire seats anyway, so I was advised to write to all the Yorkshire seats which hadn't actually selected, which I did, which amounted to about twenty, no, probably slightly less.[29]

I sent my CV to any seat that was within three hours driving distance of my home, because I reckoned three hours I could handle with an overnight or evening meeting, and getting back home, that sort of thing. I was applying for safe seats, yes. For a safe seat I was prepared to demolish my domestic life for a year or so, but not for a no-hope.[30]

You apply for everything, everybody does. Every time you get a notification about a safe seat coming up ... you then apply for that seat.[31]

Once they decide to pursue a vacancy, applicants inform Central Office, who pass biographical details to the constituency. In the 1987–92 round of selections as many as 200–400 people applied for a good 'inheritor' vacancy, while 50–100 tried for high-prospect challenger seats. In contrast, there may be only ten applicants for the more difficult contests; in the last general election the Conservatives had problems finding good candidates for the last few Scottish seats.[32] Getting an interview for the good seats is therefore highly competitive, and many remarked this was the most difficult part of the whole process:

Q: What would you say is the hardest part of getting a seat?

The first bit is getting an interview, and that is actually very, very difficult, with 200 applicants and the most they're going to interview is 20 or 30, if you can get an interview, you put yourself in with a chance ...[33]

Trying to get an interview. I have never had any problems when I've had interviews in getting straight onto the short list.[34]

It's getting interviewed, without a doubt. Get interviewed, then you've got a chance. If you can't get interviewed, then you can't get going. So the nerve-wracking thing is getting yourself interviewed and do you know anyone in the association who's likely to make sure that you will get interviewed.[35]

It's a game, it really is. I've known a lot of immensely capable people who never got a seat, or have taken three or four years to get an interview for a good seat.[36]

The curriculum vitae for constituencies has to be professional, to make an impact, with details of political and employment experience, and personal circumstances. Usually, married applicants supply details about their family, often with photographs. Since most applicants will be rejected purely on the basis of their curriculum vitae, there is considerable effort to get it right:

You simply have to have a CV which will capture the interest, the imagination, of a selection committee which is faced with 400 or 500 bits of paper to read and go through very quickly indeed. You really have to make it look smart, but not too smart. You've got to make it look impressive, but not over-impressive.[37]

... hours redoing your CV. – agonies writing, rewriting, trying to get it right...endless advice, and you never know what is a perfect CV. Political experience, campaigning experience, publishing profession, categorise it all quite clearly, and the most important thing is ease of read, and then I was told by the agent that it must all be one page.[38]

Constituency selection committee: sifting and shortlisting

Selection is a process of gradual elimination at different stages, like a game of musical chairs. The constituency has some flexibility about the procedures used but most follow the guidelines in the party's 'Model Rules'.[39] The group which does most work is the selection committee, composed of ten to twenty-five party members, depending on how active the local party is. Under the model rules the selection committee is appointed by the association's executive committee, who determine its general composition, although several places are reserved.[40]

The selection committee is briefed by the Central Office agent before the process begins so members have a clear idea of their responsibilities. The selection committee sifts all applications, possibly 200–400 in a good seat, targeting about twenty-five people for interview, before recommending no more than six to the executive. Most constituencies make a point of seeing all local applicants. Often the group establishes broad criteria about the kind of person they seek. An association in a rural Somerset constituency, for example, may decide they want someone with a farming background. In an unwinnable Glasgow seat the party may decide they want a young, energetic, candidate with local roots. Selectors use different criteria:

I marked the CVs out of 100, on the basis of education, profession, age, political experience. A person who had been an MP got marks. Or one who had fought elections, ... media, family ... humour, personality, willingness to live locally ... The cut-off point was 74 per cent.[41]

I selected X because his wife was in the photo ... [he] also seemed a caring young person because it said married with three children and gave their ages. (Interview with party member)

Experience was my number one, and the personal history of the candidate. I based my choice on experience and suitability. (Interview with party member)

Such guidelines help the committee members to sift through the large number of applications, to prioritise those for interview. But the criteria may break down in practice; several area agents mentioned that selection committees most often initially ruled out London barristers at the beginning of their deliberations, then ended up selecting one at the end. But these sorts of criteria can also result in an overly narrow shortlist.

Once the shortlist is agreed the constituency chair and area agent will visit the party vice-chairman for advice. Constituencies are recommended to choose the candidate most likely to win the seat and to serve the constituency, but they might also be advised to bear in mind the wider needs of the party in parliament, and to give special consideration to women, ethnic minority or trade union candidates. Central Office intervention does not always take place. It needs to be carefully judged as some constituencies will not accept it. The vice-chairman may draw attention to an experienced candidate who has been overlooked. At this stage important details which do not appear on the curriculum vitae will come out; for example, the constituency chair will be told that one candidate who is confined to a wheelchair does not mention his disability on his curriculum vitae, or that another candidate lives with his boyfriend. It is difficult to know the profile of applicants removed from contention at this point. Party officials suggest that generally they can probably help people to get interviews, occasionally they may be able to stop someone from being interviewed. Once the interview process begins, however, applicants are on their own.

The selection committee interviews often take place over a weekend, allowing time for social contact with applicants and their spouses. Many found the interview process daunting, but soon learnt from the experience:

I'd never been before and I was absolutely terrified. I didn't know what to expect. I believed I had to make a speech, so I mugged up lots of ... I thought, well, what sorts of things, what sorts of theme am I going to take? And they're going to ask me questions about the economy, and they're going to ask me about this and that, and, God, I'm not going to be able to answer.[42]

One gained from experience about what sort of questions one was actually going to get, and ... you got better and better at it because you had more standard answers.[43]

The fact I had a lot of interviews in a short amount of time meant that I learnt the ropes very quickly, and just finessed the act, and even got to know in advance roughly what the questions were going to be because they didn't vary so much between the constituencies.[44]

The format for interviews, usually about thirty minutes each, is a short speech followed by questions for a set time. Questions tend to cover a range of national and local issues, and are often repeated with minor variations for all applicants. As one candidate noted:

> The questions I felt were stereotyped, because I can remember two individuals read me a question, it was about economic unity within the European community, which they clearly did not understand themselves ... I felt the whole thing was stagemanaged.[45]

> As some questions are real chestnuts, plan it well in advance. They always ask you questions like what would be your private member's bill ... They always ask about capital punishment.[46]

Detailed questions about the constituency often caught out non-local applicants, even those who were carefully prepared by reading the local press and going to the library. In the Conservative party the issue of capital punishment came up with great frequency, and was perceived as a litmus test of suitability. Given the flexibility of the Model Rules, committees may occasionally use other procedures; for example, one seat asked applicants to complete a written paper with thirty questions, and to go out to canvass, to supplement the formal interview.[47] For applicants the process can be exhausting, because of the local preparation required, and because many interviews may be scheduled closely together.

At the end of the interviews each member of the selection committee votes for an agreed number of names for the shortlist, usually three to six. Any applicant receiving an overall majority goes forward to the executive committee. If there are less than the agreed number of names on the list, further ballots are held, each time eliminating the applicant at the bottom of the poll.

The executive committee: progressive elimination

As a result of this process the selection committee recommends about three to six people to go forward for interview by the executive committee. The executive consists of about 50–100 delegates from constituency branches and committees. The second interview process is similar to that used in the first stage. Each candidate is given a set time for a short speech (usually ten minutes) followed by about twenty minutes for questions and answers. At the end of this process the executive decides by plurality voting using secret ballots. If one applicant gets over 50 per cent of ballots on the first vote, the others may be eliminated, and only one name may go forward. Today this has become less common, and in good seats it is normal for two or three names to go before the general meeting.

The general meeting: approval by all party members

The final stage is approval by the general meeting of the constituency association, open to all members, which may attract anywhere from 100 to 1,000 participants. Prior to the Chelmer report in 1972, this step involved rubber-stamping; the candidate was 'presented' to the general meeting, who usually adopted the executive's recommendations without discussion.[48] In the run-up to the 1970 election, for example, there was only one occasion when the recommendation of the executive council was reversed by the general meeting.[49] After Chelmer, the general meeting was involved in a more formal process of interview and voting, although it remained common for only one candidate to be presented for approval. During the 1980s, due to dissatisfaction with this process, the general membership was usually given more choice, particularly in safe seats. By 1983 about a quarter of all Conservative general meetings had the choice of more than one finalist.[50] As one agent discussed the change:

I was a Young Conservative in the mid-fifties and my home constituency, Mid Bedfordshire, selected a new candidate to replace the retiring MP. We all trooped along to this large meeting where the man was presented to us, and we all put up our hands, and went home. And I thought, what a pointless procedure. So, ever since that early stage I have always thought that it is better to give a choice to the general membership of the association. So I always seek it, if at all possible, and so far we haven't failed in any Conservative seat. The only occasions when we have agreed that they could put forward one name to a general meeting is in some of the very small associations.[51]

The dangers of providing members with no choice were demonstrated in 1990 by the controversial selection of the black barrister, John Taylor, for Cheltenham, a Conservative marginal. There were 254 applications, which the selection committee reduced to 22, then the executive reduced to 5. With a majority of the executive vote on the first ballot, only Mr Taylor's name was submitted for approval to the general meeting. The association approved his candidacy (111 votes to 82 in his favour). But the association became bitterly and publicly divided by this process, and some local members claimed to have been steamrollered into this decision by the lack of alternatives. The Conservatives' loss of Cheltenham to the Liberal Democrats may have been due in part to these splits. To make sure most party members are behind their candidate, the Model Rules strongly recommend that more than one candidate should be put before the general meeting unless there is a clear majority for the candidate on the first ballot.[52]

At the general meeting, applicants go through the familiar process of delivering a brief speech, with a question and answer session. Members then vote by exhaustive ballot. If accepted, to avoid incurring election expenses,

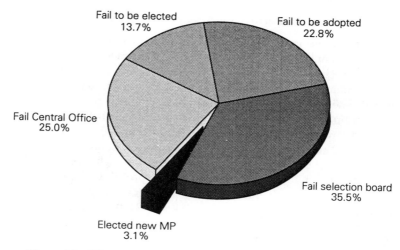

Figure 3.2   The success rate of Conservative applicants

the applicant becomes the *prospective* parliamentary candidate for the constituency. The candidate is only officially adopted when parliament is dissolved.

Thus, in the Conservative party the number of selectors increases at each stage of the process, from one party vice-chairman to a committee of assessors at the selection weekend, to the larger constituency selection committee (10–25), to a still larger executive committee (50–100), and finally to a general meeting which may involve 200–1,000 grassroots members. The process is lengthy and fairly thorough: before they can be adopted, each applicant will have been evaluated in an interview by Central Office, a weekend selection board, and at least three interviews by the constituency. The eliminating process is a series of difficult hurdles: in the 1987–92 parliament, out of the original 900 applicants, about 200 were rejected after the Central Office interview, and another 200 failed the selection board. The 500 survivors joined the total pool of eligibles on the Approved List, including 300 who had passed previous boards. Of the 800 on the Approved List about 460 failed to be adopted for a seat, and about 270 were defeated in election, leaving 61 new Conservative MPs (see figure 3.2).

The evolution of the Conservative selection process

Conservative candidates in the 1950s or 1960s, observing the selection process today, would find much that remains fairly familiar. There continues to be a process which involves four main stages: formal vetting by Conservative Central Office, application to individual constituencies, shortlisting by the local selection committee and executive council, and formal approval by party members at a special general meeting. The basic steps, outlined in previous accounts during the 1960s, remain intact.[53] Nevertheless the process of recruitment in the Conservative party has experienced three major procedural reforms in the post-war period: the Maxwell Fyfe report on party finance in 1949; the revision of 'Model Rules' following the Chelmer Report in 1972; and, as already discussed, the introduction of weekend selection boards in 1980.

Maxwell Fyfe reforms, 1948/9

The first major change in the post-war period involved financial reform. The Maxwell Fyfe committee, established in June 1948, was part of the attempt to modernise the Conservative party after its crushing post-war defeat[54]. Before the Second World War Conservative recruitment tended to follow the traditional pattern of party patronage, where the process was highly informal, and candidates required personal contacts and financial resources to secure a safe seat. In mid-Victorian Britain, there was a decline in the number of 'pocket' boroughs where local landowners could place their man in parliament, due to the extension of the franchise, the introduction of the Corrupt Practices Act and Secret Ballot, and the growth of organised parties. Nevertheless, many seats continued to maintain strong personal links with family members. As Lord Randolph Churchill wrote in 1873,

You see, both he [his father] and my mother have set their hearts on my being member for Woodstock. It is a family borough, and for years a member of the family has sat for it. The present member is a stranger, though a Conservative, and is so unpopular that he is almost sure to be beaten if he were to stand; and the fact of a Radical sitting for Woodstock is perfectly unsupportable to my family.[55]

As social influence declined, financial influence remained. In the pre-war period most Conservative MPs were expected to pay their own election expenses, as well as contributing generously towards the costs of running their local association. Sometimes this seems the only criterion of selection:

Mr Macmillan was fond of regaling younger members with an account of a selection committee he attended in the Twenties at which the chairman simply asked each applicant to write his name on a piece of paper together with the amount he was prepared to donate to the Association's funds. The highest bidder was adopted forthwith.[56]

In the aftermath of the 1945 defeat, the Maxwell Fyfe report argued that this process needed reform because it contributed towards an aristocratic image of the Conservative party, it deterred good candidates without resources from coming forward, and it weakened the party organisation by removing the incentive for mass membership contributions. As the 1945 election was seen as a rejection of Conservative politicians and policies, it was necessary to demonstrate that both were changing.[57] The interim report in 1948 recommended that the election expenses of parliamentary candidates should be the responsibility of the constituency associations; candidates should not contribute more than £25 a year to their constituencies; the question of financial contributions should not be mentioned at selection meetings until after adoption; and associations should only apply to central funds after providing proof that they had made every effort to raise enough money themselves. The reforms were introduced gradually, and were fully implemented probably only in 1955. The result was that associations were obliged to find their own money, and in order to do so they became better organised and more active. Lord Wooton, chairman of the party, claimed these measures reactivated the grassroots machinery: 'The change was revolutionary, and in my view did more than any other single factor to save the Conservative party.'[58] Although drumming up new members, making the selection process more meritocratic, and removing the practice of wealthy landowners or industrialists effectively buying a seat, the new rules had an only limited impact on changing the social background of parliamentary candidates.

The Chelmer Report (1972)

In 1970, following a period in opposition, the National Union asked Lord Chelmer to investigate how the party outside parliament could be made more democratic. Some attributed the electoral weakness of the party during the 1960s to the quality of Conservative candidates, particularly the image that they were out of touch with ordinary people. The party was also criticised for the weakness of the party organisation, and the non-involvement of party members other than in 'quadrennial canvassing and annual jumble sales'.[59] Following Chelmer's recommendations the requirement that candidates should be on the Approved List was strengthened, and the list was pruned substantially, dropping about 200 names in 1974. This culling generated substantial controversy, by alienating some long-standing party loyalists, without many positive effects.[60] The Model Rules were revised by Chelmer to make sure members had a slightly greater role in the choice of candidates at the general meeting. The report also recommended that a sitting MP threatened by non-adoption should have the right to address a full meeting of the association. The impact of the Chelmer report on candidate selection was modest, and represented a consolidation of developments which started earlier.

The impact of reform

What has been the overall impact of these changes on the process? First, the system has moved in a series of steps from an informal 'patronage' system in the pre-war period towards a more formal, rule-governed, open and 'meritocratic' process today. The process started to be formally supervised by Central Office in 1935, with the establishment of the Standing Advisory Committee on Candidates (SACC). In 1949 Maxwell Fyfe introduced the Approved List, financial reforms, and standard Model Rules. These rules remain broad guidelines, allowing some flexibility about the arrangements used by local associations. Procedures are specified in far less detail than in the Labour party. Nevertheless the rules represent a standardisation of the process.

The greatest change during the 1980s was the introduction of the weekend selection boards, which brought management practices into the selection process. As personnel officers recommend, the job is clearly defined, a range of appropriate criteria is specified for evaluation, applicants are observed in different activities, and groups of observers compare marks to standardise assessments. The overall aims of 'Sandhurst selection' are consistent with the dominant ethos within the Conservative party which lays much stress on the objectives of 'fairness' and 'equality of opportunity'. The main objective of the boards is to treat everyone fairly and equally so that the 'best' candidates win, the ones 'most likely to win the seat and to serve the constituency with distinction'.[61] The process had changed less at local level, where more idiosyncratic preferences may prevail, but here it is felt that standardisation is less important than the value of local autonomy.

Secondly, power over selection decisions has simultaneously shifted upwards and downwards within the party, away from the middle-level activists. This change should not be exaggerated, since the Selection Committee and Executive Council in local associations continue to take the major decisions about the shortlisting of individual applicants. Nevertheless, through introducing the weekend selection boards, Conservative Central Office has legitimated its authority in controlling the pool of eligible applicants. At the same time by moving towards greater choice in the final stage, grassroots party members, who attend the special general meeting, now have more influence. This represents a move towards greater 'internal party democracy', by giving all members a genuine voice in the process. As we shall see in the next chapter, there is a similar pattern within the Labour party, although there change has gone further and faster.

These reforms have produced a high degree of satisfaction with the way the process operates in the Conservative party. In the BCS participants were asked to evaluate the selection process according to whether they

Table 3.2   *Evaluation of the Conservative selection process*

'% Very'	MP	PPC	List	Officer	Member
Democratic	61	66	32	72	67
Efficient	47	53	28	57	57
Fair	61	71	30	64	60
Satisfaction Scale	87	89	74	89	85
N.	142	222	209	130	157

Note: Q. 'In your view was the procedure used in your most recent (this) selection meeting ...'
'Satisfaction' is a summary scale ranging from 0–100.
'Officer' refers to those holding local elected office.
Source: BCS, 1992.

thought it democratic, efficient and fair (using a four-point response). These criteria formed a consistent scale,[62] and the responses were summed to produce an overall measure of satisfaction. The results in table 3.2 show that most groups in the Conservative party were fairly positive about the process, with the exception of applicants on the Approved List who failed to secure a seat. About two-thirds of MPs, candidates, local officeholders and members felt the process was very democratic and very fair, and about one half thought it was very efficient. Levels of satisfaction across all criteria were significantly higher in the Conservative than Labour party.

Most participants were even more positive about the influence over the selection process exercised by Central Office and the local association. As shown in table 3.3, again with the exception of the List Applicants, over three quarters of all groups felt the role of the national party leadership and local party was about right. The List Applicants were least happy with the way the system operated, perhaps not surprisingly given that they had failed to secure a seat. But, perhaps because they failed to be shortlisted, their dissatisfaction focused on the local associations, which they felt had too much power, while in contrast they thought the hand of Central Office needed to be strengthened. For reasons discussed in the next chapter, this pattern is strikingly reversed in the Labour party, with greater dissatisfaction about the role of the NEC.

Conclusions: maintaining party unity

The recruitment process has the potential for intra-party conflict, which may prove damaging for party morale and image. In the Conservative party there have always been a handful of cases in each election where sitting MPs have not been readopted, usually on personal grounds for reasons of age, ill

Table 3.3 *Influence over the Conservative selection process (percentage)*

Influence	MP	PPC	List	Officer	Member
National party leadership					
Too great	8	9	19	9	10
About right	78	73	55	88	76
Too little	14	18	27	3	4
Local party					
Too great	14	17	33	4	8
About right	84	79	58	90	86
Too little	2	4	9	5	6
N.	141	218	209	130	157

Note: Q. 'Do you think the influence of the national party leadership has over the selection process is. . .'
'And do you think the influence the local party has over the selection process is. . .'
'Officer' refers to those holding local elected office.
Source: BCS, 1992.

health, financial improprieties or neglect of constituency duties.[63] In most cases pressure has been applied, and often the threat of deselection is sufficient to produce 'voluntary' retirements. Political grounds have also caused non-selection, for example against Powellite or Monday Club candidates in the mid-1960s and early 1970s.[64]

In the 1992 general election there were some Conservative disputes over selection, indeed slightly more than usual. These included the Cheltenham adoption of John Taylor, a black barrister; the deselection of Sir Anthony Meyer in Clwyd North West for his 'stalking horse' leadership challenge; the attempted removal of three backbenchers on personal grounds;[65] and the threatened deselection of nine Conservative MPs for voting against Mrs Thatcher in the Heseltine leadership challenge. The Cheltenham case in particular raised controversial questions about the influence of Central Office, the choice available to grassroots members attending the final general meeting, and wider questions of ethnic minority representation. The subsequent effect on party unity had serious consequences, shown by the loss of Cheltenham to the Liberal Democrats. Nevertheless, these cases are exceptional representing in total only 14 out of 645 selections.

Despite these cases, the Conservatives have usually managed to maintain a high level of party unity, with little public discord between the leadership and local associations. In the selection process disagreements have usually been resolved by a process of informal discussion between all groups. Most participants express considerable satisfaction with the way the system works. In contrast factional disputes over the adoption of candidates are far more common in the Labour party, where there have been heated conference battles over the selection rules. Why does the Conservative process function so effectively?

To some extent this reflects certain long-standing differences between the major parties. This includes the traditional role of Conservative constituency associations as loyal supporters of the parliamentary leadership, the non-federal nature of the Conservative party organisation, and the lack of deep factional or ideological splits within the grassroots membership.

More importantly, it can be argued, the Conservative selection process maintains unity through achieving a balanced division of powers between party headquarters and the constituency associations. Central Office has established legitimate authority, and complete control, over the Approved List. This defines the pool of eligibles who may apply to local vacancies. As such, the leadership can make sure that any unsuitable candidates are eliminated from consideration at an early stage, before they apply to local associations. And, if they so desire, Central Office is able to influence, albeit indirectly, the composition of the parliamentary party, for example by increasing the proportion of women or ethnic minority members in the pool of eligibles. The role of Central Office is therefore front-loaded. Further, Central Office establishes the Model Rules, and oversees their implementation at local level. Once the parameters of the process are established – the agreed rules and the pool of eligibles – the process of scrutiny, shortlisting and final selection of applicants can be safely left to largely autonomous local associations. Therefore we can conclude that the Conservatives have been effective in reforming their selection process towards a more formal meritocratic system which serves to promote party unity.

In contrast, as described in detail in the next chapter, in the Labour party the national lists of candidates are not controlled by the leadership, nor do the lists play an important role in defining the pool of eligibles. The National Executive Committee can exercise its veto powers only at the end of the process, after local constituencies have made their choice of candidate. Given the more factional nature of the party, and its federal organisation, this system is a recipe for conflict. Let us turn to how the selection process works in the Labour party.

4   Labour recruitment

This chapter has three aims. The first is to identify the principal features in the Labour party process, particularly the contrasts with the Conservatives. The second is to explain the main steps in the Labour selection process as it operated during the 1987–92 parliament, primarily from the perspective of candidates and selectors. The third is to analyse how the process has changed over time and evaluate the impact of reforms. As before, the issue of how we explain the *outcome* of the selection process will be left for later chapters.

The main features of Labour party selection

The process of selection in the Labour and Conservative parties shares many characteristics. Both involve a series of distinct stages – application, nomination, shortlisting, selection, and endorsement – with contestants gradually eliminated until a final winner emerges. In both parties the main selection decisions are taken at constituency level. Labour's National Executive Council (NEC) has formal powers to veto candidates, to establish and implement the standard rules (within general principles agreed by party conference), and to intervene more directly in selecting candidates for by-elections.[1] Most significantly, in both parties there has been a shift in selection powers in recent decades, away from the core activists in constituency committees, simultaneously downwards towards party members and upwards towards the national leadership.

Despite these similarities there remain important contrasts between the major parties. In the Labour party the federal structure gives significant powers to trade unions; the selection process has often been a major area of factional conflict between left and right; the national leadership can veto applicants only at the end of the process, and they exercise no control over the pool of eligibles; and greater dissatisfaction is expressed about the way the process operates.

The Labour selection process can be characterised as 'meritocratic' in seats which attract numerous applicants in an open competition, where the final candidate wins due to their political abilities, party experience, and interview performance. But in many safe seats the Labour party system, despite the detailed rule book, is essentially one where informal local patronage remains important. What matters, still, is who you know in these constituencies. This normally means that the favoured applicant is someone who has been around for years, sitting on half a dozen party committees in the local area, canvassing in elections, getting known by activists, local councillors, party agents and trade unionists in the seat.

This system may have certain advantages. It means, if elected, members depart for Westminster with a good understanding of the needs of their area. Local MPs may give a higher priority to constituency casework and keeping in touch with the views of their local party. Applicants are well known to the constituency, so selectors can evaluate them on their contribution to the party over many years, rather than on the basis of their performance at interview, or their brief CV.

But patronage may also have certain disadvantages. Candidates from outside the region have little chance of success in these seats. The process may be abused by powerful local factions ('fixing'), and competition is relatively closed. In the words of one candidate, in good seats few get in 'cold'. You need to know the ropes. In the Labour party a suitable applicant for these seats is seen as someone who has served an apprenticeship, learning through experience how the party works, developing networks, getting to know the constituency, serving the party. Loyalty is demonstrated rather than automatically assumed. This is not to say that patronage is confined to the Labour party. But political recruitment in the Conservatives more commonly follows the meritocratic model. The process of evaluating candidates for Westminster is seen by many Conservatives as similar to the process of managerial recruitment for a medium-sized company: a more impersonal, formal, and 'objective' competition for seats, with the job awarded to the most 'qualified' applicant.

One can speculate that perhaps the process of candidate selection reflects the dominant ethos in each party. The Labour apprenticeship process characterises a more working- class collectivist culture of loyalty to other workers, due rewards for party service, skilled apprenticeships rather than formal qualifications, and local roots rather than geographical mobility. This traditional ethos may have been diluted in recent years by middle-class entryism into the Labour party, but perhaps this has had only a lagged effect on the prevailing party culture. In contrast, the Conservatives are more concerned with the middle-class individualistic virtues of meritocracy – the importance of formal qualifications, explicit criteria for evaluation, and 'the best chap for the job' irrespective of local origin. This contrast jumps out from our interviews, and can be supported by the pattern of candidate competition revealed in the survey data. To illustrate these contrasts let us explore the main steps in the process.

The main steps in Labour selection

The Labour party began in 1900 as the Labour Representation Committee, to secure 'the representation of working-class opinion' in the Commons by 'men sympathetic with the aims and demands of the Labour movement'.[2] The Labour party was designed as a federal organisation, because of its origins in the labour movement. Affiliated organisations include trade unions, cooperative societies, local or area Trades Councils, and socialist societies.[3] The parliamentary party, including Labour MPs and peers, is headed by the party leader, chosen since 1981 by an Electoral College.[4] The party is managed centrally by the National Executive Committee, elected by annual conference. The NEC supervises the services of professional full-time staff at party headquarters in Walworth Road, London. The Director of Organisation, in day-to-day charge of administering candidate selection, is based at Walworth Road.

The role of the constituency Labour party

At local level the basic units are ward branches, workplace branches, Young Socialist branches, Women's Sections, and affiliated organisations such as socialist societies, trade unions and cooperative societies. In some constituencies there are also Black Socialist Societies.[5] All these groups are brought together under the umbrella of each Constituency Labour Party. According to official estimates,[6] the average constituency party has about 500 individual party members, making it far smaller than the average local Conservative association. Within each constituency the main organising body is the General Committee, composed of about 40 to 100 delegates who are elected annually.[7] In turn the General Committee elects a smaller Executive Committee every year, of about twenty to twenty-five members, including the main constituency officers.[8] The main steps in the selection process in constituencies are application and nomination at branch level, shortlisting by the Executive, then selection by the Electoral College (see figure 4.1). The following describes the process for new candidates in the 1987–92 parliament; the reselection process for sitting MPs is discussed later.

Application to local branches

The timetable for selecting candidates is established by the NEC, in consultation with constituencies. Normally the process starts about two years into

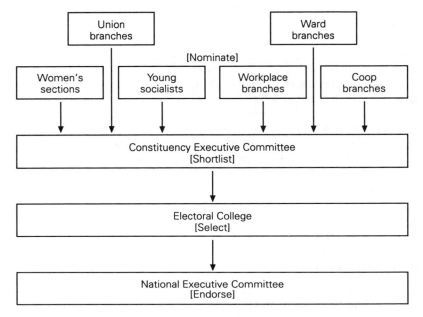

Figure 4.1   Stages in the Labour selection process

the parliament, and the best seats go first, although retirements may occur throughout the electoral cycle. Once the process starts in a constituency, party membership, and delegations to the General and Executive Committees are 'frozen', to prevent 'packing' by new members brought in just to support a contestant. Despite this rule some believe that this practice has not been entirely eliminated.[9] The local Executive Committee produces a detailed document, agreed with the NEC, specifying the timetable for all stages to selection, the procedure for nomination and shortlisting, and details of the Electoral College. The local arrangements are overseen by NEC representatives, sometimes also by regional organisers, to make sure the process follows party rules.

The first step in the selection process is application to local branches. This takes two forms. Branches can actively seek potential candidates, or individuals interested in being considered can write directly to the branch secretary. If branches seek candidates they can consult the lists of applicants from unions (A), constituencies (B), the Cooperative party (C) and women (W). The lists, maintained by Walworth Road, contained in total about 930 names in the 1987–92 parliament.

The trade union ('A') list

The 'A' list has the highest status, because it includes about 180 applicants sponsored by trade unions.[10] In the words of one applicant, 'people knowing that you're on the 'A' list – you're streets ahead'.[11] A union is allowed to contribute at most 80 per cent of the election expenses incurred by its nominee. The union can pay a maximum of £750 a year to the constituency party, or 70 per cent of an agent's salary. Other union support may be forthcoming in an election – organisation, workers, secretarial help, advice, backup. This may tip the balance towards a sponsored candidate for a local party.

It is difficult to generalise about the process of getting on this list, since Labour party rules do not control or standardise this process, leaving it to the discretion of the unions concerned. Some unions use fairly rigorous selection procedures before they endorse candidates, while others are more informal. The Transport and General Worker's Union, for example, uses regional and national interviews to scrutinise applicants. The Amalgamated Engineering Union insists nominees are employed in their trade, and use a rigorous week-long assessment process testing verbal and written skills, knowledge of Labour party policy, public speaking ability and personal interviews.[12] Others like the railway union ASLEF include 'rising stars' in any occupation whom they feel would make good Labour MPs, not just members of their union. In the last election, for example, ASLEF sponsored the actress Glenda Jackson. Some unions sponsor MPs after they have been elected, such as the Boilermaker's (GMBATU) support of Gerald Kaufman. In 1992 the unions sponsored 173 Labour candidates and 143 MPs, in both cases the highest number in the party's history (see figure 4.2). This represents about one quarter of all Labour candidates and one half of the parliamentary Labour party. Since the Conservatives' first administration, union membership has fallen dramatically, from 13.3 million in 1979 to 9.6 million at the end of 1991.[13] Nevertheless, despite the subsequent decline in revenues, union sponsorship has risen steadily in the last three elections.

The constituency 'B' list

In contrast the 'B' list includes about 650 applicants put forward by their constituency party, and enjoys lower status. In the words of one person on the 'B' list

The difference of being on the A list and the B list is like being . . . in the first division in the FA here in England and being in amateur football, because there's so many things that go with being on the A list that it's bound to sway a constituency. If you have sponsorship of a trade union that brings with it organisation and finance.[14]

The process of getting on the 'B' list is straightforward and easy. Applicants are nominated by any local unit of the party. They complete a simple constituency nomination form with details such as length of party and union membership and offices held. This form is signed by the constituency secretary, then formally rubber-stamped by the NEC.[15] The 'B' list is drawn up after every election, it does not roll forwards, so applicants need to reapply each time. As some members on the list described the routine process at ward meetings:

The lists come round, time and time and time again ... people don't have much respect for the B list, let's be honest, it comes every so often, and this time I said yes, right, I'll go on ... Of course, I think you recognise that if you're on the 'B' list you ain't got much chance ... I did expect, perhaps among some of my colleagues in the Labour party, that they might think, you know – 'who does she think she is? She's just a miner's wife, actually putting herself down on the parliamentary list.' – But no, they didn't. I was pleasantly surprised by that. They just accepted it – 'Oh, [she] wants to be an MP.'[16]

It was suggested by a number of colleagues in the party that I ought to put my name forward. Besides which, to begin with, they're always desperate to get anyone to put their names forward ... You say, alright, I'll go on the panel, and all that means is you're prepared to stand somewhere.[17]

For some, getting on the list is the first step towards Westminster, and two thirds of those on the lists actively applied to seats in the 1987–92 parliament. Going on the list may help crystallise ambition, and represents a

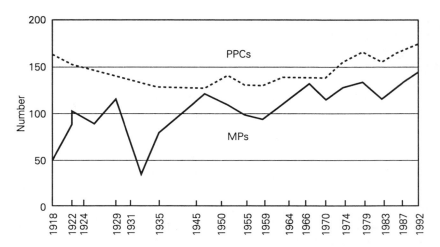

Figure 4.2   Trends in trade union sponsored candidates and MPs.
Source: F. W. S. Craig 1989.

useful stepping stone. For others it remains a formality, rather than a serious declaration of intent.[18] As one person on the 'B' list said: 'I've been on that list for donkey's years, I mean, I was surprised I was still on it. Quite frankly the B list means nothing as far as I'm concerned.'[19]

There are good reasons why the 'B' list is accorded little status. Inclusion carries no financial sponsorship, nor does it guarantee official endorsement. From 1960 to 1966 the organisation committee of the NEC vetted, and if necessary interviewed, nominees on the B list, but this practice was discontinued in part because it was poorly implemented.[20] As a result the 'B' list lacks the significance of the Conservative Approved List although some thought the openness of the 'B' list was a virtue of the Labour system, since it allowed diversity without preliminary screening.

If you say you want to be selected that's enough, as long as you've been a party member long enough. That's enough, and it's up to local parties whether they're going to trust you with the job.[21]

If branches are actively seeking applicants they may consult this list. Some people on the 'B' list reported being phoned 'out of the blue' and invited to apply for two or three constituencies, although usually for hopeless seats which might have problems attracting contestants[22]. For most going on this list represents a symbolic step, a declaration of general interest and availability.

The Cooperative party 'C' list

The 'C' list includes about one hundred applicants sponsored by the Cooperative party and cooperative societies. These are affiliated to the Labour party, reflecting the party's historical roots, although today they represent something of an anachronism. Inclusion in the Cooperative list involves individual and group interviews, public speaking and discussion exercises, and detailed scrutiny of political, union, educational and other qualifications. The Cooperative party remains influential in some seats, but they sponsor far fewer contestants than the unions. The Cooperative party reached its peak in the early 1950s, with about thirty-eight candidates and sixteen to nineteen MPs (see figure 4.3), then subsequently declined. In 1992 the Cooperative party sponsored twenty-six candidates (4.1 per cent) and fourteen MPs (5.1 per cent), which probably reflects the proportion of grassroots party members who belong to this organisation.[23]

The women's 'W' list

The 'W' list, introduced in 1989, includes the names of any women who are already on the other lists. It is available so that branches seeking women

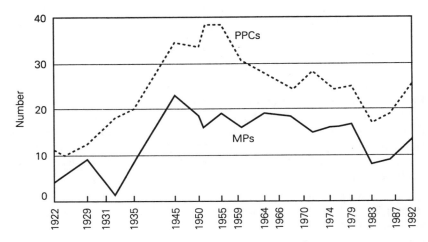

Figure 4.3   Trends in Coop party sponsored candidates and MPs.
Source: F. W. S. Craig 1989.

applicants, or all-women shortlists, can efficiently identify those who might
be available in their region. Many women's sections and some party
branches have been prepared to do this. At least three constituencies,
Hampstead and Highgate, Hornsey and Wood Green, and Birmingham
Selly Oak, selected all-woman shortlists in 1992. Between 1989 and 1992 the
list included 156 names.

Direct application to branches

Those on the list can wait to see whether they will be contacted by any
branch but more ambitious applicants directly applied for good seats.
Forthcoming selections are advertised nationally in the party press and
through the candidates' office, but most applicants learn about vacancies in
advance through the regional or local grapevine.[24] Any member of the
Labour party who is paid-up for at least a year can apply. Most people
applied to about three seats, but strategies varied substantially. As discussed
in chapter 9, some were selective, since they were only interested in representing their local constituency, while others went for seats within their
region, or any good vacancy. One of the most striking contrasts with the
Conservatives was the localised nature of candidate competition in the
Labour party. In the high-prospect challenger seats, at the time they
applied, over half the adopted Labour candidates already lived in the
constituency, about half were asked to apply, and two-thirds already knew

party members in the seat (see chapter 9, table 9.5). Many Labour candidates reflect the dominant ethos when they expressed strong disapproval of 'carpet-baggers'

I restricted my initial focus on Derbyshire seats ... Rightly or wrongly I felt at the time, and still feel to a large extent, that you have to have some understanding of the people, some knowledge of the people, and not live too far from them, so you share the same things, you share the same problems, you identify with them, your roots are connected.[25]

There were a change in the movement, not just in Sheffield but all over, saying we ought to have local candidates, people who know the constituency, people who had been educated, brought up in it, worked in it.[26]

As some Labour MPs described it, with local support they just naturally stood in their own seat:

I sort of emerged and didn't have to fight my way up really ... Friends and people I knew in the party, yes there was general encouragement. There was just an assumption I would ... I'd been around a lot. I was very active in the Labour party and it just sort of happened that way.[27]

The more we went round asking people, people were saying why don't you go. You know everybody. You know how it works. So I said right, and put my name forward.[28]

In contrast, as we have observed, Conservatives were far more likely to go for any good vacancy around the country in a national competition for seats.

Those interested in a vacancy contact the constituency secretary for a list of branches and affiliated organisations, then send their curriculum vitae to the branch secretaries. The information in the CVs is not standardised, there are no guidelines, and some include a brief political statement. Those wanting to push their case further may distribute their CV more widely to other party members, or contact them informally, although this may prove counter-productive if seen as too 'pushy'. This may be followed by phone calls to see whether branches were interested, and when meetings were planned. The official rules are meant to ban canvassing but, as some noted, in practice it was impossible to enforce these rules by preventing members talking to each other:

The system was open to abuse and was abused, and the issue of canvassing behind the scenes was the paramount example of that. A number of seats that I know fairly well, the degree of canvassing was extreme. It was open to that because nobody actually defined what is meant by canvassing, contact, and so on. It was left to interpretation.[29]

Branch nomination

Each branch can make one nomination. The total number of nominations within a constituency depends on the number of applicants and the number of branches. Poor seats such as those in Surrey or Sussex may attract only a few contestants whereas good seats in the urban North or Scotland may have far more. The number of active branches in the constituency varies substantially, including ward branches, union branches, women's organisations, socialist societies and cooperative societies. Some urban constituencies such as Birmingham Hall Green and Birmingham Edgbaston have only three wards, while others such as South Derbyshire and Ryedale have over twenty, although not all wards will have an active Labour branch. There is considerable variation, but we estimate there are about twenty-three nominating bodies in the average constituency, with almost twice as many union sections (thirteen) as ward branches (seven).[30]

Branch Interview

Party branches considering applicants may invite them for interview, although this is not required for nomination. Applicants draw lots for the order of presentation, which usually involves a brief speech plus question and answer session. The presentation is normally about 15–20 minutes per applicant. Occasionally wards used other procedures, for example a 'panel discussion' with the same questions rotated to all applicants.[31] The sort of questions varied, but most focused on policy issues, particularly those on the ideological fault-line such as public ownership, nuclear weapons or union rights.

They asked me my views on the changes in Eastern Europe ... views on nuclear weapons, views on Europe, views on the exchange rate mechanism, views on nationalisation, views on health, education, views on women. They were – and rightly so – they were quite sort of varied from meeting to meeting, but they were quite detailed and quite questioning and quite probing – and rightly so.[32]

As to the types of questions, ... they were quite clearly policy questions because there are policies that people care passionately about, and there are also policy areas that people might feel you'll be vulnerable on...There's a very important tactical element in asking questions to expose as well as to reveal...with some groups of people, having a particular stance on nuclear weapons is a big plus, and they're going to nominate you, and with another group of people it means they certainly are not going to, and so its important for whoever's in the body of the room to make jolly sure others know that. That's fair.[33]

The 'nuclear' question functioned similarly to the 'hanging' question in the Conservatives; it provided an indication of the ideological persuasion of contestants. Getting nominations may be a fairly prolonged process, involving a series of meetings around the constituency, often on different nights. From start to finish selection may take two or three months. Recent reforms have lengthened the process, thereby increasing the travel and accommodation costs for non-local contestants. But contestants can be nominated by branches without ever attending meetings.[34] The branch meetings may be scarcely attended, with less than a dozen members bothering to turn up to some wards,[35] although others drew forty to fifty members.[36]

Nomination is a critical hurdle which cannot be by-passed. Unless at least one branch nominates, applicants cannot be considered for the executive shortlist.[37] The process of being interviewed by a series of branch meetings helps applicants become better known in a constituency, which may pay off in the final Electoral College. Applicants commonly believe the key to securing nominations is having good networks among local members, particularly friends willing to push your candidacy, or union sponsorship. Some felt the ability to perform at interview, to impress people on the day with speeches, is likely to prove insufficient by itself:

I think you'd have to make a spectacular impression on the Labour party if you were coming from outside to be able to get to the shortlist because the days of some dazzling speaker turning up are gone, and people are looking for something different. Because, apart from anything else, in the age of the soundbite, the ability to declare and wave your arms about and make long speeches are a way of the past.[38]

Shortlisting: the executive committee

Once nominations are complete the executive committee of the constituency draws up a shortlist. Where there are only about five or six people nominated by branches, then this step is a formality, and all are shortlisted. One seat shortlisted all eight who had been nominated. Where there are more contestants then the Executive votes using a series of ballots. If the number of nominees is reduced from, say, fifteen to five, this stage may be a critical bottleneck.

Since 1987 there have been four principles in the shortlisting rules which regulate the process. There must be at least one woman on the shortlist, unless no women have been nominated by any branches. Sitting MPs must be included if they wish to restand. Where there is no incumbent, there must be at least five names on the shortlist, providing there are at least five nominees. Anyone who received at least one quarter of all nominations (including one from a party branch) must be shortlisted. Prior to this there were some cases where contestants won half the nominations but failed to be shortlisted, whereas union nominees with only one nomination were included, much to the annoyance of the wards.[39]

These rules regulate shortlisting to some degree. Yet at the same time since there is no requirement for interviews, no set application form, and no written report from branch interviews, the process of evaluating nominees is not standardised. It seems likely that unless contestants are already known to the executive, have union sponsorship, or fall into one of the above categories, they stand little chance. Further, as one applicant complained, there was no right of appeal for those who got some nominations but were not shortlisted.[40] The shortlist is then confirmed by the General Committee who may vote to add, substitute or delete nominees. In seats without a Labour MP, most shortlists contained about four nominees who went forward to the Electoral College.[41]

Some of these seats (about 7 per cent) used shortlists of one, which require closer scrutiny, because this provides no choice for the Electoral College. These seats fell into two categories: hopeless targets and established candidates. On the one hand, there were Conservative or Liberal seats with a solid majority, where Labour was a low prospect challenger in third place. In such places as Worthing, Esher and Wiltshire North there may be difficulties finding good nominees willing to become the Labour standard-bearer. On the other hand, some seats with one name on the shortlist were good target marginals for Labour. Where this occurred, usually the Labour candidate had already fought the previous general election or a recent by-election in the seat. The local party may have decided that they did not wish to replace a good candidate who had already become well known in the local community. Where there is a shortlist of one, party members can only rubber-stamp the decision. In most cases, however, the Electoral College is presented with a genuine choice.

Final selection: the Electoral College

In the past the final stage of selection in constituencies was decided by core activists on the General Committee. In 1989 Labour transferred this power to an Electoral College composed of all party members and affiliated organisations. The aim was to reduce the power of local activists, to give all grassroots party members a voice in the final selection, and to preserve some influence for trade unions. In the Electoral College, at least 60 per cent of the votes were allocated to local party members and a maximum of 40 per cent to affiliated organisations, mainly unions, within each constituency. The idea of an electoral college was familiar to members as it has been used since 1981 to choose the party leader. In 1993 this process was again changed, as discussed later, to one-member–one-vote (OMOV).

There were three methods of voting in the college. Affiliated organisations voted by post, after deciding whether or not to consult their members about their choice. Secondly, individual party members unable to attend the selection meeting because of domestic responsibilities, disabilities, and employment (for example, shift work) could apply in advance for a postal vote. All postal voters were circulated with brief details about each candidate, including CVs plus a 500-word political statement. Lastly, other individual members attended the final selection meeting to vote. Meetings of the Electoral College varied in size; over half attract more than 100 participants, while a few (about 12 per cent) draw more than 200.[42] Most constituencies hold one Electoral College meeting, although some have several meetings in different parts of the constituency, to maximise participation.

The interview format in the Electoral College is similar to that used by the Conservatives. Applicants are given about twenty-five minutes to present themselves to members. Normally they make a short political speech and then deal with questions from the floor. Presentations vary substantially. Some manage to engage the audience, by integrating personal experience with a few effective political points, but others read their speech straight from notes, or improvise with little evidence of preparation. Party rules restrict the range of questions which can be asked; in particular, 'racist' and 'sexist' questions are not permitted. The organisers try to ensure that all applicants are asked similar questions, for a fair comparison. Questions from the floor may be fairly predictable, reflecting current issues in the national news, items of local interest, or questions about the candidate's commitment to the constituency, loyalty to the party and ideas about campaign strategy. But others may be highly idiosyncratic, reflecting the interests of particular members rather than matters of general concern. The three- or four-hour meeting is fairly formal and usually low-key unless there is some local controversy. It usually provides a long evening for most participants, with little opportunity for real interaction with the applicants. Participants have to be present at the meeting from start to finish if they wish to vote, their membership credentials are strictly checked at the door, late entrants are disqualified, and outside observers are not permitted.

Endorsement by the National Executive Committee

Lastly, before being accepted as the official Labour candidate, the nominee needs to be endorsed by the NEC. Due to its extra-parliamentary origins, Labour has always been more of a 'bottom-up' party, while the Conservatives have a more 'top-down' tradition.[43] The role of the Labour leadership has therefore tended to be limited to the negative power of veto, implementing and reforming the rules (under principles adopted by party conference), and intervening more actively only in by-elections. The NEC has occasionally vetoed nominees. In the 1992 election it expelled two incumbents connected to the Militant Tendency, Dave Nellist (Coventry South East) and Terry Fields (Liverpool Broadgreen). Since the mid-1980s, the NEC has taken a more active role in trying to support incumbents threatened by left-wing groups with deselection.

The evolution of the Labour selection process

The Labour selection process has evolved over the years, with significant reform in the 1980s. The selection rules are national, established by party conference and implemented by the NEC, to ensure uniform and fair procedures throughout the country. Given their importance, attempts to reform party rules have been at the heart of some bitter intra-party disputes, and the subject of considerable factional conflict. There have been six main reforms: the 1933 Hastings Agreement regulating trade union sponsorship; the 1957 Wilson reforms of the financial arrangements; the introduction of mandatory reselection of sitting MPs in 1980; the 1989 changes to the rules regulating shortlisting and the introduction of the Electoral College; and the move in the 1993 conference towards one member–one vote and all-women shortlists.

1933 Hastings Agreement

Trade unions sponsored parliamentary candidates well before the Labour party was founded. In the pre-1918 period, the unions provided almost all the party's funds and workers, so almost all Labour candidates and MPs were sponsored. In the late 1920s there were calls for reform, following fears that some trade unions were effectively able to 'buy a seat'. In 1933, the Hastings Agreement was introduced to control the maximum amount which unions could contribute towards sponsored MPs. The rules stipulated that affiliated organisations could contribute no more than 80 per cent of the candidate's election expenses. Constituencies therefore have to raise at least 20 per cent of the expenses. Moreover, the sponsor could not contribute more than a maximum amount to a constituency party. The sums have been periodically revised upwards, and in 1992 the maximum was £750 per annum.

1957 Wilson financial reforms

Sponsorship of Labour candidates was not confined to unions and affiliated organisations. Between the wars there were various instances of candidates paying their own expenses.[44] In 1955 the Wilson committee on party organisation expressed concern about this practice, because of its effect on the organisation and the way it could influence the selection process. This echoed the concern of the Maxwell Fyfe report in the Conservatives just a few years earlier. As a result of the Wilson report in 1957 the Hastings Agreement was amended so Labour candidates were not allowed to contribute towards their election expenses, and they were limited to a maximum contribution of £50 towards their constituency organisation. Questions about financial contributions were banned until after selection. This removed the element of self-sponsorship from the process, although it may thereby have served to strengthen slightly the role of union sponsorship.

1980 Reselection of incumbent MPs

Internal debates within the party about reselection of sitting MPs reflect long-standing differences between left and right about the nature of party democracy.[45] Left-wing party activists had long sought to reform the candidate selection process to achieve greater control over the party leadership, including the composition of the Parliamentary Labour Party.[46] After Labour lost power in 1970 there was a shift towards the left as a result of discontent among some members with the performance of the Wilson government of 1964–70. The Campaign for Labour Party Democracy was founded in 1973, after a dispute about the party programme. Articulating the concerns of the left, this group argued that the parliamentary party needed to be made more accountable to constituency parties. The group proposed various structural changes including increasing the official status of conference resolutions, introducing an Electoral College involving constituency parties in the selection of the party leader, and implementing mandatory reselection of Labour MPs. The issue of reselection was first debated, but defeated, at the 1974 conference. This proposal gradually gained ground within the party with the rise of the left in the late 1970s, fuelled by increased disillusion with the performance of the 1974–9 Labour government.

In the aftermath of defeat, the 1980 conference introduced mandatory reselection of sitting Labour MPs before each general election. The rules stipulate that each MP has to be put through the reselection process within three years of the previous election, though all have the automatic right to be shortlisted. The change of rules ensured that the process would be routine. The left hoped that this would increase the accountability of MPs to constituency General Committees, where they were often strongly represented. Direct accountability to all party members was considered, but rejected. As the advocates argued,

It was felt that the GC – with its elected, delegate composition, its regular contact with the MP, and its representation of trade union branches – was the only body properly able to monitor the MPs actions, and therefore was best placed to be responsible for re-selection.[47]

Many on the right believed that this would lead to 'caucus control', as Ostrogorski originally feared, thereby undermining the independence of Labour MPs. This decision helped to precipitate the 'Limehouse Declaration', fuelling the breakaway movement of leading Labour MPs to found the Social Democratic Party (SDP).

Table 4.1 *Number of constituency deselections of Labour MPs*

	Total	Uncontested selection %	Contested selection	Deselected by CLP
1981–83	217	151 (69.5)	66	8
1983–87	177	135 (76.3)	42	6
1987–92	205	146 (71.2)	59	2*

Note: * includes only constituency deselections, not those by the NEC.
Source: calculated from Butler and Kavanagh 1992.

In many respects deselection proved to be a paper tiger. When first implemented, in 1981, those most at risk of constituency deselection were the more right-wing, older generation of Labour MPs. Some local battles produced bitter in-fighting. In 1981–3 Fred Mulley was deselected in Sheffield Park, Stan Cohen was dropped in Leeds South-East, and in Bradford North Ben Ford was defeated by Pat Wall of the Militant Tendency. Others like Bryan Magee, Tom McNally and Neville Sandelson defected to the SDP before being pushed. There were fewer reselection battles in subsequent parliaments, although in the 1983–7 parliament Ernie Roberts lost Hackney North and Stoke Newington to Diane Abbott, Michael Cocks was ousted in Bristol South, and Robert Kilroy-Silk resigned Knowsley North in 1986, forcing a by-election, after facing left-wing pressure. In the 1987–92 parliament, Syd Bidwell (Southall) and John Hughes (Coventry North East) were deselected by their local party. Frank Field battled in Birkenhead, and his deselection was eventually reversed by the NEC.[48] The new process precipitated some early retirements, but only a small, and diminishing, number of Labour MPs have been successfully deselected by constituencies; eight in 1980–3, six in 1983–7, and two in 1987–92.[49] This is far fewer than the number of Labour MPs who retire for traditional reasons like age or infirmity. For most Labour MPs, reselection has become a formality, as they are the only name on the short-list. Nevertheless, it may have consequences. Fear of deselection may cause MPs to keep in closer touch with their local party, with the result that they are absent from parliament. As one noted, during this period: 'MPs were away for three or four months watching their backs'.[50] Many MPs felt that the process had become a laborious rigmarole which, if there was a shortlist of one, wasted the time of party activists and elected members. The process was 'a bit lumbering'.[51] Proposals to streamline reselection are under review.

1989 selection by Electoral College

Those on the right within the Labour party had long argued that selection meetings should be reformed by opening them to all paid-up party members, on the grounds that greater participation would lead to a more representative (that is, less left-wing) outcome. This view can be traced back to Peter Paterson's argument in the 1960s in favour of party primaries.[52] A proposal along these lines was suggested in 1974, but rejected by the NEC since it would have undermined the role of unions in local parties.[53] This question reopened with renewed vigour following Labour's defeat in the 1983 election, a shift towards the centre-right in the NEC, and the election of Neil Kinnock as party leader.

During the mid-to-late 1980s, Labour experienced a radical shakeup of policy and organisation. One of Kinnock's highest priorities was to reestablish central managerial control, through a more efficient, coordinated, and modernised party. Reorganisation aimed to tackle the series of interrelated problems facing Labour – the need to prevent continued public conflict between left-wing party activists, particularly members of the Militant Tendency, and the more moderate parliamentary party; the need for a more effective campaign machine following the debacle of the 1983 general election; the need for a general modernisation of party headquarters in Walworth Road to cut costs and promote efficiency; the need to rethink the ongoing issue of the role of the unions in the party; the need for a revised machinery to produce an effective policy review; and last, but not least, the need to staunch, or reverse, the long-term erosion in the number of paid-up members at the Labour party grassroots.[54] Therefore the leadership produced a climate receptive to reform of the candidate selection process as part of this general party reorganisation. In 1987, Labour party conference passed a series of reforms to the traditional nomination, shortlisting and selection process.

Conference considered three options for reforming the selection process. First, it could have retained the old system of selection by the General Committee. Secondly, it could have opted for radical change, that is selection by one-member–one-vote of all individual party members in a constituency. Conference chose the third option; the General Committee lost its powers of selection to the Electoral College. The main impact of this change was to transfer more power from the core party activists on the General Committee down towards individual party members. Some approved of the change, believing it to be democratic in giving all members a voice in the process, while preserving a fair role for trade union supporters.[55] But most voices were extremely critical of the new system. When asked about the best features of the Labour party process, most respondents had little to say in favour of the Electoral College. Candidates identified a number of flaws with the system which caused considerable concern. First, members expressed disquiet because the system was complicated, difficult to organise, and open to abuse.

The 40 per cent trade union thing is absolutely a recipe for a nightmare. You see what can happen . . . is that a candidate could be selected for a safe seat by people not one of whom had ever seen him or heard him or met him, because you could have 10 per cent postal votes, 40 per cent trade unions, and not one need have ever met the MP.[56]

[The Electoral College] . . . was just mind-bogglingly complicated. I don't think people understood it. They just knew there was something called an 'electoral college', and they hoped to hell that the person who turned up had a calculator.[57]

The Labour party selection process is terrible; it's out of date, it's incompetent, it's inefficient, it's not representative.[58]

Secondly, there were administrative problems validating nominal levels of union affiliates. The composition of the electoral college varied considerably from constituency to constituency. The party rules stipulated that affiliated organisations, mostly unions, got at most 40 per cent of the college vote, but many got less. The exact proportion was calculated by membership and affiliation lists at the start of selection (the 'freeze date'). The Electoral College 'mirrored' the composition of the General Committee.[59] Where the affiliates' share of the General Committee exceeded 40 per cent, their votes were weighted to reduce them to the maximum allowed. Although making the relevant computations seems an arithmetic nightmare, party officials report it was relatively simple to implement. The real difficulty lay in validating membership lists and determining who was entitled to receive voting credentials. Eligibility criteria varied in complexity, with different rules for individual members and affiliate electors.[60] Unions could decide to affiliate to the maximum level. This could be checked by going through their membership records and seeing how many members lived in a constituency. But in practice this was rarely done.[61]

Thirdly, the system of postal votes proved problematic. Although they were circulated with brief details about candidates, postal voters could make their choices without much information, sometimes without ever seeing the candidates, since strict rules prevented personal canvassing. This probably created a bias towards certain types of candidates, particularly those already known in the local constituency, at the expense of aspirants of real weight who came from elsewhere in the country. Any member could get a postal vote by claiming that they met the required conditions, such as illness or work practices, which prevented them from attending the selection meeting. But this system was open to abuse by those who wanted to participate while

Table 4.2   *Proportion of Affiliates by type of seat*

	Proportion of affiliates			
	40% +	20–39%	> 20%	
Incumbents	53	41	5	100%
Inheritors	64	36	0	100%
High-prospect challengers	23	60	17	100%
Low-prospect challengers	24	58	18	100%

Source: Representation of Women in the Labour Party: NEC Consultation Document (London, The Labour Party, 1990).

avoiding a lengthy evening meeting. Other parties which use postal ballots, like the Greens and Liberal Democrats, do not stipulate any such conditions. A more consistent system would be one in which every participant voted by post, or alternatively, in which only those attending the meeting were entitled to vote. Moreover, the ban on canvassing could be lifted, allowing nominees to send postal voters information about themselves. The Greens provide details about applicants including their telephone numbers, so members can contact them to find out about their views.

Lastly, and most importantly, the appropriate role for trade unions remained controversial. In theory the 40 per cent ceiling reduced union power. But the new rules produced considerable dissatisfaction with the level of influence exercised by affiliates. The reform may have made members more aware of the power of trade unions, and the manner in which that power was exercised. Many unions determined their vote without seeing the applicant, or consulting their members. The vote of the unions was sufficient to determine the outcome in no more than about half a dozen constituencies. But their influence was more widespread, especially in the Labour heartland seats, hence they had a disproportionate impact on the composition of the Parliamentary Labour party. Candidacies can be analysed in terms of the categories used earlier: incumbents, inheritors, high-prospect challengers, and low-prospect challengers. As indicated in table 4.2, unions were entitled to their maximum vote in half of the incumbent, and two-thirds of the inheritor, contests. Therefore, unions were most influential where it mattered most – in seats which Labour was most likely to win. All these issues raised serious doubts about the workability of the electoral college and led to the debate about moves towards one-member–one-vote.

1989: women on shortlists

In 1918 four places were reserved in the NEC for women (increased to five in 1937) in early recognition that special arrangements were needed to facilitate the participation of women. In 1992 in addition to five places in the women's section of the NEC, there was one reserved place for women in the constituency section, and two in the union section. In the 1970s and 1980s the patterns of race and gender politics led to demands for quotas at all levels of the party. It remained difficult to persuade party conference that reform should be given high priority since this threatened the established interests of union affiliates and party activists. Members of constituency Executive and General Committees wanted to safeguard the principle of local autonomy in selecting 'their' prospective parliamentary candidate. Women in the party were able to use the opportunity of the debate about party reorganisation in the mid-1980s to add their own agenda: to increase the proportion of Labour women in the Commons. Groups had long argued that the selection process represented a critical barrier to women, as well as to applicants who were working class or from ethnic minorities.

In 1987, Labour party conference passed a new rule for the compulsory shortlisting of women. This rule said that, where a woman has been nominated, there must be at least one woman on the shortlist. If no woman has been shortlisted by the regular procedure followed by the Executive Committee, the final name on the shortlist is dropped, and a ballot held to determine which of the nominated women should be included. After a process of consultation by the NEC, selection under the new procedures began in January 1989.

What have been the results of these rules? Evidence from Labour selections from January 1989 to March 1990, in 219 constituencies, indicates on balance positive news for women. Seats can be classified, as before, into four types: incumbents, inheritors, high-prospect challengers and low-prospect challengers. The results in table 4.3 indicate that women were shortlisted in over three-quarters of all inheritor and high-prospect challenger seats. More than half the shortlists continued to have no women, although most of these were reselections of incumbent MPs with only one candidate. In all the selections during this period one quarter included at least one woman, while a fifth included two or more women. This does not mean women are necessarily being selected in these seats, but at least they are being interviewed by the Electoral College.

The impact of these new rules is open to interpretation. A pessimistic perspective suggests that more women may be trekking around the country to attend interviews without, in reality, standing any better chance of gaining a good seat. Since continual rejection is demoralising, the process is

Table 4.3 *Proportion of constituency shortlists including women*

Type of Seat	No women	One woman	Two or more women	% seats	Total
Incumbents	74	15	11	100	131
Inheritors	18	82	0	100	11
High-prospect challengers	27	35	38	100	52
Low-prospect challengers	40	20	40	100	25
Total	56	24	20	100	219

Source: As for table 4.2.

time-consuming, and interviews are expensive, the ultimate effect of these reforms, no matter how well intentioned, may be to discourage women's participation in the long-run. But optimists believe that at least women are surmounting one formal stage of the process, gaining interview experience, and thereby getting closer to the winning post.

1993: all-women shortlists

The 1993 conference took this process a step further, with the radical proposal that there should be all-women shortlists in half the Labour inheritor and high-prospect challenger seats. Despite some bitter attacks, this was passed in a composite motion, and also approved as part of the procedure for selection, although it remains to be seen whether and how this will be implemented. Clare Short has strongly defended this move, although other Labour MPs such as Neil Kinnock and Roy Hattersley have been outspoken in their criticism. Although in favour of positive discrimination for women and ethnic minorities, Roy Hattersley has argued that if Walworth Road tells local constituencies that they can only shortlist women applicants this is likely to back-fire and produce damaging in-fighting: 'This way of doing it will produce chaos and is just unworkable. Constituencies won't do it.'[62]

If implemented as proposed, this seems likely to produce a significant rise in the number of Labour women MPs, because women would be getting access to the good seats. Estimates of the possible effects have to remain highly approximate. To simplify matters, let us assume as our baseline that only two or three current Labour women MPs decide to retire or are defeated in the next general election. New women inheritors would swell these ranks. In the post-war period, about thirty Labour MPs have usually retired at general elections. If half these seats adopted all-women shortlists, about fifteen new Labour women candidates would inherit a seat with a gilt-edged chance of being elected. We then add the target marginals. After the 1992 election Labour are high prospect challengers in seventy-three Conservative seats. Any Labour gains depend upon the size and direction of the two-party swing, as well as the work of the Boundary Commission. These effects are unknown but post-war trends indicate that about twenty-one Conservative MPs are usually defeated by (mostly Labour) challengers every general election. Based on this approximate estimate, if the next election conforms to these trends, the number of Labour women MPs may perhaps increase from thirty-seven in 1992 to about sixty-three in 1996/7. This would be an important change within the Labour ranks although, if all other parties continued as at present, the proportion of women MPs in Parliament would probably increase from 9 per cent to around 15 per cent. This would remain below the average in comparable European parliaments, and it would take successive general elections for Labour to achieve its target. It remains to be seen if and how Labour implements these proposals.

1993: One member–one vote

The Labour selection process has experienced considerable change since 1987 as part of the general attempt to modernise the party, and move from a party of affiliates towards a party of individual members. In this process, the Electoral College was a classic Labour party fudge which left few content. In the words of one candidate, the Electoral College was neither 'fish nor fowl'. Many felt it would have been preferable either to keep the old system of selection by General Committee, or to move straight to a system of one-member–one-vote[63] . The 1990 conference supported the principle of the more democratic and straightforward system of one-member–one-vote. The 1993 conference resolved this issue, by a tight vote (47.5 per cent for, 44.4 per cent against), despite bitter opposition from John Edmunds of the GMB and Bill Morris of the transport workers, after John Smith threw his whole weight behind this principle. For the next general election candidates will be selected by one-member–one-vote, and all individual trade unionists who pay the political levy plus a £3 membership fee will be able to take part in their local constituency.

Conclusions

There was widespread dissatisfaction with the effects of the 1987 reforms. This was evident when we asked respondents how they evaluated the process in terms of being democratic, efficient and fair. The results show far less satisfaction with the system in the Labour party than in the Conservative party (see tables 4.4 and 3.2). A majority of members thought the

Table 4.4 *Evaluations of the Labour selection process*

'% Very'	MP	PPC	List	Officer	Member
Democratic	44	40	22	40	58
Efficient	29	26	13	34	44
Fair	43	33	19	37	47
Satisfaction Scale	76	78	68	76	82
N.	86	303	92	174	279

Note: Q. In your view was the procedure used in your [the] most recent selection meeting ...
'Satisfaction' is a summary scale ranging from 0–100.
'Officer' refers to those holding local elected office.
Source: BCS, 1992.

Table 4.5 *Influence over the Labour selection process*

	MP	PPC	List	Officer	Member
National Party Leadership					
Too great	9	15	42	32	22
About right	75	75	48	61	73
Too little	16	10	11	7	6
Local Party					
Too great	8	8	16	12	11
About right	83	80	54	64	74
Too little	8	13	30	24	15
N.	86	303	92	174	279

Note: Q. 'Do you think the influence the national party leadership has over the selection process is ...'
'And do you think the influence the local party has over the selection process is ...'
'Officer' refers to those holding local elected office.
Source: BCS, 1992.

system democratic, but few felt it was very efficient or fair. As in the Conservatives, List Applicants proved the most critical, although this pattern may reflect sour grapes, since they were the losers from the system.

As we have observed, the NEC have far fewer powers over selection than Conservative Central Office. Yet, most interestingly, when asked about the relative influence of the NEC and local party, the traditional suspicions of the leadership are clearly apparent (see table 4.5). Most people expressed support for the status quo, believing the current division of powers was about right, but some felt that the role of the national leadership was too great. We can conclude that the process of selection in the Labour party remains more contentious than in the Conservatives. To some extent this is attributable to traditional and long-standing features of Labour party politics, notably its federal structure, distrust of the national leadership, and factional divisions. But it also seems probable that the structure of the Labour party selection process is partly responsible for this situation. The use of an approved list, in the Conservative, Liberal Democrat and Scottish Nationalist parties, allows the leadership to determine the overall pool of suitable applicants without unduly constraining the choice of local constituencies. The role of the leadership is front-loaded. In contrast, the use of veto power by the Labour National Executive, after constituencies have already selected their candidate, is a perfect recipe for conflict. To understand alternative procedures for candidate selection, we need to consider how the process operates among the Liberal Democrats, Plaid Cymru, the Scottish National Party and the Greens.

5   Minor party recruitment

In British elections in the post-war period, as noted earlier, one of the most striking developments has been the growth of candidate competition. In the 1951 election there were 2.2 candidates per seat; over three quarters of all contests were 'straight fights' between the Labour and Conservative candidates; there were even a handful of uncontested Conservative seats. The 1951 campaign was fought by only 142 minor party candidates (109 Liberals, 10 Communists, 6 nationalists, and 17 others). In contrast, since October 1974 there have been at least three contestants for almost every seat, as the Liberals put up candidates in virtually every constituency.[1] Other parties have become more competitive until by the 1992 election there were 4.5 candidates per seat, a record number. The most serious challenge has come from the Liberal party, later the Liberal/Social Democrat Alliance, and now the Liberal Democrats. The strength of the Nationalist parties and the Greens, plus fringe and independent candidates, has also contributed towards this trend. We need to understand how recruitment operates in these parties, and whether the process and outcome differs significantly from the major parties.

There are good reasons why we might expect to find a distinctive pattern of recruitment in the minor parties, in terms of the motivation, experience and background of candidates. Many ambitious politicians seek a full-time political career on the Labour and Conservative back-benches, but it is more difficult to understand the motivation of candidates in other parties, given their chances of winning. In the 1992 general election there were 611 Liberal challengers but only four won seats (in Bath, Cheltenham, North Devon and North Cornwall). The Greens doubled their number of candidates, from 133 to 252, but failed to save a single deposit. The puzzle is to understand why any minor party candidate is willing to fight a general election given their chances of winning in this, or any subsequent, parliamentary contest. The most common explanation is that many minor party candidates are 'standard bearers', willing to help boost party support, with few illusions of entering Westminster.

Despite systematic differences, there are good reasons why we might also

	Lib Dem	SNP	PC	Green
Application form	Yes	Yes	Yes	Yes
Approved list	Yes	Yes	None	None
Nomination signatures	Self	Branch	Branch	2 members
Shortlist	Local exec.	Occasional	None	None
Selected for seat by	Members	Members	Selection conference	Members
Postal ballot	Yes	No	No	Yes
Election rules	STV	AV	AV	STV
Endorsement by leadership	None	Yes	Yes	None

Figure 5.1   The selection process in the minor parties.
Note: STV = single transferable vote, AV = alternative vote.

expect considerable similarities across parties. All operate within a common legal and electoral framework. British parties have formal mass-branch organisations where the local level controls the choice of individual candidates, although central party agencies usually play some role (except in the Greens) through scrutiny at the beginning or endorsement at the end. The main stages in the selection process are summarised in figure 5.1.

What are the differences in the recruitment process?

Recruitment in the Liberal Democrats

The Liberal Democrats have a formal selection process involving five stages: initial application with a standard form and interview; acceptance on the regional Approved List; application to a constituency; shortlisting by the local Executive Committee; and a final selection meeting where grassroots members choose their candidate. Constitutionally this is similar to the process in the Conservative party. Potential applicants start by completing a lengthy and complicated form outlining details of their political experience, campaign work, policy interests, personal back-ground, and a formal checklist of their legal eligibility. Detailed briefing notes for applicants provide a job description, and suggest that the party is looking for candidates with leadership qualities, knowledge of policy, strategic planning skills, the ability to build a public profile, and commu-nication skills.[2]

Approved List

To gain entry on the Approved List, applicants send this form to the State Candidates Committee for either England, Wales or Scotland. This division into State Parties reflects the federal nature of the organisation, and there is a Joint Candidates Committee to coordinate the work of these bodies. The state candidate committees are responsible for maintaining the approved lists, supervising and regulating the selection procedure, providing training for candidates and periodically revising the selection rules. In the 1987–92 period, the state candidates committees evaluated applicants based on their completed form, three references, and a report from sub-panels of senior activists who interviewed each applicant. The constitution recommended that in deciding whether to accept an applicant on the list the committee should take into account the support shown by the applicant for the fundamental values and objectives of the party; any available information about the ability, experience and qualifications of the applicant; the previous participation of the applicant in party work; and the need to ensure that the list contains a reasonable balance between both sexes and different age groups, as well as including representatives of different social and economic groups and of ethnic minorities.[3] Based on this information the committees recommended unconditional acceptance on the Approved List, conditional approval, deferred approval (for example, subject to training), or refusal. There is an established appeals procedure for applicants who feel they have been treated unfairly.

This stage in the process was revised after the 1992 election. The party introduced Development Centres, where about four applicants at a time are evaluated by four assessors in a series of practical exercises, tasks and interviews run by a facilitator. The assessors include long-standing party members, experienced campaigners and professionals in the field of personnel selection and training. During one day, applicants give a short presentation, plan a team project, and write a press release, as well as being evaluated by a personal interview. The aim is to see how applicants perform in the sort of situations they are likely to meet as candidates. This stage is now similar to the Conservative weekend selection boards.

Shortlisting

After approval, applicants can seek constituency vacancies, advertised in the *Liberal Democrat News*. After receiving applications in most constituencies the local Executive Committee shortlists on the basis of the curriculum vitae, but it may interview them all before deciding.[4] The rules governing the shortlist suggest it should include from two to seven names. In practice in the last election more than a quarter (29 per cent) of Liberal Democrat parties had a shortlist of only one, and very few seats (12 per cent) had more than three names, providing more limited choice than in the Labour or Conservative parties. The rules aim to ensure equal opportunities for women at this stage although positive discrimination in the form of all-women shortlists are discouraged. The use of gender shortlisting rules were pioneered by the Social Democratic Party in the run-up to the 1983 election, and subsequently revised by the Liberal Democrats. If the shortlist includes two to four names, and there are sufficient applicants, the rules suggest at least one should be of each sex. If the list contains five to seven names, the rules suggest at least two from each sex. The rules further recommend the shortlist should also be drawn up 'with regard to the desirability of securing proper representation for members of ethnic minorities', although there are no requirements for this.

Selection

During the 1950s, the Liberals often had to search for candidates willing to run in hopeless seats, rather than select them.[5] If a volunteer was found, only one name was then recommended to the general meeting of the association, which formally adopted the person as its prospective candidate.[6] In common with other parties, power has shifted downwards as the process has become more democratic. The final stage is now a meeting of all members where short-listed applicants are invited to speak. In the 1992 election, members faced a choice of 2.4 applicants on the final shortlist in most seats. One or more meetings may be held, depending on the geography of the constituency. The format is the familiar one of question and answer sessions used in other parties. About half the membership often attends these meetings, sometimes more in hotly contested candidacies. In addition, if they do not wish to vote in person, all members are entitled to apply for an optional postal vote. The SDP were the first party to introduce postal ballots, in an attempt to maximise participation. The candidate is finally selected by one-member–one-vote (OMOV). Once adopted, candidates are offered training on party policy, media presentation, and campaign skills. In cases of by-elections the selection process is reopened.

One contrast with the major parties is the way Liberal Democrats occasionally have trouble filling vacancies through the usual procedure. In preparing for the 1992 general election, the party drew up a special list of 'parachutists'; a small number of approved candidates who are unable to spend much time nursing a seat, but who are willing to run and campaign full-time for the party if asked by the national leadership to fight a seat at the last minute. The procedure is avoided by the party whenever possible, but it is used to make sure the Liberal Democrats maximise their national share of the vote by contesting all British seats.

Recruitment in Plaid Cymru (PC)

During the early 1950s Plaid Cymru fielded only a handful of candidates, but the party became more competitive following their 1966 Carmarthen by-election victory, which transformed party morale, membership and organisational strength.[7] Since the 1970 general election they have contested every Welsh seat. The most distinctive features of the selection process in Plaid Cymru are threefold: the absence of a formal role for all party members, the absence of a shortlisting stage, and the absence of a centrally approved list.

When the constituency sets the nomination process in motion, it advertises in party newsletters and publications. Any branch within the constituency may nominate a candidate. Most seats attracted between two and three applicants who go before the selection meeting. Decisions are taken by a selection conference composed of branch representatives with voting rights, and the officers of the constituency council and regional representatives who can participate as discussants. The selection conference has the usual thirty-minute question-and-answer session with each applicant, with the selection decided by a system of Alternative Votes until the winner gets over 50 per cent of the ballot. There are special procedures in the case of by-elections, where a new joint selection meeting is automatically implemented, involving the leadership of Plaid Cymru along with representatives of the local constituency.[8]

Recruitment in the Scottish National Party (SNP)

The Scottish National party was similarly quiescent in the post-war years, with only two or three parliamentary candidates fighting general elections in the early 1950s, until encouraged by some spectacular by-election results in the late 1960s. The publicity surrounding Winnie Ewing's by-election victory in Hamilton, Lanarkshire in November 1967 led to a surge of members, branches and candidates.[9] Since the 1970 general election, they have contested nearly all Scottish seats.

The first step is application to get on the approved list. The Election Committee of the SNP, a sub-committee of the National Executive Committee, maintains a list of approved applicants. Like the Conservatives, the SNP use a one-day selection board to assess the suitability of applicants for this list. During the board, applicants are tested with a series of activities, including their performance in a campaigning exercise, personal interview, discussion group, and media presentation. Applicants are assessed according to their ability to provide motivation and leadership within a constituency, and their awareness of Scottish politics and SNP policy. This supplements the information on the formal application form, which includes details of their personal background, political experience, candidate eligibility, campaign availability, references, and constituency association sponsorship. At the end of the board, the Election Committee recommends suitable applicants to the National Executive Committee, who formally approve the list.

When starting the selection process the Constituency Association invites nomination from branches and sub-branches. Only those on the Approved List can be considered by the selection meeting, and others need to apply to be approved on the list. Depending on the numbers the Association may decide to shortlist nominees, but this is not essential. In no cases did the local party attract more than six applicants, and in most cases there were less than four. Members of the Constituency Association then hold a special selection meeting, with the usual question and answer session with nominees. Voting is by successive secret ballots, with those with the lowest poll dropping out in successive rounds until one applicant receives an overall majority. There is then another vote to confirm the applicant, aiming for unanimous support. The results are passed up to the National Executive Committee, who have the formal power of veto or approval. Again in cases of by-elections there is a fresh selection process, reflecting the importance of these contests for SNP fortunes.[10]

Recruitment in the Green party

The newest party are the Greens, first founded as the Ecology party in February 1974. The number of Green parliamentary candidates has risen rapidly, from 53 in 1979 to 108 in 1983, 133 in 1987, and 252 in 1992, although they have lost every deposit. The selection process in the Greens shows several distinctive features, consistent with their radical organisational philosophy: the process is highly open and democratic with an automatic postal ballot of all members; there is no shortlisting stage – all applicants attend the selection meeting; the process is highly decentralised as there is no national endorsement/veto, there are few national rules, and no central approved list; and the outcome tends to produce more women and slightly younger candidates than the other parties. Yet at the same time evidence suggests the process is least competitive.

The first question for the Greens is whether to contest a constituency, given limited resources. Membership of the Greens reached its maximum of about 18,000 in 1990, following their success in the 1989 European elections, but subsequently fell sharply. At the time of the 1992 general election there were about 6,000 national Green party members (and an unknown number of local party members) organised in 305 local parties. In the run up to the 1992 general election, local parties therefore needed to decide whether they had the volunteers and money to mount an effective parliamentary campaign. Local Green parties often cover more than one parliamentary constituency, district or borough council so they needed to consider their strategic targets carefully.

When a local party decides to contest a constituency, it starts the process by advertising the vacancy in the party newsletter. The Green party constitution lays down no eligibility requirements for nominees: in theory anyone can apply, although some local parties stipulate a minimum duration of party membership, and the notes for guidance recommend candidates should be a paid-up member with knowledge of the party's organisation and policies.[11] Applicants require nomination from two supporters, often though not necessarily from those in the local party. Usually applicants provide a brief (100–500 word) statement about themselves and a photograph, which can be reproduced for distribution to all members along with the postal ballot paper. Normally there are fewer than four applicants per seat; in the last election 62 per cent of Green candidates were selected from a shortlist of one, and a further 25 from a shortlist of two, although there is still a ballot even if there is only a single contestant.

The selection meeting, usually attended by 20 to 100 members, follows the familiar process. There are brief speeches and questions from the floor, after which members cast their preferential vote into a ballot box at the hustings. If they do not approve of the options, members can vote to reject all nominees. Combined with the postal ballot papers, the results are calculated by the alternative vote system. Any candidate with a majority of votes on the first ballot is selected, otherwise the candidate with the least number of votes is eliminated, and the votes redistributed according to second preference. Once selected by a local party, there is no further process of central endorsement, and indeed minimum national supervision or coordination.[12] Interestingly, given the outcome, there are no constitutional rules or formal requirements about gender quotas or affirmative action. In accordance with their non-hierarchical, participatory and decentralised organisation, grassroots members in the local parties control the whole process.

What are the differences in outcome?

Are there significant differences between candidates for the minor and major parties in competition for seats, in their motivation for standing, in

Table 5.1   *Number of seat applications by candidates*

'N. of applications'	Con.	Lab.	Lib. Dem.	Nat.	Green	All
One seat	28	59	69	62	99	61
Few seats (2/4)	18	27	28	38	1	23
Some seats (5/15)	28	11	3	0	0	10
Many seats (16 +)	26	3	0	0	0	6
Mean N.	11.4	3.0	1.6	1.6	1.0	3.9
N.	218	310	314	74	138	1,054

Note: Candidates excluding MPs and List Applicants.
Source: BCS, 1992.

the background and experience of adopted candidates, and in satisfaction with the process?

Candidate competition

Given the electoral fortunes of the minor parties, it seems likely that they would attract fewer applicants. Indeed, as noted earlier, for hopeless seats where the party starts in third or fourth place volunteers may be thin on the ground, and the process may more accurately be described as one of persuasion rather than selection. Table 5.1 analyses the pattern for candidates (excluding MPs who are usually reselected and Labour and Conservative List Applicants, to produce a consistent comparison across parties). The degree of competition can be shown by focusing on the number of candidates who were adopted in the first seat they applied for, and the number who tried for a wide range of seats.

The results confirm some important, but not unexpected, contrasts. Candidate competition is greatest in the Conservative party; their candidates apply for eleven seats on average, usually in different regions across the country. Some Conservative candidates succeed in their first attempt, but half apply to at least five seats, while one quarter try for more than sixteen seats on a scatter-gun principle. In the Labour party the localised nature of the selection process, described earlier, means that few attempted a similar scatter-gun approach. The majority of Labour candidates applied to only one seat, where they were adopted. Almost two thirds of Liberal Democrats and nationalist candidates were accepted on their first application, while this practice was almost universal in the Greens. The process here can be seen as 'persuasion' as much as selection. As some of the Liberal Democrat candidates said, when asked why they first wanted to stand:

Table 5.2 *Candidate's estimates of their electoral prospects*

	Con.	Lab.	Lib. Dem	Nat.	Green
Will win seat	49	41	28	23	3
Will come second	44	40	44	45	8
Will not come first or second	7	19	29	32	89
N.	217	310	312	73	139

Note: Q. In the next general election which party do you think will win in your constituency? And which party will come second?
Source: BCS, 1992.

Because many local members urged me to do so.

[I was] persuaded by an MP that to put myself forward was an important duty to the party.

Loyalty to the party (no one else local was interested).[13]

Motivation in standing

Just as competition differs, so we might expect that the reasons why candidates stand may vary between parties. The simplest explanation for why candidates stand is the belief that they will win. Candidates were asked to rate their electoral prospects (table 5.2). Many in the Conservative and Labour parties expressed confidence that they would win, or at least come second in their constituency. Far fewer Liberal Democrat or nationalist candidates thought they would be elected, although a significant minority did believe they could beat the odds. The vast majority of Greens recognised that they would continue to trail in third or fourth place.

If most candidates for the minor parties realise they will probably lose, why do they stand? Questions about motivation will be explored in greater depth in later chapters. There are three main strategies which applicants consider when deciding which seats to pursue. Those following a *careerist* strategy seek a winnable seat which will lead to a political career at Westminster. As we have seen, the ladder of opportunities to enter the British parliament is narrow. Nevertheless, some challengers believe that they could succeed, against the odds, if they pursue good seats in any region, gain experience in a less favourable constituency, and campaign hard in a target marginal. In contrast, those following a *regional* strategy are willing to try for their local seat, those fairly close to home, or others in their region, without being prepared to travel around the country to pursue any vacancy.

Table 5.3   *Candidate motivation in applying to seats*

% 'Very important'	Con.	Lab.	Lib. Dem.	Nat.	Green	All
Thought could win seat	52	42	30	23	4	40
Thought it good experience	43	39	27	23	25	36
Seat in my region	27	39	54	23	54	38
Seat close to home	25	46	65	36	73	43
Lived in constituency	23	52	63	38	88	47
Knew party members in the seat	12	44	42	38	48	32
Was asked to apply	18	52	51	64	55	42
N.	461	443	284	78	134	1,400

Note: Q. When originally deciding to apply for a constituency, how important were the following factors in influencing your choice of seat?
Source: BCS, 1992.

Lastly those following an '*insider*' strategy only pursue seats where they already know party members, or where they are asked to stand.

Candidates were asked about the importance of different factors which influenced their strategic choice of seat. If we compare the results by party (see table 5.3), it is clear that careerist reasons are most commonly expressed by candidates in the Conservative and Labour party. More than half the Conservative candidates thought it important to apply for winnable seats, or those which provided good experience in developing a long-term political career. Far fewer Conservatives applied because of an 'insider' strategy. Almost the opposite pattern can be found in the Greens; nearly all applied for seats where they already lived or those close to home, and the majority were asked to stand. As an accurate reflection of their electoral fortunes, hardly any Greens believed they could actually win, or even that the experience would lead to a long-term political career. Candidates for the Liberal Democrats and nationalist parties struck a middle course between these extremes. Most can be classified as standard bearers, as indicated by some of their reasons for standing:

I wanted to do whatever I could to further the cause of Liberalism ... I felt I could make a contribution as a PPC and give platform for our beliefs.

I believe strongly in what my party stands for and that I might be the right choice to speak for it.

A desire to help my party.

Someone was needed for this less than hopeful seat.[14]

But still a substantial minority of minor party candidates believed they could win against the odds. As some expressed the reason why they wanted to stand:

A desire to be part of a reformist Liberal Democrat team in Parliament.

To enter full-time politics.

To get elected and change the system.

Because Parliament is where political power lies.[15]

These differences in motivation are explored further in chapter 9.

Background and experience

Who becomes a candidate for the minor parties? Do they attract a different type of political activist? If we compare the social background of candidates, as shown in table 5.4, there is a familiar pattern: the typical candidate in all parties tends to be a well-educated, professional, white male in early middle age. Nevertheless slightly greater social diversity is shown in the composition of the Labour and Green parties. These parties have the highest proportion of women, working-class and ethnic minority candidates, although these groups are under-represented in all parties compared with their numbers in the electorate. Theories of post-materialism suggest that as a new social movement, Green party activists are most likely to be drawn from the younger, better educated and more affluent sectors of society, and evidence from Britain and elsewhere tends to support this conclusion.[16] A comparison suggests that Green candidates tend to be slightly younger and less religious than others, and, somewhat unexpectedly, less affluent. Two-thirds of Green candidates are university graduates, but this is no different to most of the other parties. In contrast to the Greens, at the opposite end of the spectrum, Conservative candidates show the greatest social homogeneity, reflecting the traditional composition of parliament; overwhelmingly middle-class, male, married, middle aged, fairly affluent, Church of England, and white.

As well as social background, minor party candidates may be expected to have a distinctive profile in terms of political experience. Candidates for the major parties may be expected to have become active through work in local government or party office, and in the case of Labour candidates the trade unions, while the Greens might be expected to have participated mainly in grassroots community groups and local pressure groups. Yet the pattern shown in table 5.5 reveals considerable similarities across parties. Almost all the candidates had held office in their local party (91 per cent), and had been candidates in local government elections (79 per cent). Most had been party members for about fourteen years, slightly longer in the Labour party although for far less time, as expected, in the Greens. In addition half the candidates had been elected to local government (52 per cent), although this was less common in the Greens and nationalist parties. With the exception of the Greens, about a third had experience of standing for parliament in a

Table 5.4 *Social background of candidates*

	Con.	Lab.	Lib. Dem.	Nat.	Green	All
Male	85	74	78	79	72	78
Female	15	26	22	22	28	23
White	99	96	98	100	97	98
Non-white	1	4	2	0	3	2
Middle class	99	92	98	97	92	96
Working class	1	8	2	3	8	4
Graduate	67	72	70	76	66	70
Non-graduate	33	28	30	24	34	30
Mean age completing educ.	20	20	20	21	20	20
Older (50+)	22	21	23	15	11	20
Middle (40–50)	39	42	34	30	31	38
Younger (18–39)	39	37	43	54	58	42
Mean years of age	39	43	44	41	40	42
Religion	85	33	62	53	26	53
None	14	67	38	47	74	47
Union member	14	96	38	55	39	51
None	86	4	62	45	61	49
Income –10K	2	8	4	8	29	8
Income 10–20K	15	26	25	27	36	25
Income 20–30K	22	28	30	28	19	26
Income 30–50K	31	31	31	32	13	29
Income 50K+	31	7	11	5	3	12
Non-married	32	36	29	33	49	35
Married	68	64	71	67	51	65
N.	209	312	311	76	141	1,048

Note: Parliamentary candidates excluding incumbent MPs and List Applicants.
Source: BCS. 1992

previous election. Many had been politically active through local pressure groups and community organisations. As the summary activism scale shows, Green candidates had slightly less experience than others, mainly because fewer had been local councillors and parliamentary candidates. But overall there was relatively little difference in the experience of major and minor party candidates.

Satisfaction with the process

Given the different procedures and rules for selecting candidates, how does this affect general satisfaction with the process? As shown in table 5.6

Table 5.5   *Political experience of candidates*

	Con. (%)	Lab. (%)	Lib. Dem. (%)	Nat. (%)	Green (%)	All (%)	Weight
Stood for parliament before	31	32	30	46	20	31	[12]
Held local party office	90	95	91	93	84	91	[3]
Held regional party office	35	19	31	54	33	30	[6]
Held national party office	19	4	21	53	26	18	[9]
Candidate for local government	75	85	83	86	93	83	[6]
Elected to local government	44	66	59	30	12	50	[9]
Candidate Euro. parliament	5	6	10	7	13	8	[6]
Elected Euro. parliament	1	1	0	0	0	0	[9]
Served on local public body	57	68	52	40	20	53	[3]
Served on national public body	22	39	26	11	1	7	[9]
Local pressure group office	35	58	46	49	53	49	[3]
National pressure group office	18	20	15	22	16	18	[9]
Other community group office	36	49	44	50	44	45	[3]
Professional association office	22	24	21	18	15	21	[3]
Student organisation office	41	32	34	43	15	33	[3]
Trade union office	9	64	19	32	21	31	[3]
Women's organisation office	5	12	4	5	6	7	[3]
Years of party membership	17	19	12	18	7	15	
Summary Weighted Scale	27	31	30	34	23	29	[100]
N.	221	318	316	79	133	1,078	

Note: Q. 'Have you ever held office/served on ...'
PPCs only excluding incumbent MPs and List Applicants.
'Weight' refers to the weighting used for the summary scale of political experience.
Source: BCS, 1992.

Table 5.6   *Candidate satisfaction with the selection process*

% 'Very'	Con.	Lab.	Lib. Dem.	Nat.	Green
Fair	71	33	74	68	63
Democratic	66	40	74	79	71
Efficient	53	26	47	43	35
Complicated	4	46	3	3	3
N.	213	305	301	74	140

Note: Q. 'In your view was the procedure used in your most recent selection application ...'
This excludes incumbent MPs and List Applicants.
Source: BCS, 1992.

participants were asked to evaluate their 'most recent selection application' in terms of four qualities: was it fair, democratic, efficient and complicated? The results show that general satisfaction across these criteria was fairly high among most candidates with the exception of the Labour party.

Conclusions

A comparison of recruitment in British parties shows they share three common features. First, the system of recruitment is formalised and rule bound. That is, all parties have written guidelines set out in party handbooks and constitutions. These rules are established at national level, although there are some minor variations in England, Scotland and Wales. The rules establish the formal procedure, the schedule, the division of decision-making powers, and a process to adjudicate disputes. Compared with patronage systems, where factions or national leaders pick their team, the process is therefore relatively transparent, meritocratic and clear.

Second, the process is localised and democratic. Grassroots party members in local constituencies have the major say in determining their choice of candidate. In some cases, members are given a constrained choice, particularly in hopeless seats where minor parties often have only one volunteer. Nevertheless, where there is a choice, it is the members who decide on the basis of one member one vote. In most respects British parties can be seen to follow a 'top-down' model of party organisation but in this respect they are more 'bottom-up'.[17]

Lastly, in all parties except the Greens there is a process of central office intervention. Most commonly, central office executives (for Britain, or Scotland, Wales and England) set the general rules, supervise their implementation and adjudicate in cases of appeal, to ensure fair standards. In the Conservative, Liberal Democrat and Scottish National parties central office also establishes the pool of eligible applicants, through the use of approved lists. This constrains local choice but does not determine who is picked. The national leadership in Labour, Plaid Cymru and the Scottish National parties have veto powers at the end of the process, which allows them to withhold endorsement of any proposed candidate. The Greens have the most decentralised system, governed by minimal rules in their national constitution. We shall now consider explanations of the outcome. Why does a system which seems fair and open produce an outcome where women, ethnic minorities and working class groups continue to be significantly under-represented in all parties?

II   Who gets selected, and why?

6 Supply and demand explanations

The first part of the book has sought to explain the separate stages in the selection process in British parties, analysing the role of the key players, and describing the procedural rules and dominant ethos which govern political recruitment. We may now turn to explaining the outcome, particularly the familiar and long-standing social bias evident in most legislatures. The aims of this chapter are threefold: first, to outline briefly the major trends in the social background of the political elite, particularly changes in their occupational class, education, gender, and race; secondly, to set out the conceptual basis of the 'supply and demand' model, mentioned earlier, including how it can be operationalised; and thirdly, to examine whether supply or demand factors provide the most plausible explanation of the social bias. For the moment we reserve the question of whether the social bias *matters* – whether it has any consequences for the legislative behaviour, political attitudes, or policy priorities of members of parliament – until the last chapters.

Trends in the social bias of parliament

Observers of political elites have commonly noted that MPs tend to be drawn from the better educated and more affluent sectors of society, with few women or racial minorities. It is often claimed that as a result parliament remains 'unrepresentative', even if members are returned in accordance with the principles of fair and democratic elections. What does this claim mean?

Political 'representation' is a complex concept, its meaning contested. A. H. Birch draws a useful distinction between three main usages, each logically distinct from each other.[1] In the *'symbolic'* concept a representative serves as a concrete embodiment of a larger or more abstract entity, as when the Queen represents the nation. In the *'delegate'* concept, legislators can be regarded as spokespersons on behalf of different constituencies. These constituencies may be parties, districts or interests. As a lawyer is appointed to defend the interests of his or her client, so an MP is elected to act on behalf of his or her constituency. Lastly the *'demographic'* (sometimes referred to as the 'microcosmic') concept of representation, the focus of this book, suggests that a representative parliament should be a microcosm of the population. Just as portraits are representative if they look like the sitter, so legislatures are representative if they reflect the society from which they are drawn. In John Adams' words, the legislature 'should be an exact portrait, in miniature, of the people at large, as it should think, feel, reason and act like them'.[2] The same meaning is used in the term 'representative sample', which suggests that a small group mirrors the relevant universe. In practice, the second and third meanings often slide into each other. But the fact that a person is from a certain category of the population does not necessarily mean that they share the opinions, or represent the interests, of that group. Whether or not they do is a matter for empirical inquiry. The demographic concept does not tell us anything about the views or behaviour of the representative, merely that he or she shares the characteristics of a larger group of persons.

In practice, parliaments meet the criterion of demographic representation if they include the same proportion of each relevant sub-group as the electorate.[3] Such sub-groups vary from one society to another, depending on salient political cleavages, whether based on class, religion, age, sex, race, ethnicity, language or region. As Birch notes, advocates of demographic representation, reflecting the complacent and consensual nature of British politics of the 1960s,

have suggested that an assembly cannot be properly representative of the nation if its social composition is conspicuously different from that of the electorate. In homogeneous societies such as Britain this kind of argument, though often used as a basis for criticising existing institutions, has rarely cut much ice, but in societies divided on social or religious lines its impact has naturally been much greater.[4]

The underlying premise of this theory is that first-hand experience is intrinsically related to political interests. Where social groups have distinct political interests, it is argued that members drawn from their ranks are the most effective representatives of their interests. It is assumed that northerners are the most effective spokespersons for residents of Yorkshire, miners and dockers understand and express the problems of the working class, while women comprehend and articulate the concerns of women. As Anne Phillips puts it:

The 'interests' of pensioners or the long-term unemployed can perhaps be championed by those who fall into neither category, but the 'perspectives' of women or black Americans must surely be carried by representatives who are female or black.[5]

Since the early 1980s this theory has been most frequently articulated by advocates of affirmative action in education, employment or elected office.

But its provenance can be traced back for centuries. Bentham and the early utilitarians called for electoral reform in the 1820s on the grounds that an upper-class parliament could not represent the interests of the whole nation. The American Constitution specifies that Members of Congress must reside in their district with the assumption that only those from an area can articulate the concerns of that constituency. A similar philosophy lies behind appointed second chambers, or reserved places in elected legislatures, which are designed to include ethnic or religious minorities, women or certain economic sectors of society. World wide there are a range of practices, for example seats are reserved in New Zealand (for Maoris), Pakistan (for non-Muslims) and Bangladesh (for women).[6]

The theory of demographic representation is open to many criticisms. The most serious is that a significant link is commonly assumed between the social background of legislators and their political attitudes, beliefs and opinions. But this is rarely proved. Perhaps Labour MPs who are journalists, teachers or lawyers may articulate the concerns of the working-class community, and defend their interests, as effectively as NUM trade union officials or transport workers. Some female politicians may champion the concerns of 'women'. But equally among backbench MPs Conservative women may give less priority to such issues as childcare benefits, crèche facilities, or domestic violence than Labour men. If taken to extremes, where each particular sub-group has to be represented by a person from that group, the view quickly degenerates into solipsism. The demographic model provides only one standard by which a legislature can be judged 'representative'. Alternatives such as the 'delegate' model may provide a more coherent and plausible theory. Nevertheless, the concept of demographic representation is a pervasive one which permeates much popular thinking, and therefore deserves full examination.

It is well established that by this standard most parliaments are strikingly unrepresentative: comparative studies by Putnam, Loewenberg and others have confirmed that legislators in Western political elites tend to be drawn from a privileged social background.[7] In terms of occupational class, gender, race and education, the British parliament is no exception.

There are two ways to measure 'social bias'. Some adopt *absolute* measures. Colin Mellors, W. L. Guttsman, and others, examined the trends over time for working class candidates, or MPs educated at public school and Oxbridge, as a proportion of all parliamentary members.[8] Although the most common way of studying political elites this approach fails to set trends in their broader social, economic and political context. In the twentieth century, Britain has been transformed by demographic trends and the development of the post-industrial economy. Society has experienced a substantial decline of jobs in heavy manufacturing industry, the rise of the service sector, increased levels of post-secondary education, the mobilisation of women in the workforce, changing family structures, and greater ethnic diversity. As a result it makes little sense, for example, to discuss the decline in the number of Labour MPs drawn from manual work without at the same time measuring this against the baseline of the declining working class population. Equally, the lack of ethnic minority representatives prior to 1950 is hardly surprising, given low numbers in the population. The growth of university educated MPs may reflect rising educational standards in the general public. The composition of elites needs to be judged in the light of these broader developments.

Therefore, this study will use *relative* measures, first employed by J. F. S. Ross, to examine trends in the social background of the legislative elite compared against the baseline of social change in the British electorate.[9] This study uses a simple summary measure, the Index of Electoral Bias, calculated as follows:

$$\text{Index of Electoral Bias} = \frac{\text{Proportion of Group in the Elite}}{\text{Proportion of Group in the Electorate}}$$

For example, if women are 21 per cent of all candidates, and 53 per cent of the electorate, this produces an Index of Electoral Bias of 2.5. The number of women candidates would need to be multiplied by this figure to reflect their proportions in the electorate. Relative criteria take account of social as well as elite-level change to provide consistent comparisons over time and between groups.

Trends in occupational class

The central concern of most parliamentary elite studies has been the decline of Labour members from manual occupations, and the growth in those from the 'chattering classes', professional occupations such as lawyers, teachers, consultants and journalists.[10] Labour was first founded in 1900 to 'secure the representation of working class opinion in parliament'.[11] Ross estimates that for the 1918–35 period, although there are some problems of definition, about three-quarters of all Labour MPs (72 per cent) could be classified as rank-and-file workers – miners, metal workers, textile workers, train drivers and printers, – normally sponsored by the major unions (see figure 6.1, table 6.1).[12] This closely matched the population; from 1911 to 1931 about 70–75 per cent of the labour force worked in manual occupations.[13] The influx of new members in the post-war Attlee landslide changed the face of the Labour party. In the 1945–50 parliament, almost half the Labour members were middle class (49 per cent). The number of working-class Labour MPs

Table 6.1   *Main occupations of MPs, 1918–92*

	Conservative				Labour			
	Business	Professional	Miscel-laneous	Workers	Business	Professional	Miscel-laneous	Workers
1918–35	32	52	12	4	4	24	0	72
1945	33	61	4	3	10	49	1	41
1950	31	62	5	3	10	47	1	43
1951	37	41	22	0	9	35	19	37
1955	30	46	24	0	12	36	17	35
1959	30	46	23	1	10	38	17	35
1964	26	48	25	1	11	41	16	32
1966	29	46	23	1	9	43	18	30
1970	30	45	24	1	10	48	16	26
1974	32	44	23	1	9	46	15	30
1974	33	46	20	1	8	49	15	28
1979	34	45	20	1	7	43	14	36
1983	36	45	19	1	9	42	16	33
1987	37	42	20	1	8	40	22	29
1992	38	39	22	1	8	42	28	22

Sources: 1918–50 JFS Ross *Electors and Elected*; 1951–92 Butler 1988; Butler and Kavanagh 1992.

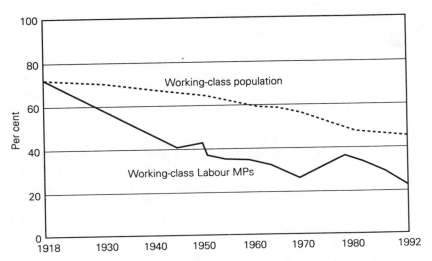

Figure 6.1   Trends in working-class Labour MPs and the working-class population, 1918–1992. *Source:* Butler 1988; Butler and Kavanagh 1992.

gradually declined throughout the 1950s and 1960s, with some fluctuations, before reaching its nadir in the last election.[14] In 1992, only one fifth (22 per cent) of Labour MPs, and one tenth (9 per cent) of adopted Labour candidates, had a working-class occupational background. The decline has been mostly among the semi-skilled and unskilled manual workers.

In the mid nineteenth century, the Conservatives were the party of the great landowners and the barons of commerce and industry.[15] In the long term, as Guttsman demonstrates, the main change has been the decline in the numbers drawn from the traditional aristocracy, and the growth of the private-sector professional middle classes.[16] Not surprisingly, there have always been few working class members in the Conservative party, at most 3–4 per cent in 1918–1951 period. Since the early 1950s this has dropped to only three or four Conservative MPs, or about 1 per cent. John Greenwood suggests this pattern existed despite strenuous efforts from 1919 to 1975 by Conservative Central Office to change the position.[17] To try to increase working-class support the Conservatives formed the Unionist Labour Movement (ULM) in 1919, when the absence of working-class Conservative MPs was considered a serious electoral liability. Several ULM members became Conservative candidates in the 1930s, but this had little effect on the class composition of the parliamentary party. Another initiative was attempted, in reaction to their post-war defeat, with the establishment of the Conservative Trade Unionists' Organisation in 1947. During the same period the Maxwell Fyfe financial reforms were intended to produce more socially diverse candidates. Neither initiative had a major effect, in part, Greenwood suggests, due to resistance to working-class applicants by constituency parties.[18]

In the post-war years, both parties have therefore seen a expansion of middle-class members, and it might appear that the parties have thereby become more homogeneous. Nevertheless, the traditional class categories are broad, and serve to disguise some significant occupational differences which continue to distinguish party elites. If we look more closely at occupational patterns from 1945 to 1992 (see table 6.2) the biggest change on the Conservative side has been the decline in the army generals and landed squires, and a steady increase in career politicians who started out as journalists, Central Office researchers or political organisers.[19] By far the largest occupational category among Conservative MPs, including about half their members, are company directors, company executives, and barristers. On the Labour benches the biggest occupational growth has come from teachers, lecturers and researchers, followed by those in local government, and in routine white-collar jobs. This pattern follows the post-war expansion of post-secondary education and the welfare services. It is most striking,

Table 6.2   *Occupational change 1945–1992*

	Labour MPs				Conservative MPs			
	1945	1964	1992	Change	1945	1964	1992	Change
PROFESSIONS								
Barristers/solicitors	11.5	14.6	6.3	−5.2	19.7	26.2	17.9	−1.9
Doctors/dentists	2.8	2.9	0.7	−2.0	1.0	1.0	1.2	0.2
Architects/surveyors/civil engin.	3.0	1.9	0.0	−3.0	1.4	1.7	1.8	0.3
Accountant	1.3	1.6	0.7	−0.5	1.9	2.0	3.6	1.6
Civil servant/local govnt.	1.0	2.2	5.9	4.9	5.3	6.0	3.0	−2.3
Armed services	0.8	0.6	0.0	−0.8	14.4	9.3	4.2	−10.3
Teachers/researchers	12.3	16.2	28.8	16.5	2.9	1.7	7.4	4.6
BUSINESS								
Company director/executive	5.5	4.1	3.7	−1.8	33.7	19.3	33.3	−0.3
Commerce/insurance	0.3	3.5	0.4	0.1	3.4	6.3	2.7	−0.7
Management/clerical/other	2.0	3.2	4.1	2.1	0.0	1.0	2.1	2.1
MISCELLANEOUS								
Misc white collar	3.3	3.5	13.3	10.0	0.0	1.7	2.7	2.7
Pol. organiser	13.3	2.2	8.9	−4.4	0.5	5.0	6.0	5.5
Publisher journalist	10.0	8.6	4.8	−5.2	2.4	6.6	8.3	5.9
Farmers	1.3	0.6	0.7	−0.5	12.0	11.6	3.0	−9.0
Housewife/student	0.8	1.6	0.0	−0.8	1.4	0.0	1.8	0.3
MANUAL WORKERS								
Skilled	13.5	16.2	15.9	2.4	0.0	0.7	0.2	−0.5
Semi/unskilled	16.8	16.5	5.9	−10.8	0.0	0.0	0.0	0.0
Total	100.0	100.0	100.0		100.0	100.0	100.0	

Sources: Colin Mellors 1978, David Butler 1992.

for example, that there were no social workers on the Labour benches until the mid-1960s.[20] These occupational patterns therefore seem to have reduced the broad class differences, but reinforced a public-private sectoral division between the major parties.

To estimate the effect of these developments on social bias we can compare these trends with occupational patterns in the electorate. As shown in figure 6.1 there has been a parallel decline in the proportion of working-class jobs in the labour force, although the decline among Labour MPs has gone faster and further. In census data the proportion of manual workers in the occupied population fell between 1911 and 1991 from 75 to 48 per cent.[21] If the most recent figure were reflected among elected representatives, parliament would include about 312 working-class MPs, not 63 as elected in 1992.

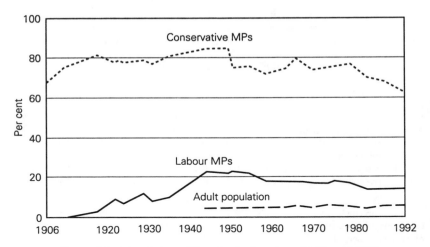

Figure 6.2   Trends in public school education of MPs and adult
population, 1906–92. *Source:* Butler 1988; Butler and Kavanagh 1992.

Trends in education

The main concern about patterns of education relates to the proportion of
members drawn from the public schools and Oxbridge, particularly the
number of Old Etonians and Harrovians. Trends indicate that from 1920 to
1950 about 80 per cent of all Conservative MPs attended a public school,
with a slight fall in the 1960s and 1970s, followed by a steady decline in the
1980s. In the 1992 general election, about 62 per cent of all Conservative
members had been public-school educated, and the figure was even lower
(55 per cent) among new Conservative MPs. As might be expected, there
have always been far fewer public school products in the Labour party,
although with the post-war intake the proportion rose to about 20 per cent,
before falling again gradually. In 1992, 40 Labour MPs (14 per cent) had
been to public school. In contrast among the British population about 5 per
cent have been to public school. If parliament reflected the population,
there would be about 33 MPs from public school, not 258 as elected in 1992.

In terms of post-secondary education the trends in Diagram 6.3 show
rising educational qualifications in parliament, with increased numbers of
university graduates. In the Conservative parliamentary party, the proportion of graduates has grown from just over half at the turn of the century (57
per cent) to almost three quarters today (73 per cent). Oxford and Cambridge retain their lead on the Conservative benches although over the years
increased proportions of MPs have attended other universities.[22] The
change has been even more dramatic on the Labour benches; there were no

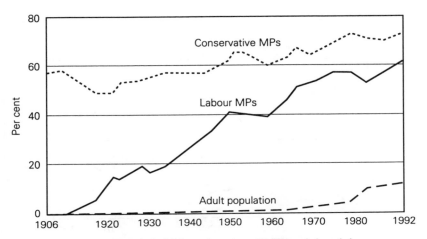

Figure 6.3   Trends in higher education of MPs and the adult population, 1906–92. *Source:* Butler 1988; Butler and Kavanagh 1992.

graduates in the early years, the proportion rose to about a third in 1945, and now stands at almost two thirds (61 per cent). Since the 1960s, Britain has experienced a significant expansion in higher education, with the growth of the 'white tile' universities and the old polytechnic/new university sector.[23] Despite this growth, the Census reports that in 1991 only 7.1 per cent of the adult population in Britain held a degree (or higher degree) as their highest qualification.[24] If parliament were as ill-educated as the nation, it would include only 46 university educated MPs, not 426.

Trends in women in parliament

Women were first allowed to stand for parliament following the Representation of the People's Act 1918 (giving the vote to women over 30) and the Equal Franchise Act of 1928 (which lowered the voting age of women to 21, the same as men). Yet from 1918 to 1983, with remarkably little progress, less than 5 per cent of all MPs were women (see figure 6.4, table 6.3). The first significant signs of change appeared in the 1987 election, when the proportion of women MPs rose to 6.3 per cent, jumping to 9.2 per cent in 1992. The Conservatives increased their number but in this election the most substantial shift occurred in the Labour party, where the number of women almost doubled from twenty-one to thirty-seven MPs, representing 13.6 per cent of the parliamentary party. In total in 1992 sixty women were elected to the Commons. This represents significant progress but neverthe-

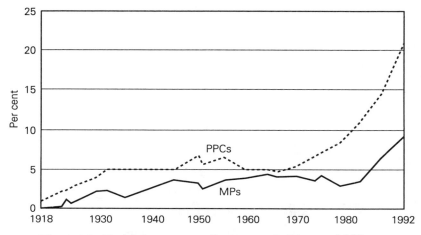

Figure 6.4   Trends in women parliamentary candidates and MPs, 1918–92. *Source:* F. W. S. Craig 1989.

less there are fewer women in the British House of Commons than in comparable legislatures in most developed democracies.[25]

The proportion of women candidates remained fairly static from 1918 until the mid-1970s; since then there has been a sharp rise, tripling from October 1974 (7.1 per cent) to 1992 (21.1 per cent). In the major parties the increase has been strongest among Labour women, although the proportion of Conservative women candidates has also doubled during this period. Due to greater longevity, and a slight tendency towards higher turnout, women constitute between 52 and 53 per cent of voters.[26] If women were represented in proportion to their numbers in the electorate, after the 1992 general election there would be 339 women in the House, not 60.

Trends in ethnic minority representation

The history of ethnic minority representation has been one of slow and modest change. In the pre war period there were three Asian Members of Parliament: the last, Shapurji Saklatvala, lost his seat in Battersea North in 1929. The post-war period saw only a few black candidates standing for the major parties: the best known was Dr (later Lord) David Pitt, fighting the Labour seat of Wandsworth Clapham, who suffered a higher-than-average swing of 10.2 per cent against him in 1970.

The situation started to change following the October 1974 election (see table 6.4) when, although overall numbers remain modest, there was a

Table 6.3 *Women MPs and candidates, 1918–1992*

	Conservative Women		Labour Women		Total all women as % all PPCs & MPs	
	PPCs	MPs	PPCs	MPs	PPCs	MPs
1918	1	0	4	0	1.0	0.1
1922	5	1	10	0	2.3	0.3
1923	7	3	14	3	2.4	1.3
1924	12	3	22	1	2.9	0.7
1929	10	3	30	9	4.0	2.3
1931	16	13	36	0	4.8	2.4
1935	19	6	33	1	5.0	1.5
1945	14	1	41	21	5.2	3.8
1950	29	6	42	14	6.8	3.4
1951	25	6	41	11	5.6	2.7
1955	33	10	43	14	6.5	3.8
1959	28	12	36	13	5.3	4.0
1964	24	11	33	18	5.1	4.6
1966	21	7	30	19	4.7	4.1
1970	26	15	29	10	5.4	4.1
1974	33	9	40	13	6.7	3.6
1974	30	7	50	18	7.1	4.3
1979	31	8	52	11	8.4	3.0
1983	40	13	78	10	10.9	3.5
1987	46	17	92	21	14.2	6.3
1992	62	20	138	37	21.1	9.2

Source: F. W. S. Craig, *British Electoral Facts, 1832–1987.*

steady rise in Conservative and Labour candidates from the ethnic minorities. In 1983 there were eighteen black candidates from all parties, although only Labour's Paul Boateng stood in a potentially winnable seat (Hertfordshire West). This led to the breakthrough in 1987 when there were twenty-eight black candidates standing for all parties, including six Labour and one Conservative selected for potentially winnable seats. As a result, for the first time since 1924, MPs were elected from black or Asian backgrounds, all Labour: Bernie Grant for Tottenham, Diane Abbott for Hackney North and Stoke Newington, Paul Boateng for Brent South and Keith Vaz for Leicester East. In all these constituencies black candidates could have been expected to do well since ethnic minorities constituted over one quarter of the electorate.[27]

In the 1992 election, Labour made little progress in increasing the number of black candidates: in addition to their four black MPs from 1987, and Ashok Kumar who won Langbaurgh in the 1991 by-election, they chose

Table 6.4   *Ethnic minority candidates and MPs, 1950–1991*

	Conservative		Labour		Total all parties	
	PPC	MP	PPC	MP	PPC	MP
1950	0	0	0	0	0	0
1951	0	0	0	0	0	0
1955	0	0	0	0	0	0
1959	0	0	1	0	1	0
1964	0	0	0	0	1	0
1966	0	0	0	0	0	0
1970	0	0	1	0	8	0
1974 Feb.	0	0	1	0	6	0
1974 Oct.	0	0	1	0	3	0
1979	2	0	1	0	12	0
1983	4	0	6	0	18	0
1987	6	0	14	4	28	4
1992	8	1	9	5	17	6
Total	20	1	34	9	95	10

Sources: M. Anwar, *Race and Politics* (London, Tavistock, 1986); BCS, 1992.

Piara Khabra for the safe Labour seat of Ealing Southall, with a significant Asian population, and three black candidates in the solid Conservative seats of Harrow West, Ashford, and Wimbledon, all leafy towns or suburbs with a small black population. Some selections proved highly controversial, with the potential for inter-party conflict over racial divisions demonstrated in the Labour selection in Birmingham Small Heath. The result was the return of five black Labour MPs, with the loss of Ashok Kumar, and the entry of Piara Khabra. Most of the 1987 Labour incumbents did well, increasing their share of the vote above the regional average swing.[28]

Conservative attempts to increase support among blacks started with the establishment in 1976 of the Anglo-Asian and Anglo-West Indian Conservative Societies, and later the One Nation Forum founded under the leadership of the party deputy chairman, Sir John Cope. The party's electoral drive was launched with the claim that Conservative values of opportunity, family life and law and order made it a natural party for ethnic minority voters, particularly Asian small businessmen. The evidence from ethnic voting patterns in the 1987 general election suggest that the Conservatives have a long way to go to mobilise support, since the black electorate is overwhelmingly likely to support Labour.[29] Partly in response to progress within the Labour party, the Conservatives selected seven black candidates to fight the 1992 general election, including John Taylor for Cheltenham and Nirj Deva for Brentford and Isleworth, both Conservative

Table 6.5   *Seats with ethnic minority candidates, 1992*

Constituency	Winner '87	Winner '92	Majority '87	NCWP	Con–Lab Swing
Conservative Candidates					
Brentford & Isleworth	Con. seat	Con. seat	14.5	13.7	− 5.3
Cheltenham	Con. seat	Lib. Dem.	7.8	2.1	
Bradford North	Lab. seat	Lab. seat	3.3	15.0	
Bradford South	Lab. seat	Lab. seat	0.6	4.5	− 4.3
Islington North	Lab. seat	Lab. seat	2.9	21.0	− 4.6
Birmingham Small Heath	Lab. seat	Lab. seat	45.2	38.8	2.5
Birmingham Sparkbrook	Lab. seat	Lab. seat	35.2	35.2	− 2.1
Mean			15.6	18.6	− 2.8
Labour candidates					
Hackney North and Stoke Newington	Lab. seat	Lab. seat	19.8	30.7	− 5.6
Brent South	Lab. seat	Lab. seat	19.5	45.7	− 3.8
Ealing Southall	Lab. seat	Lab. seat	15.3	43.7	− 0.7
Tottenham	Lab. seat	Lab. seat	8.2	37.5	− 9.2
Leicester East	Lab. seat	Lab. seat	3.7	26.3	− 9.5
Langbaurgh	Con. seat	Con. seat	3.3	0.7	
Harrow West	Con. seat	Con. seat	28.0	13.3	− 2.5
Wimbledon	Con. seat	Con. seat	23.4	9.6	0.2
Mean			15.2	25.9	− 4.4
Liberal candidates					
Ashford	Con. seat	Con. seat	29.2	1.7	
Liverpool Riverside	Lab. seat	Lab. seat	59.4	4.7	− 2.5
Hertsmere	Con. seat	Con. seat	32.8	2.6	− 1.9
Halesowen and Stourbridge	Con. seat	Con. seat	22.3	2.4	− 3.7
Cynon Valley	Lab. seat	Lab. seat	56.7	0.4	0.2
Cardiff South and Penarth	Lab. seat	Lab. seat	10.2	3.0	− 5.9
Mean			35.1	2.5	− 2.7

Note: NCWP = The % Head of Household from the New Commonwealth Population in the 1981 Census.

Source: BCS, 1992.

seats, as well as Andrew Popat for the Labour-held marginal of Bradford South (see table 6.5). In the election Nirj Deva was elected as the first Asian Conservative MP since 1900, although John Taylor lost.

There is therefore evidence of limited progress in the parliamentary representation of ethnic minorities in the post-war period. Nevertheless, this trend lags far behind the increase in the black electorate. In the 1951 and 1961 census ethnic minorities constituted less than 1 per cent of the

Table 6.6   *The ethnic minority population in Great Britain 1961–1991 (%)*

	1961	1971	1981	1991
Black	0.4	1.1	1.1	1.6
Indian	na	0.7	1.4	1.5
Pakistani/Bangladeshi	na	0.3	0.6	1.2
Mixed/Other	na	0.4	0.8	1.2
Total all minorities	1.0	2.5	3.9	5.5

Source: Heath et al. *Understanding Political Change* (Pergamon 1991); *Population Trends* (Summer 1993), vol. 72.

population of Great Britain (see table 6.6). By the 1991 Census, based on ethnic self-identity, the ethnic minority population had risen to over three million people, or 5.5 per cent of the population.[30]

It would be mistaken to assume that the black population reflects one homogeneous group: there are significant divisions in terms of language, origins, culture and religion between blacks and Asians, and indeed within the Asian population. These divisions mean that we cannot assume that ethnic minorities participate in politics as a bloc, or share a common sense of political identity. The largest single grouping is South Asian, including Indian, Pakistani and Bangladeshi, numbering 1.5 million. The black population is almost one million. The distribution of the ethnic minority population also shows wide variations, with less than 1 per cent in the North, Scotland and Wales, compared with 15 per cent in Greater London, and over a third of the residents in the London boroughs of Brent, Newham, Tower Hamlets and Hackney.

To summarise, in total there have been ten black Members of Parliament in Britain: a Liberal in the 1890s, a Conservative in the 1900s, a Communist with Labour support in the 1920s, four Labour members since 1987, one Labour member in 1991, plus one Labour MP and one Conservative MP in 1992. Based on the Index of Electoral Bias, if today's parliament reflected the social balance in the electorate we would expect the Commons to include at least thirty six MPs of black or Asian origin, not six. As the ethnic minority population has grown in Britain in recent decades, so the issue of black representation in parliament has proved increasingly controversial.

Supply-and-demand explanations of social bias

How do we explain the social bias? The 'supply-and-demand' analytical framework distinguishes between the factors influencing the 'supply' of candidates willing to come forward and the factors influencing the 'demand' of party selectors in making their decisions. On the *demand-side* the model assumes selectors choose candidates depending upon judgements about applicants. There are a wide range of factors which may enter these evaluations, including assessment of personal character, formal qualifications, and political experience. Is the person an articulate speaker, who can win the audience? Does the applicant seem confident, persuasive, clear? Does he or she appear trustworthy, honest, competent? Is he going to work hard, and campaign enthusiastically, for the local party? If elected, will she stay in touch with her constituents? All these judgements may be given different weight by different party members.

Since applicants are usually not well known by most selectors, perceptions of their abilities may be influenced by direct and imputed discrimination. The term 'discrimination' is used here in a neutral sense, to mean the evaluation of individuals by their group characteristics. Discrimination can be for or against certain groups, whether barristers, miners, trade unionists, Londoners, women or blacks.

Direct discrimination means positive or negative judgements of people on the basis of characteristics seen as common to their group, rather than as individuals. Party selectors, faced with non-local candidates, often have little information on which to choose. The curriculum vitae gives the bare bones. There may be hundreds of application forms. The interview process is relatively short and formal. Selectors may rely upon background characteristics as a proxy measure of abilities and character; prejudice functions as an information short-cut. When shortlisting candidates for interview, before selectors meet them, if someone is a barrister, it may be assumed that they are probably well-educated and articulate. It may be assumed that a woman with a career and young family has little time to spend on party work. An applicant who lives in the seat may be assumed to be more prepared to devote themselves to the local campaign than someone who has to travel from another region. These assumptions may or may not be true. The point is that the assumptions are made prior to establishing the applicant's actual ability, time or interest.

Imputed discrimination refers to the anticipated reaction among the electorate to certain social groups. Party members may personally favour a certain category of candidate ('We need more Conservative women'), or a particular applicant ('She seemed very articulate'). But members may be unwilling to choose such a candidate because they expect they would lose votes among the electorate ('But, a black candidate would never get in').

Demand-side explanations suggest the social bias in parliament reflects the direct and imputed discrimination of party selectors, the key gatekeepers in gaining access to good seats. These explanations are pervasive in popular thinking, and often reflected in the academic literature, although rarely subject to systematic evidence, in part because of the problems of establishing convincing proof of 'discrimination'.

Supply

But discrimination by selectors is not necessarily the most significant cause of the outcome. Party members frequently claim they would like to select more women, ethnic minorities, or manual workers, but few come forward. *Supply-side* explanations suggest the outcome reflects the supply of applicants wishing to pursue a political career. Constraints on resources (such as time, money and experience) and motivational factors (such as drive, ambition and interest) determine who aspires to Westminster. Most citizens are legally qualified to stand, but few do so given the risks and demands of life at Westminster. Supply-side explanations of the social bias in parliament suggest that outcome reflects the pool of applicants seeking a political career.

Supply-side and demand-side factors interact. Potential applicants may be discouraged from coming forward by perceived prejudice by party activists, complex application procedures, or anticipated failure. The concept of hidden unemployment ('Why apply? I won't get the job') is a perfect analogy for the 'discouraged political aspirant'. The outcome may well influence the pool of those who aspire to a political career.

Nevertheless despite these qualifications there remains an important distinction between the *supply* factors holding individuals back from applying for a position, ('I'm not interested', 'I don't have the right experience', 'I can't afford to move') and the *demand* factors which mean that, if they apply, they are not accepted by selectors ('He's not locally known', 'She's not got the right speaking skills', 'He would not prove popular with voters'). The supply-side and demand-side distinction therefore provides a useful analytical framework to explore alternative explanations.

How can this be tested? To operationalise this model, we can compare party strata at different levels on the ladder of recruitment. As outlined in the first chapter, we can identify five distinct groups on the ladder: voters, party members, List Applicants, candidates and MPs. Each group has progressed at different stages up the ladder.

VOTERS > MEMBERS > APPLICANTS > CANDIDATES > MPs

If supply factors are important we would expect to find significant differences between those eligible who might consider a parliamentary career (the party members) and the pool of those who come forward (the applicants on national lists). On the other hand, if demand factors are important, we would expect the main contrast to be between applicants on party lists and candidates adopted by constituencies.

Thus the central hypotheses are as follows:

(i) If demand-side factors are important, there will be a significant difference in the characteristics of applicants and candidates.

(ii) If supply-side factors are important, there will be a significant difference in the characteristics of party members and applicants.

At constituency level party selectors are choosing from among the pool of applicants. If members favour certain groups over others, the contrast would be evident in differences between applicants and candidates. On the other hand if some members lack the resources or motivation to stand, this would be apparent in differences between members and applicants.

This argument needs certain important qualifications. First, the lists are not a perfect sample of the pool of applicants. Some apply for individual constituencies who are not on the national lists, for example some local contestants. But these cases tend to be exceptional, particularly in the Conservative party due to the status of the Approved List. Moreover, some rejected aspirants never get on the list. In the Labour party, trade unions screen who goes onto the 'A' list,[31] while constituencies nominate people for the 'B' list. All nominees are added to the list after formal rubber-stamping by Walworth Road. In the Conservative party, aspirants are interviewed by Central Office and vetted by the weekend national selection boards. Only 40 per cent of those who aspire are put on the Approved List. This means there is a hidden pool of rejected aspirants not counted in our sample of those on the national lists. We can make no claims about this group although observation of the Conservative party selection boards leads us to believe that those involved make every effort not to discriminate against any particular social groups. Screening the Approved Lists does not invalidate the test of demand-side factors at constituency level.

Secondly, as mentioned earlier with the concept of 'hidden unemployment', there may be 'discouraged aspirants' who never put their name forward for consideration on to party lists, since they anticipate being unsuccessful. Some information about this group can be derived from the survey of party members. But again we make no claim to analyse the characteristics of all groups in the process. There are many steps up the ladder from party member to MP. The comparison of applicants and candidates tells us a great deal about the process, but not everything about all stages. The issue of 'discouraged aspirants' is probably least relevant in the Labour party, since there are few obstacles preventing any aspirants from adding their names to the applicant's 'B' list.

Thirdly, the sample of selectors is not perfect. In the Labour party, members may choose to participate in the Electoral College through postal voting. Since the survey of party members was conducted at selection meetings, and lists of those who took part through the post remained confidential, we have no survey data about this group of selectors.

Lastly, supply-and-demand factors operate within a broader institutional and political context.[32] The selection process works differently within each party, under certain guidelines and procedures. And in turn the parties operate within a broader political system, where opportunities to become a candidate are influenced by the legal system, the electoral system, legislative turnover, and the wider political culture. These factors are particularly important in explaining differences between countries, as explored in chapter 10, although they are less useful when focusing on the process within specific parties.

Explaining the social bias

Occupational class

The most important and complex of the background factors is occupation. As we have seen, over time parliament has become more socially homogeneous on both sides of the aisle, with a decline in Conservative landed gentry and Labour's manual workers. Today, in common with other legislatures, the House of Commons contains a disproportionate number of those drawn from the 'talking professions', notably law, journalism, and teaching.[33] Why? Previous research provides various demand-side explanations: Ranney suggests that party members, even in the Labour party, fail to choose working class candidates because of social deference.[34] Bochel and Denver found that manual workers were seen by party members as less able and articulate.[35] Greenwood argues that attempts by Conservative Central Office to increase the number of working-class trade union candidates failed because of local party resistance.[36]

On the supply-side, previous research by Ranney explained the class bias in parliament by the resources that middle-class professional occupations provide for a political career: flexible working hours, useful political skills, social status and political contacts.[37] The most illuminating supply-side explanation, by Jacob, uses the concept of 'brokerage occupations'.[38] This suggests that parliamentary careers are facilitated by jobs which combine flexibility over time, generous vacations, interrupted career-paths, professional independence, financial security, public networks, social status, policy experience and technical skills useful in political life. Brokerage jobs – barristers, teachers, trade union officials, journalists, political researchers – are complementary to politics. They minimise the costs and risks of horizontal mobility from the economic to political marketplace, and vica versa, since being a Member of Parliament is an uncertain life.

Interview evidence tended to confirm the perceived importance of brokerage occupations. Some applicants with early political ambitions consciously chose a brokerage career which they knew could be combined with pursuit of a seat. Some faced hostile employers, even the sack,[39] while others worked for companies who encouraged employees with parliamentary ambitions, since they recognised the political advantages of contacts in Westminster. The importance of flexible brokerage jobs and sympathetic employers was stressed by many applicants. Some referred to the need for suitable 'jumping off' points into politics:

Being active in politics mucks up your career like nobody's business. I mean, it really causes havoc..and if you've been an MP and then lose your seat, it again causes havoc, so you've got to say to yourself, I'm interested in politics, and I'm prepared to forego lots of career opportunities for the sake of what I believe in politics.[40]

Certain employers are quite keen to encourage their employees to do things, and I have to say that I think that unless you're lucky – the silver spoon touch – you've either got to be self-employed or work for such a company.[41]

I said at point of employment, 'My ultimate interest is to be a Member of Parliament. I always want to be able to take leave during party conferences and general elections' ... The university gave me special leave to fight my two campaigns, they were fantastic, they were good employers on that score, very good employers ... At Unilever they were very much an American-style company, where they wanted not only your heart but your soul, and I think I would have found it very difficult there in subsequent times when I wanted to fight campaigns, to be on the local council.[42]

What I thought, rightly or wrongly, was that as a solicitor in London I could earn my living there and be an MP, because my work is basically in court in the morning, whereas if you're a barrister you have all-day cases – so it would've fitted in.[43]

The brokerage explanation helps illuminate not just the class disparity, but also why women and ethnic minorities are under-represented in parliament, since they are often concentrated in low-paying skilled and semi-skilled occupations, or in family small businesses, with inflexible schedules and long-hours, in sectors which do not provide traditional routes to political life. In order to examine the importance of *occupational class* on a systematic basis party strata are compared using the respondents' occupational socioeconomic group, summarised into manual/non-manual categories. *Work status* is included, distinguishing those in paid work from others, and *trade union* membership since it was anticipated this might prove significant in the Labour party.

The analysis in table 6.7 confirms the familiar observation that MPs are drawn overwhelmingly from professional and managerial occupations. The parliamentary Labour party is dominated by public sector employees: lecturers, teachers, local government managers, and welfare officers. Another significant category draws on political career jobs: political

Table 6.7 *Social class, work status and union membership*

		Conservative					Labour				
		MPs	PPCs	List	Member	Voters	MPs	PPCs	List	Members	Voters
Class	Professional/tech.	44	46	41	33	20	61	66	56	46	13
	Manager/admin.	54	46	56	39	16	24	24	23	19	4
	Clerical/sales	1	6	1	22	30	1	5	11	14	19
	Skilled manual	0	1	1	4	15	11	5	6	12	19
	Semi-skill manual	0	1	1	2	19	3	1	3	9	45
Class summary	Non-manual	99	98	98	94	66	87	94	90	79	36
	Manual	1	2	2	6	34	14	6	10	21	64
Work status	In paid work	100	98	92	39	59	100	94	95	65	52
	Retired	0	0	1	30	20	0	1	2	20	14
	Employed in the home	0	1	3	22	16	0	1	2	6	15
	Other	0	1	3	10	6	0	4	1	8	19
Union member	TU/SA member	8	14	17	14	19	99	97	91	78	34
	Not TU member	91	86	83	87	81	1	3	9	22	65
Housing tenure	Owner occupier	99	93	96	92	83	98	91	86	82	52
	Not owner	1	7	4	8	17	2	9	14	18	48
N.		142	222	225	601	1,405	97	318	127	885	1,000

Note: PPC = Prospective Parliamentary Candidate; List = Applicant on the National List.
Source: BCS, 1992; BES, 1987

researchers, trade union officials and journalists. This category has grown substantially over time, with the rise of 'career politicians'.[44] In the Conservative ranks, there are more private sector managers, company directors, financial advisers, and barristers.

But, more importantly, the results indicate the explanation for this phenomenon: *the class bias of parliament is the product of supply rather than demand*. Within each party, the socio-economic status of MPs, candidates and applicants is almost identical. If, for argument's sake, all incumbents resigned and all applicants took their place, the social composition of the Commons would be largely unaffected. Within each party the elite has higher social status than members, while members have higher status than voters. Parliament is dominated by the professional 'chattering classes' because journalists, lawyers, self-employed businessmen, financial consultants and university lecturers have sufficient security, flexibility and income to gamble on a political career.

Education

In terms of education, we have established that parliament contains far more graduates, especially from Oxford and Cambridge, and far more from public school, than the general electorate. Despite the extensive attention given to this phenomenon, the reasons for it are not well established. Ranney suggests the explanation rests with demand: party members select the better educated because this is a sign of ability and social status, and they wish to 'choose their betters'.[45] Rush suggests Conservative selectors have an overwhelming preference for Oxbridge and public school products.[46] Many Conservative candidates we interviewed shared this perception:

A seat which is either winnable or safe looks for two things. I fear they do still go for the Old Guard – the old Etonian and the son of an MP ... if you come in that way they don't look for anything, you can go straight in.[47]

Yet, equally plausibly, on the supply-side education may influence recruitment through motivation and resources. In European elections, Holland found that selectors could not be blamed for favouring those of higher status; there was a greater public school/Oxbridge and socio-economic bias among the total pool of applicants than among those chosen.[48] The body of literature on political participation has consistently found education to be one of the best predictors of activism; it increases political knowledge, interest, confidence and skills. The influence of education continues even after controlling for income, although its effect on campaign activism is less clear-cut than other modes of participation.[49]

Table 6.8 confirms that MPs are drawn disproportionately from the

Table 6.8 *Education*

Education	Conservative					Labour				
	MPs	PPCs	List	Members	Voters	MPs	PPCs	List	Members	Voters
More than 18 yrs	70	65	74	40	13	54	66	55	51	10
16 to 18 years	29	28	22	44	42	27	23	33	25	36
Less than 16 yrs	1	7	4	16	45	19	10	12	24	54
Mean years educ.	21	20	20	18	17	20	20	20	19	16
Graduate	69	66	70	28	6	71	72	62	44	6
Non-Graduate	31	33	30	72	94	29	28	38	56	94
Oxbridge + public	26	13	15	na	na	3	2	2	na	na
N.	142	222	225	601	1,405	97	318	127	885	1,000

Source: BCS, 1992; BES, 1987.

better educated; 70 per cent of MPs are graduates compared with 6 per cent of voters. But, more interestingly, the results indicate that education affects recruitment primarily through supply rather than demand. In the Conservative party, MPs, candidates and applicants are equally well qualified. But there is a precipitous fall in the proportion of university graduates from the party elite to members, and another decline from members to voters. In the Labour party there is a similar pattern, although the graduate gap is less between applicants and members, and greater between members and voters.[50] Nor can the selectors be blamed for favouring those who have followed the traditional public school plus Oxbridge route; again this reflects the proportion of applicants who fall into this category. As with brokerage occupations, higher education influences the supply of volunteers willing to risk a political career.

Gender

The influence of gender on recruitment can be treated as a product of demand, if the selectors employ direct or imputed prejudice against women. Vallance[51] and others argue that parties have been reluctant to nominate women in winnable seats because selectors are directly prejudiced against women candidates, or because, imputedly, they fear women may lose votes.[52] Many of those we interviewed believed that men and women party members, particularly the older generation, discriminated against women candidates.

The basic problem is that selectors are not enthusiastic about women candidates. They believe the electorate does not want them. They do not see women as having the same commitment as men. They do not know how to categorise them in the same way as they can men. They fear that women might be unpredictable . . . in short, they apply different standards.[53]

There was always the assumption that if you were selecting a woman you were taking a risk. I've sat on both sides of selection committees, and nobody will ever say 'Well, I don't want a woman'. They'll never say that ever, they'll always say, 'Well I don't mind, but is this constituency ready for a woman?'[54]

Older women, they feel they couldn't do that job, and they're not going to vote for you to do it.[55]

Alternatively, gender can be seen as a supply-side effect; due to the conventional division of labour in the family, segregation in the labour market and traditional patterns of socialisation, we would expect many women to have lower resources of time and money, and lower levels of political ambition and confidence. Bochel and Denver stress supply-side factors for the dearth of women politicians; if more women came forward to pursue a parliamentary career, the study suggests, more would be nominated.[56] Based on studies of local councillors, Bristow attributed women's reluctance to a lack of volition[57] while Hills stressed life-style constraints, where politics has to be juggled with the dual demands of employment and family.[58] An earlier study by Rush found that supply-side factors were most important: in the Conservative party women comprised the majority of grassroots members but only 10 per cent of those on the Approved List.[59] Some of those we interviewed believed that many women were underconfident and reluctant to stand:

We don't have nearly enough working-class MPs and women who have had the experience of holding down a job, being a full time mother, knowing the problems of, you know, elementary things like transport for the children and when the buses run – those talents and skills that women have are so undervalued, and usually women'll say, 'Oh well, I'm only this' . . . 'but all I've ever done is . . .' and, 'this is all I can do . . .', and that sort of thing.[60]

Gender could also interact with the effects of *marital status* and *children*. On balance, married candidates would be expected to be advantaged over those who were single, since constituencies often look for a 'team', although given traditional attitudes marriage and children may prove an advantage for a man but a disadvantage for a woman.[61] As our interviewees saw it:

If you're a man, they think that if they are also getting a wife, they're getting two for the price of one, essentially. The wife will open functions, and go to fetes, and be a help in the constituency while he's down in London and all the rest of it . . . But with a woman it's the other way around. Because she is married they see her as the support to her husband.[62]

They all asked me how I would cope with my family if I was to get this seat, which I'm sure they don't ask the men. And if I turned around to them and said, 'Well, my husband will look after the family', they went, 'Oh, yeah?'.[63]

A comparison of the characteristics of party strata by gender indicates that supply is more important for Conservative women while demand plays a greater role in the Labour party (see Table 6.9). Parliament includes 20 Conservative and 37 Labour women MPs. Given this situation, some believe that Conservative party selectors, with traditional family values, must be prejudiced against women. But the proportion of women Conservative candidates and applicants is about the same, which suggests that women party members are reluctant to pursue a Westminster career. Conservative women form the majority of the grassroots party, the backbone of the organisation in terms of constituency officeholders, the participants at party conference, but they are not coming forward in equal numbers to stand for

Table 6.9 *Gender, family and race*

		Conservative					Labour				
		MPs	PPCs	List	Members	Voters	MPs	PPCs	List	Members	Voters
Gender	Male	94	85	87	48	48	91	74	63	60	48
	Female	6	15	13	52	52	9	26	37	40	52
Marital status	Married	88	68	73	71	69	78	64	70	77	63
	Not married	12	32	27	29	31	22	36	30	23	37
Family	Children under 16	37	30	46	15	31	35	48	42	34	35
	None	63	70	54	85	69	65	52	58	66	65
Ethnicity	White	100	99	98		99	98	99	96	96	93
	Non-white	0	1	2		1	2	1	4	4	7
N.		142	222	225	601	1,405	97	318	127	885	1,000

Source: BCS, 1992; BES, 1987.

parliament. The most plausible explanation is that many women members are middle-aged with traditional roles in the home, or elderly pensioners, with few formal educational qualifications. This generational difference was well expressed by a Conservative woman MP:

There was an older generation than us, who didn't approve of us being political. They thought we should do the coffee mornings and the committees and all that sort of thing. And I think we, and I would say most of us in our forties and thirties, when we came along and were stridently political, this was a shock to them.

In the Labour party women have made considerable progress in parliament, almost doubling their numbers in the last general election, to comprise 13.6 per cent of Labour MPs. Yet, contrary to popular assumptions, women seem to face greater problems from Labour than Conservative party selectors. In the Labour party, women numbered 40 per cent of individual members, and about the same proportion (37 per cent) of applicants, but only 26 per cent of candidates. Thus more Labour women are coming forward than are being selected. The main reason for this, our interviewees suggested, was that more men had trade union connections which helped in terms of sponsorship and informal constituency contacts, an explanation which needs to be explored further in later chapters.

Race

The data on race in the electorate and the party elite are derived from small numbers of cases, and as a result may prove unreliable. As noted earlier, ethnic minorities represent only about 5.5 per cent of the adult British population,[64] and the population is clustered in certain constituencies, which causes problems for any conventional election survey. Previous research suggests direct racism by party activists may have influenced some recent selections.[65] A black candidate suggested racism influenced perceptions about applicants:

A lot of people were very suspicious about black people – stereotypes – there were wrong things said about black people in the Labour party, and quite often by people who we regarded as our representatives and our leaders who should set standards. And somehow if you're black you just had a certain role that was supportive – don't come out too far. If you came out too far, you've got a chip on your shoulder, you're an extremist.

Although the evidence that non-white candidates suffer an electoral penalty is mixed (see chapter 12), imputed prejudice may count against them.[66] One Asian Labour applicant mentioned this factor when he asked why he failed to get support in a selection contest:

Table 6.10 *Age groups*

Age group		Conservative					Labour				
		MPs	PPCs	List	Members	Voters	MPs	PPCs	List	Members	Voters
Age group	Over 60	17	0	1	44	14	14	3	2	21	22
	Fifties	33	9	16	23	17	34	11	12	16	19
	Forties	43	28	47	17	20	43	39	49	24	17
	Thirties	6	43	32	7	17	8	40	31	24	16
	Under 30	1	20	5	9	33	0	6	6	15	26
	Mean Age	53	40	44	58	49	52	43	44	50	45
N.		142	222	225	601	1,405	97	318	127	885	1,000

Sources: BCS, 1992; BES, 1987.

'Well, the reason I didn't vote for you', he said, 'was because we were worried that we might lose the vote'. I said 'Well, you have a cheek to tell me to my face. Well, I'll tell you something, I would have got more votes than this person, because of my hard work, and you're underestimating the intelligence of the local people ... They would judge me on my hard work, not the colour of my skin, my name and all that. I think you are wrong.'[67]

Yet there are also supply-side explanations in the literature: Crewe noted that there have been few black candidates because few have applied in the past,[68] although this may change with increasing numbers of non-whites entering the first rungs of the political career in local government.[69] Our comparison of the characteristics of party strata confirms that in the Conservative party the main problem is probably supply-side: very few non-whites are active within the party at any level. Among those who do come forward, non-whites are relatively successful at getting on the approved list of applicants, and becoming candidates. In the Labour party the problems of supply and demand are combined. In absolute terms there are more non-white candidates and MPs in the Labour party. In relative terms, a lower proportion of black Labour applicants succeeds in becoming candidates.[70]

Age

Lastly, in terms of age, younger candidates might be most strongly motivated to ascend the greasy pole of political office. Age could also affect demand: those looking for seats in their mid- to late-thirties might be best placed, since they would have had time to establish a record of political activity, experience of public service, and good party networks. In contrast, as some of our respondents stressed, those over fifty might be considered over the hill by selectorates.[71]

A comparison of party strata suggests age affects supply and demand (see table 6.10). There were notable differences within the elite: 90 per cent of MPs, and two thirds of applicants, were over forty, while the majority of candidates were younger. Those in their late thirties and early forties may be seen as most energetic, enthusiastic and committed to the constituency, qualities seen as paramount by party selectors, as well as being sufficiently mature and experienced. In the Labour party, the age profile of members and voters was fairly similar but in contrast Conservatives members were far more elderly than their supporters.

Conclusions

To summarise the results, the influence of supply-side factors can be assessed by using multivariate regression analysis to compare the social

Table 6.11   *Impact of social background on supply and demand*

	Supply	Demand	
	List v. Members	PPC v. List	
Conservative			
Occupation	.52**	.05	Brokerage/non-brokerage
Age	.25**	.32**	Years of age
Gender	.14**	.05	Male/female
Housing tenure	.08*	.03	Owner occupier/not
Education	.07	.07	Graduate/non-graduate
Marital status	.01	.07	Married/unmarried
Children	.04	.01	Number of children
R^2	.55	.08	
Labour			
Age	.17**	.06	Years of age
Occupation	.16**	.11*	Brokerage/non-brokerage
Children	.14**	.02	Number of children
Education	.09*	.09	Graduate/non-graduate
Housing tenure	.09*	.02	Owner occupier/not
Gender	.01	.18**	Male/female
Marital status	.07	.07	Married/unmarried
R^2	.07	.05	

Note: OLS regression with standardised (beta) coefficients.
** = p. > .01 * = p. > .05.
Source: BCS, 1992.

characteristics of members and applicants (see table 6.11). The analysis suggests that in both parties the most striking supply-side contrasts were by age, occupation and housing tenure.[72] Members least likely to come forward as Conservative applicants included those in non-brokerage occupations, the elderly, women, and the non-owner occupiers. Supply-side factors proved highly significant and explained a high degree of variance in the differences between Conservative applicants and members ($R^2 = 0.55$). In the Labour party those least likely to seek office included elderly members, manual workers, the less educated, those in public housing and those with children. The social background variables explained a far lower degree of variance ($R^2 = 0.07$).

The influence of demand can be tested by using a regression model to analyse differences between applicants and candidates. In the Conservative party, age proved significant on the demand-side: as in other careers, selectors preferred younger applicants. Once Conservative members were over fifty they seem to be at a distinct disadvantage. No other social factors emerged as significant predictors of Conservative demand. In the Labour party women applicants, and those in non-brokerage jobs, seemed slightly disadvantaged. But the most striking finding was that, in most respects, candidates were very similar to the total pool of applicants. The regression analysis explained very little variance by demand. Contrary to previous studies, there is no evidence in this analysis for discrimination by party selectors on the grounds of education or marital status.

The main conclusion from this chapter is therefore that parliament includes a social bias towards the younger, better educated and those in brokerage occupations, in large part because this reflects the pool of applicants. This mirrors the well-established socio-economic bias in political participation in other forms of political activity. If other types of applicants came forward, this suggests, probably more would be selected. The next logical step in the investigation is to explore why some groups of party members fail to pursue a parliamentary career. Is this due to lack of resources – factors such as time, money, political experience, support networks, trade union sponsorship? Or is this due to motivation – psychological predispositions to become involved in political life, such as interest, drive and ambition? And, if we look more closely at the attitudes of party selectors, is there any further evidence of direct or imputed discrimination on the basis of gender or race? The following chapters consider these issues.

7   Gatekeeper attitudes

Discrimination by party gatekeepers is probably the most common explanation of the social bias in parliament. It is easy to blame the outcome on party members responsible for choosing candidates.[1] Studies by Rasmussen, Vallance and others believed the dearth of women in parliament was mainly due to prejudice by local party selection committees.[2] Similar observations have been made by Greenwood to explain the lack of Conservative working-class and trade union candidates,[3] while other studies have argued that racism within the Labour party acted as a barrier against ethnic minorities.[4] Yet although commonplace, is there good evidence for this proposition? This popular explanation needs to be critically reexamined. There has been little systematic research providing convincing proof of discrimination within parties. Most studies have examined support for another hypothesis, such as whether women face an electoral penalty. When this draws a blank, authors have fallen back on prejudice by party members as the commonsense explanation. The only detailed study of attitudes among Labour party selectors, by Bochel and Denver in the mid-1970s, found no evidence for discrimination by gender, although black applicants faced some disadvantages.[5]

As the previous chapter showed, there are good reasons to believe supplyside explanations may be more plausible. Selectors may have been presented with a limited choice. In plea of mitigation, party members frequently claim their hands were tied: they would like to short list more well-qualified woman, Asians from the local community or experienced working-class candidates, they say, but few came forward to apply. Although suspicion of prejudice is widespread, it is difficult to establish proof of discrimination.

This chapter will analyse three alternative sources of evidence to assess the possible influence of discrimination within parties. First, do applicants believe they have been discriminated against? Second, do selectors display direct evidence of sexism or racism in their expressed attitudes? Lastly, based on indirect measures, what criteria were used by party members when deciding whom to support in selection meetings, and did these tend to disadvantage certain types of candidates?

The concept of discrimination

As outlined earlier, 'discrimination' means whether applicants are judged positively or negatively by virtue of their group characteristics, not according to their individual merits, abilities and experience. Irrespective of interview performance, a barrister may be perceived as more articulate than a trade unionist; a local farmer may be seen as better informed about agricultural problems than someone from London; a woman may be expected to be more knowledgeable about child-care policy than a man. These perceptions, while influential, may be wholly erroneous judgements about the individual. In some cases, positive and negative judgements about groups may balance each other out, for example women may be seen as more caring but weaker politicians. In other cases, the weight of negative judgements may mean that Sikh, Muslim or black applicants are not evaluated fairly on their merits but in terms of racial stereotypes.

Discrimination represents a judgement for or against certain groups, whether London lawyers, northern trade unionists, or local farmers. With *direct* discrimination this judgement reflects the attitudes of the selectors. With *imputed* discrimination this reflects what the selectors perceive to be the attitudes of the electorate. In the absence of perfect information, group discrimination is an integral and unavoidable part of the selection process. Party selectors usually have minimal details on which to make their decisions. The curriculum vitae gives the bare bones. There may be hundreds of application forms. The interview process is relatively short and formal. Party members met about half the applicants (52 per cent) for the first time in the final selection meeting. Few selectors (3 per cent) were personally acquainted with applicants being interviewed, or knew them as constituency party members (see table 7.7). Almost two thirds of members (61 per cent) say they made up their minds how to vote during the final selection meeting. Some party members are experienced old-hands, but many have little knowledge of the process, especially in safe seats which have not chosen a new MP for twenty or thirty years. The majority of members who participated in the selection meetings in 1992 had not been involved in the process in the 1983 or 1987 elections. Most members, therefore, rely upon the curriculum vitae for shortlisting, and the brief interview for selection, to form snap judgements about applicants. Group stereotypes function as an information short-cut, a proxy measure of an applicant's suitability. Some stereotypes (popular images) may be accurate about the usual characteristics of members of the group, some may not.

In the shortlisting process, judgements about which groups to rule in, and which to rule out, are often implicit, reflecting tacit assumptions about the appropriate role of a parliamentary candidate, and the nature of the seat.

Sometimes the most suitable criteria may be openly discussed by shortlisting committees, or even formally standardised as they are in Conservative weekend selection boards. The Labour rules, establishing positive discrimination favouring women in the shortlisting process, takes the process a step further. But the appropriate criteria for selecting parliamentary candidates are commonly taken for granted. Party members may decide they prefer younger to older applicants, locals to carpet-baggers, those with a long experience of party work to those with community service. In the same way, to prioritise applicants for a job in the labour market, personnel managers establish certain requirements in a job specification, for example the minimal age, educational qualifications, and previous work experience. The question is not whether party selectors discriminate, they cannot avoid judging individuals by group characteristics as part of the shortlisting process. The critical question is whether these judgements consistently tend to disadvantage women, black or working class applicants.

Candidates' perceptions of discrimination

It is difficult to establish water-tight evidence of discrimination. We can start by looking at the experience of those who went through the process of being shortlisted and interviewed for a seat, – the successes and failures, – to see whether they believe they were unfairly disadvantaged, or treated differently, by party gatekeepers. Perceptions by applicants are not direct proof; there may be discrimination of which applicants are unaware, or alternatively their beliefs about prejudice may be groundless. Nevertheless, perceptions must be considered indicative grounds for further investigation. The interviews suggest certain hypotheses which deserve systematic testing. Even if entirely erroneous, these perceptions may play an important role in their own right, by discouraging some from coming forward.

What groups of applicants are thought to be ruled out, or in, by shortlisting committees? In our interviews, many believed that Conservative party members prefer well-educated, professional men in early middle age, the 'right sort' of candidates who will fit into the local party, serve the constituency, and appeal strongly to local voters. An experienced Conservative Central Office official summarised the position thirty years ago:

What most associations want is a man of solid character. Not necessarily a brilliant man, you understand; in fact they may distrust a chap who seems too brilliant or flashy or glib. They want someone with the right sort of background, someone who looks and sounds right. They want someone they can count on to do the right thing, whether as a campaigner or a leader in association affairs or a Member of Parliament. They want someone who, by his business career or his war record or his party service or his social standing, has proved he is this kind of man.[6]

The search for the 'right chap' has broadened somewhat in the Conservative party since the post-war period, at least from army majors to merchant bankers, but similar echoes can be heard today in many interviews. Conservative MPs and candidates explained, in different ways, how selectors approached the task. Members may adopt fairly arbitrary criteria to help the shortlisting process:

People start with prejudices about the candidates. In the old days, they used to band them and say 'We're not having anybody under 40, nobody over 50, or we're not having a lawyer, or we're not having somebody from the south-east, or whatever it might be. Whatever prejudice they decided to start with knocked out a whole lot of people many of whom might have been exactly what they really wanted.[7]

Conservative committees ... look for candidates in their own image. They look for candidates who will have a fair bit of money, preferably a county background, connections, and if he happens to be a barrister, or something important in the City of London, then they think he's an ideal chap![8]

You're much more likely to go for the same options – to pick the merchant bankers, the solicitors, and the people from Eton and Harrow and Cambridge and Oxford, because they've been through the system and know what to expect. Why on earth would you interview a housewife from a seaside town whose photo looks quite nice and someone said she's awfully good at public speaking. But where did she go to school, what's her background? You haven't got the accreditation, have you?[9]

In the Labour party, applicants tended to be more uncertain about what selectors sought, probably, they speculated, someone 'whose face fits', or who was prepared to work hard for the constituency. Applicants often experience only one or two interviews, so they find it difficult to generalise. But many believed Labour members were commonly attracted to those with trade union experience, while local connections were frequently cited as extremely important.

Q. What were party members looking for?

Somebody who knew the area. Somebody local and somebody who knew the people.[10]

I think they were looking for people from Sheffield, ... people in Sheffield were saying yes, we ought to have some born and bred people...people who knew the constituency, people who had been educated, brought up in it, worked in it.[11]

I think its quite difficult these days for someone from outside the constituency, miles and miles away, to actually get local support ... I would think it would be ludicrous to think of someone from Inverness thinking of a seat in Edinburgh, or someone from Newcastle thinking maybe, of well, maybe a Carlisle seat.[12]

It sounds as if anyone can have a go, in fact they can't. If they get union backing, and that's more than just their name on the list – if they get financial support, if they get training support, they're gonna be at an advantage.[13]

If selectors base their assumptions about suitable applicants on their image of established MPs this may produce a systematic bias in favour of maintaining the status quo. Some Conservative MPs believed this was particularly true in inheritor seats, where most members were largely inexperienced in selecting candidates:

When you're looking for a Member of Parliament, you probably haven't done it for thirty years or twenty years or whatever, so you're much less used to it. You're much more likely to look at all the CVs and go for the same options.[14]

Most comfortable seats with good majorities have had a sitting member for quite some time. They probably haven't gone through the selection procedure for twenty, thirty years. You have a group of people, tending to be middle-aged, if not elderly, ... and so there are people who have never in their lives made such a choice, the most they may have ever chosen is who was going to be their cleaning lady. And they're faced with the prospect of replacing someone who was a very powerful image in their world, because they were engaged in politics, and their image of politics was the MP, so they naturally relate to that image ... what they're looking for subconsciously is a younger version, if that member was successful, of what they had before.[15]

The existing characteristics of MPs may define the dominant role model used for evaluating new applicants, which can build an inherent conservatism into the process. Applicants who conform to the model will be seen as suitable (for example, in the Labour party middle-aged teachers and local government officers with trade union experience, or company directors and financial consultants in the Conservatives). Others with a different background will be perceived as less appropriate (for example, those with experience of looking after children, or unpaid voluntary work for charity). Although the party membership may change, such as the entry of more black Labour activists during the 1980s, this role model may act as a brake on the social composition of parliament.

Candidates' perceptions of gender discrimination

Opinions were divided about whether women experienced direct discrimination. Most women politicians stressed support from other women within the party, with informal networks providing information, encouragement and mutual assistance. Some felt that today women applicants were treated fairly, or were perhaps at an advantage with party selectors. 'I think, at the moment, it's extremely open for women, they're looking for women, they want more women to come forward.'[16] Where people thought the process was fair, they tended to explain the paucity of women in parliament by structural constraints such as the problems of combining a parliamentary life with family responsibilities, or women's lack of confidence.

Yet not all agreed. Others (both women and men) were strongly convinced that party selectors were prejudiced against women applicants, or at least treated women differently.

> I think the problem stems from the fact that local Labour parties for all their talk about women, when the chips are down, they don't select women ... I think it's easy to say 'I support the rights of women in the party', and then they don't act on it.[17]

> It doesn't help being a woman. Over and over again that's the case ... I can think of one or two seats where they wouldn't interview a woman at all.[18]

In the Conservative party some believed that older women members were the least inclined to support female applicants, due to traditional attitudes:

> Selection committees tend to be biased, and it's dreadful women who are the worst. Women are against other women.[19]

> Unfortunately it's the other women who break you down. It's not the men ... its the generation of women, kind of fifty upwards, who didn't have a career themselves. They're resentful of your having such a wonderful career. The younger women I think have actually been rather good.[20]

> He eventually got it by two votes, because they felt that a woman, it wouldn't be right for a woman to fight in the rougher ends of [the constituency]. The two old ladies came up and said how sorry they were, but they were the two who finally decided.[21]

> I was a single woman ... it certainly came across very strongly that those doing the selection process at the initial stages were happier with somebody who was married and had, as they saw it, a stable home life ... most of the people sitting on that committee were retired, elderly people, and invariably those are the voluntary workers of our party, and they've been brought up with the old idea, of the old ideology, [of] ... a woman's role.[22]

Nevertheless, this reaction was by no means universal. Another Conservative women candidate thought that being divorced was an advantage with the selectors in her seat, since they were not looking for 'married-with-kids'.[23] Generally there were few statements of clear sexist treatment of most women applicants; in most cases Conservative women were not asked any personal questions about their family, or marital status, which were not asked equally of men. This indicates a substantial change since the practices reported as common in the 1950s.[24] In the Labour party such questions are formally banned by the rules. There was one exceptional case, however, illustrating the culture clash between women's roles and traditional attitudes among the Asian community, when a Conservative woman candidate addressed a campaign (not selection) meeting:

> I went to meet the Asian community in Huddersfield where the opening gambit from the men – I had to wear a yashmak and couldn't show any flesh and had to sit in a lotus position because they wouldn't let a woman stand in front of them – [was] 'Why do you want to be in a man's world?' 'Where are your babies?' 'Where is your husband?' Once you got over that, then you could talk about the issues.[25]

Perceptions of racial discrimination

There was a more widespread consensus that ethnic minorities tended to be disadvantaged by racism within parties. An Asian Labour applicant said he thought he fell at the first hurdle, he was not given the chance to perform at interview, because of his name: 'You read my letter, you read my application, you tore it off, and it's gone in the dustbin. You know, those are the Patels and Singhs and the Mohammeds, they all go. So all you got, the Smiths and Jones and MacDonalds.'[26] Another applicant, a trade unionist originally from Guyana, felt that attitudes towards race within the Labour party had changed substantially during the last decades. During the 1960s, he felt:

A lot of people were very suspicious about black people, stereotypes, there were wrong things said about black people within the Labour party, and often by people who we regard as our representatives and our leaders who should set standards ... They felt uncomfortable debating racism..they didn't know whether to call people blacks, or coloureds, or immigrants, or whatever. Very difficult...The Labour party then, and to some extent today, was dominated by middle-to-aging men, white men, and pretty working class, with a few people from education. Now it's very much the middle class, younger elements, larger numbers of white women, and the situation has changed a bit. We have a number of black councillors and black candidates. But racism hasn't disappeared.[27]

The main reason why black applicants were not adopted, many suggested, was imputed discrimination: party members feared an electoral penalty. Party members may favour a certain category of candidate ('I'd like to vote for a woman', 'We need more blacks in parliament'). But selectors may be unwilling to choose such a candidate because they expect they would lose votes among the electorate ('But, she'd never get in', 'There aren't enough black voters in Cheltenham'). Some ethnic minority, and a few women, applicants felt fear of electoral unpopularity influenced their political careers. Some expressed their experiences as follows:

People quite often send me long letters saying why they didn't vote for me, [in selection meetings] but I was the best candidate, and that I really touched their hearts and minds, but they felt a black radical, an ex-trade union officer, in that particular constituency, may not win. And if it's a marginal seat even more so they need a white, respectable person who comes across very moderate.[28]

Well the reason I didn't vote for you, he said, because we were worried about we might lose the vote. I say, well you have a cheek to tell me to my face. Well, I'll tell you something. I would have got more votes than this person, because of my hard work ... The local people ... would judge me on my hard work, not the colour of my skin, my name and all that. I think you are wrong.[29]

A number of Labour party members, one family said: 'Come take your poster away. I'm a Labour member but I could never bring myself to vote for you.' ... In fact a number of votes we lost, but we picked up many others.[30]

There was always the assumption that if you were selecting a woman you were taking a risk . . . I mean, I've sat on both sides of selection committees, and nobody will ever say if they sit on a selection committee, 'Well, I don't want a woman'. They'll never say that, ever, they'll always say, 'Well I don't mind but is this constituency ready for a woman?'[31]

Whether these fears are groundless, or whether women and ethnic minorities do lose votes, is explored below in chapter 12.

While the issues of race and gender have become more important in recent decades, concern about discrimination against working class applicants is rarely expressed today, even in the Labour party. Some regretted the middle class take-over of the party, but attributed this to structural factors handicapping working class applicants, not attitudinal barriers.[32] In the Conservative party there was a vague suspicion that members preferred certain types of occupation, such as lawyers and merchant bankers, but this issue produced little concern.

This evidence from personal interviews illuminates perceptions by applicants but it requires more systematic confirmation to provide a convincing case for or against discrimination. The interviews drew on the experience of only a sub-sample of cases. Often applicants sent conflicting messages expressing uncertainty about whether party members had treated them fairly. Most importantly, applicants may suspect prejudice but this does not constitute proof; the belief may be erroneous, or a rationalisation of failure.

To see whether these perceptions are broadly representative, we examined whether the process was seen as fair by most groups of participants. As mentioned in chapters 3 and 4, respondents were asked to indicate whether they felt that in their most recent application, the selection process had proved democratic, efficient, complicated and fair. As table 7.1 shows, overall the majority of MPs (55 per cent) and candidates (59 per cent) felt the selection meeting which adopted them used a very fair process. The majority of candidates in all social groups, – women and men, young and old, middle and working class, black and white – thought the process was very fair, with the single exception of candidates for the Labour party. In some ways this is unsurprising, because candidates are the winners in the selection game of musical chairs. To acknowledge that the process was not fair would serve to delegitimize their position. When asked whether the process was fair, one new woman MP confessed somewhat cynically: 'Yes. I don't know if my opponent would. I have too much knowledge, too many contacts, knew too many people. I had all the addresses of everybody important and they didn't. But that's the way life goes.'[33] The least satisfaction groups were the List Applicants, who failed to secure a seat; only one quarter (26 per cent) thought the process very fair. Although there is a need for caution given the limited number in the sample, among the pool of list applicants, women tended to be more critical than men, as were non-white

Table 7.1   *Perceptions of fairness among MPs, candidates and applicants*

% saying 'very fair'	MPa	PPCs	List applicants
All	55	59	26
Con.	61	71	30
Lab.	43	33	19
Lib. Dem.	83	74	...
SNP + PC	...	67	...
Green	...	63	...
Men	55	60	29
Women	44	58	16
Middle class	55	59	26
Working class	39	68	40
Twenties	...	54	38
Thirties	39	56	28
Forties	45	62	23
Fifties	67	65	28
Sixties	61	79	33
White	54	59	27
Non-white	...	67	14
Graduates	56	62	26
Non-graduates	54	58	26
N.	222	1,025	292

Note: Q. 'In your view was the procedure used in your most recent selection application ...
fair?'
[Very/quite/not very/Not at all]
Source: BCS, 1992.

applicants, although working-class applicants were slightly more positive. Therefore, this provides some support for the argument that women and black list applicants felt they were treated unfairly by the selection process, although to some extent the assessments may reflect *post-hoc* rationalisations, 'sour grapes', among those who tried but failed.

In general, irrespective of their personal experiences, do applicants believe that parties block the opportunities of women and ethnic minorities to stand? Participants were asked to evaluate different explanations of why there were few women and black members in parliament. Respondents were asked to agree or disagree with a series of eight possible explanations, including supply-side factors ('Women don't come forward as candidates', 'Women are not interested in politics') or demand side ('Women are not given the opportunities by political parties', 'Women lose votes') (see table 7.2). The results indicate that over half (55 per cent) thought that women were not given the opportunity by parties to stand. Yet the most common

Table 7.2   *Explanations for gender parliamentary under-representation*

Women MPs ...	Agree	Neither	Disagree	%	N.	PDI (*)
Don't come forward	73	8	19	100	1,613	54
Are not given opportunity by parties	55	14	32	100	1,628	23
Don't have confidence	28	13	59	100	1,629	−32
Don't fit into parliament	9	8	83	100	1,614	−75
Lose votes	4	9	88	100	1,617	−84
Are not interested	4	7	89	100	1,636	−85
Lack the right experience	3	4	93	100	1,620	−91
Not suited to the job	2	4	94	100	1,641	−93

Note: Q. 'Would you agree or disagree with the following explanations of why there are few women MPs?'
(*) The Percentage Difference Index (PDI) summarises agreement minus disagreement.
Source: BCS, 1992, 'Survey of MPs, PPCs and Applicants'.

Table 7.3   *Explanations for ethnic parliamentary under-representation*

Asian and Black MPs ...	Agree	Neither	Disagree	%	PDI (*)
Don't come forward	67	13	20	100	47
Are not given opportunity by parties	66	11	23	100	43
Lose votes	31	23	46	100	−16
Don't have confidence	22	11	62	100	−40
Lack the right experience	8	13	79	100	−71
Don't fit into parliament	5	9	87	100	−82
Are not interested	3	9	87	100	−84
Not suited to the job	1	8	91	100	−90

Note: Q. 'Would you agree or disagree with the following explanations of why there are few Asian and Afro-Caribbean MPs?'
(*) The Percentage Difference Index (PDI) summarises agreement minus disagreement.
Source: BCS, 1992 – 'Survey of MPs, PPCs and Applicants'.

explanation for women's under-representation was the widespread belief that women do not come forward to stand; three quarters agreed with this view. None of the other explanations, such as women's lack of experience or interest, was seen as particularly plausible. The pattern of responses was fairly similar for explanations of racial underrepresentation (see table 7.3); two thirds agreed equally with the arguments that black applicants do not come forward, and that, if they do so, parties do not give them the opportunity to stand. These explanations commanded similar levels of agreement among party members.

This suggests some important conclusions about the perception of applicants. Most MPs and candidates thought that the process had treated them fairly. But at the same time many believe that the social bias in parliament reflects, at least in part, the lack of opportunities provided by party selectors. Opinion is divided about the effects of gender, although there is a greater consensus about the influence of racism. To understand these issues more directly we can examine the attitudes of selectors to see whether they are guilty of discrimination, as critics charge. There are three indicators from the membership survey: attitudes towards women in politics, gender stereotypes about candidates, and anticipated electoral penalties.

Selectors' attitudes towards women in office

First we can see whether party members say they support the idea of having more women in office, and hence whether they are concerned about the current composition of parliament. In the 1970s, Bochel and Denver's survey of Labour party selectors asked whether, other things being equal, members supported the idea of selecting more women and more 'coloured' Labour candidates. Overall the survey found 60 per cent of party members agreed with the idea that more women should be selected, and women were not perceived by members as an electoral liability. Therefore, the authors concluded, women were not disadvantaged by local Labour parties: 'the common allegation that selection committees have a prejudice against women candidates receives no support from this evidence'.[34] In terms of race, Labour selectors were divided almost evenly about whether more black candidates should be selected. The greater reluctance to choose them, Bochel and Denver suggests, rested with the widespread belief that black candidates would lose votes.

During the 1980s there were stronger demands for greater social diversity within parliament, particularly within the Labour party as women mobilised around this issue, and black sections became organised. One would expect that concern about this issue would have grown over time. To update the Bochel and Denver data, the BCS survey asked party members whether they felt there should be more women in parliament, whether there should be fewer, or about the same as now. The results, in table 7.4, suggest that support for increased numbers of women politicians has become the overwhelming consensus among members of the Labour party, where 95 per cent supported this proposition. There was slightly lower support in the Conservatives but still three quarters of all party members expressed approval. Generally the response was fairly uniform across social groups although support was slightly stronger among the better educated and younger members, as might be expected, and there was also a modest difference by gender. Moreover, this evidence debunks the common myth,

Table 7.4   *Members' attitudes towards women in parliament*

| | Conservative | | | Labour | | |
	More	Same	Fewer	More	Same	Fewer
All members	75	24	1	94	4	1
Office-holders	76	22	2	93	6	1
Non-officers	70	30	0	95	4	2
Men	73	25	2	92	7	2
Women	76	24	0	98	1	1
Older	72	27	1	91	8	1
Middle	76	23	0	95	3	1
Younger	83	17	0	96	3	0
Older women	77	23	0	96	2	2
Older men	67	32	2	88	12	0
Graduate	85	14	2	96	3	2
Non-graduate	73	26	1	93	6	1
Middle class	76	23	1	96	3	1
Working class	82	18	0	90	7	3

Note: Q. . . 'Do you feel there should be more women in parliament, fewer women in parliament, or about the same as now?'
Source: BCS, 1992, 'Members Survey'.

sometimes echoed in our interviews, that older Conservative women members were the strongest opponents of women's active involvement in public life. Not so. This evidence shows older men had more traditional attitudes than older women within both major parties.

Gender stereotypes about candidates

Popular stereotypes about women politicians may prove a mixed blessing. On the one hand, women may be seen as more honest, caring and less aggressive than men, which may be useful if politicians want to campaign as 'outsiders' bringing a fresh perspective to politics as usual. But women may also be seen as unsuitable for politics if it is believed that they are less strong and decisive leaders, less knowledgeable about foreign policy issues, or that they have less time for campaigning. Either way, the female applicant is being judged on the basis of characteristics assumed about women as a group which may have no bearing on her personality and abilities. To understand perceptions of women politicians, and the impact of gender stereotypes, members were presented with a series of characteristics, such as the qualities of honesty, toughness and ambition. Members were asked whether they felt that women or men candidates would be more likely to

Table 7.5   *Gender images of candidates among party members*

		Women more	No difference	Men more	N.
Caring	Con.	36	63	1	288
	Lab.	35	64	2	482
Practical	Con.	24	60	16	289
	Lab.	24	70	6	481
Approachable	Con.	17	73	10	289
	Lab.	31	66	3	480
Honest	Con.	14	82	3	292
	Lab.	21	78	2	495
Principled	Con.	17	77	6	287
	Lab.	14	84	3	484
Hardworking	Con.	15	80	5	292
	Lab.	15	83	2	490
Decisive	Con.	11	66	24	284
	Lab.	6	85	9	483
Effective	Con.	3	84	14	285
	Lab.	8	86	6	479
Tough	Con.	12	60	28	287
	Lab.	7	79	14	480
Ambitious	Con.	14	58	28	290
	Lab.	7	68	25	482
Ruthless	Con.	15	50	36	285
	Lab.	7	65	29	475

Note: Q. 'In general do you think that a woman candidate or a man candidate is more likely to have the following qualities, or would there be no difference?'
Source: BCS, 1992, 'Members Survey'.

have these qualities, or whether there would be no difference. If gender stereotypes explain why women were not picked, members should display traditional attitudes.

As table 7.5 indicates, the most popular response across these items was gender neutral; the majority of members said they thought there was no difference between women and men across these qualities. But where there were differences, they were in the expected direction of gender stereotypes, that is, women were more likely than men to be seen as caring, approachable, practical, honest and principled. In contrast, men were more likely to be seen as ruthless, ambitious, and tough. These traditional images were particularly widespread among Conservative members. This confirms that gender stereotypes remain common, but it is not clear that these necessarily disadvantage women. If selectors place a high priority on the case-work aspect of an MP's job, dealing with the practical problems of individual constituents, as many do, then stereotypes about women may be a positive advantage.

Members' perceptions of electoral risks

To examine imputed discrimination we need evidence of member's perceptions of the electoral risks of adopting certain types of candidates. To assess perceived 'risks', members were asked whether certain types of candidates might gain or lose votes in their constituency (see table 7.6). In the Conservative party, reflecting the dominant image of the MPs, candidates who were local, white, middle class, and male were thought likely vote winners. Women and working-class candidates were perceived as electorally slightly positive, while black or trade union applicants were seen as vote losers. In the Labour party, candidates from the local area were seen as a considerable electoral asset, as emphasised in our interviews. White, female and middle-class candidates were seen as positive electoral assets. Strikingly, even in the Labour party, middle-class candidates were thought more popular than working-class candidates. Again, black candidates were seen as posing the greatest electoral risk. As some regional officers noted:

What they [party members] say is 'We don't have prejudice, but all those awful people out on the streets, we know they have got prejudice. So it wouldn't be fair to inflict them on this chap or woman.'[35]

One of the brightest people on the list is an ethnic. He's extremely bright, he's very cultured, he's very educated. I got him an interview but they made it clear to me that they wouldn't select him on the grounds he wouldn't be accepted locally. Very much a case of 'We're not prejudiced, but ...'[36]

Perceptions of anticipated electoral gains and losses reflect, and thereby reinforce, the dominant class and racial biases within parliament. Those who conform to the standard social background of an MP tend to be seen as the least risky choices, while ethnic minority applicants are widely perceived as unpopular with the electorate.

This evidence suggests three main conclusions about members' attitudes. First, when asked directly, most party members say they favour bringing more women into politics. Support for this proposition seems to have increased since previous studies in the mid-1970s. Second, gender stereotypes about candidates remain fairly pervasive. Nevertheless, it is not clear that these necessarily disadvantage women, perhaps the reverse. Lastly, women are now seen as a positive electoral asset, although ethnic minority candidates were seen as electoral risks.

The problem of interpretation is what weight should be placed on these results. These questions tend to be very simple and direct. Party activists are relatively politically sophisticated. In this sensitive area the results may reflect the 'politically correct' response, since few party members may wish to acknowledge being seen as openly sexist or racist. Direct questions on race have proved misleading in other contexts; for example, opinion polls in

Table 7.6   *Anticipated electoral gains and losses*

Candidates who were ...	Gain many	Gain some	No difference	Lose some	Lose many	PDI (*)
Conservative party						
Local	32	35	20	9	4	55
White	20	33	46	0	0	52
Middle class	11	29	55	5	0	35
Man	11	23	66	0	0	34
Woman	5	18	62	15	1	7
Working class	5	21	53	20	2	4
Black or Asian	9	9	17	43	22	−47
Trade union	3	11	22	42	22	−51
Labour party						
Local	45	43	11	0	0	88
White	13	28	58	1	0	40
Woman	11	32	50	7	1	35
Middle class	9	29	51	10	2	26
Man	6	13	77	4	0	15
Working class	10	19	52	18	1	11
Trade union	6	18	59	16	1	7
Black or Asian	3	18	26	42	11	−33

Note: Q. 'Do you think that for your party in this constituency certain candidates would ...'
(*) The Percentage Difference Index (PDI) is the net gains minus losses.
Source: BCS, 1992, 'Members Survey'.

the United States which ask about voting intentions for black gubernatorial or Senate candidates have tended to produce a systematic over-estimate of their support. Respondents may feel pressured to provide answers which conform to the dominant social norms. There may be little relation between responses to hypothetical questions ('Should there be more women selected ...?') and actual support for applicants. This evidence therefore needs supplementing with alternative approaches to analysing discrimination.

What criteria influence selection?
Questions referring directly to sexist or racist attitudes are open to the dangers of rationalisation. To overcome this, we aimed to find out how Labour and Conservative selectors ranked applicants when they were being interviewed. At the start of selection meetings members were given a form for self-completion which was collected at the end of the evening. Members were asked to evaluate each applicant during the interview, in the order in which they appeared, according to a checklist of qualities. There was one column per applicant. This included a range of eighteen items, for example

Table 7.7   *Factor analysis of evaluations of candidate qualities*

	Campaigning abilities	Personal character	Constituency links
Good speaker	0.77		
Political experience	0.74		
Knowledgeable about issues	0.69		
Personal energy and enthusiasm	0.66		
Likely to win votes	0.63		
Effective	0.62		
Experienced party worker	0.60		0.47
Good personal appearance	0.59		
Well educated	0.55		
Tough	0.52		
Caring		0.76	
Honest		0.76	
Principled		0.73	
Supports political views		0.59	
Stable home life		0.55	
Local candidate			0.81
Nationally well known			−0.44
Committed to constituency	0.43		0.45
Percentage variance explained	42.5	7.5	5.7

Note: The coefficients are produced by principal components factor analysis with a minimum eigenvalue of 0.40.
Source: BCS, 1992, 'Members Survey'.

whether applicants were good speakers, knowledgeable about the issues, committed to the constituency, politically experienced, honest, principled, well educated, and likely to win votes. At the end members were also asked to indicate who they judged overall to be the best candidate, second best, and third best. This provides a reliable indication of how members actually voted in the meeting, since nearly all (93 per cent) said they voted for the candidate they thought best. Few voted tactically (5 per cent), or because they were mandated how to vote by their branch (2 per cent). Respondents were also asked how they knew each candidate. Finally, for purposes of analysis, the background characteristics (age, gender, class, marital status, and race) of the interviewees (N. = 101) were merged with the survey data.[37] It should be noted that these questions made no reference to the social background of applicants; these data were added later.

To establish how applicants were being evaluated, we employed factor analysis to see which characteristics were closely associated with each other.

Table 7.8   *Important qualities in selecting candidates*

	Beta
Likely to win votes	0.16**
Good speaker	0.16**
Personal energy and enthusiasm	0.12**
Supports your political views	0.11**
Knowledgeable about issues	0.10**
Political experience	0.10**
R^2	0.32

Note: The dependent variable was whether the respondent ranked the applicant best (4), second (3), third (2) or other (1).
The model uses OLS regression with standardised beta coefficients. ** = sig.p. > .01
Source: BCS, 1992, 'Members Survey'.

The results in table 7.7 indicate three underlying factors, explaining 42 per cent of the variance in the evaluations. The most important of these can be termed 'campaigning abilities', such as whether applicants were good speakers, had political experience, proved knowledgeable about issues, and were likely to win votes. The second group of characteristics revolved around judgements about an applicant's 'personal character', such as whether they seemed caring, honest, and principled. Lastly, 'constituency links' also proved to be closely clustered evaluations, namely whether applicants were locally or nationally well known, and whether they were committed to the constituency.

To explore which qualities were important in determining members' choice, these qualities were entered into a regression analysis. The ranked preference for the applicant (best, second best, third best, and other) were scaled as the dependent variable. As table 7.8 shows, overall campaigning qualities proved most important; members voted for candidates according to judgements about their ability to win votes, speaking ability, personal energy and enthusiasm, knowledge about the issues, and political experience. In addition, whether applicants supported the members' political views also proved important. Altogether these qualities explained a fairly high proportion of variance ($R^2 = 0.32$). Other campaigning qualities also proved statistically significant in stepwise regressions, but were excluded from the final model on the grounds of parsimony, since they added little to the proportion of explained variance. This evidence confirms that what members want, above all else, is someone who can win votes for the party. Other factors which some believed influence members, such as educational qualifications, family status, the personal character of applicants, or local connections, proved relatively unimportant in this model.

In one regard this was puzzling. In interviews Labour candidates had often stressed the importance of local connections. So it seemed worthwhile to investigate the issue of constituency links more closely. Members were asked how they knew each candidate being interviewed, and this was compared with the way they were ranked. The results in table 7.9 show that, contrary to expectations, most members had little prior acquaintance with those being interviewed. In general half (52 per cent) of the applicants were first seen by members at the final selection meeting, while 18 per cent were familiar through an earlier stage in the selection process. Another 18 per cent were already known through local politics, but few (less than 6 per cent in total) were familiar as personal acquaintances or constituency party members.

How did this affect the final choice? The results confirm that personal familiarity was an advantage; although this was a small group, 61 per cent who already knew the applicant personally ranked him or her first. But it was rarely a decisive advantage. In general the selection process proved remarkably open; there was little difference in the relative ranking of applicants by familiarity. Being known through local politics was only a slight help. This supports the remarks of some applicants who suggested that being already known in the seat may prove a two-edged sword, since people may have made political enemies as well as friends. At an earlier stage personal contacts with the key officers in a constituency may perhaps help secure an interview. But most grassroots members attending the final meeting have never met the applicants until the selection process began. The impression made during the half-hour interview was decisive to success or failure.

If campaigning qualities are the most important criteria for selection, are women seen as less effective campaigners? The evidence is mixed. As shown in table 7.10 when interviewees were ranked by members in selection meetings, women attracted slightly higher support than men. Overall, 28 per cent of the women interviewees were ranked first as 'best' applicant, compared with 25 per cent of men. The difference is not large, but the direction suggests if anything positive discrimination by the selectorate.

Yet when we analysed how members evaluated the qualities of interviewees in the final selection meetings, women were rated slightly less highly on the most important campaigning qualities; they were generally seen as less good speakers, and less likely to win votes (see table 7.11). The apparent contradiction between this result and the earlier findings is probably explained, at least in part, by the difference between direct questions about support for women politicians, where there may be a tendency to

Table 7.9   *The effect of familiarity on applicant ranking*

| | Rank of applicant | | | |
	First	Second	Third	All
First saw at this meeting	46	37	17	52
Saw at earlier selection meeting	49	35	16	18
Through local politics	56	33	11	18
By national reputation	53	35	12	6
Personal acquaintance	61	30	8	3
Constituency party member	44	34	22	3
All	49	35	15	100

Note: Q. 'How do you know each candidate?' (Multiple response)
Source: BCS, 1992, 'Members Survey'.

Table 7.10   *Ranking of applicants by gender*

	Best	Second best	Third best	Other
Women applicants	28	19	8	46
Men applicants	25	18	8	49

Source: BCS, 1992, 'Members Survey'.

express a politically correct view consistent with the dominant social norms within the party, and the indirect measure of evaluations for applicants, which were gender-neutral items. Perhaps members *say* they would like more women in office, but in practice when they evaluate interviewees they may see women in a slightly more negative light, as less effective campaigners.

In conclusion, critics commonly believe that gatekeepers are to blame for the social bias in parliament, if traditional attitudes have produced the under representation of women and black MPs. The evidence from this analysis reveals little discrimination against women applicants; members say they support the idea of having more women in parliament; there is no evidence that gender stereotypes necessarily disadvantage women candidates; and members believe nowadays women are vote winners. In practice, when interviewing individual applicants, women tended to be evaluated slightly less positively on the critical campaigning qualities which help determine who gets selected. Nevertheless, the difference is not great, and in the final interview women tended to be ranked the same, or slightly

Table 7.11   *Candidate qualities by gender of applicants*

	Applicants		
	Men	Women	Diff.
Good speaker	65	53	13
Likely to win votes	43	33	10
Supports own views	42	33	9
Personal energy	62	55	7
Knowledgeable	58	57	1
Political experience	55	54	1

Source: BCS, 1992, 'Members Survey'.

higher, than men. The evidence concerning ethnic minority applicants is more limited, given the number in the survey. Nevertheless, the available results suggest that black applicants seem to suffer greater disadvantages than women, primarily because Labour and Conservative members continue to believe that their selection poses electoral risks. Since the most important quality when choosing candidates is their ability to win votes, this seems likely to pose a serious obstacle to black representation. Imputed rather than direct discrimination is the main barrier facing black and Asian candidates. In general, this suggests that gatekeeper attitudes are not the main reason for the lack of women in parliament, and we need to consider supply-side explanations for a more plausible explanation.

8   Candidate resources

This chapter compares the resources of actors on the ladder of recruitment. 'Resources' are understood as a range of assets which can be employed to advantage in pursuing a political career. This includes personal income, union sponsorship, time, political experience, and support networks. In the analytical model, outlined in figure 8.1, it is a combination of resources plus motivation which form the necessary and sufficient conditions for seeking a parliamentary seat. Many people have the time and money to run for office, but without commitment they will not use these resources for political objectives. Others may have nursed a long-standing ambition to be in Westminster, but without the experience or contacts they may never succeed. Resources could be expected to influence either the supply or demand-side of the candidate selection process, or both.

On the *supply-side*, resources may place aspirants in a stronger position to pursue a political career, should they aspire to Westminster. Studies of mass political participation have commonly found individual and group-based resources to be strongly associated with different forms of activism, in political parties, interest and community groups.[1] Resources may influence which party members enter the pool of applicants. The impact of certain resources like household income can be tested in the most straightforward way, by comparing the characteristics of members and applicants, as in the previous chapters. With some other resources, information about party members is not available, or is simply inappropriate, since certain questions about recruitment can only be asked of the political elite.[2] In these cases supply-side explanations are tested by comparing the characteristics of groups on the ladder of recruitment.

On the other hand, *demand-side* explanations may be equally plausible, if party selectors are most strongly attracted to applicants with considerable time and energy to invest in the constituency campaign, plus relevant experience, financial sponsorship, useful political skills, and a good network of contacts. Evidence supporting this explanation would be significant differences in the resources of applicants and candidates. Based on our understanding of the process, we would also expect the importance of

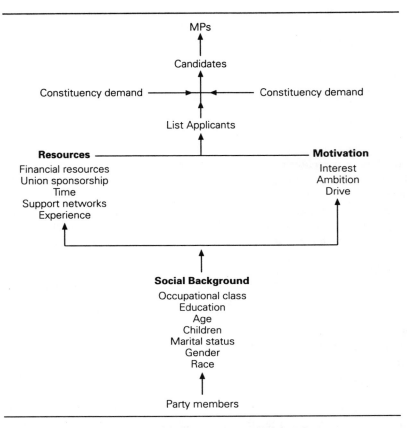

Figure 8.1   The supply and demand model of recruitment.

different types of resources to vary by party, and the nature of the contest. Trade union sponsorship, for example, may be critical in safe Labour constituencies, while financial resources may be most important for Conservative challengers fighting geographically distant seats. This chapter will examine these issues, then weigh the relative influence of resources against social background factors.

Personal financial resources

In Britain, personal expenditure by aspirants has become less significant today than in the prewar period, when contemporary accounts suggest that this was sometimes decisive in gaining good seats.[3] Reform of the campaign finance laws in the 1880s, combined with the 1949 Maxwell Fyfe rules in the Conservative party, and the 1957 Wilson reforms in the Labour party, strictly limited the nature and amount of money individual candidates could contribute to their election expenses and the constituency association. Legally, a candidate may spend up to £600 on his or her personal expenses during a campaign, including travel and accommodation. Any personal expenses above this limit must be paid by the agent although this is not included in the legal maximum for the election campaign. Financial barriers for British candidates do not provide the formidable hurdle faced in some other countries, such as by Congressional candidates in the United States.[4] Nevertheless, more hidden personal expenses which must be met by a candidate may be a problem, as one Conservative women candidate remarked: 'The financial side of it is, I think, prohibitive, because it's almost selective in itself, as I said, if I had had children, and been in a different situation financially, then there's no way I could've contemplated it.'[5]

Interview costs

Applicants first face interview costs, the initial expenses associated with pursuing a seat: travel to successive meetings in different constituencies, suitable clothes for interviews, local research, overnight or weekend accommodation, attending regional training sessions and party conferences. Unlike standard practices in the private sector, applicants attending interviews around the country usually pay their own expenses. The Conservative Model Rules recommend that, although the constituency association should be ready to help with transportation and hospitality, it is not desirable that the association should refund an applicant's travelling and hotel expenses. If necessary, Central Office can help in this regard, although it is not apparent how often this happens in practice, and there may be a stigma attached to applying for funds.[6] Some Labour constituencies offer to pay travel costs for interviews, meals and even childcare, but this is discretionary.[7] Recent Labour party reforms have had the unintended consequence of lengthening the process, and increasing the number of branch and constituency meetings that candidates must attend. The interview costs may seem modest, but they proved sufficient to deter at least one Labour 'B' list woman we interviewed from going any further in the process:

I did see many obstacles. I thought at the time, well . . . you've made people aware that, yes, you could do it, that you're prepared to do it. But deep down, I knew that I'm a working-class woman, that I don't have money. I couldn't travel the country seeking nomination. I couldn't run around to constituencies, I have a lot of problems at home, I've got a sick husband, I've got a daughter who two years ago had the little laddie there, she's a single mother, I've got a lot of domestic problems. We haven't got a lot of money. And I do think there's got to be some sort of funding to enable people like me to travel to Milton Keynes, or Coventry Southwest I think it was – I got an invitation from a ward there . . . My name had been shortlisted, and I was quite thrilled . . . I said I will make every effort, and then I actually thought about the money – it was money.[8]

Campaign costs

If adopted, candidates face personal campaign costs in nursing the constituency, often for one or two years before the election. Unlike MPs, challengers face direct expenses including telephone, mail, photocopying, and possibly secretarial costs to deal with letters from constituents, and transportation for regular party meetings and local campaigning, plus the hidden costs of time away from work, possibly child-care or home help. Well-resourced local parties can help with some of these costs, and other office expenses can be deferred through sympathetic employers for those like union officials. Emily's List in the Labour party may also help meet some of this expenditure for Labour women. How much does it all cost? Estimates varied. Local candidates already resident in the constituency, or those sponsored by their trade union, thought it cost little, at most a few hundred pounds: 'The most cost I've ever encountered was petrol from home to the constituency . . . getting on the list, perhaps there would be £70 to £80 for your hotel, your overnight stay. You could probably add in going to conference every year, that sort of thing, but in a way it's a bit like a holiday.'[9] Those with more distant seats thought it cost them anywhere from £3,000 to £10,000 per campaign, which could be multiplied two or three times in successive elections. For some this proved prohibitive. An adopted candidate who became unemployed had to withdraw from his constituency before the election. As MPs noted:

To get myself selected was a very cheap process. It took a couple of letters and one visit. But then it took a hell of a lot of money to be a candidate. Up and down, up and down. Just on rail fares alone . . . It was about £2,000 or £3,000 then, which is a lot of money now.[10]

The costs of selection are borne by you, the costs of nursing the seat are borne by you . . . I should think about £10,000 over the three year period. I was selected in '76, and fought the seat in '79 – there was travel and accommodation and subsistence . . . I ran up a very large overdraft, nursing the seat and fighting the election of '79, and I could not afford to fight in '83.[11]

The costs, I suppose, if you get selected long before an election, you have to start nurturing it, cultivating it, nursing it. You can spend £4,000 or £5,000 easy-peasy 'cos you have to go there every weekend, or quite a lot . . . It's very expensive and some people do find it a terrible strain, and then, of course, they don't win the damn seat at the end of it. And £5,000 in a couple of years out of someone's life can be very big money.[12]

Career displacement costs

Lastly, there are displacement costs, since many MPs had flourishing professional or business careers before they entered the House. Some careers such as journalism or the law can be maintained in parliament, or even enhanced with professional and business contacts. But it may prove difficult to combine a career in public service, or a small business with the demands of Westminster. In the long term, except in safe seats, a political life usually entails considerable financial risks, given the chances of electoral failure, and the uncertainties of government office. As one Conservative MP said,

Financially, it's an enormous sacrifice, because in my company by then I had a very successful business, my personal income would make most people in this place green with envy, also I was very much free to go anywhere in the world because my business took me everywhere in the world, I had a very good lifestyle.[13]

In comparative terms, British MPs are not generously rewarded in terms of salary, allowances, services and general facilities.[14] Since 1983, MPs' pay has been linked to Civil Service rates. In 1992/3, backbench members were paid £30,854 per annum. Those with a London constituency have an additional supplement (£1,222). For members outside of London, there is an annual allowance to cover the expenses of staying overnight away from home, up to the maximum of £10,901, which recognises the need for many members to maintain a domestic base at Westminster as well as in the constituency. Members may also claim costs (up to £40,380) for office expenses, equipment, secretarial and research assistance, and most maintain about two employees.[15] In addition there are a few subsidies with the job, including free travel to their constituency and home for the member and their family, official postage and telephone.

A precise comparison of the financial rewards of office in different legislatures is difficult since many costs and benefits are an integral part of the wider political system. Despite the growth of legislative business, the increased number of 'career' politicians,[16] and periodic debates about reforms, the British parliament continues to work on the assumption of 'gentleman amateurs'. The hours of sitting assume that members should be able to maintain professional careers in private practice. Parliamentary rules assume that members should be able to maintain company directorships, or other forms of sponsorship, so long as such interests are officially disclosed. Members are allowed to vote on any business before the House except private legislation where they have a direct pecuniary interest.[17] Despite some improvements, office facilities and the research support provided for MPs assume that the main business of parliament is carried out on the floor of the house.[18] By contrast, in a professional legislature, such as the US Congress, members have far more generous resources for staffing, research, official expenses and constituency service (a maximum of $713,069 per annum, or £469,124 per Member of the House of Representatives in 1987).[19] Compared with the salaries of many European counterparts, and of American members of Congress, British MPs are not generously rewarded (see chapter 10).

The impact of financial resources

To assess the impact of personal financial resources, party strata were compared by the household's total *income*, divided into seven bands (see table 8.1). Since most party selectors can only infer the personal income of applicants when selecting them at interview, it seems most plausible to expect financial resources to influence supply, and indeed this receives confirmation. The results show List Applicants had very similar incomes to adopted candidates. The most striking contrast was between all the political elite and the non-elite: two thirds of Labour voters were in households with incomes of under £10,000, compared with one third of members, and only 8 per cent of the Labour elite. In the Conservative party, 42 per cent of voters had incomes of under £10,000, compared with almost none of the party elite. As we might expect, there were also noticeable differences between parties, with Conservative MPs by far the most affluent group. The evidence supports the thesis that financial resources affect the supply of those who come forward to seek a Westminster career. Those without a comfortable income may feel they just cannot afford the financial investment required to nurse a seat, and the financial risks of a political life, particularly given the chances of electoral failure.

Trade union sponsorship

As discussed earlier, in the Labour party sponsorship by trade unions is commonly perceived by applicants as a critical advantage, which could swing the decision with under-funded local parties. There are two significant issues to be considered here. How important is union sponsorship for the success of Labour applicants? And does union sponsorship make a difference to the composition of the Labour party, that is, do the unions continue to provide an avenue for working-class candidates?

Table 8.1   *Financial resources (in percentages)*

| | Conservative | | | | Labour | | | | |
Pounds	MP	PPC	List	Voters	MP	PPC	List	Member	Voters
> 5,000	0	1	1	18	0	0	5	16	36
5–10,000	0	1	1	24	0	7	11	21	31
10–20,000	0	15	9	39	2	26	24	32	27
20–30,000	5	22	19	13	31	28	30	17	5
30–40,000	12	16	17	6	37	21	15	8	1
40–50,000	22	14	11		20	11	11	4	
< 50,000	61	31	43		10	7	4		
	100	100	100	100	100	100	100	100	100

Note: The scale for voters only extends to £30,000 + and for Labour Party Members to
£40,000 +
Source: BCS, 1992; BES, 1987; Labour Party Membership Survey, 1989.

How influential is union sponsorship?

In recent years, the influence of unions over the selection process has proved
controversial, as Labour has reexamined its links with the organised labour
movement. As part of the process of party modernisation, the party leadership, under Neil Kinnock and John Smith, has attempted to move the
balance of power in the party in favour of individual members. Trade
unions sponsored parliamentary candidates long before the Labour party
was founded, to assist working-class representatives.[20] In the last decade,
union sponsorship has grown, so that by the 1992 parliament over half of all
Labour MPs were sponsored by unions, 143 out of 271, the highest number
in the party's history. Most Labour candidates we interviewed felt that
unions should have some role in selection, but the way their power was
exercised needed reform.[21] There was a broad consensus that union support
provided a substantial, often decisive, advantage for applicants:

I didn't get a safe seat. I felt for those you had to have far greater backing than I did
... Either you had to be the union favoured person, which I wasn't, or you had to be
absolutely local in the area with a good council background.[22]

I've been a trade unionist all my life, but I do have reservations about the union
clout, and the union involvement in selections ... they determine what's going on in a
constituency, they determine who is the candidate.[23]

If you're not either a local candidate, or on a trade union sponsored list, nor, more
importantly, on the list of a union which is very well organised in the constituency
you're aiming at, then it is very difficult indeed.[24]

In a few constituencies, some suggested, union power was abused, as seats were sewn up in advance for favourite applicants, and the process of selection was undemocratic:

I think the worst feature is – it doesn't happen in my constituency – when unions start fixing things, and there's a lot of evidence to suggest it's happening all over Birmingham.[25]

In my old constituency up till 1983, it was the NUM that dominated. Then, [I] moved into this new constituency, and its the GMB that predominates. They can get anything through, 'cos its GMB. XXX, he was last selected, everybody knew he would get it. He's a good lad, I'm not saying he's not. But if you've got the votes before you go into a selection, you determine whether your caucus meeting says 'We've got the votes, we're supporting him because he's one of ours' ... They don't assess and judge people on their merits. I do now believe in one-person one-vote.[26]

Others felt that the influence of the unions was exaggerated, since they could usually only recommend, rather than impose their choice on local constituencies:

I've always had the full support of the Transport and General Workers Union. They always like me to get a chance somewhere but they can only recommend. They even recommended at one stage to XXXXXXXX that they were willing to pay all the election expenses towards me – that means, up to £25,000, but ... the rule is that the members select, so I didn't even get the chance to go to the final selection.[27]

Unions can seek to exercise direct and indirect influence over the selection process. Most directly, union delegates and branch secretaries can play a critical role through branch nominations, constituency shortlisting, and voting for their preferred applicant in the final Electoral College. Some unions swing all their nominations behind one applicant in a constituency,[28] while others are more ad hoc, leaving the decision to individual union delegates attending branch meetings.[29] Yet, as noted earlier, in the final Electoral College union-sponsored candidates must also win support from individual party members in the constituency, since the unions have, at most, 40 per cent of the weighted vote. In the 1987–92 parliament, union affiliates cast, on average, 30 per cent of the Electoral College vote. There were only a handful of seats where union votes were decisive for the outcome. More indirectly, union-backed applicants may prove attractive to party selectors. Sponsorship may bring support with office facilities, campaign staff, candidate training, organisational help, as well as contributing up to £750 per annum towards the costs of maintaining the constituency party, or 70 per cent of the agent's salary:

People knowing you're on the A list, ... They expect, rightly or wrongly, you're going to bring all sorts of goodies with you – backup in terms of personnel, workers, money, organisation[30]

Table 8.2   *Union sponsored Labour candidates*

	Union sponsored	Non-sponsored		N.
Incumbent MPs	67	33	100	95
Inheritors	46	54	100	13
Strong challengers	26	74	100	78
Weak challengers	11	89	100	206
List Applicants	16	84	100	127

Note: See appendix for definitions of categories.
Source: BCS, 1992.

Table 8.3   *Union sponsorship and nominations*

	PPCs		List	
Union sponsored	Yes	No	Yes	No
Branch nominations per seat				
Nominations received	4	3	2	3
Total number of branch nominations	9	7	7	8
Percentage	48.8	42.0	27.5	34.2
Union nominations per seat				
Nominations received	7	3	4	1
Total number of union nominations	15	10	9	12
Percentage	47.1	31.7	45.5	10.7
Total nominations per seat				
Total nominations received	11	6	6	4
Total number of nominations	24	17	16	20
Percentage	47.7	35.9	37.6	20.0

Note: Q. 'How many of the following bodies nominated you in your most recent short-listing? And how many are there in the constituency?'
Source: BCS, 1992.

It sounds as if anyone can have a go, in fact they can't. If they get union backing, and that's more than just their name on the list – if they get financial support, if they get training support, then they're going to be at an advantage.[31]

Although demand-side explanations are common, sponsorship may also affect the supply of candidates. Unions may provide an avenue which encourages working-class party members to consider a political career, and they may help subsidise the personal expenses of interviews and campaigning. Experience in the organised labour movement may provide members with an informal network of party contacts, practice with formal meetings and conferences, public speaking skills, and involvement in public life.

What is the evidence that union sponsorship is a critical asset for Labour applicants, as widely assumed? If it is we would expect that candidates with union support would be more successful in being nominated and adopted, particularly for good Labour seats. The results in table 8.2 confirm that sponsored applicants are more successful at every stage in the Labour ladder of recruitment. In the Labour party, union sponsored candidates represented about two thirds of all incumbent MPs, about one half of the inheritors, and one quarter of the high-prospect challengers in good Labour target seats. In contrast union sponsored candidates were only one in ten of the low prospect challengers. There was a strong and significant correlation ($r = 0.47$ p > 0.01) between whether a candidate was sponsored by a union, and the winnability of the seat, measured by the strength of the Labour vote in the 1987 election.

Moreover if we look more closely at the different stages in the selection process it is apparent that sponsored candidates proved far more successful in gaining direct union nominations within constituencies; on average they received fifteen union nominations per seat, while other candidates got about ten. More surprisingly, sponsored candidates also proved more successful in getting other branch nominations, about 9 per seat (see table 8.3). Furthermore, those with union sponsorship were slightly more successful at the critical shortlisting stage. Those on the 'A' list were shortlisted for 1.7 seats, compared with 1.2 seats for those on the 'B' list. This evidence therefore tends to confirm the conventional wisdom within the party about the advantages which sponsorship brings, in direct union votes, and indirect incentives for constituency support.

Who receives union sponsorship?

If it is important, what difference does sponsorship make to the kind of person who becomes Labour MPs? In particular, do the unions continue to provide an important pathway of recruitment for working-class aspirants? Previous studies have commonly found considerable contrasts in the social profile of union sponsored candidates and those financed by their constituency party. In particular, in the 1950s and early 1960s unions tended to support those who had devoted long service to the organised labour movement, coupled with faithful support of the party, and who often had experience of local government. As a result union candidates were normally older, less well-educated, with a manual occupation, and lengthy Labour party membership.[32] Does this remain the case?

The results in table 8.4 confirm that union sponsored applicants, candi-

Table 8.4 *Social profile of union sponsored labour candidates*

Union sponsored		MPs Yes	MPs No	PPCs Yes	PPCs No	List Yes	List No
Occupational Class	Middle	72	84	75	86	60	74
	Working	28	16	25	14	40	26
Subjective Class	Middle	37	55	38	58	8	43
	Working	63	46	62	42	92	57
Income	Less than 30K	33	33	69	61	85	68
	More than 30K	67	67	31	39	15	32
Gender	Men	88	97	69	75	75	61
	Women	12	3	31	25	5	39
Education	Graduate	66	81	60	74	42	65
	Non-graduate	34	19	40	26	58	35
	Mean Years Edu.	19	21	20	21	18	20
Age	Mean Age	51	53	44	43	46	43
Officeholders	Union	66	56	71	62	70	61
Experience	Regional party	57	28	25	18	45	19
N.		66	32	52	261	20	104

Source: BCS, 1992.

dates and MPs continue to display a distinctive social profile. Those with union backing are more likely to come from manual occupations, to be less well educated and less affluent, as well as having a stronger subjective working-class identification, than those financed by their constituency party. Nevertheless, this distinctive profile has become heavily diluted over the years. In the period 1950–66, the vast majority of union sponsored MPs and PPCs (82–85 per cent) came from a working-class occupational background.[33] Today the proportion is 25–28 per cent. Thus trade unions have played a role in the embourgeoisment of the parliamentary Labour party. The rise of the teachers, lawyers, and local government officers, at the expense of the miners, textile workers and plant operatives, cannot be attributed simply to the middle-class take-over of constituency parties.

Nevertheless, this pattern varied substantially by union. Some continued to sponsor mostly manual workers and union officers drawn from their own trade, particularly the National Union of Mineworkers (NUM), Amalgamated Engineering Union (AEU), the National Union of Public Employees (NUPE), and the National Communications Union (NCU). These unions provide an avenue for working-class aspirants; in the last election, for example, the AEU list included planning engineers, draughtsmen, mechanical engineers, toolmakers, marine fitters, and fitter machinists, as well as union officials. It is partly the decline in the number of NUM-sponsored candidates which has produced the dilution of working-class Labour MPs; at their height, in the 1920s, the NUM sponsored one fifth to one quarter of the parliamentary Labour party, over forty MPs, but this number had declined to fourteen MPs in the last election.[34] In marked contrast, other unions supported candidates from a diverse range of occupations, with only a tenuous, formal connection, with their membership. Unions following this pattern included the Transport and General Worker's Union (T&GW), the General Municipal and Boilermaker's Union (GMB), and the National Union of Rail, Maritime and Transport Workers (NUR/RMT), and the Electrical, Electronic, Telecommunications and Plumbing Union (EEPTU). The social profile of nominees from these unions is little different from non-sponsored Labour MPs, including university lecturers, solicitors, scientists and consultants. In these cases, as one member remarked, union backing may be just a 'flag of convenience':

The trade union influence in this place (Westminster) now, and I'm talking about genuine trade unionists, is becoming less and less. They are flags of convenience, they're not people who've come through their various trades and know what working 21 shifts is like, or working three shifts or working nights in the melting shop or down at pit. There's very little experience at that now, and I think the place is poorer for it.[35]

Where the unions support any rising talent within the party, for instance sponsorship of Glenda Jackson by the Associated Society of Locomotive Engineers and Firemen (ASLEF),[36] then the unions may get articulate spokespersons to defend their concerns, and they may improve the quality of Labour's frontbench team, but they do not provide a unique avenue for working-class recruitment.

In terms of age and gender, as well as class, union-sponsored candidates have become less distinctive today than in the past. In a study of candidates in the 1951–64 elections, Ranney concluded that the unions often stocked their parliamentary list with union officials who had given many years of faithful service in the Labour movement, and who were slightly older than other candidates.[37] Yet by 1992 there were no significant differences for sponsored candidates in terms of age, although they were slightly more likely to have held union office. Previous studies noted some gender bias in the union lists: during the 1950s women represented 2 per cent of the union sponsored candidates compared with 6 per cent of the unsponsored.[38] Although they have increased in numbers, women continue to be less well represented on the 'A' list than on the less competitive 'B' list. Women's under-representation was particularly evident in unions with a predomin-

Table 8.5 *Union sponsored Lists by gender*

	Men N.	Women N.	Total N.	Women %	Women members %
NUPE	3	2	5	40	77
GMB	11	7	18	39	30
UCW	5	1	6	17	26
TGWU	34	5	39	13	18
USDAW	15	2	17	12	61
EETPU	13	1	14	7	
NCU	15	1	16	6	20
AEU	20	0	20	0	10
UCATT	7	0	7	0	1
NGA	3	0	3	0	8
ISTC	7	0	7	0	
NUM	18	0	18	0	4
NUR	6	0	6	0	5
TSS	12	0	12	0	
Total	169	19	188	10	24

antly male membership located in traditional, heavy manufacturing industries, like the AEU, NUM and RMT/NUR (see table 8.5). However, white-collar unions with a higher female membership, such as NUPE, tended to support more women on their list, and those women who were on the 'A' list were disproportionately successful in being adopted, and elected. Women represent one third of all sponsored candidates, compared with one quarter of non-sponsored candidates. Among Labour MPs, a far higher proportion of women than men were sponsored.

We can conclude that the unions continue to exercise considerable influence over the selection process. Does this make a difference for the social composition of the party? Union sponsorship may have produced 'two Labour parties' in the past, and today they continue to support slightly more working-class candidates than constituency parties do. Nevertheless, the differences between the social characteristics of the sponsored and unsponsored candidates have diminished over time, leaving only a relatively faint, albeit significant, imprint on the party.

Time

Time may be among the most important resources common to candidates in all parties. Standing for office is a demanding activity requiring attendance at regular constituency meetings, social and fund-raising events, local 'surgeries', public speaking engagements, door-to-door leafletting, canvassing and campaigning in local as well as general elections.[39] Applicants need to invest time at different stages of political recruitment: in attending selection interviews, in the lengthy process of nursing a seat, and, if elected, in the demands of Westminster life.

Securing a seat

In the Conservative party, where applicants trail around the country for any vacancy, the interview process can be time-consuming and gruelling, as a Conservative MP recalled:

I was doing something like about five interviews a weekend, so you would start in Cornwall, you would go up to Lancashire, you would come back to Suffolk, you would go back to Yorkshire, you would end up in Devon. And I did that and I never said no to an interview, unless there was a direct clash and I couldn't sort it ... I never said no. I'd go anywhere, I'd go to Inverness, I'd go to Anglsey, I was so single-minded I'd have gone anywhere.[40]

Given the more local nature of the Labour process, their applicants may spend less time on travelling. But they may need to attend far more meetings on different evenings within a constituency – maybe ten to fifteen – to secure nominations in different wards and union branches. The complete selection process in a constituency may go on for four or five months.[41] Preparation for an interview, finding out about the constituency, also required time:

Every time I went for an interview, the research took an enormous amount of time. I went round to everyone from headteachers to the police ... Four interviews, four rounds, and each time I went back and back seeing more people ... the time it takes, you've no idea.

The long campaign

Once adopted by a seat, even a hopeless one, candidates need to spend one or two years' campaigning. Indeed, Conservative Central Office recommends not selecting candidates too early, so that they will not get burnt out before the general election. The formal general election campaign requires the most intensive period of full-time work but before that there is the investment in constituency casework, organising and canvassing, and local publicity, as well as regular party meetings:

If one's working full-time, the stress and strain that it puts candidates under – travelling and commitments ... I mean, they spend a good two-and-a-half, maybe three years, all their free time..at night time you're on the phone, you're perhaps travelling and staying over night, every weekend, to win a constituency ... and (afterwards) I suspect a lot of them are forgotten – they've got no guarantee of being picked again for that constituency even if they wanted to.[42]

I met a girl from Fulham, and I do not understand it … She was standing [for Labour] for somewhere round, it was a bit of Lincolnshire which was totally Tory – Brigg and something or other I think – ten to twenty thousand majority. The local party had total funds of £43 at the time that I met her, and she was going up every weekend under her own steam, and paying her own fare, to fight a seat like that. I thought, my gosh, I hope your dedication pays off with a better seat next time.[43]

The workload of MPs

For elected members, the workload is heavy, with multiple demands on their time. MPs estimated spending 66 hours per week on their work at Westminster and in their constituencies.[44] This estimate, based on different activities during an average week when the house is sitting, is very close to previous ones.[45] The workload included, on average, about 25 hours a week on constituency work – surgeries (3 hours), local party meetings (3 hours), casework (14 hours), and other local functions (5 hours). Travelling time back and forth from the constituency absorbed another 6.5 hours, although this obviously varied substantially by location. The remaining time at Westminster was spent on parliamentary debates (8 hours), select, standing and backbench committees (9 hours), meeting group representatives (4 hours), informal meetings with other members (6 hours), and other parliamentary business (7 hours). One official review suggests that the basic elements of an MP's job have changed little, but the pressure upon members has increased significantly in the last decade. Greater demands by constituents have been generated by television coverage of parliament, the impact of local radio, and more sophisticated lobbying techniques by interest groups.[46]

Therefore, all aspects of seeking a Westminster career make considerable demands on time. In the light of these demands, applicants with more time to invest in a political career should find it easier to move up the ladder of recruitment. While plausible, there are problems about testing this hypothesis. It is difficult to establish an accurate gauge of the time spent on political activity by grassroots members and candidates, given the flexibility of the concept of 'political work', the range of tasks which can fall into this heading and season variations. For example, local elections, party conferences, council and parliamentary sittings impose heavier demands in certain months. Subjective estimates can only be treated as an approximate guide to the hours spent on any task, and there may be a tendency to exaggerate. One also needs to be cautious in distinguishing the direction of causality: are candidates spending more time on party work by virtue of their role, or did they become candidates partly because they were willing to invest more time in helping the party? Moreover, what may matter is not just the amount of time available, and also flexibility over scheduling. Blocks of time – paid leave of absence from work and/or child-care during the month-long formal

Table 8.6   *Time resources (in percentages)*

| | Conservative | | | Labour | | | |
	MP	PPC	List	MP	PPC	List	Member
0 hours	0	0	0	0	0	0	50
0–5 hours	7	1	18	0	0	12	30
5–10 hours	10	5	18	9	2	15	9
10–15 hours	10	3	18	17	7	12	4
15–20 hours	10	5	12	14	9	10	2
< 20 hours	64	87	35	60	83	53	4
	100	100	100	100	100	100	100

Note: Q.'How much time do you usually devote to party activities in the average month?'
Source: BCS, 1992, Labour Party Membership Survey, 1989.

campaign – may be as important as free evenings and weekends.[47] Bearing in mind these qualifications, in this analysis *time* is measured by the number of hours devoted to party activities, in categories ranging from less than 5 hours, to more than 20 hours, in the average month. It should be remembered that this was a mid-term period and that fieldwork was 6–12 months before candidates devoted themselves full-time to the hectic activity of the formal campaign.

The results indicate a substantial difference in the time invested in party work by these groups, although there are problems about how this can be explained (see table 8.6). On the demand-side, there is a significant distinction in the amount of time spent on party work by candidates and list applicants. In the Conservative party, nearly all candidates (87 per cent), but only a third of applicants, were in the most active group, devoting over twenty hours per month to party activities. In a similar pattern in the Labour party 83 per cent of candidates, compared with 53 per cent of applicants, fell into this category. In contrast, the least active category included almost no candidates, but quite a few Labour and Conservative applicants (12 and 18 per cent respectively). This finding remains open to interpretation. It may be, as some other evidence suggests, that selectors favour candidates with considerable reserves of time and energy to spend on constituency campaigning. Selectors placed these qualities high on their list of priorities when interviewing applicants. Many believe local parties look for candidates with the commitment to invest time in their seat. One applicant with young children was told she was not adopted because selectors felt she would not have time to balance the demands of a family and constituency campaign.[48] On the other hand, it may be that by virtue of their office candidates subsequently spend a lot of time on party work, since they need to devote themselves wholeheartedly to the task well before the start of the official campaign.

Moreover, there are significant time differences on the supply-side. The greatest contrasts were between the elite and members, since half the Labour members were entirely passive, spending no time on party work.[49] Given this limited evidence it seems most plausible to conclude that time resources probably affect both supply and demand: those able to spend more time on party work have the opportunity to get more involved in the demanding activity of standing for parliament, spending evenings and free weekends going up to organise their campaign, sort out casework problems, and keep in touch with local party functions. At the same time applicants willing to devote themselves to such activities probably prove more attractive to party selectors.

Political experience

Political experience may be another vital resource. Members who have already held public office can be expected to have developed political expertise, speaking skills, practical knowledge of government, and social contacts, useful in gaining a seat. A parliamentary career is usually the apex of years involved in ward, constituency and executive party meetings, the local or county council, the trade union movement, community work or public service. As one Conservative MP described the process it was a gradual escalator:

After I'd been a councillor for a while – a borough councillor – I started to see some of the decisions taken a bit further away at County Council. I became a County Councillor immediately after that and then, of course, one sees all the big decisions taken in Parliament, and I became more and more interested in that.[50]

Most noted how many overlapping political commitments they had, which gradually took over their lives, as one northern Conservative candidate remarked:

I'm on the town council, I'm on the district council, I'm on the county council, I'm on various voluntary bodies – the community health council, Relate, the Council for Voluntary Services – I'm a governor of the local radio station ... it's a merry-go-round. When I started in politics I had a full-time job, eventually it became a part-time job, and eventually the job virtually became non-existent[51]

Ranney suggests long-standing party or union service is particularly important in the Labour party.[52] Candidates often assume they have to be 'blooded' by fighting a hopeless seat before they will be considered for a good one, although too many consecutive failures may count against applicants.

We can compare the political *experience* of party strata by measuring a range of different types of activism including: whether party members had

Table 8.7 *Political experience*

	Conservative (%)				Labour (%)				Scale Weight
	MP	PPC	List	Member	MP	PPC	List	Member	
Stood for parliament before	100	31	49		100	32	22		[12]
PPC how many times?	4.5	1.5	1.4		3.3	1.3	1.3		
Held local party office	87	90	90	32	96	95	96	50	[3]
Held regional party office	38	35	36	8	47	19	24	4	[6]
Held national party office	31	19	21	2	19	4	8	1	[9]
Candidate for local government	61	75	70	14	79	85	81	20	[6]
Been elected to local government	50	44	57	15	65	66	61	19	[9]
Been candidate European parliament	4	5	6		9	6	4		[6]
Been elected European parliament	3	1	1		6	1	0		[9]
Served on local public body	47	57	62		67	68	76		[3]
Served on national public body	28	8	12		34	9	13		[9]
Held office in local pressure group	39	35	36		56	58	61		[3]
Held office in national pressure group	39	18	21		36	20	24		[9]
Held office in other community group	30	36	42		43	49	55		[3]
Held office in professional association	22	22	26		25	24	24		[3]
Held office in student organisation	28	41	39		22	32	31		[3]
Held office in trade union	8	9	11		63	63	61		[3]
Held office in women's organisation	3	4	6		5	11	20		[3]
Summary Weighted Scale	39	27	32		45	31	31		[100]

Note: Q. 'Have you ever held office/served on ...'
Source: BCS, 1992.

ever held local, regional or national party office; whether they had ever considered standing, been a candidate or elected to the local council; and whether they had ever been a candidate at a previous general election. These items were added for a summary scale, weighted according to the level of office (see table 8.7). Nearly all the elite had been active in their local party, and over 90 per cent had held some local office. About three-quarters or more had been candidates for local government, and over half had been elected as local councillors. The local connection was particularly strong in the Labour party where two-thirds of the candidates had experience of serving on local government and local public bodies, and about half had held office in another community group.

The most striking finding about the results is that, contrary to popular wisdom, general political experience fails to explain why some are more successful than others in being adopted by a seat. Candidates were no more experienced than applicants. Indeed, in the Conservative party the reverse held true: applicants had slightly *more* experience of standing for parliament and holding local office. Once more the main contrast, where comparisons could be drawn, was between members and the party elite; for example, less than one fifth of members had run for local government compared with 80 per cent of the elite. We can conclude that candidates need to demonstrate some political experience, to have 'done their bit', to get adopted by a seat, but no more is required. As one Conservative MP noted applicants have a good chance: 'So long as you fulfil the criteria of having done something to help the party – been a local councillor, done a bit of work in a constituency, and you've got the backing of one or two people who are prepared to say you are a fairly sane and rational human being.'[53]

Yet at the same time this conclusion needs an important qualification. The conventional wisdom is that candidates usually need to be 'blooded' by fighting a hopeless marginal as the party standard-bearer, to demonstrate their loyalty and learn the ropes, before they will be given a better seat in subsequent elections. As one remarked: 'I was told that you have to do the unwinnables before you get to the winnables.'[54] There is evidence which suggests political experience adds to the chances of securing a *good* seat. As table 8.8 shows, three-quarters of the Conservative candidates who inherited a good seat, and almost half of the strong Conservative challengers already had experience of standing for parliament, compared with only a quarter of Conservative challengers in weak seats. There was a similar distinction between high- and low-prospect challengers in the Labour party, although many of the inheritors, like Peter Mandelson in Hartlepool, were elected on their first attempt. There was a moderate but significant correlation in the Conservative party ($R = 0.31$ p > 0.01) and the Labour party ($R = 0.27$ p > 0.01) between whether a candidate had fought a

Table 8.8 *Previous experience of standing for parliament*

	Conservative				Labour			
Stood before	Yes	No		N.	Yes	No		N.
Incumbent MPs	100	0	100	142	100	0	100	97
Inheritors	76	24	100	46	33	67	100	12
High prospect challengers	46	55	100	22	53	47	100	78
Low prospect challengers	26	74	100	181	25	75	100	206
List Applicants	49	51	100	224	22	78	100	127

Note: Q. 'Have you stood before for Parliament?'
Source: BCS, 1992.

previous campaign, and the winnability of the seat, measured by the strength of their party's vote in the 1987 election.

Support networks

Support networks may be an important source of information, advice and direct endorsements. Those who received widespread encouragement from close friends, party members, party agents, community groups, business associates, trade unionists and employers, as well as their immediate family, should be more likely to consider a parliamentary career, and better placed to secure a good seat. In the Labour party, many stressed the importance of local contacts, and the informal grapevine to find out about vacancies in advance, especially within trade union branches:

One candidate in the last selection I was in was asked how it was he'd got thirty-three nominations. He very honestly explained that he'd been around a long time, he knew a lot of these people, he often went out drinking with them, and therefore when he phoned them up to say, 'Ow about the NUPE or the T&GWU?' – or whatever the nomination – 'Yeah, all right, I'll send you the form'.[55]

Through having worked in the area I did develop a lot of contacts and a lot of friends, and especially the person who encouraged me to go for seats in the first place, and so he was there, and actually on the ground, and knew what was happening, and there was therefore very much of a support network available.[56]

A lot of men come up through the trade union movement, and therefore they're known. It's just actually that people know of them. They hear them. They see them. They go to conferences and these people are taking a very active part.[57]

The Labour party gets seats because they gossip. You talk about seats way in advance, all you know in that area, how many votes you're likely to get, and so on, trade unions sympathetic to you, that kind of thing.[58]

Table 8.9   *Support networks*

	Conservative			Labour		
	MP	PPC	List	MP	PPC	List
Spouse or partner	4.2	4.2	3.9	4.2	4.1	3.9
Other family members	4.0	4.0	3.8	4.0	3.8	3.7
Personal friends	4.1	4.2	4.0	4.3	4.2	4.2
Women's groups	3.3	3.5	3.5	3.5	3.8	3.5
Community groups	3.4	3.5	3.5	3.9	3.7	3.6
Business associates	3.5	3.7	3.5	3.4	3.4	3.1
Trade unionists	2.9	3.2	3.1	4.5	4.1	3.8
Party members	4.5	4.6	4.4	4.6	4.4	4.2
Party agents	4.4	4.4	4.2	4.3	4.0	3.4
Employers	3.3	3.4	3.2	2.9	3.0	2.7
Summary index	26.0	28.0	28.0	30.0	32.0	30.0

Note: Q. 'Some people receive encouragement from those around them when they decide to stand for public office, while others experience indifference or disapproval. How positive or negative were the following people in encouraging you to become a candidate in the next election?' Scaled from 5 (very positive) to 1 (very negative). The summary index is scored from 0 (very negative) to 50 (very positive). Figures represent the mean response.
Source: BCS, 1992.

In the Conservative party social networks, developed through party conference, constituency work, or Central Office, were seen as invaluable in identifying good opportunities, getting advice about procedures, or simply as a source of encouragement, a steer in the right direction:

When you get to a certain level these contacts really can be very, very useful to you. Very useful. One word from the right person in the right place can actually open a door. Can't get you a seat, but it can open a door. Just draw your attention to opportunities.[59]

The secret of networking is finding someone who's on that [selection] committee, or close to that committee, who can tell you the prejudice of the people on that committee, and [you] try to pander to them.[60]

The social *networks* of party strata are compared using a 50–point scale summarising the level of support which applicants reported from ten different groups, ranging from family to friends, employers and party members. Despite the interview evidence, the results in table 8.9 reveal minimal differences between candidates and applicants; all perceived fairly positive support from most groups.

Table 8.10   *Demand-side model predicting whether respondents were candidates or applicants*

	Conservative	Labour
Social variables		
Age	0.14**	0.04
Children	0.13**	0.05
Marital status	0.09**	0.07
Social class	0.06	0.07
Education (years)	0.02	0.09*
Public + Oxbridge	0.01	0.03
Gender	0.01	0.08*
Resource variables		
Time on party work	0.50**	0.42**
Political experience	0.14**	0.08
Networks	0.03	0.12*
Financial resources	0.03	0.04
Union sponsorship	n.a.	0.02
R^2	0.32	0.18

Note: The figures represent OLS standardised regression estimates (Beta) predicting whether respondents were candidates or list applicants.
** = $p > .01$ * = $p > .05$
Source: BCS, 1992.

Conclusion

The impact of resources can be analysed to predict the difference between applicants and candidates on the demand-side. The regression analysis models, in table 8.10, were run for the major parties controlling for the core demographic variables established earlier. The results indicate that in the Conservative party the resources of time and political experience proved to be most significant, along with the demographic variables, noted earlier, of age, children and marital status. Applicants who could devote time to party work, and who had some political experience, particularly if they had stood for a seat before, were more likely to be adopted by a constituency. In the Labour party, time also proved significant along with social networks. It may be that the more local nature of the selection process in the Labour party means that, as many have suggested, to secure branch nominations it is important to have established some links with activists within the constituency before applying. The resource variables explained a higher degree of variance than the demographic factors. Nevertheless, financial resources in both parties, and union sponsorship in the Labour party, proved insignificant predictors of demand. This confirms the previous evidence that these factors mainly operate through influencing the supply of applicants, by reducing the costs of pursuing a Westminster career. The next step is to consider how resources interact with motivation, – the other half of the equation.

9 Candidate motivation

Motivation – political ambition, drive, determination – could be expected to play a critical role in recruitment. As one MP expressed the drive: 'It was a longterm aim to be a Member of Parliament, and I devoted a hell of a lot of mental energy to that because you don't get there if you don't'.[1] Most British citizens are legally qualified to stand. There are thousands of lawyers, teachers and company directors in brokerage occupations with sufficient career flexibility, financial security and leisure time to run for elected office. Many have experience on the first rungs of the political ladder, in party office, local government, voluntary groups, and public bodies; there are about 100,000 elected local councillors in Britain.[2] And many have good local networks among community groups, business associations and trade unions. Yet few seriously consider a parliamentary career, while even fewer run. Conservative Central Office receives only 2,000 applicants every election from a pool of about 750,000 members. Why? In the supply-side model developed earlier a combination of motivation plus resources produces the necessary and sufficient conditions for pursuing a political career.

The aims of this chapter are threefold. First, to consider alternative ways of understanding political motivation based on biographical, social psychological and behavioural approaches. Second, to analyse whether evidence of drive helps to explain the progressive political ambition of candidates. Lastly, to consider how motivation relates to different underlying notions of political representation in the Labour and Conservative parties.

Understanding political motivation

Motivational factors can be understood as psychological predispositions to run for office which become catalysts for action within a given opportunity structure. Why do applicants pursue a parliamentary career? Earlier chapters have documented how most candidates, particularly in the Labour and Conservative parties, pay considerable costs in pursuit of office: travelling to a series of interviews, nursing the seat, risking careers, campaigning in successive elections. The reasons for running are complex and varied. On the one hand, there are ministerial aspirants, such as a young Conservative lawyer single-mindedly pursuing safe seats across the country as the launching pad for a front-bench career. On the other, there are minor party standard bearers, for example a middle-aged teacher fighting a hopeless local campaign for the Greens. As well as understanding the decision to stand, there is the converse question why most party members choose *not* to pursue a political career.

Although motivation seems likely to prove an important factor in recruitment, there has been little work on the political ambition of British parliamentary candidates. One reason for the neglect is widespread skepticism about whether it is possible to understand ambition on a systematic basis, since motivations are hidden, complex, fluid, and open to the problems of rationalisation. As one review concludes: 'The proposition that personality factors are likely to be a major recruitment-relevent variable is intuitively appealing but efforts to demonstrate the relevance of predispositions in recruitment have been neither numerous nor very successful.'[3] Another reason is the conventional wisdom that demand by party selectors is probably more important than the supply of applicants in the British system. If one applicant is picked out of 200, the reasons why the applicant won seem more important than the reasons why the other 199 stood.

In theory, if ambition is important it should distinguish strata at all levels on the ladder of recruitment: party members who are eligible to stand, applicants on central party lists, interviewees short-listed by seats, low-prospect challengers, high-prospect challengers, inheritors, and incumbent MPs. If there is a simple linear relationship between ambition and success, ambition should increase with every level. The problem is to design consistent measures of ambition which are appropriate for all different strata. Standard indicators of mass political participation show little variance among the elite. In particular, little is known about why a few party members take the first step to apply for party lists. To overcome this difficulty, studies can focus on *progressive* ambition within the elite. Progressive ambition means how and why candidates move from one position to another in their careers. For example, how list applicants become low-prospect challengers. Or how challengers become inheritors. Motivation can be explored through biographical, social psychological, and behavioural approaches.

Biographies of political careers

The traditional approach to understanding political ambition in Britain is the literature charting the careers of MPs, leading cabinet members and prime ministers as they move from party activists and junior backbenchers to become leading members of the government and elder statesmen. This approach describes how early ambitions crystallise, develop and evolve during a politician's lifetime, drawing on historical sources such as personal diaries, memoirs, letters, official government papers, and interviews with contemporaries. Personal accounts by insiders describe the experience of life at Westminster.[4] Drawing on this approach, Anthony King, Peter Riddell and others have explored how a range of British MPs see their work as backbenchers.[5]

This literature provides many insights into the complexities of political ambition, but for those interested in patterns of recruitment it has certain limitations. This approach tells us most about leading politicians, occasionally about backbench MPs, but remains silent about those who drop off the lower rungs of the recruitment ladder including candidates who failed to be elected, applicants who were never selected, and grassroots party members. Moreover, although this provides a detailed and thorough account of the motivation of individual politicians, based on their own perceptions, it provides few generalisable or testable propositions about patterns of political careers. Many politicians say they first became interested in a Westminster career in their early youth, but the precise factors sparking this ambition are lost in hazy recollections. Memoirs provide vague clues, little more.[6]

To look for more systematic patterns, the BCS survey asked politicians to tell us in an open-ended question 'the single most important reason why you first wanted to stand for parliament?'. This was explored in greater depth in the group of personal interviews. Survey responses were coded into six major categories, which can be illustrated by some of the reasons candidates gave for standing. Some expressed a desire to enter politics as a *personal career* move:

It was the natural next step after local government.

I wished to further my political career.

To be involved in politics full-time.

Ideological reasons were put forward by others:

To fight the extremism of the Labour party.

To help build an international society free from the scourges of war and poverty.

A belief that the Conservative approach works and that socialism does not.

To make Britain a capitalist, successful democracy.

Concern for others with a fervant hope that socialists like me could utilise the parliamentary system for radical and fundamental changes in society.

The third category expressed a *public service* role:

To serve my country.

To play a part in public life.

In order to change society parliament was the place to be.

Some gave priority to one or two *single issues*:

Wish to reform health service and legal system.

To get independence for Scotland.

To promote education as a major issue.

To make the other parties think, talk and get serious about planetary survival.

The last category stressed the *representation of a group*:

As a small businessman I felt that parliament needed more representatives from the business sector.

Previous MPs have been based in London and have been totally out of contact with local issues and attitudes. I felt I could represent the area much better.

The party needed more able women candidates.

Wanted to see a trade union influence.

To present and represent working people and their priorities.

When these responses were classified, the results in table 9.1 suggest a party difference: perhaps due to party culture. Conservatives tended to stress the public service role while more Labour politicians tended to see themselves as group representatives. Overall, personal ambition, political ideology and public service emerged as the most important reasons given by politicians, in that order. By this measure there was no major difference in the motivation of incumbents, candidates and applicants. The problem with interpreting this evidence is the danger of accepting *post-hoc* justifications and self-delusions in politicians' own accounts. Motivation is hidden; older MPs may have forgotten their initial impetus; candidates may disguise naked ambition under the cloak of public service; bitter failure may produce plausible rationalisations. In short, this provides some clues to the common reasons given for pursuing parliamentary seats, but we would be hesitant to place great weight on this evidence.

Rather than asking politicians, as an alternative approach, the motivation of grassroots activists was explored in the BCS survey by asking party members whether they would like to stand for parliament. Only one in ten party members expressed any interest in becoming a parliamentary candidate (see table 9.2), and this response varied significantly by age, education, gender, and party, although not, somewhat surprisingly, by class. To test

Table 9.1   *Motivation (in percentages)*

	Conservative			Labour		
	MP	PPC	List	MP	PPC	List
Personal ambition	46	42	51	45	40	37
Ideology	20	20	21	25	18	21
Public service	20	22	16	14	9	11
Party standard-bearer	6	12	5	4	12	7
Single issue	6	2	4	1	4	4
Group representative	0	1	3	1	12	19
Invited	2	2	1	9	4	1

Note: Q. 'What was the most important reason why you first wanted to stand for parliament?'
Source: BCS, 1992.

the relative importance of these factors they were entered into a multivariate regression model, with willingness to stand for parliament as the dependent variable. In addition, we wanted to test whether standing for parliament was related to other indicators of mass political participation. The model therefore included summary measures of political activism and efficacy. These were measured on a 14-point scale according to whether members had actually participated, or would be willing to participate in, a series of political activities ranging from signing a petition, and joining a pressure group, to proposing a motion at party conference. The results (see table 9.3) indicate that the strongest predictors of willingness to consider a parliamentary career were age, gender and political activism, in that order. Other factors in the model proved insignificant. That is, the groups least willing to become a candidate were older party members, women, and those with little prior history of political activism.

To explore this further we asked party members why they were reluctant to stand. Respondents could select multiple choice answers from a list of possible reasons, such as not having the time and energy, lacking the right experience, or putting the family first. The results, in table 9.4, show a complex pattern. Members most commonly said that they lacked the time and energy (43 per cent), or the right sort of experience (39 per cent). Lack of experience was a particularly common reason given by working class, women, and the less educated party members. Women members were also more likely than men to give a slightly higher priority to their family. Another common reason was that members anticipated failure, that is, they believed they would not be selected, but this response was fairly uniform across social groups. This suggests woman and working-class members are

Table 9.2 *Willingness of party members to stand for parliament*

	Yes	No	Don't Know
All party members	11	81	7
Conservatives	9	88	3
Labour	13	78	10
Younger	24	64	12
Middle-aged	15	77	8
Older	4	93	3
Middle class	12	81	7
Working class	12	79	9
Graduate	16	76	8
Non-graduate	9	84	7
Men	15	75	10
Women	7	88	5

Note: Q. 'Would you like to stand for parliament?'
Source: BCS, 1992.

Table 9.3 *Predictors of willingness to stand*

	Con.	Lab.
Age	.30**	.18**
Class	.06	.02
Gender	.06	.14**
Experience	.01	.16**
Education	.04	.10
R^2	.09	.06

Note: Regression analysis of party members' willingness to stand for parliament. Figures represent standardized beta coefficients.
Source: BCS, 1992.

not discouraged aspirants who feel that they would face special barriers in being accepted by selectors. Rather they saw themselves as unqualified for the job. This evidence helps provide another clue to the puzzle why some groups are less willing to come forward. But these results also need to be interpreted with considerable caution, since members were responding to a series of structured options. Perhaps other reasons not listed, for example lack of financial resources, would have proved equally important.

Table 9.4   *Reasons why party members were unwilling to stand*

	Time and energy	Experience	Not be Selected	Family	Interest	Career
All party members	43	39	30	24	22	11
Conservatives	38	38	28	20	19	10
Labour	47	39	32	27	24	11
Younger	44	40	34	39	13	24
Middle-aged	41	41	29	31	27	16
Older	44	37	31	16	17	4
Middle class	44	36	30	25	32	13
Working class	39	58	30	29	20	6
Graduate	53	35	30	27	21	18
Non-graduate	37	42	32	24	22	7
Men	42	35	31	23	23	12
Women	44	44	30	28	19	10

Note: Q. 'Would you like to stand for parliament? If not, why is that?'
This was a multiple choice answer where members could tick as many reasons from the list as they chose.
Source: BCS, 1992.

Social psychology; personalities, incentives, roles, drive

A body of literature developed in the United States, based on social psychology, could provide an alternative theoretical framework for British studies. The earliest study, by Harold Lasswell, was derived from social psychological theories which assume that politicians have certain needs or drives developed through socialisation in early childhood, which they seek to fulfil through political activism. For Lasswell, politicians have a distinctive kind of personality which causes them to seek office. In a series of studies during the 1930s Lasswell argued that politicians are characterised by intense cravings for deference, which are rationalised in terms of the public interest.[7] The practical and methodological problems of studying political personalities mean that few have tried to follow Lasswell's footsteps except in 'psycho-biographies' of politicians.[8]

In the mid-1960s, one of the most influential studies in this tradition, by James David Barber, was based on members of the Connecticut legislature.[9] Barber divided politicians into four types depending upon their activity and willingness to continue to serve. 'Spectators' were defined as those who enjoy the conviviality and excitement of the legislature, but take little part in its substantive work. 'Advertisers' were the upwardly mobile younger careerists who found that the work provided beneficial business contacts.

'Reluctants' were the more passive elderly members motivated primarily by a sense of duty. Lastly, 'lawmakers' were the active members who made government work. Later, a similar approach was applied by Barber to presidential personality, based on another four-fold classification.[10] Barber concluded that individuals adapt to being politicians in ways which meet their personal needs, and the early personality developed in childhood has a major impact on later political behaviour. Given the inherent problems of understanding such a complex phenomenon as 'personality' for a wide range of politicians, subsequent work in this field has looked more narrowly at 'incentives', defined as needs such as status or sociability which politicians seek to meet through political work.[11]

Since the early 1970s the social psychological approach has tended to fall out of favour since its weaknesses have become more apparent. Early studies suffer from ill-defined, imprecise and unmeasurable variables, which are difficult to replicate in subsequent work. Reducing complex personalities with complicated, multiple and overlapping motives to a few simple types seems crude and inadequate. Usually the assumed link between personality types and legislative behaviour is not clearly demonstrated. Accounts which have classified personality or incentives have often failed to explain the origins of these predispositions.[12] If we accept that individuals do pursue certain dominant goals such as status or sociability, it is not clear why they should turn to political life, rather than another avenue, to meet this need. Attempts to understand the early ambitions of established politicians suffer from the problems of circularity and *post-hoc* rationalisations. As Anthony King summarised the position:

Politicians are said to displace private emotions on to public objects, to suffer from lack of self-esteem, to experience difficulty in making meaningful relationships, to be hungry for power, to be hungry for acclaim, to be hungry for personal recognition, to be hungry for all sorts of things. But in fact no one has the faintest idea of whether or not any of this is true.[13]

After reviewing the literature, Matthews concludes that politicians have a wide variety of personalities, rather than a few simple types, and there are few well-established and reliable generalisations derived from this body of research.[14]

Faced with this barrage of criticisms, many studies of recruitment and members of parliament have simply played safe, adopted an institutional framework, and avoided discussing political ambition.[15] Following Schlesinger, others have used rational choice theories of office-seeking.[16] This assumes *a priori* that all politicians are equally ambitious to seek higher office, and then analyses the institutional and political environment to predict how politicians will react to the structure of opportunities.

Behavioural evidence of drive

Rather than trying to establish the psychological reasons for applicants wanting to run, with all the acknowledged problems this entails, or abandoning the attempt to understand how ambition varies from one politician to the next, as rational choice theories suggest, it seems preferable to use behavioural measures of drive. The concept of '*drive*' refers to how strongly individuals pursue office: the persistence, vigour and intensity with which applicants try to get selected and elected within a particular opportunity structure. Not all candidates are alike. Interviews revealed that some are simply political amateurs 'having a go' in half-hearted fashion, while others declared themselves to be single-minded careerists. Drive operates in the context of an opportunity structure within each party. Parties vary by their rates of candidate competition, the rules and procedures governing selection, their internal culture, and their electoral fortunes. The opportunities to become a candidate for the Greens, for example, are far easier than securing a good seat in the Conservative party. We would expect drive to be important, since within each party candidates who were more tenacious might be expected to be more successful. One Labour MP suggested one of the main difficulties in the initial stages was persistence:

Keeping going. There were lots of reasons why I shouldn't go on, like ... thinking life's passing you by and you should be getting on with your career. It's ups and downs. The hardest part was keeping determined during the troughs. You know you've tried – what does it matter? The most difficult thing is getting yourself back and trying again.[17]

Another MP echoed the need to overcome self-doubts and discouragements, and just plough on:

You've got to decide whether you want it and, if you do, every time you feel doubtful and you're not going to go for it, you've got to remind yourself that you want it ... every time I nearly dropped out, it was because I had rationalised it.[18]

Logically, the more committed the applicant, it can be assumed, the better their chances within their party of being interviewed and adopted for a good seat.

In this study drive is operationalised within each party in terms of three primary dimensions. First, there are the *number* of applications; some apply for one or two seats while others send their curriculum vitae to dozens. Second, there are the *strategic reasons* for applying; some restrict their applications to seats close to home while others pursue any good vacancy up and down the country; some are invited to apply while others try for hopeless seats because they believe it will provide good experience. Lastly, there are *career histories*; some novices try once and never again, while other seasoned veterans fight repeated battles in successive general elections. Some pursue seats in their late twenties while others start late in life. These behavioural indicators of drive are more reliable than attitudinal data; for example, we can verify how many times candidates have stood for office from published records. By definition, the measure of drive cannot be used to distinguish the pool of eligibles and applicants, the first step on the ladder. But it can be used to analyse differences in progressive ambition between strata, such as applicants, low-prospect challengers, and strong challengers, within each party. If ambition is important we would expect those with the greatest drive within each party to be most likely to move up the career ladder to Westminster: is this so?

The number of applications

The number, spread and range of seats which applicants tried for varied substantially. In interviews some stressed they wanted to represent their local constituency, but not to pursue any and every available opportunity. This view was particularly common in the Labour party:

I lived there. I wouldn't trail around the country looking for a seat. I'm not interested in that.[19]

No, I wouldn't have gone for any other seat. I'd been asked to stand for other seats before and had said no.[20]

I was only prepared to consider this seat. I would never go for another seat, and if I didn't get it, I would never try again.[21]

I wanted to be the MP for [this constituency], I didn't just want to be an MP, I didn't want to go to Westminster – I mean, I know enough MPs, I mean I read enough newspapers, it's not that brilliant being a backbench MP, it's not so special.[22]

I don't want to do it anywhere but X [local constituency] ... People say that if you want to be an MP you've really got to be very hungry for it, and I would never really describe myself as very hungry for being an MP. I wanted to be the MP for X [local constituency].[23]

In contrast many Conservatives said they chased any available vacancy up and down the country:

I think all I did was choose seats that came up..if someone was looking for a candidate, I just bunged in an application.[24]

I applied for every seat with one or two exceptions.[25]

Ticking the box – I applied for anything – we were told – apply for anything, tick the box, you know...

Mind you, I sent my CV anywhere as long as I thought I had a chance of winning – so I had loads and loads of CV's sent all over the place.[26]

Table 9.5   *Number of seat applications*

	Conservative				Labour			
	Inheritors	Strong chal.	Weak chal.	List	Inheritors	Strong chal.	Weak chal.	List
No seats	0	0	0	10	0	0	0	32
One seat	30	53	26	4	93	75	55	20
Few seats	7	13	22	12	7	20	29	27
Some seats	37	13	23	34	0	5	12	16
Many seats	26	21	29	40	0	0	5	4
%	100	100	100	100	100	100	100	100
Mean N. Seats	9.4	8.7	11.7	16.9	1.1	3.0	2.7	3.2
N.	46	38	139	210	14	40	253	127

Note: Number of applications: Few = 2/4, some = 5/15, many = 16 + seats.
Source: BCS, 1992.

To measure drive the *number* of applications in the 1992 general election were analysed, controlling for party. To compare different groups on the ladder of recruitment we focused, as before, on four strata: inheritors, high-prospect challengers, low-prospect challengers, and List Applicants[27]. Incumbent MPs were excluded since all applied and were reselected for their own seat. If simple persistence was rewarded, we expected that within each party inheritors who got the best seats would have made the greatest number of applications, while List Applicants would have made the least.

The results in table 9.5 clearly proved this assumption to be faulty. Contrary to expectations, the number of applications was inversely correlated with candidate success. In the Conservative party, multiple applications (to five or more constituencies) were made by three-quarters of List Applicants, half the low-prospect challengers, and one third of the high-prospect challengers, although two thirds of the inheritors also applied widely. List Applicants in the Conservatives tried on average for seventeen vacancies, compared with nine applications by inheritors and high-prospect challengers. In the Labour party there was an even more striking pattern: almost all inheritors (93 per cent) only applied to one seat, as did three quarters of the strong challengers, over half of the low-prospect challengers and one fifth of the List Applicants. This suggests that multiple applications were characteristic of applicants who *lack* the personal contacts, political experience or ability to land a good seat. Instead of a focused and strategic campaign in one or two good seats, the weaker applicants 'bunged in a CV' on the off-chance it might magically rise to the top of the short-listing pile.

Table 9.6   *Important factors influencing original choice of seat applications*

'Very important'	Conservative					Labour				
	MP	Inher.	Strong chal.	Weak chal.	List	MP	Inher.	Strong chal.	Weak chal.	List
Insider strategies										
Asked to apply	23	8	27	20	14	69	77	64	49	37
Knew members	16	3	15	14	8	49	75	73	42	25
Already lived in seat	13	6	36	25	7	50	39	47	60	5
Regional strategies										
Chose seats close to ...										
... my region	29	17	35	29	26	38	30	54	36	42
... my home	20	14	37	27	25	33	36	50	50	47
... Westminster	2	0	0	2	2	2	0	3	1	0
Electoral strategies										
Winnable	62	81	68	27	54	62	75	71	31	35
Good experience	43	17	29	63	38	25	20	11	45	46
N.	104	42	34	122	199	80	14	36	226	91

Note: Q. 'When originally deciding to apply for a constituency, how important were the following factors in influencing your choice of seat?'
Source: BCS, 1992.

Strikingly, in the Labour party, the most successful group who stepped into safe Labour seats, possibly for life, were adopted on their first attempt. The results confirm that applicants faced the fiercest competition for seats in the Conservative party. In contrast, as noted in chapter 5, it proved relatively easy to be adopted by the Liberal Democrats, Greens or nationalist parties, where three quarters of all candidates were selected for the only seat to which they applied. These results throw doubt on the idea that most applicants on the major party lists are not actively pursuing vacancies. Particularly in the Conservative party, applicants are usually trying hard, but failing. The puzzle, therefore, is why applicants are less successful than candidates, despite their persistence.

To throw light on this we can turn to the *strategic reasons* for applying for seats. As noted earlier, we expected considerable differences in the pattern of recruitment in hopeless seats, where parties are trying to drum up a local standard bearer, and close marginals, where candidates have a real chance of success. Accordingly we asked respondents to rate the importance of certain factors influencing their choice of seats when they originally decided to apply (see table 9.6). These eight items were subject to factor analysis, to see whether responses were structured in a consistent fashion. The factor analysis revealed that when applying for seats candidates followed 'electoral', 'insider', and 'regional' strategies. In total these factors accounted for 60 per cent of variance in response.

Electoral strategies

Not surprisingly the highest priority in selecting seats was electoral: were they winnable? And would standing provide good experience for subsequent elections? Some developed their application strategy quite carefully:

I basically looked at the Labour seats which hadn't been selected and divided them into three categories: those which I thought I could make a good impression on and which had a sustainable Conservative vote, and those which were a bit in-between, and those which were really no-hoper seats, which I discounted. I wanted to go for one of the better seats.[28]

It was widely assumed that candidates have to be 'blooded', fighting a hopeless seat in a two-stage process before they can hope to be considered for a good one.

If you are starting from scratch, as I was then, you do have to have at least one election contest behind you to be thought of as any good.[29]

I realised I was not going to get selected obviously for a Conservative constituency at that age, but I wanted to get the experience under my belt ... I subsequently went on to be the candidate there in the second election of 1974 ... the next stage was applying for winnable seats.[30]

Some strategically chose hopeless seats the first time round, they said, in case they were accused of losing a target marginal. In general, those who were strong challengers tended to emphasise the importance of applying for winnable prospects, while low-prospect challengers gave greater weight to the importance of applying for constituencies which provided campaign experience, although it seems likely that this provides at least a partial rationalisation for their own situation.

Insider strategies

Those who followed 'insider' strategies placed a high priority on going for one or two local seats, particularly if they were invited to apply, if they already knew some party members, or if they were already part of the local community. The invitation to apply proved particularly important in distinguishing Labour candidates who secured good seats from those who failed to be adopted. Insider strategies seem less important in the Conservative party, since candidates are more likely to pursue seats across the country, but still some Conservative candidates mentioned that this influenced their own decision to run:

The local MP intimated that he would be retiring, and local people said they would have liked me to have taken the position because they felt I knew the constituency. That is when I thought well, if that is how people feel, I'll see how it goes.[31]

They virtually decided they wanted me, it was a very paternalistic association.[32]

This was echoed strongly among Labour candidates:

After a busy fifteen years in local government I wanted to become involved at a higher level, initially in Europe. My local party supported me strongly in this, and when our MP [a local man] died, they invited me to stand as his natural successor.[33]

I was encouraged to go for it by some people in the party . . .[34]

I was then approached..would I stand[35]

I knew the agent. She said, 'Why don't you apply?' . . . I mean, I realised there was no chance, because there was a strong local contender – and I got it by one vote. Everyone was absolutely flabbergasted.

Regional strategies

Regional considerations – applying only for seats within the same county or area – was less important in predicting differences between party strata. But it was still a consideration mentioned by many candidates in selecting seats:

I determined that it was going to be Yorkshire. I wanted to find a Yorkshire seat to start.[36]

I don't think any Scottish seats came up, but I don't think I would've applied for any of those. I didn't apply for any Welsh seats, and I also restricted myself geographically as to how far north I would go – Manchester and Leeds were included.[37]

This analysis suggests that electoral strategies were the most important considerations for Conservative applicants, who saw the experience as a two-stage process, a gradual progress from hopeless to safe seats over successive elections. The process of applying for good seats is regarded as a national competition, where there is no particular stigma attached to 'carpet baggers'. Conservative recruitment is widely perceived by most participants as a competitive search for the best talent throughout the country, albeit one fraught with uncertainty, where the lucky break in securing a good interview may prove decisive for a lifetime career in parliament. 'Normally you're just a carpet bagger. You go round and pray that a seat with a decent majority selects you.' By contrast, in the Labour party there is more emphasis on choosing representatives who come from the community, and this restricts the breadth of the search. Party activists living in Surrey or

Table 9.7   *Number of previous general elections fought by candidate*

	Conservative					Labour				
	Incumbent	Inher.	Strong PPCs	Weak PPCs	List	Incumbent	Inher.	Strong PPCs	Weak PPCs	List
None	0	24	61	83	52	0	57	35	73	78
One	8	33	24	15	32	26	7	45	22	17
Two	20	15	8	2	12	20	21	18	3	4
Three	16	2	3	0	3	17	0	0	1	2
Four	12	2	3	0	0	9	7	0	0	0
Five +	44	24	3	0	2	28	7	3	0	0
%	100	100	100	100	100	100	100	100	100	100
Mean selected	3.6	2.0	0.7	0.2	0.7	2.9	1.1	0.9	0.3	0.0
Mean elected	3.3	1.6	0.1	0.0	0.1	2.9	0.9	0.1	0.0	0.0
N.	133	46	38	139	210	96	14	40	261	127

Note: General Elections 1945–1987.
'Strong PPCs' = candidates who are second place in marginal seats
'Weak PPCs' = all other candidates
Source: BCS, 1992.

Sussex, where there are few good seats, are discouraged from applying in the marginal-rich Midlands or North-west. The Labour party process tends to be more pro-active: party agents and local officers do more to encourage applicants. The dominant Labour party ethos discourages overt careerism. When asking for possible names to be considered for nomination, the self-starter seems to be actively discouraged as a sign of personal ambition. 'I was actually asked to put my hat in the ring . . . that [in the] Labour party is a law unto itself, it is not seen as nice to tout yourself, it's very distasteful.'[38] As a result the local insider enjoys a considerable advantage in the Labour party: members who already lived in the seat were more successful on the ladder of recruitment.

Campaign histories

The third measure of political drive is based on campaign careers. Some try, try and try again, no matter the knock-backs of successive rejections at interview and electoral defeat, while others give up after the first few attempts. As discussed, some assume that the appropriate pattern is one of an honourable defeat in a hopeless seat, proving loyalty to the party and gaining campaign experience, followed by the the opportunity to fight a stronger prospect. In order to measure this we need to consider the lifetime histories of candidates: how often they had been adopted and elected in general elections prior to 1992. As shown in table 9.7, there was a clear difference in the campaign experience of different strata on the ladder of recruitment. As would be expected, incumbents in both major parties had the longest track record: more than half the Conservative MPs, and one third the Labour MPs, had stood in five or more previous general elections, or back to February 1974. Contrary to expectations, many inheritors were adopted for a safe seat without ever fighting a previous general election; this was true for one quarter of the Conservative inheritors and more than half the Labour inheritors. Inheritors therefore remain a puzzle: in the Labour party, many succeeded on first interview, even without prior experience in a general election contest. Campaign experience does differentiate more successfully between high- and low-prospect challengers, although not between low-prospect challengers and list applicants who failed to be adopted.

Conclusions

This study has examined whether behavioural indicators of motivation help to predict the position of individuals on the ladder of recruitment. Drive, meaning how strongly applicants pursued office, was conceptualised as having three main dimensions: the number of seats applied for in the 1992 general election, the strategy of applicants, and the campaign histories of candidates. Drive operates within a particular opportunity structure, which was partially controlled for by comparisons within each party. The expectation was that those with the greatest drive within each party would be most likely to succeed.

The results suggest that a complex pattern operates within the major parties. The most interesting results concerned inheritors. These had the highest chance of electoral success – remember, 93 per cent of inheritors were sent to Westminster. Inheritor seats offer a lifetime parliamentary career; 92 per cent of MPs who chose to stand again were returned. Yet many who became inheritors did so, particularly in the Labour party, without any previous experience as a candidate in a general election, and on their first application. The reasons are that most Labour inheritors followed an 'insider strategy': most were asked to apply and already knew members in the seat. This confirms the earlier observation that patronage – meaning informal contacts, local knowledge and personal networks – continues to play an important role in Labour party recruitment. The traditional solidaristic loyalties in the Labour movement have reinforced a party culture emphasising *local* representation. It is important for Labour party members that the candidate is 'one of us', sent from the community to parliament to represent the distinct local concerns of a Liverpool Riverside or a Glasgow Springburn. This follows one of the oldest traditions of parliamentary representation, and indeed is the original basis for divisions into local constituencies.

By contrast, in the Conservative party the recruitment process lays greater emphasis on meritocratic criteria, whether the candidate is 'the best person for the job'. Most Conservative inheritors have some experience of previous general election campaigns, are adopted for a constituency after a series of applications to vacancies around the country, and follow electoralist strategies when targeting applications. The key question Conservative inheritors ask when choosing to apply is not whether they already knew members or lived in the constituency, but whether the seat was winnable. The underlying concept of representation behind this meritocratic model is that Westminster is a national forum for the debate of issues facing the country. The Conservative party culture therefore emphasises that politicians need to be drawn from 'the brightest and the best', irrespective of local origins.

This conclusion needs to be qualified. There are elements of the patronage and meritocratic model in both major parties. Local contacts may help secure an interview in the Conservatives, while Labour party members also see themselves as selecting good candidates on their merits. Yet there is a clear distinction in the emphasis which the Labour and the Conservative parties put on localism. Neither model should be seen as inherently preferable, since our evaluation depends on perceptions of the job of an MP. If an MP is regarded primarily as a local representative of the constituency, so that each place has its own voice at Westminster, then the Labour model may be preferable. If members are seen as policymakers concerned with issues of national politics, and potential Ministers of State, then the Conservative approach may be preferable. But what is clear is that the dominant model may well shape the type of politician who is successful, and in turn this may perhaps influence the calibre and strengths of politicians in the House of Commons, and ultimately the quality of the leadership of the major parties. Accordingly the last section of the book will examine the consequences of selection decisions on Westminster.

10   Comparative candidate recruitment

This chapter seeks to understand recruitment within a wider cross-national context. We have established that there are few women and working-class MPs in the British parliament: is this a universal phenomenon? To compare countries a distinction can be drawn between four levels of analysis (see figure 10.1). First, there are systematic factors which set the broad context within any country – the legal system, electoral system, party system and structure of opportunities. Secondly, there are factors which set the context within any particular political party – the party organisation, rules and ideology. Thirdly, there are factors which most directly influence the recruitment of individuals within the selection process – the resources and motivation of candidates, and the attitudes of gatekeepers. Lastly, there is the outcome of the process for the composition of parliaments.

The aim of this chapter is fourfold: first, to see whether the social bias in the British parliament is a universal phenomenon; secondly, to consider how the legal system, electoral system, party system and structure of opportunities influence the recruitment process; thirdly, to analyse how decisions over recruitment vary with different party organisations; lastly, to consider what strategies have been employed by parties to overcome the social bias of legislatures. To set Britain in context, this chapter compares recruitment to the lower house of national legislatures in twenty-five established liberal democracies.[1]

The outcome of the recruitment process

Comparative research has established that political elites tend to be drawn from higher status professional occupations worldwide, although there is considerable cross-national variation in the particular professions which are most heavily represented in each country.[2] Table 10.1, showing the pattern in twelve liberal democracies, where recent information is available, confirms the over-representation of higher status occupations. In these systems, lawyers form the highest proportion of members (18 per cent), with business executives and managers close behind as the next largest group

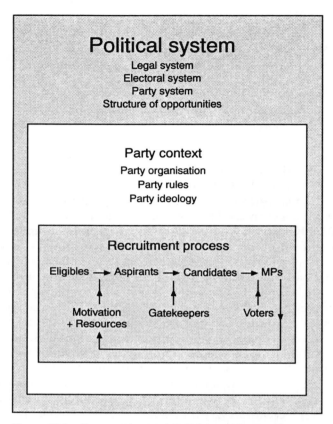

Figure 10.1   Comparative model of the recruitment process.

(17 per cent). Administrators and professional members of the chattering classes – teachers, journalists, social scientists – are also over-represented. The main avenues for working-class recruitment lie through Labour, Social Democratic and Communist parties.[3] Although systematic cross-national data are unavailable, the fall in the number of working-class candidates in Britain reflects similar trends evident in Germany, France, Norway, Australia, and elsewhere.[4] Indeed, even in the 1993 Russian parliamentary elections, only 1 per cent of candidates came from a working-class occupation.[5]

The position of women in legislative elites is well established (see table 10.2). In recent years, women have been relatively well represented in Scandinavian countries and the Netherlands, where they form over a third

Table 10.1a *Comparative occupations of parliamentarians (Lower House) (in percentages)*

	Total	Australia	Canada	France	Greece	Israel	Japan	Malta	NZ	Portugal	Switzerland	USA	UK
Lawmaking professions													
Legal profession	18	11	19	6	38	18	6	27	14	21	17	35	13
Civil servants & administrators	11	8	10	20		5	33	6		8		11	11
Politicians & party officials	10	11	1				33			1	30		7
Business & finance													
Commercial and business	17	22	22	6		18	13	4	20	15	12	30	24
Accountants/financial consultants	1		3					4	6				2
Chattering professions													
Educational profession	14	18	15	26	11	14	2	4	12	19	13	11	16
Journalism/media/writers	3	2	5	3		3	1	3		1	7	5	7
Social scientists	2		2		6	10		3		6			
Literary and artistic	1	1		2		4					3		1
Other professions													
Medical profession	5	4	4	12	14	1	1	20	3	6		1	1
Agriculture & farmers	3		5	3		8	3		15		13	4	2
Engineering/architects	3	2	1	2	10	4		13	3	10	7	1	1
Other white collar	3	10	3	13				6					
Armed forces	1	1	1		3				1	1			2
Clergy						4							
Manual trades													
Manual workers	3	5		3						4			10
Trade unionists	1	5							5			1	
Not available	6		10	4	20	12	7	10	21	8		1	1
Total	100	100	100	100	100	100	100	100	100	100	100	100	100
Election year		1987	1988	1986	1990	1992	1990	1992	1990	1987	1991	1990	1992

Source: Chronicle of Parliamentary Elections and Developments, Geneva, InterParliamentary Union, 1990–1992.

Table 10.1b *Summary occupations of parliamentarians (Lower House) (in percantages)*

	Total	Australia	Canada	France	Greece	Israel	Japan	Malta	NZ	Portugal	Switzerland	USA	UK
Lawmaking professions	39	31	30	26	38	23	73	33	14	30	47	47	32
Business & finance	17	22	25	6		18	13	9	26	15	12	30	26
Chattering professions	20	20	21	31	17	32	3	10	12	26	22	16	24
Other professions	15	17	14	30	26	17	4	39	22	17	19	7	6
Manual workers	3	10		3					5	4		1	10
Not available	6		10	4	20	12	7	10	21	8		1	1
	100	100	100	100	100	100	100	100	100	100	100	100	100

Source: Chronicle of Parliamentary Elections and Developments, Geneva, InterParliamentary Union, 1990–1992.

Table 10.2   *Women candidates and MPs in the Lower House (in percentages)*

		Year	Women MPs	Election Year	Women MPs	Change	Electoral System
1	Finland	1987	31.5	1991	38.5	7.0	List
2	Norway	1985	34.4	1989	35.8	1.4	List
3	Sweden	1988	38.1	1991	33.5	−4.6	List
4	Denmark	1988	30.7	1990	33.0	2.3	List
5	Netherlands	1986	20.0	1989	29.3	9.3	List
6	Iceland	1987	20.6	1991	23.8	3.2	List
7	Austria	1986	10.9	1990	21.8	10.9	List
8	Germany	1987	15.4	1990	20.4	5.0	List/AMS
9	Switzerland	1987	14.0	1991	17.5	3.5	List
10	New Zealand	1987	14.4	1990	16.5	2.1	FPTP
11	Spain	1989	14.6	1993	16.0	1.4	List
12	Luxembourg	1984	11.7	1989	13.3	1.6	List
13	Canada	1984	9.4	1988	13.2	3.8	FPTP
14	Ireland	1989	7.8	1992	12.1	4.3	STV
15	USA	1990	6.4	1992	10.8	4.4	FPTP
16	Belgium	1987	8.5	1991	9.4	.9	List
17	Israel	1988	6.7	1992	9.2	2.5	List
18	UK	1987	6.3	1992	9.2	2.9	FPTP
19	Australia	1990	6.7	1993	8.2	1.5	AV
20	Italy	1987	12.8	1992	8.1	−4.7	List
21	Portugal	1985	6.4	1987	7.6	1.2	List
22	France	1988	5.7	1993	6.1	.4	SB
23	Greece	1989	6.7	1990	5.3	−1.4	List
24	Japan	1986	1.4	1990	2.3	.9	SNTV
25	Malta	1987	2.9	1992	1.5	−1.4	STV
	Average		13.8		16.1	2.3	

Note: Alternative Vote (AV), Single Transferable Vote (STV), First-past-the-post (FPTP),
Party List (List), Single Non Transferable Vote (SNTV), Second Ballot (SB), Additional
Member System (AMS)
*Source: Inter-Parliamentary Union Distribution of Seats Between Men and Women as at 30 June
1993* (IPU, Geneva, 1993).

of all members of parliament, with substantial growth in their numbers
since the mid-1970s. Women constitute about one fifth of elected politicians
in Germany and Austria; they are least well represented in Malta, Japan,
Greece, France and Portugal. Liberal democracies have experienced a
modest increase in women's representation in recent elections, on average
about 2.3 per cent from one election to the next, although there was a sharp
fall in the number of women politicians in the first democratic elections in
Eastern and Central Europe, following the abolition of gender quotas.

The age pattern of legislatures shows little change over time (see table 10.3).

Table 10.3   *Age of parliamentarians (Lower House)*

	Under 30 (%)	30s (%)	40s (%)	50s (%)	60 + (%)	Election
1 Austria	0	17	42	32	6	1990
2 Belgium	2	21	38	38	1	1991
3 Denmark	4	11	46	25	15	1988
4 Germany	2	25	50	22	1	1990
5 Greece		26	32	33	9	1990
6 Iceland		24	41	25	10	1991
7 Israel		14	37	33	16	1992
8 Japan		5	24	31	39	1990
9 Luxembourg	3	13	32	23	28	1989
10 Malta	2	27	30	24	16	1992
11 New Zealand	3	21	51	23	3	1990
12 Portugal	8	27	38	18	9	1987
13 UK	0	12	39	33	15	1992
14 USA		9	35	31	25	1990
Mean	3	18	38	28	14	

Source: Chronicle of Parliamentary Elections and Developments Geneva, InterParliamentary Union, 1990–1992.

Most members tend to be in their mid-forties, although there are some cross-national variations. The issues of class and gender have attracted more attention. Nevertheless, the lack of younger legislators may also be important for political representation if there are, as Inglehart suggests, significant generational differences in basic values.[6] Many parties have youth organisations, aiming to attract new blood into the party. The age of aspirants is one of the factors which party leaders may take into consideration in balancing party lists. Therefore, as this review confirms, the social biases of legislative elites are long-standing and well established. But there is less agreement about how to explain the outcome.

The context of the political system

The first set of explanations for cross-national differences could rest with contextual variables: the legal system, electoral system, and party system. Unless there is a significant change under debate, such as constitutional or electoral reform, systemic factors are often overlooked by studies focusing on particular parties. But they play a critical function since they set the general 'rules of the game', which a comparative perspective makes strikingly apparent.

The legal system

The legal system specifies the criteria of eligibility for candidates in all liberal democracies, and regulates the detailed recruitment process in just a few. Today the most common legal criteria for candidates concern age, nationality, residence, personal conduct, and holding public office (see table 10.4). The age requirements vary: in most countries candidates must be at least 18, 21 or 25, although a few set the minimum age higher (30 for the US Senate, Canadian Senate, Japan House of Councillors, 35 for the French Senate, and 40 for the Belgian and Italian Senates).[7] Citizenship is an almost universal requirement, and sometimes for a long period, occasionally from birth. Local residency requirements are uncommon, although they do affect candidates in Canada (for the Senate), Luxembourg, New Zealand, and the United States.[8]

The law establishes certain standards for politicians. Candidates can often be disqualified on the grounds of insanity, criminal convictions, undischarged bankruptcy, and, in some under-developed countries, educational and literacy disqualifications. Certain occupations are commonly seen as incompatible with membership of parliament, to prevent a conflict of interest, secure the independence of MPs, and prevent a threat to the separation of powers. Disqualified occupations include membership of other assemblies, public office, members of the armed forces, judiciary and police, and executives of public corporations.[9] These eligibility requirements exclude some but mean that most citizens in a country are usually legally qualified to run for office, should they so choose. After the universal enfranchisement of women in liberal democracies, the legal system cannot explain the social bias within legislative elites, except possibly for a modest effect on the age of members.

The legal system only regulates the recruitment process in detail in the United States, Germany, Norway, Finland, Turkey and Argentina. In the United States state laws closely regulate the selection of candidates for Congress and most other offices. Direct primaries became widespread during the 1960s, minimising the selection powers of parties. Most primaries are closed (allowing only those registered for a party to vote in that contest), but some are open (allowing any citizen to participate).[10]

In *Germany*, Article 21 of the 1949 Constitution provided public funding of parties, and required them to select candidates for the Bundestag by a direct secret vote of all enrolled party members in each district, or by a district nominating committee.[11] *Finland's* 1969 Party Act requires that parties keep democratic principles in their activities. *Norway's* 1921 Nomination Act states that electoral lists must be decided by party conventions in each constituency, although this is interpreted quite flexibly.[12] In *Turkey*,

Table 10.4   *Legal Eligibility for Legislative Candidates (Lower House)*

	Minimum age	Residency requirement	Reasons for disqualification				
			Criminal record	Insanity offence	Election	Bankrupt	Other
1 Australia	18	Country	Y		Y		
2 Austria	21	Country	Y				
3 Belgium	25	Country	Y	Y			
4 Canada	18	None	Y	Y	Y		
5 Denmark	18	Country					Y
6 Finland	18	None					
7 France	23	None					
8 Germany	18	None	Y				
9 Greece	25	None	Y				
10 Iceland							
11 Ireland	21	None	Y	Y		Y	
12 Israel	21	None	Y		Y		
13 Italy	25	None	Y	Y			
14 Japan	25	None	Y				
15 Luxembourg	21	Local	Y	Y	Y		
16 Malta	18	Country	Y	Y	Y	Y	
17 Netherlands	21	None	Y	Y			
18 New Zealand	18	Local	Y	Y	Y		Y
19 Norway	18	Country	Y	Y			
20 Portugal	18	None	Y	Y			Y
21 Spain	18	None					
22 Sweden	18	None					
23 Switzerland	20			Y			
24 UK	21	None	Y	Y	Y	Y	Y
25 USA	25	Local					
Mean	21		17	12	7	3	4

Source: Inter-Parliamentary Union, 'Parliaments of the World' (Hants, Gower 1986, 2nd edn).

the 1965 Political Parties Law requires that 95 per cent of candidates are selected by the direct vote of due-paying members in each district.[13] Lastly, in *Argentina* the 1991 Electoral Law established a compulsory 30 per cent quota for female candidatures for all elective posts, which constrains the choice of parties, although the effects of this reform are not yet clearly established.[14] Elsewhere, selection processes are regulated not by law but by party constitutions, internal rules, and informal practices.

The party system

Candidate competition – the number who run for election, and their chances of winning – varies substantially cross-nationally (see table 10.5). In

Table 10.5 *Rate of candidate competition*

	Candidates N.	MPs N.	Elected (%)	Year
1 Iceland	1,029	63	6.1	1991
2 Sweden	5,256	349	6.6	1988
3 Israel	1,700	120	7.1	1988
4 Italy	8,631	630	7.3	1987
5 Switzerland	2,411	200	8.3	1987
6 India	6,160	545	8.8	1989
7 Belgium	2,114	212	10.0	1987
8 Finland	1,911	200	10.5	1991
9 New Zealand	677	97	14.3	1990
10 Canada	1,574	295	18.7	1988
11 Australia	782	148	18.9	1990
12 France	2,788	577	20.7	1988
13 Spain	1,663	350	21.0	1989
14 UK	2,946	651	22.1	1991
15 Denmark	606	179	29.5	1990
16 Malta	173	69	39.9	1987
17 Ireland	370	166	44.9	1989
18 Japan	953	512	53.7	1990
19 USA	836	435	52.0	1992
	2,238	305	13.6	

Source: Inter-Parliamentary Union, 'Distribution of Seats Between Men and Women in National Parliaments' (Geneva, TPU, 1991).

Sweden, for example, 5,256 candidates contested 349 positions in the 1988 general election. In contrast, in the US general election there were 836 Democratic and Republican candidates running for 435 districts in the House of Representatives. Opportunities to become a candidate are influenced by the party system, the relatively enduring structure of party competition which persists across a series of elections. Party competition has two principal dimensions: the *strength* of parties, conventionally measured by their number of seats in the legislature (or votes in elections), and the *ideological position* of parties across the left–right spectrum (see figure 10.2). Opportunities for candidates might be expected to be influenced by three factors: the number of parties in the system; the growth of new parties; and the strength of left-wing and Green parties.

There are three main types of party system. *Limited party 'catch-all' systems* are exemplified by Ireland, the USA and Canada. In these systems there are few major parties represented in the national legislature and these tend to be 'catch-all', appealing widely across the ideological and social spectrum.[15] In the United States, the Democrats and Republicans provide classic exemplars of loosely organised and weak 'catch-all' parties, although third 'party' independents periodically challenge the system.

Polarised two-party systems are exemplified by Australia and the UK. The UK system has become more fragmented among the electorate, with substantial if uneven support for the minor parties, but in parliament over 90 per cent of seats continue to be held by Labour and the Conservatives. The Australian parliament is dominated by Labour and the Liberals, with the National party and Australian Democrats minor players.[16] Lastly, *fragmented party systems* are illustrated by Italy, Norway, the Netherlands and France, where there are multiple parties represented in the legislature and considerable divisions across the ideological spectrum. Post-unification Germany also falls into this category.[17]

Increased opportunities for candidates may be generated by the growth of new parties in the system. This includes the fluctuating fortunes of the Greens, increased support for the far-right in Italy, France, Belgium and Germany, and revived regional parties such as the Bloc Québecois in Canada, the Scottish National party in the UK, and the Northern League in Italy. Party fragmentation has increased substantially in recent years in Sweden, Italy and Japan, following the decline of dominant one-party systems.

How does the party system therefore influence the outcome? Multiparty systems tend to have a higher proportion of women candidates than systems with few parties. Yet the pattern is not clear-cut: Israel, Belgium and France are classically seen as having a fragmented multi-party system yet these countries have relatively few women in office. In terms of new parties, the growth of the Greens has contributed towards greater social diversity among candidates; they usually have the highest proportion of women and

	Few parties	Many parties
'Catch-all' centerist	Ireland USA Canada	
Ideologically polarised	Britain Australia	Sweden Italy Netherlands France Norway Germany

Figure 10.2   Comparative model of party competition.

younger candidates. But on the other hand the growth of far-right parties has produced the contrary tendency, for example, the extreme religious parties in Israel have no women members, let alone women candidates. And the decline of communist parties has restricted opportunities for working-class mobilisation. In general, this indicates that the relationship between party systems and legislative elites is complex, and we need to avoid drawing simple inferences about the relationship between recruitment and party systems.

Electoral system

Theoretically the electoral system could influence recruitment in various ways. Czudnowski, amongst others, suggests the main influence concerns the centralisation of the selection process:

Party selection seems to be closely related to the electoral system. When a candidate has to be elected by a local or regional constituency, he will tend to be selected by the local or regional party organisation. In large multi-member constituencies ... central party organisations have a far greater influence, if not a monopoly, on candidate selection.[18]

Yet Gallagher found no support for the proposition that proportional systems with party lists are associated with centralised selection.[19] National party leaders have more influence over recruitment decisions in some majoritarian systems, such as New Zealand and Japan, than in some countries with regional or national party lists such as Norway, Germany, and the Netherlands.

The influence of the electoral system on the social composition of legislative elites, particularly the representation of women, is better established.[20] The effects of the electoral system on class, ethnic, linguistic or religious minorities depend on the spatial distribution of support, the system of boundary revisions, and other issues.[21] Electoral systems vary substantially in different countries but the main alternatives are Simple Plurality First-past-the-post, Alternative Vote, the Second Ballot, Single Transferable Vote, Additional Member System, and Party List.[22] What difference would these systems make for candidate recruitment?

Comparative studies suggest that three main factors in electoral systems influence recruitment, namely, in order of priority: the ballot structure (whether party list or single candidate); district magnitude (the number of seats per district); and, the degree of proportionality (the allocation of votes to seats). All other things being equal, women tend to do best under multi-member constituencies with a high number of seats per district. Therefore, party list systems tend to be the most favourable for women. The effect of STV proves variable, depending upon district magnitude. In contrast, plurality and majoritarian systems – first-past-the-post, second ballot and alternative vote – are least favourable to the representation of women.

What evidence is there for this? In the same country, in simultaneous elections, women do far better under party list systems. Australia uses the alternative majoritarian vote in single-member electoral divisions for the House of Representatives, and multi-member state-level districts using proportional quotas for the Senate. In the 1993 general election, women constituted 8 per cent of House members but one quarter of the Senate. The classic case to confirm this is Germany. In federal elections to the Bundestag, half the seats are allocated by majoritarian single-member districts and half by proportional Land (regional) party lists. In 1990, 136 women were elected to the Bundestag, of whom 109 entered through Land lists. The importance of proportional systems for women's representation is confirmed by evidence from countries such as France which changed their electoral system over time.[23]

Moreover, we can compare the proportion of women MPs in the most recent election results (1989–93) across all liberal democracies (see table 10.2). All the countries where women constitute more than 20 per cent of MPs use regional or national party lists, with the variation of the additional member system in Germany. In contrast, most countries at the bottom of the table use majoritarian or plurality systems. The main exceptions are Malta which uses the single transferable vote in small, multi-member constituencies, and the southern Mediterranean democracies of Greece, Italy and Portugal. In the middle strata, the pattern is not wholly uniform, for example, New Zealand under first-past-the-post has more women MPs than many party list systems.

Electoral systems with a high number of seats in multi-member constituencies facilitate the entry of women. But it would be misleading to see this factor in isolation from its broader context. A party list system is perhaps a necessary, but certainly not a sufficient, condition for high levels of female representation. In Scandinavia, the electoral system is conducive to women's representation but, since the electoral system has remained stable, by itself this factor cannot account for change over time. In Israel, Italy and Greece the electoral system should be favourable to women, yet without party initiatives or wider political pressures from the women's movement, few are selected or elected. It is therefore necessary to understand the interaction of the political system in a comprehensive model, rather than relying upon simple, deterministic and monocausal explanations.

Why would party list systems facilitate women's entry? There are three main reasons. In single-member constituencies local parties pick one standard bearer. Therefore, selection committees may hesitate to choose a woman or ethnic minority candidate, if they are considered an electoral risk. As we have established, electability is a major consideration in the choice of candidates. In contrast, there is a different 'logic of choice' under proportional systems where voters are presented with a list of candidates for each party. Here, parties have a rational incentive to present a 'balanced ticket'. With a list of names it is unlikely that any votes will be lost by the presence of women candidates on the list. And their absence may cause offence, by advertising party prejudice, thereby narrowing the party's appeal. Second, there is the strategic argument. If parties want to help women by affirmative action programmes, selection quotas, positive training mechanisms, or financial assistance, this is easiest where there are national or regional lists of candidates. Lastly, there is the argument that greater proportionality increases the number of seats which change hands and party competition. This improves access for under-represented groups in parliament, including women.

The structure of opportunities

As discussed in chapter 2, the 'structure of opportunities' includes a range of factors influencing candidate competition.[24] The number of contestants for nomination and election may be affected by different costs and benefits: the status, power and rewards of legislative office compared with other positions; the number of elected offices available within the system; the career structure in government; the function and powers of the parliament; the full- or part-time demands of the legislature; the ability to combine a legislative career with outside occupations; the salary, fringe benefits, and powers of patronage associated with the post; and lastly, the risks and costs of standing. The basic underlying hypothesis is that where the rewards of office are less, this reduces candidate competition, so challengers seeking entry stand a better chance of getting elected. Where competition for seats is strong, challengers face more difficulties gaining access.

Comparative information about basic salaries and facilities has to be treated with considerable caution; there are differences in daily allowances, travel and secretarial expenses, and regulations on other forms of income.[25] Nevertheless, as shown by table 10.6, basic annual salaries for legislators in the Lower House in the mid-1980s ranged from US$75,000 for US Congressional representatives down to less than US$15,000 in Israel, Portugal and Malta. As Mezey notes, American legislators are more generously rewarded than any others.[26] Current information is more sparse, but that which is available suggests that legislative salaries tended to roughly double from 1985/6 to 1990/1 in six countries. Salaries increased to US$125,100 for

Table 10.6 *Salaries for members of parliament (Lower House)*

	1985/86 ($)
1 USA	75,100
2 Japan	46,710
3 Canada	40,900
4 Italy	37,800
5 Germany	35,000
6 Belgium	33,700
7 Austria	30,140
8 Australia	28,800
9 Norway	25,000
10 Luxembourg	23,300
11 France	23,000
12 New Zealand	23,000
13 UK	21,700
14 Denmark	20,272
15 Ireland	19,039
16 Netherlands	18,540
17 Finland	18,375
18 Sweden	18,000
19 Greece	17,740
20 Israel	15,300
21 Portugal	7,500
22 Malta	5,900
Average	26,583

Source: Inter-Parliamentary Union 'Parliaments of the World' (Hants, Gower 1986, 2nd edn).

Congressional Representatives, to US$68,000 for members of the German Bundestag, and to US$39,500 for British MPs.[27] To some extent the contrasts in remuneration reflect national differences in per capita income. But after controlling for this we still find considerable contrasts; for example, Scandinavian countries have some of the highest per capita incomes, yet MPs from these countries receive fairly low basic annual salaries, although this is supplemented by regular allowances when parliament is in session.

Low levels of incumbency turnover, measured by the percentage of new members every election, is often seen as a significant barrier to change in the established legislative elite. In the US House of Representatives and the British House of Commons, over 90 per cent of incumbents who choose to run again are normally returned.[28] But total turnover is far greater, produced by by-elections, defeats and retirements. About three-quarters of all British MPs are returned from one parliament to the next, and this level of

Table 10.7 *MPs and Cabinet posts*

Ministers must be MPs
1 Australia
2 Ireland
3 Japan
4 Malta
5 New Zealand
6 UK
Ministers are usually MPs
1 Belgium
2 Canada
3 Germany
Ministers not necessarily MPs
1 Austria
2 Denmark
3 Finland
4 Greece
5 Israel
6 Italy
7 Norway
8 Spain
Ministers cannot be MPs
1 Luxembourg
2 Netherlands
3 France
4 Portugal
5 Sweden
6 Switzerland
7 USA

Source: Interparliamentary Union *Parliaments of the World* (Hants, Gower 1986 2nd edn.)

turnover is fairly similar to other countries. Matland estimates that in twenty-three developed democracies the average turnover of members in national parliaments was 68.8 per cent in general elections during the 1980s, and 72.4 per cent in countries using single member districts.[29] Incumbency represents a bottleneck to change where women and ethnic minorities are gaining political experience at local and state level faster than the opportunities for good parliamentary seats.

The constitutional context may influence the chances of promotion from the backbenches. In about one third of the countries under comparison, including Britain, Australia, Japan and New Zealand, cabinet ministers are drawn from the ranks of parliamentary backbenchers (see table 10.7). In these systems, there is a narrow career track for political life: a parliamentary seat is an essential prerequisite for ministerial office. Another third of these countries have mixed systems. In the remaining nations, constitutional restrictions prevent members of the executive from simultaneously holding legislative office.

The constitutional structure of government influences other opportunities for candidates, including the territorial and functional division of powers, whether the parliament is bicameral or unicameral, the number of parliamentary seats, electoral thresholds for minor parties, and the frequency of elections. The centralisation of power at Westminster, for example, means there are few other channels for elected politicians with ambition.[30] In federal systems such as Germany and Australia, powerful state governments provide an alternative avenue into political office.

Party organisations

The political system sets the general context of recruitment but in liberal democracies parties are the main gatekeepers. The key selectors may be grassroots party members, delegates at local party conventions, regional officers, factions, affiliated interest groups, or national party leaders, depending on the centralisation of the system. Different actors may influence different stages of the process, such nomination, ranking, voting on the final selection, and formal endorsement. Decisions by gatekeepers take place within the context of formal party rules, and informal norms and practices, which limit their choice.

Cross-national comparisons of recruitment are hindered by the complexities of the decision making process within each party. Reviews have attempted to summarise the primary 'selecting agency' in each country, such as the national executive or constituency committee.[31] But this often represents a considerable oversimplification: in practice, many groups play a role at different stages of the recruitment process; a series of decisions, not one, produces the eventual outcome; practices vary substantially between different parties in a country; and formal constitutional powers may disguise *de facto* control.[32] It is meaningless to ask whether the 'real' power rests with those who propose, sponsor, promote, shortlist, select, prioritise or endorse. All participants play some role. These issues indicate the complexities of analysing power within the recruitment process.

Decision-making within parties varies depending on the degree of institutionalisation and centralisation, producing four main types of recruitment process (see figure 10.3). In this classification, the first criteria is the *institutionalisation* of the process. In formal systems, the application process is defined by internal party rules which are detailed, bureaucratic, explicit, standardised, implemented by party officials, and authorised in party documents. The steps in the decision making process are relatively transparent to outside observers. There are formal appeal procedures. The significance of the rules for the distribution of internal party power may produce heated conflict over proposed changes.

In contrast, in informal systems the nomination procedure is relatively closed, the steps in the application process are familiar to participants but rarely made explicit, and procedure may vary from one selection to another. Any guidelines in official party regulations or constitutions tend to have *de jure* not *de facto* power. Since formal rules are rarely implemented, there are few effective courts of appeal. The process is less bureaucratic and more open to personal patronage by 'party notables'.

The second dimension of this typology concerns the *centralisation* of decision making. In *centralised* systems the key players are national authorities within the party. This category can be defined as including executives, party and faction leaders at the national level. In *regional* systems, the key players are party leaders at state or regional level. In contrast, in *localised* systems the key players are within constituencies,[33] including local officers, constituency executives, local factions, grassroots members and voters. Defining the key players is a complex issue, because power over selection can be exercised by many bodies which interact. Systems vary on a continuum from the highly centralised to the highly localised, rather than as discrete categories. The selection process will be influenced by those who set, implement and adjudicate over the rules of the game, as well as those who participate at different stages in directly picking individual candidates. Bearing these qualifications in mind, differences between systems can be illustrated by examples of each type.[34]

	Centralised decisions	Localised decisions
Formal rules	Dutch VVD French PC Italian PCI NZ Labour Austrian Soc Japan LDP	British Cons German SDP Swedish SDP Norwegian Lab Dutch PvdA
Informal rules	Italian DC Italian PSI French UDF	US Democrats Canadian Libs

Figure 10.3   The recruitment process within parties.

Informal-centralised recruitment

Informal-centralised recruitment characterised the unreformed Italian Christian Democrat (subsequently the Popular Party) and the Italian Socialist Party (PSI).[35] In these fragmented parties, selection was decided by a process of bargaining between the leadership of competing factions. Local officials try to ensure their interests are heard, but they are often overruled.[36]

In *France*, the UDF are characterised as a 'caucus-cadre' organisation, a loose network of like-minded followers coalesced around local and national notables. In the UDF, the key gatekeepers are the national party leaders and regional notables who can 'place' favoured candidate in good positions, after taking account of proposals from departmental organisations. With no tradition of internal party democracy, grassroots members play almost no role in the process.[37] The French Socialist Party (PS), which developed a more organised mass base, provides a weaker exemplar of this type. In PS, candidate selection in principle is decentralised, with local constituencies choosing their own candidates by secret ballots of members. Yet in practice, Appleton and Mazur suggest that national party organisation has very significant powers of supervision which it has used to change nominations during the final stage of candidate ratification.[38] The party has adopted quota requirements for candidate selection since the mid-1970s, but in practice these have not been implemented, except in recruitment to the European Parliament. Quota rules have proved rhetorical gestures rather than effective regulations. The proportion of women party members, leaders, candidates and elected officials in the Socialists is similar to the position in the Rassemblement pour la République (RPR), without any such quota rules.

In informal-centralised systems of recruitment, if party leaders wish to promote certain groups or individuals to balance the ticket, they have considerable power to do so. Through patronage, party leaders can improve the position of candidates on party lists to create a balanced ticket, or place them in good constituencies. As a result under this system of 'benevolent autocracy' change can be implemented relatively quickly, although without institutional safeguards the gains can be quickly reversed. On the other hand, if the leadership resists change to the status quo, they can block opportunities for challengers. Under this system positive discrimination strategies to increase social diversity will probably prove ineffective, since any regulations or guidelines will not be implemented. Since the process is not rule-governed, changing the rules will not alter the outcome.

Informal-localised recruitment

In contrast, in informal-localised systems it is difficult for the central party leadership to play a major role – whether positive or negative – in the recruitment process. The most extreme exemplar of this type is the *United States*. Traditionally, American party organisations were relatively weak 'caucus-cadre' rather than 'mass-branch' organisations. The decline of the power of party bosses to choose their candidates in the proverbial smoke-filled rooms, due to the introduction of primary elections by state law, produced the rise of entrepreneurial candidates with their own independent funding, organisation and campaign. Any candidate who wishes to run in a party primary can do so, once they fulfil the minimal legal requirements, although parties in a few states retain a residual formal role. In the countries under comparison, in this regard, as in much else, American parties are atypical. Elsewhere few parties have made use of direct voter primaries. In Canada, some ridings have occasionally opened the selection process to open voter meetings.[39] Primaries were also used by the People's Party in Austria in the early 1970s, and at the same time the Christian Democrats experimented with them in Rhineland-Pfalz.[40] Nevertheless, voters have some role in legislative recruitment in all systems, since all candidates need electoral support. This role can be particularly influential in open party list systems, where voters can prioritise candidates within parties.

The use of primaries in the United States has led many observers to stress that 'self-recruitment' is the norm. Yet this overlooks the way all but self-financed candidates face other powerful 'gatekeepers'. Political Action Committees carefully evaluate candidates before they are prepared to offer funding. Candidates may be interviewed by PACs in a formal process, and may have to provide documentation to support their application, or pledge certain policy positions. Other actors who play a gatekeeping role include the local media, individual financial contributors, campaign professionals and local volunteers. Unless candidates are seen as strong and credible contenders by these gatekeepers they may be unable to run an effective campaign. Accordingly, in the United States party organisations can no longer block, but neither can they do much to promote, candidacies at the nomination stage.[41]

The closest example of an informal-localised process is probably *Canada*, where local party members in the Progressive Conservative party determine most of their own rules and practices for choosing their nominee.[42] As a result, some constituency parties open the selection process to the whole membership, while others give a greater role to elected party officers. National leaders have formal veto power over the final choice of names, but in the last two decades this has been used only twice by the major parties.

The leaders of the major parties have encouraged women to run, assisted ridings searching for prospective candidates, and provided some training conferences, but Erickson concludes their hands have been tied by the localised nature of the process.[43] In recent years, following concern about possible abuse of the system, there have been moves to formalise the local selection rules in Canada.

Under 'informal-localised' systems opportunities for candidates are not restricted by the central party leadership. At the same time it is difficult to see what steps, beyond rhetorical encouragement, these parties would take to improve the social balance of their slate. If the final decision rests in the hands of each local constituency party, and there are no standardised party rules concerning the nomination process, or reviews of the overall party list, this seems to exclude positive action guidelines, financial assistance, or shortlisting targets.

Formal-localised recruitment

The most common system in liberal parties is 'formal-localised' recruitment, where explicit bureaucratic rules are established and implemented to standardise the selection process throughout the party organisation at national or state level. Within this framework decisions about which individuals get chosen are taken largely at constituency level, although regional bodies may play a part. The major parties in Britain, Sweden, Ireland and Germany exemplify this type.

In the *Swedish* Social Democrats, Conservatives and Liberals there are three stages: putting forward names, ranking nominees, and adopting the list.[44] The middle stage is most critical. Here the non-socialist parties often rely on meetings of activist members at the local and constituency level. In the Social Democrats the local nominating committees and the constituency executives play a decisive role. The party lists are based on large, multi-member constituencies. In ranking candidates on the party list, the party aims to produce a balanced ticket in terms of region, age, occupation and gender. The Social Democrats recommend that at least 40 per cent of candidates should be women, and every other place on the party list should be allocated to the opposite sex.

In *Ireland*, candidates for Fianne Fail and Fine Gael are chosen by selection conferences of party members. These meetings select a party ticket with three to five candidates in multi-member constituencies. While the main decisions are taken at local level, party leaders may impose additional candidates. This power is not widely exercised but is occasionally used to balance the party ticket in terms of locality, age, electoral appeal and gender.[45]

Lastly, *Germany* provides a weaker exemplar of this type, with a party

system based on formal 'mass-branch' organisations. The process of candidate selection in constituencies, established by electoral law, follows two
models. Either a meeting is held in a constituency where all party members
may vote. Or party members elect delegates who in turn vote on candidates.
The local parties determine recruitment for parliamentary elections but
regional party organisations influence the process, particularly in nominations on the Lander lists. Kolinsky notes that the regional and national
party leaders have played a significant role in persuading local constituencies to accept more women.[46] The names of nominees for constituencies
and regional lists are compiled by the constituency and the regional executive, then passed to local parties for confirmation by party members. Gender
quotas in the Social Democrats and Greens regulate the composition of
party lists, while in other parties certain positions near the top of the list are
ear-marked for women.

Formal-centralised recruitment

The decline of what Duverger termed 'caucus-cadre' and 'militant-cell'
party organisations means that today few parties in liberal democracies use a
formal-centralised recruitment process. In this system, national party
leaders have the constitutional authority to decide which candidates are
placed on the party ticket. In the past this system operated most clearly in
traditional communist parties organised according to the principle of democratic centralism, such as the PCF in France and the PCI in Italy.[47]
Elsewhere, a comprehensive review of the evidence suggests the national
leadership or executive is the main selector of candidates in the Austrian
Socialist Party, in the Dutch Liberal party, in many Israeli parties before
1977, in the New Zealand Labour party, in the Greek PASOK and New
Democracy parties, and in the Japanese Liberal Democratic party.[48]
Pressures towards internal party democracy have produced a decline in the
number of parties which continue to use this system in liberal democracies.

Conclusions: implementing equal opportunity strategies

What are the implications of this typology for changing the outcome?
Parties have implemented three types of recruitment policies. *Rhetorical
strategies*, articulated in leadership speeches, official statements, and party
platforms, aim to change the party ethos by affirming the need for social
balance in the slate of candidates. *Affirmative action* programmes aim to
encourage groups to run by providing training sessions, advisory group
targets, special conferences, financial assistance, and group monitoring.
Positive discrimination sets mandatory group quotas, at a specific level –
whether 20, 40 or 50 per cent – applied to internal party bodies, shortlists of

applicants, or lists of candidates. The distinction between advisory targets and mandatory quotas is often blurred in practice, particularly if quota rules are not implemented. The term 'quotas' is often employed quite loosely, and may have different crosscultural connotations. But this does not invalidate the basic distinction between formal regulation and informal guidelines.[49]

The typology suggests each type of party can employ rhetorical and affirmative action strategies, but positive discrimination operates most effectively in formal-localised systems. It makes little sense to think about using positive discrimination in the major parties in the United States or Canada. And, even if rules are passed, they are not likely to be implemented in the French UDF or the Italian Christian Democrats. Accordingly positive discrimination quotas are taken seriously in a rule-bound and bureaucratic culture where decisions by different bodies within an organisation need to be standardised. In the German Social Democrats, the decisions about who gets nominated are taken at local level, but they are taken within a framework of positive discrimination which has been effective in raising the proportion of women candidates, and their position on party lists. In Sweden, positive action guidelines have been equally effective in most parties. Accordingly, the nature of party organisations is one factor, among others, which seems worth exploring further to understand the strategies social groups can employ to increase their representation.

One question raised by this discussion is why some parties have favoured one strategy over others. One answer lies in the role of party ideology. Social Democratic and Green parties are more likely to believe positive discrimination is justified to bring about short-term change. Parties of the right and centre are more likely to rely upon rhetorical strategies, and possibly affirmative action, in the belief that women should be encouraged to stand, and party members should be encouraged to select them, but the recruitment process has to involve 'fair' and open competition. Greater intervention in the recruitment process in left-wing parties, via different mechanisms, is evident in the use of positive gender discrimination in candidate selection by the Socialists in France (20 per cent quotas), Labour in Britain (for shortlisting only), the Socialist Left and Labour in Norway (40 per cent quotas), Labour (PvdA) in the Netherlands (25 per cent quotas), and the Social Democrats in Germany (40 per cent quotas). Such mechanisms have become more widespread with appointments to internal party bodies. Just as right-wing parties favour a minimal role for government in the free market economy, so they prefer non-intervention in the recruitment process.

This generalisation needs one major qualification: once positive discrimination is successfully implemented by left-wing and Green parties, others within the political system may follow suit. As Sainsbury suggests, in Sweden the Social Democrats were the first to favour women's elections in the late 1960, setting advisory guidelines where each sex should have representation of at least 40 per cent, and their dominant position led the other parties to compete, and even outbid, the Social Democrats as champions of equality.[50] The result has been a convergence of trends across Swedish parties. In Norway, however, Skjeie notes the Conservatives and Christian People's parties have not, so far, followed the gender quotas adopted by the left and centre.[51]

III   Does the social bias matter?

11 The values, priorities and roles of MPs

The 'demographic' model of representation, discussed in chapter 6, requires elected bodies to reflect the social composition of the population from which they are drawn. This view was perfectly expressed by Alexander Hamilton in the Federalist papers when he questioned whether a representative body composed of 'landholders, merchants and men of the learned professions' could legitimately speak for all the people: 'It is said to be necessary, that all classes of citizens should have some of their own numbers in the representative body, in order that their feelings and interests may be better understood and attended to.'[1] Similar concerns are echoed today. In recent decades many have claimed that contemporary democracies are 'unrepresentative' since universal rights of citizenship have often failed to be translated into comparable gains at elite level. The salient political cleavages vary in different countries; for example, linguistic and regional divisions are critical in Belgium and Canada, race is important in the United States, while religion and ethnicity define the political communities in Pakistan and Northern Ireland. In Britain during the post-war period, the greatest concern was expressed about the growing proportion of MPs from the professional middle classes, at the expense of the traditional aristocracy and manual workers. Reflecting the changing politics of the 1980s, more recent debates have focused on the issues of race and gender.[2]

The social composition of parliament raises symbolic as well as substantive issues. Exclusion may undermine the moral legitimacy and authority of democratic bodies. For example, it is difficult for the British parliament to claim to understand the needs and defend the interests of the Muslim or Sikh communities if it includes few members. MPs who are not from these groups, no matter how sympathetic to their interests, may not be seen as legitimate spokespersons by these communities on issues such as the Rushdie affair or religious education. Most would agree that the British parliament needs to be more socially representative on these grounds alone. What is more controversial is the stronger claim that if Westminster became more socially diverse this would make a *substantive* political difference. This theory rests on the premise that the class, gender and race of politicians have a significant influence on their values, policy priorities, and/or legislative behaviour. The aim of this chapter is to explore the empirical basis of this claim.

Some remain skeptical about this claim. A wide-ranging survey of research in different countries, by Matthews, found little evidence of a strong and consistent relationship between the social background and policy attitudes of legislative elites.[3] In Britain, Mellors concluded that it is difficult to prove a link between biographical data and political attitudes.[4] Numerous studies counting the social background of MPs may indicate availability rather than the significance of these data. Structural variables, which are commonplace explanations of mass political behaviour, may prove an inadequate guide to the beliefs and actions of the elite. Politicians may acquire their values from a lifetime's experience working within parties and the local community, debating issues with colleagues at Westminster, and interacting with officials and interest groups in Whitehall, so that it is hard to discern the more distant imprint of their social origins. As Kavanagh expresses the sceptical position:

> From all the available data on social background it is not immediately obvious what its implications are for the behaviour and values of politicians. Will a better educated ... House be more ideological, more interested in abstract ideas? In the case of Labour, does the decline in the numbers of former manual workers and the embourgeoisiement (when elected) of former workers lead to a deradicalisation of views, as Michels claimed at the beginning of the century? Has the reduction of MPs from upper class backgrounds led to a decline of the 'One Nation' outlook on the Conservative benches? ... We do not know, but it seems most implausible that there should be a strong correlation between broad social background characteristics and values.[5]

Even if there are significant gender differences in society, it cannot be assumed that these will necessarily be reflected in members of political elites. Women MPs may be more divided by party and generation than united by gender.[6] The strength of party discipline controlling backbench behaviour may override any differences in personal preferences. A review of the literature by Czudnowski concludes that a connection between the social background and attitudes of elites is frequently assumed, but rarely demonstrated.[7]

Yet socialisation theory suggests that, although there is no simple relationship, the attitudes and values of politicians will probably reflect their formative experience in early childhood, formal education, the workplace and family. Politicians typically enter parliament in mid-life, well after their basic values might be expected to be well entrenched. Some previous studies suggest a link between social class and attitudes among British MPs, although the nature of the relationship remains a matter of dispute. Hindess argued that Labour had a more radical socialist outlook when it was largely working class, and the progressive embourgeoisement of the party has led to a de-radicalisation.[8]

In the post-war period, pioneering work on legislative behaviour in the British parliament was developed by Finer, Berrington and Bartholomew.[9] The authors found a significant association between voting on Early Day Motions and the occupational and educational background of MPs. The analysis divided motions into two categories. 'Ideological' issues included those such as pacifism, civil liberties, foreign policy, and humanitarianism, while 'materialist' issues included welfare benefits, the cost of living, health and education. In the Labour party, Berrington found that working-class MPs with elementary education and trade union sponsorship were relatively rightwing on a range of 'ideological' issues. In contrast, white-collar occupations such as journalism, social work and party organisation proved the most leftwing, while the university-educated professionals such as lawyers, teachers and doctors were roughly in the middle. In contrast, on the 'materialist' issues there were significant differences between leftwing workers and rightwing MPs in the professions and white-collar occupations. This analysis was limited by the strength of party discipline in voting for all major legislation in the Commons, and this avenue was not explored further in Britain.

A link between class and attitudes has also been found among party members. Parkin found middle-class political activists to be more radical on the goals of pacifism, humanitarianism and equality.[10] Seyd and Whiteley's recent survey of Labour members reported that middle-class members tended to be relatively leftwing on issues such as the environment and nuclear weapons, and relatively rightwing on issues such as nationalisation and the role of trade unions.[11] Heath and Evans suggest a pattern of working-class authoritarianism among the electorate.[12] It has not been established whether differences at mass-level are reflected in similar patterns among parliamentarians.

A growing literature suggests women politicians make a substantive impact in other countries, particularly on 'women's issues'. Vallance and Davies found that women members of the European Parliament played a major role in raising the equality directives on the political agenda in the late 1970s.[13] Studies in Scandinavia found that women and men politicians gave a different priority to policies on childcare, welfare support, and equal opportunities, based on their dissimilar experiences within the family, welfare state and labour market.[14] In the United States, research has established that the gender of elected representatives influences their legislative priorities and roll call votes, in Congress and State Houses.[15] Unfortunately, in the absence of good evidence, it cannot necessarily be assumed that the same relationship holds in the British political system. The strongest version of this claim suggests that the presence of women in political forums is necessary to defend issues where women have a direct interest, and also to bring a different understanding of justice, power and morality to the polity.[16]

The small number of black MPs in British politics hinders a systematic study of their political ideology. Some leading black Labour MPs are perceived as fairly left wing, such as Bernie Grant and Diane Abbott, but this may be a product of the media's treatment of black politicians, or the politics of their constituencies, and there are too few cases to generalise. Others, like Keith Vaz, have played a leading role articulating the concerns of the Asian community, for example in the Rushdie affair. The ethnic community is also itself sub divided by region and religion, so that it cannot be assumed that black MPs can necessarily express the interests of the Muslim, Hindu or Sikh communities.[17] It can be argued that black representation may be necessary to defend the interests of the ethnic community, on issues such as religious education, immigration policy or welfare rights, and also as a way of changing racism in society.

To evaluate this controversy we can explore whether values, policy priorities, and legislative roles are influenced by social background. By *values* we mean general orientations towards social and political goals. Values are durable beliefs about broad principles; should government be interventionist or *laissez faire* on the economy? Should we give greater priority to economic growth or environmental protection? Should society be traditional or liberal on moral issues? These principles may not be raised as explicit issues in election campaigns but they may help form broad images of politicians and parties. By *policy priorities* we mean level of concern about more specific policy issues such as unemployment, interest rates, education, or Britain's role in the European Community. By *legislative roles* we mean the activities which politicians perceive as appropriate, and the priorities they allocate to different aspects of their work in parliament.[18] Theoretically we might expect social background to have the greatest influence on general social and political values, although in turn these may affect more specific policy priorities, and ultimately legislative behaviour.

Throughout our study the pool of politicians was analysed controlling for the effects of party and incumbency. Politicians were classified as Conservative or opposition, since this can be seen as the dominant division in party competition in British politics.[19] As established earlier, despite growing homogenisation over the years, parties continue to display a distinctive social profile with differences in gender, race, class,[20] education, household income, religiosity, union membership and age, (see table 11.1), and these factors were entered into the analysis.[21] There is a need for caution when interpreting the analysis by race and class, given the small number of cases

Table 11.1 *Social background of the political elite.*

	Conservative	Labour	Lib. Dem.	Nat.	Green	All
Male	88	74	78	79	72	80
Female	12	26	22	22	28	20
White	99	96	98	100	97	98
Non-white	1	4	2	0	3	2
Middle class	99	92	98	97	92	96
Working class	1	8	2	3	8	4
Graduate	69	69	70	77	66	69
Non-graduate	32	31	30	23	34	31
Older (50 +)	22	21	23	15	11	20
Middle (40–50)	39	42	34	30	31	38
Younger (18–39)	39	37	43	54	58	42
Religion	87	36	62	55	26	59
None	13	64	38	45	74	41
Union member	15	97	38	54	39	50
None	85	3	62	46	61	50
Income <10K	1	8	4	8	29	7
Income 10–30K	26	51	54	53	55	43
Income 30–50K	30	35	31	35	13	31
Income 50K +	43	7	11	5	3	19
N.	553	510	311	77	129	1,681

Note: The elite sample includes MPs, Parliamentary Candidates and List Applicants.
Source: BCS, 1992.

in the sample. Our model assumes that party is the primary cleavage in parliament, and analyses the indirect effects of gender, class and race on values, attitudes and behaviour.

Social values

To see whether social background shapes underlying social and political values we use Likert-type scales to measure values along four dimensions: left–right, liberal–authoritarian, post-materialist, and feminist. The left–right scale included six items about the general principles of equality, collectivism and government intervention, with agree–disagree statements such as: 'There is one law for the rich and one for the poor', 'Major public services and industries ought to be in state ownership', and 'It is the government's responsibility to provide a job for everyone who wants one'.

Table 11.2   *Party and value scales*

	Conservative	Lib. Dem.	Nat.	Green	Labour	All
Left–right scale	20	49	62	58	65	45
Liberal–authoritarian	46	59	61	65	61	56
Feminism scale	61	71	75	76	80	71
Post-materialist	2	55	61	70	49	36
N.	553	311	77	129	510	1,681

Note: See text for construction of the scales. The scales are scored from least left/liberal/feminist (0) to most left/liberal/feminist (100).
Source: BCS, 1992.

Table 11.3   Social background and values

	Left–right	Liberalism	Post mat.	Feminism	
Party	0.68**	0.50**	0.63**	0.26**	Conservative/other party
Incumbency	0.04	0.08*	0.08**	0.06*	MP/Non-elected
Gender	0.08**	0.01	0.04	0.18**	Male/female
Race	0.01	0.07*	0.02	0.02	White/non-white
Class	0.03	0.01	0.03	0.01	Working/middle class
Graduate	0.03	0.05*	0.03	0.02	Graduate degree/none
Age	0.02	0.17**	0.05*	0.10**	Years of age
Religion	0.07**	0.19**	0.01	0.22**	Belong to religion/none
Union	0.21**	0.01	0.02	0.15**	Union member/not
Income	0.07**	0.04	0.01	0.01	Household income (categories)
R^2	0.77	0.36	0.44	0.27	Total variance

Note: OLS regression analysis with standardised beta coefficients. See text for the construction of the scales.
** = sig. p. > 0.01 * = sig. p. > 0.05.
Source: BCS, 1992 (N. = 1681).

The liberal–authoritarianism scale concerns the values of tolerance and freedom of expression, with statements such as 'Homosexual relations are always wrong' and 'Young people today don't have enough respect for traditional British values'. The post-materialism scale used the standard item developed by Inglehart. The feminist scale used five items on values associated with the second-wave women's movement. (For details of all the scales, see appendix A). These scales proved reliable when tested for internal consistency using Cronbach's alpha,[22] with a low kurtosis and skew. After being arithmetically standardised these systematic 100-point scales can be used to compare the position of politicians across all parties.

Left–right values

The effects of occupational class and income may be expected to be most evident on the classic left–right values of the redistribution of wealth, government intervention in the economy, and trade union rights. Berrington found working-class Labour members had the strongest leftwing values on these sorts of 'materialist' issues.[23] The conventional wisdom about gender is that women voters are more rightwing than men in Britain. The gender gap among the electorate during the 1980s has become more complex. A 'gender-generation' gap was evident in the last British general election, with younger women slightly more 'leftwing', and older women slightly more Conservative, than their male equivalents.[24] During the 1980s most of the studies in the United States and Scandinavia have found that women politicians in state and national legislatures tend to be slightly less 'rightwing' than their male colleagues.

As we would expect, the left–right scale proved a strong predictor of party, with the Conservative elite on the right (with a mean score of 20 per cent), the Liberal Democrats in the centre (49 per cent), and Labour on the left (65 per cent) (see table 11.2). After controlling for party, the demographic variables which proved most significant in table 11.3 were union membership, gender, religiosity, and income. Conservative and Liberal Democratic women tended to be slightly more leftwing than their male colleagues, although there were no significant differences within the Labour party. In total, the model explained a remarkably high degree of variance (77 per cent) in the position of politicians on this scale. Most strikingly, occupational class and race failed to predict left–right values among politicians, after controlling for party.[25] This contradicts the argument made by Hindess and suggests that Labour's shift towards the moderate centre ground during the post-war period has to be explained by political and electoral developments, not the progressive embourgeoisement of the parliamentary Labour party.

Liberal–authoritarian values

Studies have commonly found education, religion and age to be strongly associated with authoritarian values among the electorate, with older, less educated and more religious voters among the least liberal.[26] We might therefore expect these factors would also prove significant at elite level. Social class might also be thought to play a role since, as mentioned earlier, working-class Labour MPs have been found to be relatively rightwing on 'humanitarian' issues.[27] Given the experience of many women as the main 'carers' within the family, responsible for children and elderly parents, it is often assumed that women are more 'tender' than 'tough' on moral values, such as tolerance of minority rights, respect for authority, and use of the death penalty.

As we might expect, the scale divided the political elite by party, with Conservative politicians the most authoritarian and the Greens the most libertarian (see table 11.2).[28] Incumbency status also proved significant. In terms of the demographic variables, the regression analysis shows that the strongest and most consistent predictors of the respondent's position on the liberal–authoritarian scale were, respectively, religiosity, age, race, and education (see table 11.3). The influence of religion and age proved consistent across all the major parties. The model successfully explained a fairly high degree of variance (36 per cent). Contrary to expectations, there were no significant and consistent differences by gender or class on this scale, after controlling for political party. Insofar as personal values have an impact on parliamentary activities, the growing proportion of slightly younger and better educated MPs over the years may therefore have tilted the balance of opinion within the Commons in a slightly more liberal direction, especially where personal preferences may be expressed in free votes on such moral issues as abortion, homosexual rights, capital punishment and civil liberties.

Post-materialist values

These scales represent some of the classic divisions within British politics. Following Inglehart, other studies of values amongst the mass electorate have suggested that the emerging cleavage in politics consists of divisions over post-materialist values, relating to issues such as nuclear power stations, the deployment of troops, sexual and racial equality, and protection of the environment. Studies suggest that post-materialism is particularly strong among the younger generation, the more affluent, the better educated and women.[29] To explore this the study used Inglehart's standard battery of items designed to classify respondents into the categories of materialist, mixed, and post-materialist.

Scores on this scale show substantial differences by party (see table 11.2). Over half the Conservative politicians were materialists (54 per cent) while hardly any (2 per cent) were post-materialist. In contrast, about half the Labour, Liberal Democrat, and Nationalist politicians were post-materialist, as were 70 per cent of the Greens. As well as party, incumbency status also proved significant. The analysis in table 11.3 suggests, however, that after controlling for party the only background variable which proved important was age. Over time, generational change may produce a gradual shift within the Commons towards post-materialist concerns, although a change in the electoral fortunes of the opposition parties would produce a far swifter transformation of British politics. Contrary to expectations, gender, class and education proved insignificant predictors on this scale at the elite level.[30]

'Feminist' values

The literature on gender politics suggests that women politicians may prove most distinctive in the area of 'feminist' values. Many of the concerns of the women's movement – such as reproductive rights, domestic violence and rape – raise moral questions which cut across traditional party lines. Studies of support for feminism at the mass level have commonly found age, religiosity, and education to be important.[31] In particular, the younger generation of women politicians might be expected to take a distinctive stance on these issues, since they became active in political life during the mid-1960s, after the rise of the modern women's movement.

The 'feminist' scale incorporates support for five issues central to the agenda of the women's movement: equal opportunities for women, the availability of abortion on the NHS, the right to abortion within the first trimester, punishments for domestic violence, and the issue of rape in marriage. These items produced a feminist values scale, scored from 0 to 100, with a satisfactory degree of reliability (Cronbach's Alpha = 0.70). As the results indicate, party proved less strongly associated with the feminist scale than with the more traditional left–right cleavages in British politics. After controlling for party, the most significant predictors of support for feminist values among politicians were religiosity, gender, union membership and age, explaining 27 per cent of variance. Within each party, women were more feminist than their male colleagues, and this gender gap over-rode some conventional party divisions: for example, Conservative women were more feminist than Liberal Democrat men.

This analysis suggests that across these four different indicators party proved, not unexpectedly, the most significant predictor of social and political values. The results also suggest that religiosity and age played a role in influencing many of these values. But the influence of the central variables under analysis was relatively modest. The strongest case can be made for the impact of gender, which proved significant on two scales (feminism and left–right). In contrast race was significant on only one (liberalism–authoritarianism), and class on none. Income and education, which are usually alternative indicators of social class, also proved very weak predictors. The case for the 'demographic' theory of representation receives limited support from this evidence in terms of women MPs, but in general scepticism seems largely justified.

Policy priorities and attitudes

Defenders of the 'substantive' case could argue, however, that many of the values we have been analysing represent general principles which are shared so widely among Labour and Conservative politicians that we would not expect social background to make much difference. The stronger claim is that the background of members has an impact on their policy priorities. In Scandinavia it has been found that women legislators tabled far more parliamentary motions on issues such as family policy, childcare support, education and welfare, and raised these concerns in parliamentary questions.[32] Nevertheless, given cross-cultural differences, and the higher proportion of women in Scandinavian legislatures, similar patterns may not necessarily be evident in Westminster. If class plays a role in policy priorities, we might expect working-class members to place greater emphasis on issues such as welfare benefits, trade union rights and low wages.

To examine policy priorities the BCS survey used an open-ended question asking politicians to specify the 'three most important problems facing the country at the present time ... in order of priority'. These responses were classified into ninety minor sub-categories, then collapsed into three major categories concerning economic, social and foreign policy issues. The results were then transformed into weighted scales reflecting the priority given to the issue and the number of times it was mentioned. For example, someone who said that unemployment (3), interest rates (2) and inflation(1) were the three most important issues, in that order, was scored highly on the economic priority scale (6).[33] Another who thought education (3), unemployment(2) and electoral reform (1) were the most important would be weighted lower on the economic priority scale (2). The scales were then used as dependent variables in a standard regression analysis with the same controls used earlier.

The results in table 11.4 indicate that party proved a good predictor of the priorities given to problems, with each party emphasising their areas of greatest strength. Not surprisingly, Labour politicians were far more likely to express concern about social issues like education, pensions and the health service, while the Conservatives were more likely to rate foreign and defence issues such as European Monetary Union and Eastern Europe more highly. Similarly, the minor parties emphasised issues such as the environment (the Greens) or constitutional reform (the Liberal Democrats and the Scottish Nationalists).

After controlling for party and incumbency, gender proved to be significantly associated with the priority given to social policy; in the open-ended questions, women were more likely to express concern about such issues as welfare services, poverty and health. It should be noted that these

Table 11.4 *Social background and policy priorities*

	Economic	Social	Foreign	
Party	0.35**	0.30**	0.15**	Conservative/other party
Incumbency	0.18**	0.04	0.03	MP/non-elected
Gender	0.07	0.11**	0.04	Male/female
Race	0.05	0.01	0.01	White/non-white
Class	0.02	0.01	0.03	Working/middle class
Graduate	0.05	0.06*	0.06*	Graduate degree/none
Age	0.03	0.06*	0.02	Years of age
Religion	0.02	0.04	0.01	Belong to religion/none
Union	0.09*	0.07*	0.01	Union member/not
Income	0.06	0.09*	0.05	Household income (categories)
R2	0.17	0.12	0.04	Total variance

Note: OLS regression analysis with standardized beta coefficients. See text for the construction of the scales.
Q. 'What would you say are the three most important problems facing the country at the present time? Please list in order of priority ...'.
** = sig. p. > 0.01 * = sig. p. > 0.05.
Source: BCS, 1992 (N. = 1,681).

were general policy references. Only two or three women politicians spontaneously mentioned issues which related more specifically to the agenda of the women's movement, such as equal opportunities for women or tax relief for childcare. Politicians therefore tended to reflect the main issues on the public agenda during the general election campaign, since 'women's issues' were not a major part of the debate. The results also indicate that education and union membership were significant in two dimensions, although class and race were not associated with policy priorities. Interestingly, there is no evidence here that working-class members are more likely to articulate concern about social policy matters such as welfare services.

Legislative behaviour

Lastly, in the final and most decisive test, does background affect behaviour? Studies in Britain have noted significant differences in the roles members adopt, and hence the priorities they give to activities such as individual casework, committee work, and attending debates. These differences have been explained by party affiliation, type of constituency, and political generation.[34] But it is possible that the social background of legislators also influences the roles they adopt. There are a range of plausible hypotheses to be tested; do women members give a higher priority to background committee work while men tend to prefer the arena of parliamentary debate? Does education influence the way politicians see their role as influencing the formulation of party policy? Do working-class politicians give a high priority to constituency concerns?

The focus on legislative 'roles' seeks to understand motivation by linking cognitive goals with personality predispositions. Legislative roles refers to the way applicants see the job of an MP in terms of appropriate goals and activities. Roles shape what politicians do, how they do it, and why they think it appropriate behaviour. Work at Westminster involves many different tasks: attending parliamentary debates, dealing with individual casework, appearing on the media, developing party policy, answering constituency mail, holding surgeries, scrutinising legislation in select committees, attending local party meetings, and so on. Political careers are not clearly defined, there are no established qualifications or agreed job specifications. Given a hundred-and-one demands on their time and attention, MPs can prioritise their roles in many different ways.

The most systematic research on how British backbenchers perceived their roles, and the behavioural consequences, was by Donald Searing in the early 1970s.[35] His study seeks to conceptualise backbench roles along commonsense lines, using everyday language, as the roles were commonly understood by MPs themselves.[36] Following this general approach the BCS study explored how respondents saw the role of an MP. Questions about the nature of legislative work, including what politicians considered the most and least rewarding parts of the job, were discussed in the personal semi-structured interviews. The study then measured how politicians prioritised fourteen different tasks ranging from speaking in parliament to holding constituency surgeries, supporting the party leader, working with interest groups, and dealing with the press.[37] Responses were subject to factor analysis to see if they were structured in a consistent fashion.[38] The analysis (see table 11.5) revealed three primary dimensions of legislative roles, which accounted for 43 per cent of variance. Respondents saw themselves primarily as constituency members, party loyalists or parliamentarians.

Constituency workers

The largest group, constituency workers, gave the highest priority to helping people with individual problems, holding regular constituency surgeries, and representing local interests in parliament. This pattern was also evident in the personal interviews. Often Labour and Conservative MPs mentioned that public service to the community, helping with particular problems of social services or pensions, and looking after people, were some of the most rewarding aspects of the job:

Table 11.5   *Factor analysis of legislative roles*

	Constituency member	Party loyalist	Parliamentarian
Helping with individual problems	0.68		
Holding surgeries	0.68		
Attending community functions	0.65		
Attending local party meetings	0.54		
Representing constituency	0.53		
Supporting party leader		0.82	
Defending party policy		0.69	
Voting the party line		0.83	
Representing regional interests			0.62
Developing party policy		0.35	0.58
Working with interest groups	0.38		0.56
Parliamentary committee work			0.56
Speaking to national media			0.48

Note: Scores represent the factor loadings, greater than 0.30. Total variance explained by these factors is 42.8%.
Source: BCS, 1992

First of all there's the constituency work. I enjoy it, the social worker side of it, looking after people's individual problems. That's a chore for a lot of colleagues. It's not a chore for me; it's a pleasure.[39]

As I say, I was very,very attracted to the life, and I've never seen the necessity to hide that, and to try to find some great rational reason – when in fact, I'm attracted to public life and to taking up causes, to looking after people, to being everybody's great protective umbrella when they need it – I'm very attracted to that ... I do take up some pretty obscure stuff, and I do like to feel that I can hold out a wing for little chicks to come under.[40]

I think I've got abilities to help people – part of my job, I mean, I'm a lawyer, and I'm a commercial lawyer, but inevitably in the law there's quite a strong element of helping people, whether you're acting for people or whether you're assisting, and I enjoy that aspect of it, and as I went on with being a candidate and doing more and more constituency related work, the more I realised that I really enjoyed that element – the element of assisting people.[41]

Another Labour MP also referred to 'helping people' at the grassroots level as one of the more productive parts of the job:

You're meant to be in politics to change things and to help people, and I think I learnt through being a councillor that I might not change the world, but I could influence a family's and an individual's life for the better -- and that I'm still finding as an MP.[42]

Possibly the clearest articulation of the 'public service' model came from this Conservative candidate:

I've always had a great desire to be of service, I feel this very strongly – service to the public. I don't profess to be very skilled at lots of things but one thing ... I always like to help people, so I think perhaps the constituency side has more attractions than anything within the executive as it were, so I think the key thing was public service.[43]

Parliamentarians

In contrast, 'parliamentarians' gave greater priority to broader legislative activities within the House such as speaking in debate, working in parliamentary committees and dealing with the media. For these people, parliament was seen as the place to get things done, the national forum to debate the great issues of state, the main check on the power of the executive. The clearest expressions of the 'parliamentary' category occurred in remarks by Conservative MPs:

Power, in so far as one ever has power in any democracy, is at the centre and if I want to influence the nation's affairs this is the place I have to get to.[44]

One sees all the big decisions taken in Parliament, and I became more and more interested in that ... I think that's where you get things done, where you change things, where you can work for people most effectively.[45]

Since I came down here with my father ... I watched him do his job. I thought I'd like to do that too – but more than that, I think with a, d'you know, an excitement, it's the emotional bit as well – I liked what I saw him doing, I liked the atmosphere down here, I love debating, I like the excitement of political activity.[46]

Some liked debates while others preferred the quieter committee work behind the scenes, whether select or standing committees. Some found this one of the most rewarding parts of the job:

I do a lot of standing committees, bills going through line by line ... I enjoy these more than I enjoy the chamber. Chamber's quite fun, but it's a theatrical thing rather than, in my view, about government.[47]

Party loyalists

Party loyalists placed the greatest stress on their role as party representatives, whether as standard bearers at election or supporters in the Commons. This group gave high priority to sustaining the party leader, defending and developing party policy, and voting the party line in divisions. As some applicants emphasised, the election was primarily about party not personal victory:

I felt that I'd something to offer the Labour party. I felt that the experience that I'd got on the City Council, my energy and enthusiasm – I felt that I could win a seat for Labour.[48]

Table 11.6   *Social background and legislative roles*

	Constituency worker	Party loyalist	Parliament	
Party	0.03	0.21**	0.01	Conservative/other party
Incumbency	0.03	0.01	0.10*	MP/non-elected
Gender	0.11**	0.06*	0.11**	Male/female
Race	0.01	0.01	0.04	White/non-white
Class	0.04	0.06	0.03	Working/middle class
Graduate	0.05	0.03	0.05	Graduate degree/none
Age	0.01	0.05*	0.05	Years of age
Religion	0.08*	0.07*	0.03	Belong to religion/none
Union	0.13**	0.17**	0.12**	Union member/not
Income	0.04	0.11**	0.02	Household income (categories)
R^2	0.03	0.07	0.04	Total variance

Note: OLS regression analysis with standardized beta coefficients. See text for the construction of the scales.
Q. 'In your view, how important are the following parts of an MP's job?'
** = sig. p. > 0.01 * = sig p. = 0.05
Source: BCS, 1992 (N. = 1,681).

I thought that I could win the seat for the Labour party – proved to be right, and I feel I can do the job as well as anybody else can.[49]

I mean the most important thing was the Labour party, to me, and getting somebody in who could represent Labour – and if I felt I couldn't have won the election, I wouldn't have stood.[50]

In order to examine whether social background had an impact on the roles politicians thought appropriate, the battery of items on legislative activities were used to develop standardised summary scales, based on each role, ranging from 0–100. The results of the regression analysis in table 11.6 show that the model was unable to explain as much variance in legislative roles as in the previous analysis of values and policy priorities. The main reason for this was the insignificance of party differences among constituency workers and parliamentarians. Social background tended to be only weakly related to legislative roles, although gender proved significant across all three indicators. Women in every party expressed a far higher priority for constituency work than men, and this pattern was confirmed by behavioural evidence. When we examined the number of hours which members said they devoted to constituency casework while at Westminster, male MPs thought they devoted about fourteen hours per week to this while women MPs estimated they spent about twenty-five hours per week on casework.[51]

Conclusions

The debate about changing the social composition of parliament raises complex issues. There is a strong argument that the legitimacy and authority of parliament is undermined if it fails to reflect the social diversity of British society. In the classic view of representative government, parliament should be the main debating chamber for the nation, the forum where all voices are heard. On symbolic grounds alone the case can be made for increasing the number of women, working-class and black MPs in Britain. Yet the substantive argument is harder to sustain with good evidence. The results of this study suggest that in most respects social class failed to have a substantive impact. The occupational class of politicians was not strongly associated with their social values, policy priorities, or legislative roles. On the basis of this evidence the impact of race appears to be limited, although it must be acknowledged that this analysis is severely restricted by the number of cases, and by the range of measures in the study which might be most appropriate to measure divisions on ethnic politics. Ideally, the approach of this research needs to be replicated with a larger sample of black politicians, perhaps in local government, before the results can be treated with confidence. Lastly, the evidence suggests that gender influences all three dimensions: women tended to give slightly stronger support for feminist and leftwing values, to express stronger concern about social policy issues, and to give higher priority to constituency casework. This gender difference should not be exaggerated, since party proved by far the stronger indicator of values and policy priorities. The gender gap among politicians was modest and not evident on every indicator. Nevertheless, this suggests that the election of more women to Westminster has the potential to make more than just a symbolic difference.

APPENDIX   Scale measures

(i) The *socialism-laissez faire* scale included the following six agree/disagree items:
Ordinary people get their fair share of the nation's wealth.
There is one law for the rich and one law for the poor.
There is no need for strong trade unions to protect employees' working conditions and wages.
It is government's responsibility to provide a job for everyone who wants one.
Private enterprise is the best way to solve Britain's economic problems.
Major public services and industries ought to be in state ownership.

(ii) The *libertarian-authoritarian* scale included the following six agree/disagree items:

Young people today don't have enough respect for traditional British values.

Censorship of films and magazines is necessary to uphold moral standards.

People in Britain should be more tolerant of those who lead unconventional lives.

Homosexual relations are always wrong.

People should be allowed to organize public meetings to protest against the government.

Even political parties which wish to overthrow democracy should not be banned.

(iii) The *feminist* scale was constructed from the following five items:

'Next we want to ask you about some changes which have been happening over the years. For each one can you say whether it has gone too far, not far enough, or is it about right'?

* Attempts to give equal opportunities to women in Britain?

* The availability of abortion on the NHS?

'Can you tell me how far you agree or disagree with the following statements'?

* There should be more severe punishments for domestic violence.

* Rape in marriage should be a crime.

* During the first 12 weeks of pregnancy the law should not restrict a woman having an abortion.

(iv) The *post-materialism* scale was constructed from the standard Inglehart question:

'There is a lot of talk these days about what the aims of the country should be for the next ten years. If you had to choose between the following items, which seems most important, and next most important, to you'?

a. * Maintaining order in the nation

b. * Giving people more say in important government decisions

c. * Fighting rising prices

d. * Protecting freedom of speech

Following Inglehart postmaterialist are classified as responses b and d. materialist as a and c, mixed are the rest.

12 The personal vote

The aim of this chapter is to examine the claim that there is a 'personal vote'. If MPs invest time in constituency service do they strengthen their support? If parties selected more black or women candidates, would they experience an electoral benefit or penalty? In short, do candidates matter electorally?

Incumbency effects

The consensus in the literature is that any personal vote for incumbents is fairly modest, with most British voters tending to 'vote the party'. Byron Criddle expressed this common view: 'Candidates, despite a necessary belief in their own importance, contribute little to the outcome of British general elections.'[1] The most extensive exploration of the personal vote, by Cain, Ferejohn and Fiorina, tested whether constituency service produced incumbency effects.[2] The study compared level of constituency work with swings experienced by incumbent MPs in the 1979 election. Constituency activity was measured by whether MPs encouraged casework, publicised successful cases, handled local casework, and held regular surgeries. The authors concluded that in 1979 variations in constituency work accounted for swings of 1.5 to 2 per cent for the Conservative MPs (750–1,000 votes) and between 3 and 3.5 per cent for Labour MPs (1,500–2,000 votes).[3]

As regards successive general elections, Curtice and Steed's estimates of the effects of a personal vote are similar, in the region of 750 to 1,000 votes, based on a different approach.[4] Curtice and Steed analysed vote change for 'second-term MPs': successful challengers facing re-election. When similar seats are compared, the authors found that second-term MPs enjoyed a boost worth about 1.5 to 2 per cent of the vote in the 1979, 1987 and 1992 elections, although not in 1983.

Lastly, Norton and Wood compared elections from 1983–87 by cohort of entry into parliament.[5] The authors found significant variations in the size of the personal vote, with the 'second-term' cohort performing particularly well. One reason for this, the authors suggest, is that new MPs, particularly in marginal seats, may work harder to shore up their support than seasoned veterans. In sum, the literature suggests that there is an incumbency advantage, albeit modest, for British MPs, although there is disagreement about the precise explanation and nature of this phenomenon.

Incumbency is a complex phenomenon, open to a number of interpretations. To explore the different dimensions we can analyse the possible benefits of office, the length of parliamentary careers, the amount of constituency service, and finally the effects of retirements on election results.

The benefits of office

The first proposition predicts that by virtue of their office, other things being equal, incumbents will do better than challengers within the same party. Voters may perceive MPs as having greater political authority, status, expertise and credibility than challengers, due to their experience on the backbenches, as well as greater name recognition and publicity. Most MPs we interviewed thought that incumbency was a clear advantage for these reasons, provided the member had been visible and hardworking. One woman Conservative thought that televising parliament helped the sitting MP: 'I wear a lot of red and pink. Constituents can pick me out ... they say "We saw you on television".'[6] Another agreed about the publicity value of incumbency: Provided you're sensible and conscientious once you're in place, you have vast opportunities to project yourself. On the other hand, as another Conservative pointed out, once you had been the MP, your record is public and not everyone likes everything you have done or said: You have to be infinitely more cautious because the position you take or undertakings you give have to be upheld, whereas the new boys and girls can afford to be more irresponsible. This first proposition stresses that the institutional advantages of the office apply to all MPs, irrespective of their behaviour. What matters is the fact that they are an MP, not how hard they campaign, how much time they devote to constituency service, or how well they represent the local area.

If office-holding provides an advantage in itself, all other things being equal, we would expect MPs to do better than challengers within their party. Yet when we consider elections since 1955, the pattern is one of trendless fluctuation: in some elections, incumbents do better, in others challengers (see table 12.1). Variations are caused by swings against the government and regional trends. When the government becomes unpopular, as in 1964–66 or 1959–64, the strongest swings are against sitting MPs. This explains most of the variance. Regional trends play a more minor part. In 1992 the Labour vote increased by 3.1 per cent for Labour MPs, but by 4.8 per cent for Labour challengers. Conversely, Conservative MPs lost

Table 12.1   *Change in vote for challengers and incumbents*

	Conservative			Labour		
	Challengers	Incumbent	Diff.	Challengers	Incumbent	Diff.
1955–59	0.6	−3.7	−4.3	−4.1	−1.8	2.3
1959–64	−4.3	−7.9	−3.6	0.2	1.9	1.7
1964–66	−2.4	−1.2	1.2	4.5	4.4	−0.1
1966–70	3.6	5.1	1.5	−3.7	−5.2	−1.5
1970–74	−5.9	−8.1	−2.2	−6.6	−5.3	1.3
1983–87	−1.8	0.3	2.1	2.6	6.1	3.5
1987–92	−0.6	−1.0	−0.4	4.8	3.1	−1.7
Mean	−1.5	−2.4	−0.7	−0.3	0.5	0.7

Note: 1979–83 excluded because of boundary changes excluding inheritors.

slightly more votes than Conservative challengers. Why? Because Labour MPs were concentrated in Scotland and the North, while the party's share of the vote increased more strongly outside of these areas. This underlines the need to take into account a range of factors which affect election results, and to compare trends over successive contests, before assessing the strength of any residual incumbency effect. We can conclude that office-holding *per se* does not necessarily produce an electoral advantage. When the government becomes unpopular, their MPs often face a stronger than average electoral penalty.

The length of parliamentary career

The second proposition is that some, not all, incumbents will enjoy a personal vote. In particular MPs who have represented their constituency during successive parliaments, sometimes for twenty or thirty years, may build up a loyal personal following.[7] Over time, members may be expected to become well known in their constituencies, through individual casework, local publicity, door-to-door campaigning as well as representing the concerns of the constituency in the house. Members may gradually accumulate a loyal personal following which builds up over the years. If correct, the personal vote should increase according to the accumulated years of a lifetime in parliament.

The results indicate, contrary to expectations, that length of parliamentary service was not related in a simple linear fashion to increased electoral support for incumbents (see table 12.2). There was a modest correlation among Conservative MPs but not among Labour MPs. Indeed, among Liberal Democrat MPs the longer their years of service, the greater

Table 12.2 *Length of years in parliament and change in vote share*

	r	Mean years	N.
Conservative MP	0.15*	11.9	319
Labour MP	0.03	10.5	204
Liberal Democrat MP	−0.24	11.5	20
Nationalist MP	0.06	10.2	5

Note: Pearson product moment correlations (r) between the number of years an incumbent has served in a constituency and the percentage change in their vote, 1987–92.
* = Sig. p. > 0.05.

the loss of votes; there was a modest negative correlation (probably due in part to the effects of regional swings). On reflection, the lack of a significant positive relationship may not be so surprising after all. Length of parliamentary service is a simple measure which cannot distinguish between assiduous MPs who invested years helping constituents and others who spent most of their time in Annie's Bar.

Amount of constituency service

This leads to the third proposition, that the incumbency effect relates to the amount of time MPs devote to constituency service. We might expect that hardworking MPs who concentrate on local casework develop a greater personal vote than those who focus on backbench committees or parliamentary debates. To examine this proposition, constituency work is measured according to the number of hours in the average week which MPs say they devote to constituency casework, constituency surgeries, local party meetings and other constituency functions. It is always difficult to gauge the accuracy of these sorts of measures, since members may consistently inflate the time spent on work, or simply misjudge it. Nevertheless, there is no reason to believe that any exaggeration produces biases in a systematic direction. The estimates of workload in this survey were very similar to previous studies.[8] This hypothesis predicts that the more assiduous the constituency service, the greater the electoral benefits.

MPs claimed to spend about sixty-six hours on parliamentary business in the average week, including about fourteen hours for constituency casework, three for constituency surgeries, two and a half for local party meetings, and five for other functions in the constituency. Constituency work would therefore absorb about one third of an MP's work (or 24.5 hours per week). Previous studies suggest that members in marginal seats have the greatest incentive for constituency service, and new MPs will be more active

Table 12.3   *Constituency service and change in incumbent vote share*

	% change in vote	
	Conservative MPs	Labour MPs
Least active	− 0.7	2.4
Moderately active	− 1.1	3.9
Most active	− 0.7	3.6
Correlation (r)	0.09	0.17*
N.	121	78

Note: Pearson correlations (r) between the number of hours per week MPs spend on constituency service and the change in their vote 1987–92.
* = sig. > 0.05

during their first term than more seasoned members.[9] Yet this receives no support from the evidence: the amount of constituency service bore no significant relationship to the marginality of the seat or the cohort of entry. The cohort of new MPs who entered in 1987 spent twenty-seven hours per week on constituency service, compared with twenty-five hours for all others.

Does constituency service bring any direct electoral rewards? MPs were classified into those who were most, moderately and least active. For Conservative MPs there was no significant correlation between constituency service and the change in their vote between 1987 and 1992 (see table 12.3). Labour MPs received more tangible electoral benefits, – the greater the constituency service, the more favourable the change in their vote – although even here the relationship remained modest (Pearson correlation r = 0.17 sig. p > 0.05). Labour MPs who spent most time on constituency . service gained a boost of at most about 1.2 per cent in their share of the vote over the least active, a modest effect, although one which may be significant in a few marginal seats.

The effects of retirements

Following the literature on the US Congress,[10] the final proposition relates incumbency effects to two stages in the legislator's career-cycle. This predicts that when an MP leaves office there will be a modest 'retirement slump' in the party's share of the vote, lasting for one election. Inheritors lack the status, political credibility, and public recognition which the office bestows on MPs. For the subsequent general elections the theory predicts a 'second-term surge', an extra boost which restores the personal vote as the new MP develops visibility and experience. After this surge, the incumbency

Table 12.4   *Retirement slump 1955–92.*

| | % change in Conservative vote | | | % change in Labour vote | | |
	Incumbent	Inheritor	Diff.	Incumbent	Inheritor	Diff.
1955–59	−3.7	−3.5	0.2	−1.8	−3.6	−1.8
1959–64	−7.9	−8.3	−0.4	1.9	1.8	−0.1
1964–66	−1.2	−2.3	−1.1	4.4	3.8	−0.6
1966–70	5.1	6.5	1.4	−5.2	−5.9	−0.7
1970–74	−8.1	−8.2	−0.1	−5.3	−3.3	2.0
1974–79	6.9	8.2	1.3	0.5	0.4	−0.1
1983–87	0.3	−0.6	−0.9	6.1	5.2	−0.9
1987–92	−1.0	−1.6	−0.6	3.1	−0.5	−3.6
Mean	−1.2	−1.2	0.0	0.5	0.3	−0.7

Note: 1979–83 excluded because of boundary changes in many seats where MPs retired in 1983.

effect may be expected to stabilise over successive elections. It should be stressed that the second-term surge is independent of constituency service; it is not the result of the new MPs' efforts but rather an automatic return to the 'normal party vote' in a constituency. To test the 'retirement slump' we can analyse the change in the vote for incumbents and inheritors. For 'second-term surge' we can look at the change in the vote for second-term incumbents with other cohorts of MPs.

If we compare the vote change for MPs and inheritors in elections from 1955–92 (see table 12.4), the evidence confirms a retirement slump. The results suggest that in seven out of eight elections the Labour vote fell more for Labour inheritors than for Labour incumbents. The difference was small, in the region of 0.7 per cent or 400 votes, but fairly consistent. In the Conservative party, the pattern was more erratic, but a small retirement slump was evident in five out of eight elections. The results in 1992 confirm this pattern; the retirement slump was particularly evident among Labour inheritors, who won 1,800 votes less than Labour incumbents on average.[11] In the Conservative party, too, incumbents did better than inheritors although the difference was more modest – only 0.6 per cent.

Evidence also confirms the 'second-term surge'; a better than average performance for new MPs facing reelection (see table 12.5). In the main parties, as the analysis shows, the second-termers who entered in 1983 proved the strongest cohort in 1987, and the second-termers who entered in 1987 proved the strongest cohort in 1992.[12]

Yet the results presented so far cannot be treated as conclusive. Any apparent incumbency effect may be the result of other factors, for example,

Table 12.5 *Parliamentary cohort by voting change*

MP first elected	% change in vote 1983–7		% change in vote 1987–92	
	Con.	Lab.	Con.	Lab.
Pre-1970	−0.3	4.5	−1.9	2.8
1974	−0.1	3.5	−1.0	3.8
1979	0.9	6.4	−0.9	1.4
1983	1.2	7.7	−0.8	3.5
1987*	0.4	4.2	0.2	4.0
1987**	−1.0	5.2		
1992*	...	...	−1.6	−0.5
1992**	...	...	−0.5	6.2
All	0.3	5.9	−1.0	3.3

Note: * Inheritors. ** Challengers who won

more Conservative MPs may have retired in regions with strong pro-Labour swings. For a multivariate analysis the measures of constituency service, length of parliamentary careers, and retirement effects were entered into the model of voting behaviour. The dependent variable is the change in the Labour and Conservative share of the vote (1987–92) in their own seats controlling for factors which produced significant variations in constituency results, including regional swing, the tactical battleground and by-election interventions.[13]

The results in figure 12.1 indicate slightly different patterns for each major party. The strongest predictors of Labour's share of the vote in 1992 were, as expected, Labour's share of the vote in 1987 and the regional swing. After controlling for these factors, the retirement slump, and to a lesser extent the effects of constituency service, continued to prove fairly significant. The importance of these factors is therefore not simply the product of the type of seats where Labour MPs resigned in this election.

We have already observed that incumbency effects tend to be weaker, and less consistent, for Conservative MPs. Hence, it is not surprising that the model confirms this pattern. For Conservative MPs the strongest predictors of their share of the 1992 vote were, in order of importance, the 1987 Conservative vote, the tactical contest, and the regional swing, as expected. After controlling for these factors the length of service in parliament continued to prove modestly significant, although other measures dropped out of the equation. Why length of parliamentary career should prove more important for Conservative MPs, while constituency service and the retirement slump prove more important for Labour MPs, is a puzzle which

Conservative seats

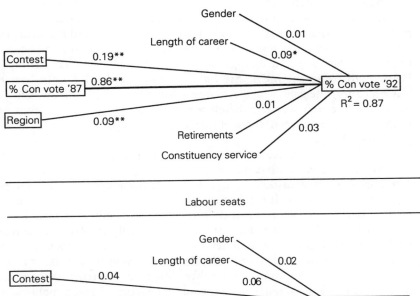

Labour seats

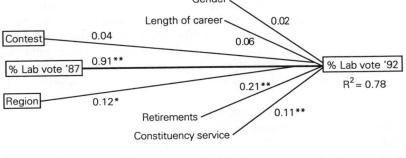

Figure 12.1   Model of voting choice. *Notes:* figure entries are
standardised regression coefficients (Betas) that measure the independent
impact of each predictor while controlling for the effects of other
predictors in the model. ** = sig. > 0.01; * = 0.05.

deserves further attention. It is not inconsistent with party differences
found in previous work,[14] but the reasons remain unclear at this stage.

Do women candidates lose votes?

If there is a personal vote due to incumbency, is there also one due to the
social background of candidates? Here we need to turn to the question of
whether women and ethnic minority candidates face significant electoral

penalties or benefits. Most previous studies have found no voter discrimination against women[15] , although these findings have not gone without challenge.[16] The literature is more divided about whether voters are biased against ethnic minority candidates.[17] Since there are few cases for comparison, it is perhaps not surprising that studies have produced inconclusive results. Moreover, the term 'ethnic minorities' encompasses candidates originally from disparate backgrounds – the Caribbean, East Africans, Pakistan, Bangladesh, India, Sri Lanka – each subdivided into diverse classes, castes, allegiances, and religions – Muslims, Hindus, Sikhs, Christians. 'Black' candidates may therefore experience quite different levels of support depending upon their ethnic background and the social composition of the seat.

Did politicians perceive any electoral bias against candidates who were women or from an ethnic minority? According to women politicians, voters are not misogynists. Indeed, says Emma Nicholson, 'The electorate is profoundly impartial, it is selection committees which are hypersensitive on this one'.[18] Elizabeth Peacock suggests that being a woman is an advantage: 'People like the fact that you're practically involved in the real world: not many guys push a trolley round Tescos'.[19] Kate Hoey believes that women may like to be represented by another woman, and as for men, 'Increasingly they don't oppose it either. Margaret Thatcher changed all that.'[20] This view is fairly widespread. The survey asked politicians whether they believed women were disadvantaged by the electorate: a few (4 per cent) thought that women lost votes but the vast majority (87 per cent) disagreed.

Did women candidates experience voter discrimination? There were 336 women candidates standing for the three main parties in the 1992 general election, including 41 incumbents, 10 inheritors, and 32 Labour and Conservative strong challengers. Comparing the change of their share of the vote (1987–92), in the Labour and Conservative parties, women did slightly better than men as incumbents, marginally worse as inheritors, and about the same as challengers. Yet once gender was entered into the model of voting choice (controlling for the type of seat, region and incumbency), sex proved irrelevant for the Labour and Conservative results. We can conclude that it is the lack of women inheritors and strong challengers, not voter discrimination, that is responsible for the under-representation of women in the Commons.

Do ethnic minority candidates lose votes?

Ethnicity may be more of an electoral hurdle. An Asian MP thought there were some advantages and disadvantages to his background.

Table 12.6   *Gender and voting change, 1987–92.*

	% change in vote (N.)			
	Men		Women	
Conservative incumbents	− 1.1	(303)	− 0.1	(16)
Conservative inheritors	− 1.5	(52)	− 2.7	(6)
Conservative challengers	− 0.5	(219)	− 0.7	(37)
Labour incumbents	+ 2.8	(181)	+ 4.8	(23)
Labour inheritors	− 0.2	(21)	− 2.7	(3)
Labour challengers	+ 4.9	(293)	+ 4.5	(112)
Lib. Dem. incumbents	− 7.7	(20)	− 2.3	(1)
Lib. Dem. inheritors	...	...	− 0.5	(1)
Lib. Dem. Challengers	− 4.9	(491)	− 5.4	(140)

Note: The number of candidates is given in parenthesis.

In the beginning, there was a lot of curiosity about who this man was. Most people's only experience of an Asian would be the person who sold them their newspaper. My people were asked, 'Can he speak English?' – I simply went back to the person and said, 'I've come to put your mind at rest. I believe you have some worries about my ability to communicate in English.'

There were some positive benefits too, with 14,000 Asian voters in the constituency. A lot of Asians who were Labour party supporters, even members, said they voted for me.

Yet in our survey almost a third of all politicians (29 per cent) believed that ethnic minority candidates lost votes, including almost half the Conservative MPs (44 per cent).

In total, twenty-two ethnic minority candidates stood for the main parties in 1992, a slight decline on 1987.[21] The results for the Conservatives, with one exception, were disappointing. The exception was the election of the first Asian Conservative MP this century, Nirj Joseph Deva, for Brentford and Isleworth. The result which received most publicity was the defeat of John Taylor in Cheltenham, which fell to the Liberal Democrats on a swing of − 5.2 per cent. In the aftermath John Taylor refused to admit in public that racism was to blame. The Liberal Democrats' strength in the south-west, the marginality of the seat, and internal divisions within the local Conservative party may all have been important. Nevertheless, compared with swings in a neighbouring constituency such as Cirencester and Tewksbury, racism seems to have played a part. Black Conservative challengers did slightly worse than average: for example in Islington North the anti-Conservative swing was − 4.6 per cent compared with − 3.0 per cent for inner London.

In contrast Labour ethnic minority incumbents did particularly well, with one exception. In Langbaurgh Ashok Kumar failed to hold his by-election gain, although the result was very close. Three Labour MPs elected in 1987 all experienced second-term swings above the regional average, with a substantially increased Labour vote for Bernie Grant (+13 per cent), Keith Vaz (+10 per cent) and Diane Abbott (+9 per cent). Piara Khambra was elected for Ealing Southall, increasing the total number of black MPs to six. In sum, the 1992 election represents mixed results for ethnic minorities: the total number of candidates fell while slightly more MPs were elected. Conservative challengers seem to have faced a slight electoral penalty, although black Labour incumbents did well.

Conclusions

If there is a modest personal vote, the question remains how politically significant this is. In Britain about half of all constituencies can be judged very safe, with majorities over 20 per cent, and in these – seats such as Glasgow Maryhill, Rhondda, Esher or Surrey North West – the gain or loss of a few hundred votes is irrelevant to the outcome. But some seats turn on the personal vote. How many?

If we use a fairly conventional measure, we can define very marginal two-party seats as those won by the Conservative or Labour parties where the difference between the winner and runner up was less than 5 percent, or about 2,500 votes in the average constituency. From 1955 to 1992 about 10 to 15 per cent of all constituencies, or between 60 to 100 seats, generally fall into this category in every election. In 1992, the Conservative majority rested on 21 seats with majorities of less than 2.4 per cent. In marginals the personal vote will rarely be sufficient to tip the balance in more than, at most, a handful of seats. Nevertheless, this handful may be critical for maintaining the government majority in parliament, as in 1950, 1964 and 1974. Moreover, the pattern of 'retirement slump' and 'second-term surge' has widespread effects making many seats slightly more or less safe than they might appear from the simple majorities. As one source of electoral change helping to explain variations in constituency results, alongside regional swing and tactical voting, the personal vote needs to be built into our equations.

13 Reforming recruitment

During the 1980s more women and black MPs entered the House of Commons. Nevertheless, the pace of change remains slow. If current trends are projected forwards on a linear basis, the number of women MPs would be only 100 by the year 2000, and would not achieve parity with men until the middle of the twenty-first century. The number of black MPs rose from four to six in the last general election, but this figure needs to more than quintuple to keep pace with the size of the ethnic population. MPs from the chattering class continue to expand at the expense of traditional working-class trade unionist. Any transformation in the social composition of parliament is a slow process of incremental change, which lags behind demands for political inclusion. The structure of opportunities in the British political system is narrowly constrained by low levels of incumbency turnover. Very few people become Labour or Conservative inheritors, or strong challengers, with serious prospects of being elected.

If the pace of change is to be quickened, in order to produce more women and black MPs before the year 2000, what else can be done? Whether, and how, this situation is perceived as a problem, and the alternative solutions acceptable to each party, depend upon each party's general values and ideology. Alternative models of recruitment to both the private and public spheres provide different ways of evaluating the selection process. This concluding chapter will compare these alternatives, consider what further steps could be taken by parties if they wish to increase the social diversity of parliament, and summarise the main results of this study.

Evaluative models of recruitment

The patronage model of recruitment

The traditional form of recruitment is based on patronage, through personal friendship, social links, family ties or financial influence. In traditional societies, particularly close-knit communities, the most important access to opportunities depends on personal contacts, that is, *who*, rather than *what*, you know. In eighteenth century Britain it was taken for granted that positions such as apprenticeships in factories, farm labourers, clerks in the civil service, seats on company boards, or political constituencies, should be handed down within families. It was assumed that the technical knowledge required for political life could be acquired on the job, whereas political skills and ability were questions of character. Applicants were evaluated on the basis of long familiarity within the same local community or social circles, not by formal interviews.

Recruitment by patronage is based on criteria of *acceptability*, meaning whether a person will fit into the organisation, based on informal, implicit and 'subjective' judgements. In political recruitment, the key question by these criteria is whether the applicant is 'one of us': party loyalty and personal character are seen as more important than policy expertise or formal qualifications. In most large-scale companies the influence of patronage has gradually although not wholly declined over the years. Patronage continues to remain important in political recruitment, however, due to the nature of the job. It is difficult to define the appropriate formal qualifications, or to specify the particular skills which might count, given the range of tasks politicians undertake. A legal training may seem most appropriate for legislators, but far from essential.

The meritocratic model of recruitment

In large-scale companies, the patronage model has been gradually displaced in advanced industrial societies by the meritocratic model. This suggests that as far as possible appointments should be made on the basis of 'objective' suitability at formal interview, not 'subjective' acceptability. Criteria of *suitability* means formal, functionally specific standards of performance, involving the technical, educational, or experiential qualifications required for a job. Such criteria tend to be 'objective' (i.e. externally validated), explicit, and standardised. Whether someone can be employed as a barrister, accountant or civil engineer, depends on criteria established by professional or technical bodies. These define the eligible population for a job, and set the minimum threshold barrier for rejecting applicants. The emphasis on formal qualifications and standardised entry procedures has increased over time with the rise of large-scale bureaucratic organisations, the increased specialisation of knowledge, the growth of higher education, the expansion of the professional and service sector, and also the demand for equal opportunities.

The meritocratic model has become so pervasive that its premises usually go unchallenged, and most other approaches are commonly seen as 'unfair'.

The model derives from theories of economic liberalism which give centrality to the market place. Recruitment decisions are conceptualised as selections of individuals who freely compete with each other for the desired post. Criteria of suitability are seen as formal and absolute, measured in terms of, say, certificates of education, completed apprenticeships or professional qualifications. Talent and ability are conceived as individual attributes. Meritocratic equal opportunities policies are about standardising practices, specifying the requirements of the job, reducing the role of tacit judgements, and devising mechanisms which ensure the enforcement of those rules. A classic example in the Victorian period was the replacement of nepotism and patronage in the British civil service by standardised entrance examinations.

Evidence for unfair recruitment in the meritocratic model would be a significant disparity between the supply of certain categories of applicants and their adoption as candidates. The meritocratic strategy suggests that spelling out the criteria of selection, and following through the implications, will prevent deliberate prejudice. In this model employers should advertise the qualifications for a vacancy, and judge applicants in the light of the formal job specification. In the meritocratic model, if two people come forward for a vacancy, it is seen as only fair that the applicant with more formal qualifications and work experience should be given the job, irrespective of any other considerations. The answer to any remaining inequalities of recruitment is to remove any obstacles to the free operation of the market, for example, by advertising vacancies more widely.

Yet the assumptions underlying the meritocratic model are open to serious criticism. Its results are often minimal increases in the recruitment of members of disadvantaged groups. It implies that the recruitment decision is reducible to technical requirements and denies the social basis in the acquisition of skill and qualifications.

Perhaps most importantly, it overlooks the fact that inequalities of power and authority in an organisation give groups different capacities to specify, interpret and operationalise rules in such a way that procedures may well reproduce inequalities. In the case of racial inequality, the meritocratic model assumes that ethnic minorities are denied opportunities because of stereotyped beliefs about their capacities. The meritocratic solution tries to correct this by adopting procedures which require employers to look objectively at candidates as individuals, rather than as exemplars of a group. For example, appointment committees are encouraged to evaluate applicants against an agreed check-list of job specifications, to formalise the requirements. Because the problem is defined as procedural, certain causes of inequality are untouched, and certain possible solutions are ruled out.

The affirmative action model of recruitment

Critics of the meritocratic model argue that formal criteria of suitability may be socially biased: power-holders may define knowledge and skills which the educational system institutionalises into qualifications. Such criteria may appear fair in theory, but in practice they are far from neutral. Just as there is not free competition in the labour market, so there is not free competition in the prior educational market. Proponents argue further that the acceptability criteria for jobs may also be socially biased, since terms such as 'talent' and 'ability' conceal a series of value judgements whereby they refer to behaviours and skills which are mainly possessed by the dominant group.

The affirmative action model suggests it is legitimate to waive criteria of suitability and acceptability to get the desired outcome. If the same number of men and women with 'identical' formal qualifications come forward for a management post, in a company which has employed few women in the past, in the affirmative action model it is fair to appoint only women until there is gender parity. These strategies are for the most part illegal in Britain, where it is widely believed that discrimination for or against women or ethnic minorities is unfair to those who possess the formal qualifications for the position. The strength of belief in the meritocratic model means that it is difficult to get such strategies accepted.

The radical model of recruitment

The meritocratic and affirmative action models were developed to achieve the goals of racial and class equality. Although there are many analogies between inequalities of race, class and gender, there are unique elements of each. Some argue that even if acceptable, policy based upon affirmative action would not bring about equal opportunity because it continues to give too much credence to the legitimacy of the basis on which jobs are offered.[1] It says that the only route to equality is to promote the less qualified. But this may misrepresent the nature of selection criteria. In the case of gender, Webb and Liff draw on feminist studies of occupational sectorialisation to show that women fail to be recruited, not because they cannot perform the required tasks, but because the formal suitability qualifications are defined in a gendered way! The characteristics of the labour market are such that men and women have different experience, training, education and work, as well as unequal domestic responsibilities. Meritocratic equal opportunities policies cannot get at the inappropriate definition of jobs because the strategy requires only that criteria of suitability are applied consistently.

The radical model suggests jobs need to be audited to establish the appropriate qualifications. This would involve restructuring the jobs, questioning the terms upon which they are offered, and challenging the full-time, continuous career model which characterises most high-status occupations. Especially for complex professional and managerial employment the specification of qualification criteria involves value judgements about skills and working practices which establish certain criteria as indicators of suitability. Question time and parliamentary debates are often given most publicity, nowadays through television. In contrast, far less attention is given to other activities which are a major part of MPs' work, such as detailed scrutiny of legislative bills in committee, or individual casework. The job of an MP may be defined in terms of aggressive debating ability, and applicants may be judged in this light. This gets fed back into the recruitment process, and further perpetuates the characteristics of those who hold office. If women are less comfortable with such debate, as some we interviewed suggested, this entrenches the gender division as the specifications lead to the recruitment of only one sex. We need to understand how political careers have been conventionally defined which might discourage certain categories of applicants. The radical model suggests we reanalyse the nature of the job of an MP, for example, reforming working conditions at Westminster.

The implications for party reform

What are the implications of these models for legislative recruitment? Each provides a different set of normative standards to evaluate the selection process, and a different range of solutions to overcome the social bias of parliament.

Reforms under the meritocratic model

The Conservative party provides the clearest example of a gradual transition from a patronage system based upon informal criteria of acceptability ('one of us') towards a more meritocratic system based on more formal criteria of suitability ('The right person for the job'). This change is clearly exemplified by the introduction of weekend selection boards, introduced due to concern about the influence of the 'old-school tie' on the image of the Conservative party, and the need to attract good quality candidates. The boards have many features of the meritocratic model: the criteria for evaluation are clearly listed on a check-list of qualities (communication skills, range of political experience, ability to get on with people, etc.) Applicants are evaluated by teams representing different parts of the party (MPs, regional agents, private sector advisors) so that standards are homogenised across the organisation. Boards use a series of tasks in different environments, so applicants are evaluated according to a range of social, communication and political skills. The full review process to get on the Approved List takes into account references, the formal application form, and a personal interview, as well as the board's activities. And, by meritocratic standards, as noted earlier, the outcome is fair. The proportion of women and ethnic minorities who applied to get on the Approved List is about the same as those who pass. The basic limitation of the system, however, is that few apply. In stressing equality of opportunity, the Conservatives have acknowledged the need to encourage more women to come forward for parliamentary seats, although they remain firmly opposed to any affirmative action to achieve this objective.

Information

What alternatives are available, within the meritocratic model, which might increase the proportion of women and ethnic minority candidates? The most acceptable proposals are about the provision of information, training, resources and revisions to the final selection interview. If competition for candidacies is to be fair, the selection process has to be transparent and clear. Accordingly a candidate advisory office could be established, and information leaflets could be produced, telling party members about the opportunities to become a parliamentary candidate, the main steps in the process, and providing detailed briefing packs about particular constituencies as vacancies arise. There would need to be a clear division of labour between the advisory office, concerned to let applicants know about opportunities, organise training sessions, and otherwise encourage participants, and the officers concerned with selection. Many candidates remarked that they depended upon informal networks, 'the grapevine', to learn about forthcoming selection meetings. Those well integrated with the party were able to seek advice from old hands at an early stage, for example about their interview presentation or which seats to pursue. Others we interviewed were clearly in the dark, occasionally trying for seats on an *ad hoc* basis.

Information and advice could make the process more efficient for everyone, and it could improve the quality of applicants willing to come forward, but it might also be of particular benefit for any 'out-groups'. Communications structures directed explicitly at women tend to be poorly articulated, underfunded and often channelled through overburdened branch secretaries and regional officers who may not prioritise information to women activists. Similar problems are faced by men, but at least some are redressed by union and business networks. As a result it may take more effort for women to link into the grapevine. The 300 Group provides a bi-partisan support network, sharing practical information and advice. In the Labour party the Labour Women's Network (LWN) helps with infor-

Table 13.1 *Approval of proposals by candidates*

% Approve/approve strongly	Con.	Lab.	Lib. Dem.	SNP	PC	Green	All
Party training programmes for women	71	97	92	93	90	91	86
Better childcare facilities in Parliament	62	99	98	98	95	96	86
Changing the hours of Parliamentary sittings	58	92	95	100	100	97	82
Positive quotas/affirmative action for women	6	75	49	42	53	52	42
Financial support for women candidates	6	59	32	47	42	55	34

Note: Q. 'Do you approve or disapprove of the following proposals for increasing the number of women in Parliament?'
Source: BCS, 1992.

mation and training, while Emily's List, UK (Early Money is Like Yeast) has recently been developed, following the American model, to assist women with the financial costs of candidacy.

Training
All parties offer some training for candidates, although practices vary. Most parties usually have one- or two-day sessions advising candidates about public speaking, media relations, television presentations, campaign strategy and organisation, and the legal requirements for elections. As shown in table 13.1, in all parties candidates expressed widespread approval of party training programmes to increase the number of women in parliament; indeed, this proved the most consensual option. Parties could take training further by four steps: giving guidance to applicants as well as candidates; expanding the length of training sessions; investing greater resources in this process rather than expecting participants to pay their own way; and last, but by no means least, training key selectors such as party agents and constituency officers.

Resources
As noted earlier, one factor discouraging some applicants from coming forward is the cost of attending interviews, especially those around the country where there may be expensive personal costs in travel and overnight accommodation, for a succession of meetings. More substantial personal expenses can be incurred once adopted, for regular trips to canvass or attend party meetings. At present most of these expenses are expected to be paid for by the applicants or candidates. There are discretionary funds available in the Conservative party, but there may be some reluctance to apply for

these. Some constituencies assist with local accommodation or travel, but there are no guarantees. Emily's List, UK is designed to help Labour women. If parties are concerned to attract the best applicants then they need to set aside resources so that, as with interviews in the private sector, some personal expenses are automatically covered.

Selection interviews

Lastly, the weekend selection boards used by the Conservatives and the Scottish National Party use a variety of exercises to test different skills among applicants: debates, group work, personal interviews, written work. Yet at the final stage all parties use a standard format: a half hour interview for each applicant in turn, with a brief speech followed by a question and answer session with party members. This short session may be decisive for the outcome. Yet the ability to perform well at interview may have little relation to the ability to perform as a candidate, still less as an MP or even cabinet minister. Speaking ability is only one of the qualities required for successful politicians. The process often involves a fairly lengthy meeting for members. Parties could consider alternative formats for the final interview, for example using brief speeches by each applicant followed by small 'Question Time' group discussions. Or supplementing interviews by asking applicants to write a two- or three-page briefing paper about an issue of local concern. Or, after interviews, bringing the top two candidates together for a 'presidential debate'. Different formats would reveal different skills and strengths, and, if carefully adjudicated, would be fair to all participants.

Reforms under the affirmative action model

Demands for increased representation by women and ethnic minorities grew significantly in all parties during the 1970s and 1980s. The greatest impact of this pressure has been felt by the Labour party, given the strength of the organised women's movement and black activists within this party, and to a lesser extent by the Liberal Democrats and Greens. As shown in table 13.1, few Conservatives, but three quarters of the Labour candidates, and about half of the Liberal Democrats and Greens, expressed approval for positive quotas or affirmative action to increase the number of women in parliament. The ideology within these parties made them most sympathetic to the idea of using these strategies.

Affirmative action has been applied in different ways. In the early 1980s the Social Democratic Party and the Liberals, later the Liberal Democrats, introduced gender quotas at the shortlisting stage. As discussed earlier, the Labour party followed suit in 1988. In June 1990 the Labour Women's

Conference adopted a far-reaching policy of positive action to increase the representation of women at all levels of the party. The conference called on the party to draw up a phased programme over the next ten years, or three general elections, so that at least 40 per cent of the parliamentary Labour party seats, and internal party posts, would be held by women. This was developed further in the NES women's committee until October 1993, when the Labour party conference passed a resolution to require all-women shortlists in half the party's inheritor and high prospect challenger seats, although it remains to be seen how this may be implemented. The use of gender quotas in elections to Labour's shadow cabinet also strengthened, with backbench MPs required to vote for four rather than three contestants in the women's section. There has been something of a backlash against these moves, but it is too early to say whether these will be reversed. On the basis of post-war trends in incumbency turnover, we can estimate that if Labour women candidates were adopted in half their inheritors and strong challengers seats, the number of Labour women MPs could perhaps rise from thirty-seven in 1992 to about sixty to seventy-five in the next general election, although this has to remain extremely approximate since the extent of the change depends upon the way the rules are implemented, the size of the two-party swing, the impact of redistricting, and the rate of Labour retirements.

What else could be done under this model? At present affirmative action has been applied most clearly at the shortlisting stage, and will perhaps be extended to the use of all-woman shortlists in good seats. In addition, affirmative action can also be used at the early stages of the process, by targeting resources, training and information to help encourage more women and ethnic minorities to come forward. Rather than helping with the personal expenses of all applicants, as the meritocratic model suggests, this would use limited resources more effectively to help certain under-represented groups.

A more radical proposal would be to change the status and composition of the national lists of Labour applicants, to allow affirmative action to operate here. At present there is no requirement that candidates must be drawn from an officially approved list or panel. If Labour leaders would like to increase the opportunities for women or ethnic minorities, this restricts their capacity to do so. The Labour party could give serious consideration to introducing one centrally approved official list from which all nominees would normally be drawn, as was the case in the 1950s. A national list would have several potential advantages. By itself it would not automatically help women, but it would allow the party to introduce minimum quotas on the list for women and ethnic minorities. This might be less controversial than establishing constituency-level quotas, for example, at the nomination or selection stages. It would allow the party to offer support services for candidates on the list, such as training programmes, or financial assistance for attending nomination meetings. It would enable the party to establish minimum qualifications for candidacy which could be widely known and understood, in order to reduce idiosyncratic selection decisions. Since candidates would already have official endorsement by the NEC, it would reduce the potential for intra-party conflict at the end of the candidate selection process, when constituencies feel committed to their choice and resent any attempted veto by the NEC.

At the same time, the system would still leave the final choice of candidate to the local constituency. Party headquarters could shape the overall balance of candidates on the approved list, but the final decision about who would represent the constituency would continue to be taken at local level. Constituencies would therefore retain their autonomy. Trade union involvement might be maintained by the simple requirement that trade union sponsored candidates would have to qualify for inclusion on the party's list as well as for approval by the unions. It would deliver more power over selection to the party centre: for this reason it might prove controversial and be difficult to get accepted. But it has significant advantages for the implementation of affirmative action.

Reforms under the radical model

Lastly the radical model suggests that the most fundamental reform needs to consider the nature of a parliamentary career, the demands of work at Westminster, and the way that the job is conventionally defined. Many working conditions in the House of Commons have slowly evolved from the 'gentleman's club' of the nineteenth century, when many MPs without independent incomes held outside practices as barristers in the Inner Temple or as financiers in the City. The hours of parliamentary business, starting in the early afternoon with occasional all night sittings, were designed to allow dual careers. Office facilities were minimal, on the assumption that members would spend most of their time debating in the main chamber, working in committees, or engaged in social meetings. Backup services, in the form of secretarial allowances and research facilities, are not generous by international standards. Although successive committees have considered reforms of these working conditions, fundamental changes have been put on the back burner.[2]

These conditions affect all candidates, but may have a greater impact in discouraging women, who may find it more difficult to combine the demands of a normal family life with the demands of Westminster. As we have seen women who do succeed in politics tend to be those who are either childless, or whose children have grown up and left home, whereas men MPs were far more likely to have young children at home. As shown in table 13.1, there was overwhelming bi-partisan support among candidates for improving childcare facilities in parliament, as well as changing the hours of parliamentary sittings. It can be argued that until the conditions and workload of a parliamentary career become more attractive for women, most of whom continue to have primary responsibilities for the family, many will be reluctant to come forward.

The most radical proposal would be to change the British political system. Proposed reforms to the electoral system are under discussion within the opposition parties. The Liberal Democrats have long pressed the case for changing to a system of Single Transferable Vote with small, multi-member seats. The Scottish Convention is debating the most appropriate arrangements for elections to a proposed Scottish Parliament, including among its objectives far greater participation by women. The Labour party is considering alternative systems for elections to the European and Westminster parliaments, including the majoritarian Supplementary Vote, and the more innovative Additional Member System, as used in Germany. John Smith favoured retaining the present system, but at the same time he proposed holding a referendum to put the issue before the public, following the New Zealand example. If a more proportional system of electoral reform were to be implemented, such as the Additional Member System with regional party lists, comparative evidence suggests this would probably lead to a rapid increase in women's representation. It remains to be seen how far the opposition parties will travel down the road towards wholesale reform, or whether they will be content with merely tinkering with the first-past-the-post system.

Conclusions

This book has sought to explore how and why the recruitment process produces a legislative elite which fails to reflect the diversity of British society. The primary results from this study suggest that on balance supply-side factors are the most persuasive explanation for this social bias. If we analyse the background of strata on the ladder of recruitment, adopted candidates usually reflect the pool of applicants who come forward. The gap between the lives of grassroots party members and applicants is far greater than the difference between applicants and candidates. This is clearest with the class and educational bias of the legislative elite, which can be attributed to the way well-educated, professional 'brokerage' jobs provide the career flexibility, financial resources, occupational security, and work conditions which facilitate the pursuit of a political career.

The pattern is more complex in terms of gender and race. Older women are the backbone of activists in the Conservative party but, perhaps because of traditional attitudes, lifestyle, and experience, few come forward as applicants. In contrast, in the Labour party more younger and middle-aged women are seeking candidacies, although they face difficulties securing inheritor seats. There are few black activists within the Conservative ranks, at any level, while in the Labour party applicants from the ethnic minorities may face problems from selectors, largely because of concerns about their electability. The power to pick the real winners who will get into parliament – the inheritors and strong challengers – lies largely in the hands of the grassroots Conservative and Labour party members rather than the electorate. But these members exercise choice within constraints, with supply-side factors tending to drive the outcome.

It follows that policy options directed at changing the resources and motivation of potential applicants, which encourage party members to consider seeking a parliamentary career, will probably prove most effective. But what would achieve this objective? Here there is no unanimity. The provision of more information and advice about the selection process, training for applicants and candidates, and resources to cover personal expenses could all help, and these options would probably command fairly widespread support, although they are unlikely to make more than a modest difference in the short term. Affirmative action would provide more targeted help for women and ethnic minorities, whether applied to approved lists or the shortlisting stage, although this may prove more controversial. Lastly, more radical reform of the nature of parliamentary work, which rethinks the demands of political careers, may make political life more attractive for many of those who are politically experienced, well qualified, talented and capable, who could make a valuable contribution to public life, but who currently never consider Westminster. Parliamentary representation is important for both symbolic and substantive reasons, for the legitimacy and vitality of British democracy and for the quality of the decisionmaking process. In the classic words of John Stuart Mill,

Parliament has an office ... to be at once the nation's Committee of Grievances, and its Congress of Opinions; an arena in which not only the general opinion of the nation, but that of every section in it, and as far as possible every eminent individual whom it contains, can produce itself in full light and challenge discussion; where every person in the country may count upon finding somebody who speaks for his mind.[3]

Or her mind. Until Westminster includes greater social diversity, reflecting the electorate at large, it will fail to be a parliament of all talents.

APPENDIX A

British Candidate Survey, 1992

(1) *Party members*: The survey of party members includes 1,634 Labour and Conservative activists who attended twenty-six selection meetings in constituencies throughout Britain. The constituencies to which we had access were chosen to be broadly representative in terms of party, major census region, and marginality. The seats were: Beckenham, Sutton and Cheam, Feltham and Heston, Croydon North East, Putney, Brentford and Isleworth, Eastleigh, Milton Keynes North East, Gloucester, Bristol West, Colne Valley, Ashfield, Dudley West, Stoke on Trent South, Warley East, Monmouth, Manchester Withington, Glanford and Scunthorpe, Leeds South and Morley, Oldham Central and Royton, Littleborough and Saddleworth, Edinburgh Central, Tweeddale, Ettrick and Lauderdale, Caithness and Sutherland, and Dumfries. Fieldwork was conducted from January 1990 to October 1991. The main questionnaire was distributed in person to members at meetings, and collected there, producing a response rate of 74 per cent. A more detailed follow-up postal questionnaire was given out for self-completion (with a response rate of 43 per cent of all members at the meeting).

(2) *MPs and candidates*: This survey includes 1,320 MPs and prospective parliamentary candidates who were selected by constituencies for the April 1992 general election at the time of the fieldwork. We included MPs and PPCs for the Conservative, Labour, Liberal Democrat, Scottish National, Plaid Cymru and Green parties. We excluded incumbent MPs who were retiring and independents. Fieldwork was conducted in two main waves, from April 1990 to October 1991. Respondents were sent a postal questionnaire with covering letter, a postcard reminder, and a full reminder a month later. Out of 1913 names, we received completed replies from 1,320, which represents a response rate of 69 per cent.

(3) *Applicants*: This survey includes 361 applicants who failed to be selected to become candidates. Respondents were selected using a random sample of one in three applicants on the Labour party 'A' and 'B' lists, and one in two names on the Conservative party Approved List, who had not been adopted by parliamentary constituencies. Respondents were sent the same questionnaire as above, following the same procedure. Out of 656 names we received replies from 361, which represents a response rate of 55 per cent.

(4) *Personal interviews*: To pursue questions about their experiences and motivation in greater depth the study includes thirty-nine hour-long personal interviews with MPs, PPCs and applicants. The list of respondents who agreed to a further interview was stratified by party, type (MP, PPC or

Appendix table 1   *MPs' and PPCs' response rate*

	Total	Surveyed	Replied	% response rate
Conservative	645	606	364	60
Labour	634	603	415	69
Liberal Democrat	632	399	320	80
Scottish National	72	66	59	89
Plaid Cymru	35	22	18	82
Green	250	217	144	66
Total	2,268	1,913	1,320	69

Appendix table 2   *Applicants' response rate*

	Total 1992	Sampled	Replied	% response rate
Conservative	800	400	232	58
Labour	768	256	129	50
Total	1,730	656	361	55

applicant) and gender. Using a stratified random sample we selected thirty-nine names for further interview after the election, from April to October 1992. During the course of the project we also conducted personal interviews with constituency activists, party agents and national party managers in all parties. To preserve anonymity, interviews are attributed by reference number.

(5) *Official documents:* The project included a review of official documents outlining party rules and procedures.

(6) *Meetings:* Research included observations of a range of Labour and Conservative selection meetings at different stages in the process, including Conservative weekend selection boards.

(7) *Voters:* Survey items were designed to be identical across different levels of party strata, as well as to be comparable with the British Election Study 1992, conducted by Anthony Heath et al.

(8) *Constituencies:* Aggregate data from constituencies was merged with the candidate file, including such factors as the demographic characteristics of the seat and its marginality.

The research focused on the Labour and Conservative parties, given two-party dominance in parliament, although the study of candidates includes all British parties for contrast and comparison. The surveys measured the social background, political experience and attitudes of the main actors involved in the process. Personal interviews allowed the opportunity to explore some of the findings of the survey data in greater depth. Throughout party officials gave us the fullest cooperation, assistance and support. The constituency meetings to which we had access were selected as broadly representative in terms of party, region and marginality. The response rate met, or often exceeded, expected standards for a postal survey.

APPENDIX B

Questionnaire: British Candidate Survey, 1992

SECTION A: POLITICAL BACKGROUND

First, we would like to ask you some questions about your political background.

1.   What is your current party affiliation?

Conservative 35.1
Labour/Coop 32.3
Liberal Democrat 19.2
Scottish Nationalist 3.6
Plaid Cymru 1.1
Green 8.6

2.   Are you currently an elected Member of Parliament?

Yes 14.8
No 85.2

3.   Are you a prospective parliamentary candidate for the coming general election?

Yes 78.1
No 21.9

If 'Yes', for which constituency are you standing:

_____

4.   When did you **first** join your present political party? 1974

5.   Has your party membership been **continuous** since then?

Yes 92.2
No 7.8

6. Have you ever been a member of another British political party?

Yes 20.0
No 80.0

If 'Yes', which one?

Conservative 6.0
Labour/Coop 18.6
Liberal 34.4
SDP 15.0
Scottish Nationalist 1.5
Plaid Cymru 1.5
Green 0.9
Other (please specify) _____ 20.0

7. What was your single **most important reason for joining** your present political party?

PLEASE WRITE IN

_____

_____

_____

_____

_____

8. Please tick if you have ever . . .

Held a local Party office 91.1
Held regional Party office 32.3
Held national Party office 19.4

Been a candidate for local government 78.9
Been elected to local government 52.3

Been a candidate for the European Parliament 7.2
Been elected to the European Parliament 1.0

Served on a local public body 55.7
Served on a national public body 11.6
Held office in a local pressure group 47.3
Held office in a national pressure group 21.8
Held office in other community groups 43.6

Held office in a professional body 22.1
Held office in a student organisation 32.4
Held office in a trade union 30.5
(For women only)
Held office in a women's organisation? 7.0

9. What are the **two** most responsible **political** positions you have held
outside of Parliament?

_____

_____

10. How much time do you usually devote to party activities in the
average month?

Up to 5 hours 5.1
From 5 to 10 hours 8.4
From 10 to 15 hours 9.7
From 15 to 20 hours 10.3
More than 20 hours 66.4

11. If you belong to any **party groups**, (for example the Fabian Society,
the Bow Group or the Tawney Society) could you please say which ones?

_____

_____

12. If you belong to any **pressure groups** (for example the Electoral Reform Society, the National Council for Civil Liberties, the Chamber of Commerce, the Trade's Council or Greenpeace) could you please say which ones?

_____

_____

13. Has anyone in your family been active in public life, or held political office? If so, please give details.

_____

_____

_____

14. Have you **stood** for Parliament before?

Yes 42.4
No 57.6

If '**Yes**' could you give brief details below?

	Candidate?	Elected?	Name of Constituency?
1945	Yes____	Yes____	_____
1950	Yes____	Yes____	_____
1951	Yes____	Yes____	_____
1955	Yes____	Yes____	_____
1959	Yes____	Yes____	_____
1964	Yes____	Yes____	_____
1966	Yes____	Yes____	_____
1970	Yes____	Yes____	_____
1974 (F)	Yes____	Yes____	_____
1974 (O)	Yes____	Yes____	_____
1979	Yes____	Yes____	_____
1983	Yes____	Yes____	_____
1987	Yes____	Yes____	_____
By-election 19__	Yes____	Yes____	_____

15.   Have your mother and father ever been **party members?**

	Mother	Father
Yes	44.0	42.4
No	56.0	57.6

If 'Yes', for which party?

	Mother	Father
Conservative	55.7	50.7
Labour/Coop	20.5	28.3
Liberal/Lib Dem/SD	14.6	11.7
Scottish Nationalist	2.0	1.8
Plaid Cymru	0.7	0.6
Green	1.0	0.1
Other	5.5	6.8

SECTION B: YOUR EXPERIENCE OF SELECTION

16.   What was the single most important reason why you **first** wanted to stand for Parliament?

PLEASE WRITE IN

_____

_____

_____

17.   Some people receive encouragement from those around them when they decide to stand for public office, while others experience indifference or disapproval.

How positive or negative were the following people in encouraging you to become a candidate in the next election?

	VERY POSITIVE	POSITIVE	NEUTRAL	NEGATIVE	VERY NEGATIVE
Your spouse or partner	42.8	33.5	15.7	5.4	2.6
Other family members	26.0	39.7	28.4	4.7	1.2
Personal friends	36.9	44.1	17.3	1.5	0.2
Women's groups/networks	22.4	24.6	48.5	2.6	2.0
Community groups	13.8	37.3	46.5	1.5	1.0
Business associates	11.3	33.6	44.0	8.6	2.4
Fellow trade unionists	23.7	30.8	39.6	3.4	2.5
Party members	59.1	35.0	4.9	0.6	0.4
Party agents	49.2	31.9	16.6	1.3	1.0
Employers	8.5	23.3	50.7	10.0	7.5

18.   For the coming general election:

For how many seats did you **apply**? 5.1

For how many were you **interviewed**? 2.0

For how many were you on the **final short-list**? 1.4

19.   In your **most recent shortlisting**:

How many were on the final shortlist? 3.0

How many were women? 0.6

How many were of Asian background? 0.1

How many were of Afro-Caribbean background? 0.1

20.   When originally deciding to apply for a constituency, how important were the following factors in influencing your choice of seats?

	VERY IMPORTANT	QUITE IMPORTANT	NOT VERY IMPORTANT	NOT AT ALL IMPORTANT
I already lived in the constituency	47.2	9.5	11.6	31.6
I chose seats close to my home	43.3	27.1	11.4	18.2
I chose seats in my region	37.7	29.7	11.9	20.7
I chose seats close to Westminster	1.5	3.6	12.9	82.1
I knew party members in the seat ..	32.0	21.2	14.7	32.0
I was asked to apply	41.6	19.1	9.7	29.6
I thought I could win the seat	39.5	21.4	15.5	23.5
I thought it would be good experience	35.9	29.9	12.7	21.6

FOR LABOUR PARTY ONLY:

21.   How many of the following branches nominated you in your most recent short-listing? And how many branches are there in the constituency?

	Total Who Nominated You	Total in Constituency
Branch sections	3.7	7.5
Trade Union sections	5.2	12.8
Cooperative sections	0.6	0.8
Women's sections	0.9	1.0
Socialist Societies	0.6	0.7
Other_____	0.7	0.7

FOR ALL RESPONDENTS:

22.   In your experience how important are the following qualities to party members when selecting their parliamentary candidate?

	VERY IMPORTANT	QUITE IMPORTANT	NOT VERY IMPORTANT	NOT AT ALL IMPORTANT
Good speaker	50.0	46.5	3.2	0.2
Personal energy/enthusiasm	77.3	21.5	1.0	0.2
Good personal appearance	26.5	57.6	14.4	1.6
Political experience	33.8	50.1	14.1	1.9
Stable home life	16.0	41.6	29.8	12.5
Supports members' views	24.4	55.2	18.1	2.3
Likely to win votes	50.9	39.3	7.7	2.1
Committed to constituency	63.2	30.2	5.9	0.6
Nationally well known	4.6	13.6	44.0	37.8
Local candidate	31.1	37.8	22.9	8.2
Well educated	10.2	51.9	31.3	6.7
Knowledgeable about issues	43.9	50.3	4.9	0.9
Experienced party worker	24.7	51.1	20.4	3.9

23.   In your view was the procedure used in your most recent selection application . . .

	VERY	QUITE	NOT VERY	NOT AT ALL
Democratic	54.9	35.0	8.5	1.6
Efficient	36.9	43.4	15.7	4.1
Complicated	16.6	34.1	33.0	32.8
Fair	52.3	37.9	7.1	2.7

24.   Do you think the influence the **national party leadership** has over the selection of Parliamentary is generally . . .

Far too great	4.2
Too great	8.7
About right	74.4
Too little	10.3
Far too little	2.4

25. Do think that the influence the **local party** has over the selection of parliamentary candidates is generally ...

Far too great	2.4
Too great	9.9
About right	79.7
Too little	6.7
Far too little	1.3

26. In your view how important are the following parts of an MP's job?

	VERY IMPORTANT	QUITE IMPORTANT	NOT VERY IMPORTANT	NOT AT ALL IMPORTANT
Speaking in parliament	22.7	58.0	17.7	1.6
Holding regular constituency surgeries	80.1	18.5	1.2	0.2
Attending local party meetings	40.3	51.0	7.6	1.2
Parliamentary committee work	35.4	52.2	11.2	1.1
Representing regional interests	32.2	48.7	16.1	3.0
Helping with individual problems	70.6	26.5	2.8	0.1
Supporting the party leader	21.7	52.7	19.0	6.6
Developing party policy	35.9	48.8	12.8	2.5
Voting the party line in parliament	20.7	51.8	17.8	9.7
Speaking to the national press & TV	29.2	50.5	18.2	2.0
Attending local community functions	42.0	50.2	7.1	0.8
Representing the constituency in parliament	83.3	16.1	0.5	0.2
Working with interest groups	18.9	55.3	22.5	3.3
Defending party policy	31.6	57.8	8.8	1.8

FOR ALL PROSPECTIVE CANDIDATES:

27a. In the next general election which party do you think
will **win** in your constituency?

Conservative	48.1
Labour	38.6
Liberal Democrat	8.8
SNP/PC	2.1
Other	2.4

27b. And which party do you think
will come **second**

Conservative	36.2
Labour	26.5
Liberal Democrat	27.7
SNP/PC	5.0
Other	4.6

28. Do you think the result in this seat will be
close or will one party win easily?

Close result	47.3
Win easily	45.7
Don't know	7.0

FOR MEMBERS OF PARLIAMENT ONLY:

29.   Can you tell me whether you agree or disagree with the following
statements about the work of Members of Parliament:

	AGREE STRONGLY	AGREE	DISAGREE	DISAGREE STRONGLY
MPs' casework has increased too much and ought to be reduced	15.8	39.0	38.6	6.6
Solving constituents' problems is one of the most worthwhile parts of my job	48.6	43.8	7.6	0.0
An active MP can increase his or her personal vote	51.0	44.6	4.4	0.0
MPs are elected to participate in government, not to act as unpaid social workers	13.6	36.6	40.3	9.5
Most people vote for the party not the individual candidate	44.6	50.2	4.4	0.8

FOR MEMBERS OF PARLIAMENT ONLY:

30.   Roughly about how many hours do you think you usually devote to the
following activities in the **average week** when the house is sitting?

Work in the Palace of Westminster:

Dealing with constituency casework .... 14.6 hours
Attending parliamentary debates on the floor of the House .... 7.9 hours
Working in parliamentary select committees .... 2.2 hours
Working in parliamentary standing committees .... 3.9 hours
Working in backbench party committees .... 2.6 hours
Informal meetings with other MPs .... 5.7 hours
Meeting with group representatives and delegates .... 3.6 hours

Work in your constituency

Holding constituency surgeries .... 3.1 hours
Attending local party meetings .... 2.4 hours
Attending other constituency functions .... 5.0 hours
Time travelling between Westminster and your constituency   6.7 hours

Total hours per week devoted to your work as an MP .... 66.1 hours

31. Turning to your political **correspondence**, in the average week about how many letters do you receive from **constituents**? 89.9
And about how many letters do you receive from **others**? 96.5

FOR ALL RESPONDENTS:

32. Which of the following two statements comes closest to your views about politicians?

Politicians should spend **more time listening to the views of ordinary people** 69.1

Or politicians should rely more on their **own judgement,** instead of on public opinion 27.2

Doesn't matter either way 3.2

33. Do you feel that there should be **many** more women in parliament, a **few** more, about the **same** as now, or **fewer** women in parliament?

Many more women 74.7
A few more women 18.0
Same as now 3.8
Fewer women 2.7

34. Would you agree or disagree with the following **explanations** of why there are few women in parliament?

	AGREE STRONGLY	AGREE	NEITHER	DISAGREE	DISAGREE STRONGLY	DK
Women don't come forward to be considered	19.6	51.6	7.9	14.0	4.5	2.4
Women lose votes	0.5	3.2	8.6	27.9	58.7	1.1
Women are not given the opportunity by parties	18.9	34.8	13.7	22.6	8.4	1.5
Women put their families above a career in parliament	12.7	54.4	17.0	9.0	2.9	4.1
Women don't have the right experience and education	0.2	2.3	4.3	25.0	67.9	0.3

Women are not suited to the job	0.5	1.1	3.9	20.5	73.5	0.4
Women don't have the confidence	2.4	24.9	12.9	25.2	33.7	1.0
Parliamentary life is impractical for women	1.6	6.7	8.1	25.3	56.2	2.0
Women are not interested in politics	0.3	3.9	6.4	27.4	61.2	0.7

35.   Do you approve or disapprove of the following **proposals** for increasing the number of women in parliament?

	APPROVE STRONGLY	APPROVE	DISAPPROVE	DISAPPROVE STRONGLY
Party training programmes for women	48.3	37.9	10.2	3.5
Positive quotas/affirmative action for women	20.4	21.9	24.9	32.8
Better childcare facilities in parliament	52.1	33.9	9.1	4.8
Changing the hours of parliamentary sittings	56.5	25.0	12.0	6.4
Financial support for women candidates	17.0	17.3	37.8	27.9

36.   Concerning MPs or Asian and Afro-Caribbean background, do you feel that there should be **many more**, a **few** more, about the **same** as now or **fewer** MPs?

Many more	44.1
A few more	43.4
Same as now	8.3
Fewer	1.1
Doesn't matter either way	3.1

37.   Would you agree or disagree with the following **explanations** of why there are so few Asian and Afro-Caribbean MPs?

	AGREE STRONGLY	AGREE	NEITHER	DISAGREE	DISAGREE STRONGLY	DK
They don't come forward to be considered	12.7	47.1	11.2	13.7	4.1	11.3
They lose votes	3.8	25.2	21.8	28.6	15.4	5.1
They are not given opportunity by parties	18.4	45.0	10.8	17.5	4.2	4.1
They don't have the right experience and education	0.7	7.3	12.5	39.6	37.4	2.5
They are not suited to the job	0.5	0.7	7.4	36.5	53.4	1.5
They don't have the confidence	1.4	19.4	15.4	29.3	28.8	5.7
They don't fit in to Parliament	0.8	3.7	8.6	34.4	50.1	2.4
They are not interested in politics	0.2	3.1	8.4	33.4	51.2	3.8

C: YOUR POLITICAL ATTITUDES

38.   What would you say are the **three** most urgent problems facing the country at the present time? Please list in order of priority.

i.   _____

ii.   _____

iii. _____

39.   In political matters some people talk about 'left' and 'right'. Where would you place **your views** on this scale?

Left						Right
4.9	22.9	25.6	13.0	17.3	14.6	1.6
1	2	3	4	5	6	7

40. And where would you place the views of your **constituency party** on this scale?

Left						Right
2.8	17.5	23.4	17.1	17.4	18.2	3.6
1	2	3	4	5	6	7

41. And lastly where would you place the views of your **party leader**?

Left						Right
0.9	9.2	29.4	23.7	26.6	9.2	1.1
1	2	3	4	5	6	7

42. Do you think the **government should or should not** do each of the following things, or doesn't it matter either way?

	DEFINITELY SHOULD	POSSIBLY SHOULD	DOES NOT MATTER	POSSIBLY SHOULD NOT	DEFINITELY SHOULD NOT
Spend more money to get rid of poverty	60.7	17.3	6.4	9.4	5.8
Encourage the growth of private medicine	15.0	13.1	8.4	12.1	50.1
Put more money into the NHS	59.7	22.0	6.8	8.2	2.9
Introduce stricter laws to regulate trade unions ...	7.1	15.3	17.2	24.9	34.1
Spend less on defence	39.2	27.8	3.3	15.4	14.0

43. Are you generally in favour of ...

More **nationalisation** of companies by government 32.9

More **privatisation** of companies by government 37.4

Or leaving things as they are now 28.9

44.   Suppose the government had to choose between the following three options. Which do you think it should choose?

Reduce taxes and spend less on health, education, and social benefits 4.7

Or keep taxes and spending on these services at the same level as now 26.8

Or increase taxes and spend more on health, education and social benefits 68.4

45.   If the government had to choose between keeping down inflation or keeping down unemployment, to which do you think it should give highest priority?

Keeping down inflation 33.5

Keeping down unemployment 20.4

Or both equally 45.6

46.   Do you think that trade unions in this country have:

Far too much power 3.7

Too much power 22.4

About right 42.6

Too little power 27.1

Far too little power 4.2

47.   And do you think that business and industry have:

Far too much power 24.1

Too much power 33.7

About right 33.4

Too little power 8.0

Far too little power 0.7

48.   Which, if either, of these two statements comes closest to your own opinion on British nuclear weapons?

Britain should rid itself of nuclear weapons while persuading others to do the same 32.9

Or Britain should keep its nuclear weapons until we persuade others to reduce theirs 33.3

Or neither of these 32.8

49. On the whole, do you think the UK's interests are better served by

closer links with **Western Europe** 61.1

or closer links with **America?** 3.6

or – **both equally** 35.2

50. People hold different views about how they would like to see the **European Community** develop. Which of these statements comes closest to your own view?

A **fully integrated Europe** with most major decisions
taken by a European government 18.8

A Europe **more integrated than now** but with decisions
that mainly affect Britain staying in British hands 60.2

The **situation much as it is now**, with Britain retaining
a veto over major policy changes it does not like 17.1

Complete **British withdrawal** from the European Commu-
nity 3.9

51. There is a lot of talk these days about what the aims of the country should be for the next ten years. If you had to choose between the following items, which seems **most important**, and **next most important**, to you?

	Most Impt	Next Most Impt
Maintaining order in the nation	14.9	17.1
Giving people more say in important government decisions	49.1	15.4
Fighting rising prices	20.4	24.1
Protecting freedom of speech	15.6	43.4

52. Can you tell me how far you agree or disagree with the following statements:

	AGREE STRONGLY	AGREE	NEITHER	DISAGREE	DISAGREE STRONGLY	DK
Young people today don't have enough respect for traditional British values	4.8	18.5	31.2	31.3	10.8	3.5
Censorship of films and magazines is necessary to uphold moral standards	5.8	26.9	12.9	35.6	17.8	1.0
People should be allowed to organise public meetings to protest against the government	60.4	36.2	1.3	1.3	0.9	0.1
Homosexual relations are always wrong	4.9	6.9	12.9	29.6	44.6	1.1
People in Britain should be more tolerant of those who lead unconventional lives	35.9	42.0	14.4	5.7	1.7	0.4
Even political parties which wish to overthrow democracy should not be banned	12.5	41.7	8.0	22.9	13.4	1.5
The death penalty is never an appropriate sentence	53.5	17.1	2.7	14.6	11.7	0.4
Schools should teach children to obey authority	12.8	34.5	21.1	21.7	9.0	0.8
Ordinary people get their fair share of the nation's wealth	7.1	21.5	9.4	23.0	38.0	0.9
There is one law for the rich and one for the poor	32.6	29.8	7.3	16.3	13.7	0.4
There is no need for strong trade unions to protect employees' working conditions and wages	4.0	14.2	9.5	37.1	35.2	0.1
Private enterprise is the best way to solve Britain's economic resources	24.2	20.5	13.7	21.3	18.8	1.4

Major public services and industries ought to be in state ownership	17.0	24.3	14.8	17.5	25.4	1.0
It is government's responsibility to provide a job for everyone who wants one	8.2	22.3	14.9	28.5	25.6	0.6
There should be more severe punishments	14.1	50.4	20.3	12.1	1.5	1.6
Rape in marriage should be a crime	36.9	45.8	8.2	6.3	1.5	1.4
During the first 12 weeks of pregnancy the law should not restrict a woman having an abortion	35.6	33.5	7.1	11.9	10.4	1.6

53. An issue in **Scotland and Wales** is the question of an elected Assembly – a special parliaments dealing with Scottish and Welsh affairs. Which of these statements comes closest to your view?

	Scotland	Wales
Scotland and Wales should become **independent,** separate from the UK and the European Community	2.4	2.2
Scotland and Wales should become **independent,** separate from the UK **but part of the European Community**	13.9	11.6
Scotland and Wales should remain part of the UK but with their own **devolved Assemblies** with some taxation and spending powers	55.7	54.2
There should be **no change** from the present system	28.0	32.1

54.   Next we want to ask you about some changes that have been happening in Britain over the years. For each one can you say whether it has gone too far, not far enough, or is it about right.

	GONE MUCH TOO FAR	GONE TOO FAR	ABOUT RIGHT	NOT FAR ENOUGH	NOT NEARLY FAR ENOUGH
Welfare benefits that are available to people today?	6.2	6.5	27.7	37.4	21.8
Attempts to give equal opportunities to women in Britain?	3.0	4.8	27.0	38.6	26.5
The building of nuclear power stations?	44.8	14.2	23.0	13.6	3.1
Attempts to give equal opportunities to black people and Asians in Britain?	3.4	6.0	27.3	38.1	24.4
The availability of abortion on the NHS?	11.1	9.7	43.4	22.5	8.7

D: YOUR PERSONAL BACKGROUND

Finally we would like to ask you some questions about your social background.

55.   In what **year** were you born? 1948

56.   Are you   Male 79.9
                              Female 20.1

57.   What is your present **marital status?**

                              Married 69.6
                              Widowed 1.0
                              Divorced 6.4
                              Single 20.6
                              Separated 2.3

58. Do you have any **children** in your care who are aged

	Under 5	5–15 yrs
No	79.7	62.6
Yes	20.2	37.4
If 'Yes' how many?	1.4	1.8

59. How old were you when you completed continuous **education**?   20.3

60. Have you a university or polytechnic **degree**?

No	30.7
Yes	69.3

If 'Yes', where did you take your first degree?

_____

61. Which type of **school** did you last attend full-time?

Secondary Modern	9.1
Technical	3.1
Comprehensive	15.2
Grammar	35.5
Direct Grant	6.3
Junior Secondary	0.5
Senior Secondary	4.3
Grant aided	1.2
Independent Freepaying	23.1
Primary/Elementary	0.4
Other	1.5

If **private** (fee-paying), which school?

_____

62. Are your currently a **member** of trade union or staff association?

Yes Trade Union	46.9
Yes Staff Assoc.	2.9
No	50.2

63.   Are you a **union sponsored** candidate?

Yes 8.5

No 91.5

If Yes, which union?_____

64.   Which of these best describes what you were doing last week? If you are an MP, which best describes your occupation immediately prior to being elected?

In full-time education 0.8

In paid work 93.4

Registered unemployed 2.4

Wholly retired from work 1.0

Looking after the home 1.7

Other ...... _____ 0.8

65.   If currently employed, please describe your occupation and employer. If an MP, please describe your occupation and employer immediately prior to being elected.

Occupation: _____

_____

Employer: _____

66. Please tick to show which best describes the sort of work you, and your partner/spouse, do. **If you are an MP,** or not working now, please indicate what you did in your job immediately prior to being elected.

	Self	Spouse
Farmer or farm manager	1.9	1.2
Farm worker	0.0	0.2
Skilled manual work (for example: plumber, electrician, fitter, train driver, cook, hairdresser).	3.0	2.4
Semi-skilled or unskilled manual work (for example: machine operator, postman, waitress, cleaner, labourer)	1.2	2.6
Professional or technical work (for example: doctor, accountant, school teacher, social worker)	57.0	52.8
Manager or administrator (for example: company director, manager, executive, local authority officer)	32.4	16.8
Clerical (for example: clerk, secretary, telephone operator)	2.4	10.8
Sales (for example: commercial traveller, shop assistant)	1.4	2.1
Other (please describe). _____	0.7	11.0

67. Which **sector** you are employed in? If an MP, which sector were you employed in immediately **prior** to being elected?

Small business	32.4
Large business	19.9
Central government	2.3
Local government	9.5
Law	7.5
Education	9.5
Health service	21.2
Nationalised industry	2.5

68. Do you ever think of your self as belonging to any particular **social class?**

Yes	51.9
No	48.1

If 'Yes', which class is that?

_____

69. In your main **accommodation** do you, or your household:

Own the property	91.8
Rent from your Local Authority	1.9
Rent from a private landlord	5.5
Rent from a Housing Association	0.7

70. Which **ethnic** grouping do you belong to?

White	97.9
Black-Caribbean	0.2
Black-African	0.1
Black-Other	0.6
Indian	0.1
Pakistani	0.1
Bangladeshi	0.1
Chinese	0.1
Any other ethnic group	1.0

71. Do you regard yourself as belonging to any particular **religion?**

Yes	58.9
No	40.9

If 'Yes' which one?_____

72. Is your household's total **income?**..

Less than £5,000	2.0
£5,000 – 10,000	4.7
£10,000 – 20,000	19.1
£20,000 – 30,000	24.2
£30,000 – 40,000	18.4
£40,000 – 50,000	12.1
£50,000 +	19.4

73.   Where were you living when you were 14?

Village, town, city _____   County_____

And where do you live now?

Village, town, city _____   County_____

74.   Would you be willing to help the project further with a brief interview?

Yes   _____
No   _____

If 'Yes' could you give a telephone number:

Tel Home: _____   Tel Work: _____

75.   If you would like to know about the results when they are published please tick here   _____

Many thanks for completing the questionnaire.

Notes

1. PUZZLES IN POLITICAL RECRUITMENT

1 For reviews of the comparative literature see Moshe M. Czudnowski 'Political Recruitment' in Fred I. Greenstein and Nelson Polsby (eds.), *Handbook of Political Science*, Vol 2, *Micropolitial Theory* (Reading MA, Addison-Wesley, 1975); Donald Matthews, 'Legislative Recruitment and Legislative Careers' in Gerhard Loewenberg, Samuel Patterson and Malcolm Jewell (eds.), *Handbook of Legislative Research* (Cambridge MA, Harvard University Press, 1985); Linda Fowler, *Candidates, Congress and the American Democracy* (Ann Arbor MI, University of Michigan Press, 1993); Leon Epstein, *Political Parties in Western Democracies* (New Brunswick NJ, Transaction Books, 1980); M. Gallagher and M. Marsh (eds.), *Candidate Selection in Comparative Perspective* (London, Sage, 1988); Gerhard Loewenberg and Samuel C. Patterson, *Comparing Legislatures* (Boston, Little, Brown and Company, 1979); Michael Mezey, *Comparative Legislatures* (Durham, NC, Duke University Press, 1979); Pippa Norris, R. K. Carty, Lynda Erickson, Joni Lovenduski and Marian Simms, 'Party Selectorates in Australia, Britain and Canada: Prolegomena for Research in the 1990s', *The Journal of Commonwealth and Comparative Politics*, 28, (2 July 1990), pp. 219–45; Austin Ranney 'Candidate Selection', in D. Butler, H. Penniman and A. Ranney, *Democracy at the Polls* (Washington DC, American Enterprise Institute, 1981); Lyn Ragsdale, 'Legislative Elections' in Loewenberg, Patterson and Jewell, *Handbook of Legislative Research*.

2 For a review of elitist theory see Robert Putnam, *The Comparative Study of Political Elites* (Englewood Cliffs NJ, Prentice-Hall, 1976); T. B. Bottomore *Elites and Society* (New York, Basic Books, 1964); Geraint Parry, *Political Elites* (New York, Praeger, 1969). For a recent summary of the neo-marxist perspective see John Scott, *Who Rules Britain?* (Oxford, Polity Press, 1991).

3 For an overview of the literature on women see Vicky Randall, *Women and Politics*, 2nd edn (London, Macmillan, 1989) and on race see Muhammad Anwar, *Race and Politics* (London, Tavistock, 1986).

4 Harold Lasswell, David Lerner and C. Easton Rothwell, *The Comparative Study of Elites* (Stanford CA, Stanford University Press, 1952).

5 See Bruce Cain, John Ferejohn and Morris Fiorina, *The Personal Vote: Constituency Service and Electoral Independence* (Cambridge MA, Harvard University Press, 1987).

6 Gordon Black, 'A Theory of Political Ambition: Career Choices and the Role of Structural Incentives', *American Political Science Review*, 66 (1972) pp. 144–159;

Jeffrey Banks and D. Roderick Kiewiet 'Explaining Patterns of Candidate Competition in Congressional Elections', *American Journal of Political Science*, 33 (1989) pp. 997–1015; Paul Abramson, John H. Aldrich and David W. Rohde 'Progressive Ambition amoung United States Senators', *Journal of Politics*, 48 (1986) pp. 433–9.

7 See Philip W. Buck, *Amateurs and Professionals in British Politics, 1918–59* (Chicago, University of Chicago Press, 1963); Anthony King, 'The Rise of Career Politicians in Britain – and its Consequences', *British Journal of Political Science* (July 1981), pp. 249–63.

8 For comprehensive reviews of the literature see Moshe M.Czudnowski, 'Political Recruitment' in Fred Greenstein and Nelson Polsby (eds.), *Handbook of Political Science: Micropolitical Theory* (Reading MA, Addison-Wesley, 1985), pp. 178–86; Donald Matthews, 'Legislative Recruitment and Legislative Careers' in Gerhard Loewenberg, Samuel Patterson and Malcolm Jewell (eds.) *Handbook of Legislative Research* pp. 24–6; Lynda L. Fowler, *Candidates, Congress and the American Democracy.*

9 This definition refers to multi-party marginals, that is those where the difference between the parties in first and second place is less than 10 per cent. From 1955 to 1992 about 73 per cent of seats can be seen as safe by this definition. See Pippa Norris and Ivor Crewe, 'The British Marginals Never Vanished: Proportionality and Exaggeration in the British Electoral System Revisited', *Electoral Studies*, (June 1994).

10 It should be noted that the only exceptions for Cabinet office are entry via the House of Lords.

11 M. Ostrogorski *Democracy and the Organization of Political Parties* (New Brunswick NJ, Transaction Books, 1982).

12 E. E. Schnatterschneider, *Party Government* (New York, Holt, Rinehart and Winston, 1942) p. 64.

13 Austin Ranney, 'Candidate Selection' in David Butler, Howard R. Penniman and Austin Ranney, *Democracy at the Polls*, p. 103.

14 See chapter 10.

15 For studies of the process in Italy and France see chapters 4 and 7 in Michael Gallagher and Michael Marsh (eds.), *Candidate Selection in Comparative Perspective* (London, Sage, 1988).

16 M. Ostrogorski, *Democracy and the Organization of Political Parties.*

17 See Norman Gash, 'From the Origins to Sir Robert Peel' in Lord Blake (eds.), *The Conservatives: A History of their Origins to 1965* (London, George Allen and Unwin, 1977), pp. 66–9; Robert Stewart, *The Foundation of the Conservative Party* (London, Longman, 1978) pp. 142–6; G. K. Roberts, *Political Parties and Pressure Groups in Britain* (London, Weidenfeld and Nicolson, 1970); A. Beattie (ed.), *English Party Politics*, (London, Weidenfeld and Nicolson, 1970); David Judge, *The Parliamentary State* (London, Sage, 1993) pp. 73–85; F. O'Gorman, *Voters, Patrons and Parties* (Oxford, Clarendon Press, 1989).

18 Samuel H. Beer *Modern British Politics* (London, Faber and Faber, 1982) pp. 48–52.

19 M. Ostrogorski *Democracy and the Organization of Political Parties.*

20 See H. J. Hanham, *Elections and Party Management: Politics in the Time of Disraeli and Gladstone*, 2nd edn. (London, Harvester Press, 1978) pp. 125–54;

J. R. Vincent, *The Formation of the British Liberal Party, 1857–1868* (The Harvester Press, 1976).

21 Samuel H. Beer, *Modern British Politics* p. 53.

22 R. T. McKenzie *British Political Parties*, 2nd edn. (London, Mercury Books, 1963).

23 R. T. McKenzie *British Political Parties*, pp. 253, 556.

24 See Peter Richards, *Honourable Members* (London, Faber and Faber, 1964) ch 7.

25 In *Pathways to Parliament* Austin Ranney interviewed about forty party officials, candidates and MPs from 1961 to 1962. He combined this information with the political characteristics of their constituencies, and the social background of candidates adopted from 1951 to 1964, using aggregate data. See Austin Ranney, *Pathways to Parliament* (London, Macmillan, 1965). See also Austin Ranney, 'Candidate Selection and Party Cohesion in Britain and the United States' in William J. Crotty, *Approaches to the Study of Party Organisation* (Boston, Allyn and Bacon, 1968); Austin Ranney, 'Candidate Selection' in David Butler et al., *Democracy at the Polls* (Washington DC, American Enterprise Institute, 1981). Michael Rush studied the social background of Conservative and Labour parliamentary candidates from April 1950 to March 1966, along with detailed case-studies of the process in particular constituencies, for *The Selection of Parliamentary Candidates* (London, Nelson 1969); see also Michael Rush, 'The Selectorate Revisited', *Teaching Politics*, 15:1, (1986).
See also Edward G. Janosik *Constituency Labour Parties in Britain* (London, Pall Mall Press, 1968) ch. 5. For a comparative study at this time see Leon Epstein, 'Chapter VIII: Candidate Selection' in *Political Parties in Western Democracies* (London, Pall Mall Press, 1967).

26 Peter Paterson, *The Selectorate* (London, Macmillan, 1966).

27 *Report of the Hansard Society Commission on Electoral Reform* (London, Hansard Society, 1976) pp. 18–19. See also S. E. Finer, *The Changing British Party System, 1945–1979* (Washington DC, AEI Press, 1980) pp. 213–4.

28 Eric Shaw, *Discipline and Discord in the Labour Party* (Manchester, Manchester University Press, 1988); D. Kogan and M. Kogan, *The Battle for the Labour Party* (London, Fontana, 1982); Patrick Seyd, *The Rise and Fall of the Labour Left* (London, Macmillan, 1987). For a detailed account of one de-selection battle see Robert Kilroy-Silk, *Hard Labour* (London, Chatto and Windus, 1986).

29 For the party debate about mandatory reselection see Alison Young, *The Reselection of MPs* (London, Heinemann, 1983).

30 See Louis Minkin, *The Contentious Alliance* (Edinburgh, Edinburgh University Press, 1992).

31 See R. T. McKenzie, *British Political Parties*, 2nd edn (London, Mercury Books, 1963) pp. 250–3, 549–57.

32 See John Bochel and David Denver, 'Candidate Selection in the Labour Party: What the Selectors Seek' in *British Journal of Political Science*, 13, (1988), pp. 45–69; David Denver, 'Britain: Centralised Parties with Decentralised Selection' in M. Gallagher and M. Marsh (eds.), *Candidate Selection in Comparative Perspective* (London, Sage, 1988).

33 There have been major membership surveys of all the main parties: Labour, Conservative, Liberal Democrat, SDP, the SNP and the Greens. The main publications from these studies are as follows: Patrick Seyd and Paul Whiteley,

Labour's Grass Roots: The Politics of Party Membership (Clarendon Press, Oxford, 1992); Paul Whiteley and Patrick Seyd, *True Blues: The Politics of Conservative Party Membership* (Clarendon Press, Oxford, 1994); Lynn G. Bennie, John Curtice and Wolfgang Rudig, 'Liberal, Social Democrat or Liberal Democrat? Political Identity and British Center Party Politics', Paper presented at the Annual Conference of the PSA Specialist Group on Elections, Parties and Public Opinion, University of Lancaster, 17–19 September 1993; John Curtice, Wolfgang Rudig and Lynn Bennie, *Liberal Democrats Reveal All* (Glasgow, Strathclyde Paper No. 96, 1993); David Denver and Hugh Bochel, 'Merger or Bust: Whatever Happened to Members of the SDP?' Paper presented at the Annual Conference of the PSA Specialist Group on Elections, Parties and Public Opinion, University of Lancaster, 17–19 September 1993; Wolfgang Rudig, Lynn Bennie and Mark Franklin, *Green Party Members: A Profile* (Glasgow, Delta Publications, 1991).

34 For a review of elite theory see Geraint Parry, *Political Elites*.

35 J. A. Thomas, *The House of Commons, 1832–1901: A Study of its Economic and Functional Character* (Cardiff, University of Wales Press, 1939).

36 J. F. S. Ross *Parliamentary Representation* (New Haven CT, Yale University Press, 1944), p. 116; J. F. S. Ross, *Elections and Electors* (London, Eyre and Spottiswoode, 1955).

37 See W. L. Guttsman, *The British Political Elite* (London, MacGibbon and Kee, 1968); Geraint Parry, *Political Elites*; T. B. Bottomore, *Elites and Society*; Anthony Samson, *The Anatomy of Britain* (London, Hodder and Stoughton, 1962).

38 No mention of the underrepresentation of women in Parliament could be identified throughout the book, except for one concerning the membership of Royal Commissions and government committees. Nor was Guttsman alone in the neglect of gender representation. For a review see S. Borque and J. Grossholtz, 'Politics an Unnatural Practice: Political Science Looks at Female Participation', *Politics and Society*, 4, 4 (1974).

39 Colin Mellors, *The British MP: A Socio-economic study of the House of Commons* (Hants, Saxon House, 1978).

40 See Martin Burch and Michael Moran, 'The Changing Political Elite', *Parliamentary Affairs*, 38, 1 (1985), pp. 1–15; Dennis Kavanagh, 'The Political Class and Its Culture,' *Parliamentary Affairs* 45, 1 (January 1992) 18–32; Peter Richards *The Backbenchers* (London, Faber and Faber, 1972), pp. 11–23; John Scott, *Who Rules Britain?* (Cambridge, Polity Press, 1991), pp. 124–152; Byron Criddle, 'MPs and Candidates', in David Butler and Dennis Kavanagh (eds.), *The British General Election of 1992* (London, Macmillan, 1992). See also previous chapters in Nuffield series by David Butler et al., *The British General Election* (London, Macmillan, 1950–); Anthony Sampson *The Changing Anatomy of Britain*.

41 R. D. Putnam, *The Comparative Study of Political Elites*; G. Loewenberg and S. C. Patterson, *Comparing Legislatures*; J. D. Aberbach, R. D. Putnam and B. A. Rockman, *Bureaucrats and Politicians in Western Democracies* (Cambridge MA, Harvard University Press, 1981), pp. 40–83.

42 See Martin Burch and Michael Moran, 'The Changing Political Elite'.

43 In 1945, 83 per cent of Conservative MPs and 19 per cent of Labour MPs had attended public school. In 1992 the figures were 62 per cent and 14 per cent respectively. There has also been a decline in the number from Oxford and

Cambridge although in 1992 one third of all MPs had been educated there. See Burch and Moran, 'The Changing Political Elite'; Criddle, 'MPs and Candidates'; George Borthwick, Daniel Ellingworth, Colin Bell and Donald MacKenzie, 'The Social Background of British MPs' *Sociology*, 25, 4 (November 1991), pp. 713–17.

44 It should be noted that the term 'black' will be used to refer to ethnic identification based on the 1991 Census definitions including Black Caribbean, Black African and Black other.

45 See W. L. Guttsman, *The British Political Elite*.

46 See Martin Holland, 'The Selection of Parliamentary Candidates: Contemporary Developments and the Impact of the European Elections', *Parliamentary Affairs*, 34, 2 (1981).

47 Jenny Chapman, *Politics, Feminism and the Reformation of Gender* (London, Routledge, 1993).

48 S. E. Finer, H. B. Berrington and D. J. Bartholomew, *Backbench Opinion in the House of Commons, 1955–59* (Oxford, Pergamon Press, 1961); Hugh Berrington *Backbench Opinion in the House of Commons 1945–55*, (Oxford, Pergamon Press, 1973).

49 Philip Norton, *Conservative Dissidents* (London, Temple Smith, 1978); Philip Norton, 'The House of Commons: Behavioural Changes' in Philip Norton (ed.) *Parliament in the 1980s* (Oxford, Basil Blackwell, 1985), pp. 22–47; Philip Norton, 'Independence, Scrutiny and Rationalisation: A Decade of Changes in the House of Commons', *Teaching Politics* 15, 1 (1986), pp. 69–98; Philip Norton, *Dissension in the House of Commons 1945–1979* (Oxford, Clarendon Press, 1980).

50 See Susan Welch, 'Are Women More Liberal than Men in the US Congress?' *Legislative Studies Quarterly*, (February 1985), pp. 125–34.

51 See Donald D. Searing, 'New Roles for Postwar British Politics: Ideologues, Generalists, Specialists and the Progress of Professionalisation of Parliament', *Comparative Politics*, (1987) 19, 4 pp. 431–53; Donald Searing, 'The Role of the Good Constituency Member and the Practice of Representation in Great Britain', *Journal of Politics*, 47 (May 1985), pp. 348–81; J. Vincent Buck and Bruce E. Cain, 'British MPs in Their Constituencies' *Legislative Studies Quarterly*, 15 (February 1990), pp. 127–43; Bruce E. Cain, John A. Ferejohn and Morris P. Fiorina, *The Personal Vote: Constituency Service and Electoral Independence* (Cambridge MA, Harvard University Press, 1987); Philip Norton and David Wood, 'Constituency Service by Members of Parliament: Does it Contribute to a Personal Vote?' *Parliamentary Affairs*, 43, 2 (April 199)), pp. 196–208.

52 Moshe M. Czudnowski, 'Political Recruitment'.

53 See Donald Matthews, 'Legislative Recruitment and Legislative Careers'.

54 The BCS survey was compared with the larger Whiteley and Seyd survey of Labour party members (N = 5071). This confirmed that selectors are broadly socially representative of all members. Pat Seyd and Paul Whiteley, *Labour's Grassroots*.

55 It should be noted that throughout this book the term 'applicant' refers to those on the national lists of applicants. It does not refer to those who apply to particular constituencies. Further, the Labour and Conservative lists are not wholly comparable. The Conservative list is based on candidates approved by Conservative Central Office, therefore some 'applicants' have already been

weeded out. In contrast the Labour 'A' (Trade Union nominees) and 'B' (constituency nominees) has not been approved by the National Executive Council.
56 The authors are most grateful to the principal investigators for this data: Anthony Heath, Roger Jowell and John Curtice.
57 Derived from Ivor Crewe and Anthony Fox, *British Parliamentary Constituencies* (London, Faber, 1984).

2. THE STRUCTURE OF POLITICAL RECRUITMENT

1 Gordon Black, 'A Theory of Political Ambition: Career Choices and the Role of Structural Incentives', *American Political Science Review*, 66(1972), pp. 144–59; David Rohde, 'Risk Bearing and Progressive Ambition: The Case of Members of the United States House of Representatives', *American Journal of Political Science*, 23(1979), pp. 1–26; Linda Fowler and Robert McClure, *Political Ambition: Who Decides to Run for Congress* (New Haven CT, Yale University Press, 1989); Linda Fowler, *Candidates, Congress and the American Democracy* (Ann Arbor MI, University of Michigan Press, 1993).
2 Joseph Schlesinger, *Ambition and Politics: Political Careers in the United States* (Chicago, Rand McNally and Co, 1966); Joseph Schlesinger, *Political Parties and the Winning of Office* (Ann Arbor MI, University of Michigan Press, 1991).
3 David Rohde, 'Risk bearing and progressive ambition'.
4 John R.Hibbing, 'The Career Paths of Members of Congress', in Shirley Williams and Edward Lascher, *Ambition and Beyond* (Berkeley CA, University of Berkeley Press, 1993), pp. 130–1.
5 See, for example, Alan Ehrenhalt, *The United States of Ambition* (New York, Times Books, 1992).
6 Joseph A. Schlesinger, *Political Parties and the Winning of Office*, ch 9.
7 Labour MP No. 30.
8 Interview No. 20.
9 Pippa Norris, Andrew Geddes and Joni Lovenduski, 'Race and Parliamentary Representation', in Pippa Norris et al. (eds.), *British Elections and Parties Yearbook, 1992* (Hemel Hempstead, Harvester Wheatsheaf, 1992), p. 94.
10 Shirley Williams, 'Introduction', in *Ambition and Beyond*, p. 1.
11 It should be noted that in the 1992 election the division of Milton Keynes into two constituencies created an open seat without an incumbent or inheritor.
12 It should be noted that others entered through the by-election route, as discussed later.
13 For full details see J. A. G. Griffith and Michael Ryle, *Parliament: Functions, Practice and Procedures* (London Sweet and Maxwell, 1989), pp. 47–8.
14 The last case of an election being declared void due to bribery or corrupt practices was Oxford in 1923. F. W. S. Craig, *British Electoral Facts 1832–1987* (Aldershot: Parliamentary Research Services/Gower, 1989), appendix 12.
15 In the last case in 1955 P. C. Clarke (Fermanagh and South Tyrone) was disqualified as a felon.
16 This was established in the *Peerage Act 1963* after Tony Benn (Viscount Stansgate) was disqualified when elected the Labour MP in the 1961 Bristol South East by-election.
17 Matthew Cole, *Parliamentary Affairs*, January 1992.

18 See Pippa Norris, *British Byelections: The Volatile Electorate* (Oxford, Oxford University Press, 1991).
19 For details see F. W. S. Craig, *British Electoral Facts*, appendix 12–16.
20 Michael Gallagher, 'Conclusion', in Michael Gallagher and Michael Marsh, *Candidate Selection in Comparative Perspective* (London, Sage, 1988), p. 257; see also Austin Ranney, 'Candidate Selection', in David Butler, Howard R. Penniman and Austin Ranney, *Democracy at the Polls* (Washington DC, American Enterprise Institute, 1981).
21 These connections may not be very strong in Britain, but in countries with party list systems the ties between citizens and their representatives would be weakened, or even severed, since MPs owe their allegiances to the party not to the district. See Ivor Crewe, 'MPs and their Constituents in Britain: How Strong are the Links?' in Vernon Bogdanor, *Representatives of the People?* (Hants, Gower, 1985).
22 'Wider empirical evidence, too, does not lend support to the view that PR, in whatever format, gives more power to central party agencies than single-member systems.' Michael Gallagher in Gallagher and Marsh *Candidate Selection*, p. 259.
23 It should be noted that New Zealand changed its electoral system from first past the post to an additional member system following the 1993 referendum.
24 See Pippa Norris, *British By-Elections*, chapter 2.
25 Anthony King, 'The Rise of the Career Politician in Britain – And its Consequences', *British Journal of Political Science* (July 1981), pp. 249–63.
26 For a discussion of these factors see Pippa Norris and Ivor Crewe, 'Did the British Marginals Vanish? Proportionality and Exaggeration in the British Electoral System Revisited', *Electoral Studies* 11,2 (June 1994).
27 See Anthony King, *Britain at the Polls, 1992* (Chatham NJ; Chatham House, 1992), chapter 7.
28 See Chris Cook, *A Short History of the Liberal Party, 1900–92*, 4th edn (London, Macmillan, 1993); John Stevenson, *Third Party Politics Since 1945* (Oxford, Blackwell, 1993).

3. CONSERVATIVE RECRUITMENT

1 For more details see, for example, S. E. Finer, *The Changing British Party System, 1945–79* (Washington DC, American Enterprise Institute, 1980), pp. 79–80; Richard Rose, *The Problem of Party Government* (New York, The Free Press, 1974), pp. 133–66.
2 It should be noted that the selection process operates in an identical fashion in Scotland but there is a separate organisation with Scottish Central Office headquarters in Edinburgh. There is a separate Scottish Approved List with about 100 names. Candidates can apply for, and be accepted by, both the Scottish and English lists simultaneously. For details see Gerald Warner, *The Scottish Tory Party: A History* (London, Weidenfeld and Nicolson, 1988).
3 For details see Philip Norton and Arthur Aughey, *Conservatives and Conservatism* (London, Temple Smith, 1981), p. 222–32; Michael Pinto-Duschinsky, 'Central Office and 'power' in the Conservative Party', *Political Studies*, 20, 1 (1980), pp. 1–16.
4 The Standing Advisory Committee on Candidates (SACC) is a sub-committee of

the executive Committee of the National Union of Conservatives. Established in 1935, SACC's role was considerably strengthened by the Maxwell–Fyfe report in 1949. Today SACC is empowered to examine the qualifications and records of all who wish to be included in the official Approved List of candidates. SACC may also withhold approval from any other candidate that constituencies wish to consider. The committee contains twelve members including the Chairman of the National Union and leader of the parliamentary party. The vice chairman responsible for candidates attends in an advisory capacity.

5 Austin Ranney, *Pathways to Parliament* (London, Macmillan, 1965), p. 27.
6 For details see J. A. G. Griffith and Michael Ryle, *Parliament: Functions, Practice and Procedures*, pp. 47–9.
7 Interview with Mr Balfour, Scottish Central Office, June 1989.
8 Interview No. 39.
9 Interview No. 30.
10 Interview No. 30.
11 *Notes on Procedure for the Adoption of Conservative Parliamentary Candidates in England and Wales* (London, Conservative Central Office, 1981).
12 Central Office had sought the advice of management selection consultants as early as 1966, when seeking to prune the approved list, but they did not adopt substantially new procedures for fear of offending candidates and constituency associations. Michael Pinto-Duschinsky, 'Central Office', p. 15.
13 Anyone on the approved list for ten years without being selected by a constituency must also go through the residential selection board.
14 Interview No. 15.
15 Interview No. 22.
16 Interview No. 20.
17 Interview No. 30.
18 Interview No. 20.
19 Interview No. 39.
20 It should be noted that information was not directly available about applicants who failed the board, who might be expected to be more critical, although most party members expressed a high level of satisfaction with the general role of Central Office in the selection process.
21 Interview No 31.
22 As noted earlier the Scottish Approved List contains about 100 names, and candidates may be on both lists simultaneously.
23 Lord Houghton, *Report of the Committee on Financial Aid to Political Parties* (London, HMSO, 1976).
24 Patrick Seyd, Paul Whiteley and Jeremy Richardson, 'Who Are the True Blues? The Conservative Party Members' Paper presented at the Annual Meeting of the Political Studies Association, Leicester, April 1993, p. 4.
25 Philip Tether, 'Recruiting Conservative Party Members: A Changing Role for Central Office', *Parliamentary Affairs* 44, 1 (January 1991).
26 See Philip Norton and Arthur Aughey, *Conservatives and Conservatism*, pp. 222–32.
27 Interview No. 30.
28 Interview No. 39.
29 Interview No. 25.

30 Interview No. 38.
31 Interview No. 26.
32 Personal interview in June 1989 with the Scottish Vice Chairman, Mr Balfour.
33 Interview No. 35.
34 Interview No. 21.
35 Interview No. 26.
36 Interview No. 7.
37 Interview No. 7.
38 Interview No. 20.
39 *Notes on Procedure for the Adoption of Conservative Parliamentary Candidates in England, Wales and Northern Ireland* (London, Conservative and Unionist Central Office, 1990), p. 4.
40 At a minimum the standing selection committee normally includes key officers of the association (the president, chairman and treasurer), a woman elected by the women's constituency committee, a Young Conservative, at least five representatives of branches, and at most three co-opted members. The constituency agent is secretary to the committee, and the area agent (or deputy) attends meetings in an advisory capacity.
41 Interview No. 30.
42 Interview No. 23
43 Interview No. 35
44 Interview No. 24.
45 Interview No. 22.
46 Interview No. 26.
47 Interview No. 22.
48 Austin Ranney, *Pathways to Parliament*, p. 61.
49 This occurred in Nelson and Colne where David Waddington was selected over the Executive Committee's choice of David Penfold. See David Butler and Michael Pinto-Duschinsky, *The British General Election of 1970* (London, Macmillan, 1971), p. 292.
50 Byron Criddle in D. Butler and D. Kavanagh, *The British General Election of 1983* (London, Macmillan, 1984), fn. 23.
51 Interview with Area Agent.
52 *Notes on Procedure* (1990), p. 4.
53 See Austin Ranney, *Pathways to Parliament*.
54 T. F. Lindsay and Michael Harrington, *The Conservative Party*, pp. 156–63.
55 Quoted in Michael Rush, *The Selection of Parliamentary Candidates* pp. 28–9.
56 Michael Rush, *The Selection of Parliamentary Candidates* p. 29.
57 John Ramsden, 'From Churchill to Heath', in Lord Butler (ed.), *The Conservatives: A History of their Origins to 1965* (London, George Allen and Unwin, 1977).
58 Quoted in Lindsay and Harrington *The Conservative Party*, p. 161.
59 Sarah Morrison, 'Remaking the Party Machine', *Crossbow* (October 1973).
60 Zig Layton Henry, 'Constituency Autonomy in the Conservative Party', *Parliamentary Affairs*, 29, 4 (autumn 1976), pp. 399–400.
61 *Notes on Procedure*, (1990), p. 4.
62 When the satisfaction scale was tested for reliability Cronbach's Alpha was 80.0, indicating a consistent scale measure.

63 See, for example, David Butler, 'The Renomination of MPs', *Parliamentary Affairs*, (Spring 1978); Byron Criddle, 'Candidates', in David Butler and Dennis Kavanagh, *The British General Election of 1987*, pp. 195–7; Byron Criddle, 'Candidates', in David Butler and Dennis Kavanagh, *The British General Election of 1983*, pp. 225–9.

64 David Butler and Dennis Kavanagh, *The British General Election of February 1974*, p. 205.

65 Sir Trevor Skeet (North Bedfordshire) was unsuccessfully threatened with deselection on grounds of age. John Browne (Winchester) withdrew under threat of deselection for non-disclosure of financial interests, while Sir John Stradling-Thomas (Monmouth) withdrew under pressure on the grounds of ill health. For details see Byron Criddle 'MPs and Candidates', pp. 217–18.

4. LABOUR RECRUITMENT

1 Details are specified in the Labour party *Rule Book, 1991–2* (London, The Labour Party, 1992), pp. 40–1.

2 Statement of the founders at the Memorial Hall meeting quoted in Robert Mckenzie, *British Political Parties*, pp. 456–7.

3 According to the party's Rule Book, at constituency level affiliated organisations may consist of:

    a. trade unions or branches thereof affiliated to the Trades Union Congress or recognised by the General Council of the Trades Union Congress as bona fide trade unions and affiliated to the Labour Party.

    b. Co-operative societies, branches of the Co-operative Party and other co-operative organisations.

    c. Other categories including branches of socialist societies affiliated to the Labour Party nationally; branches of other organisations whose affiliation has been approved by the Party's National Executive Committee; local or area Trades Councils; and other NEC approved organisations.

4 The Electoral College for the party leader, introduced in 1981, includes weighted votes for the parliamentary party (30 per cent), constituency delegates (30 per cent) and affiliated organisations (40 per cent). See Malcolm Punnett, *Selecting the Party Leader* (Hemel Hempstead, Harvester Wheatsheaf, 1992).

5 In 1986 one report estimates there were black sections in over thirty constituencies, with about 1,500 members, and delegate status on some General Committees. See Steve Ingle, *The British Party System* (Oxford, Basil Blackwell, 1987), p. 134. The Seyd and Whiteley survey found that 0.4 per cent of members belonged to Black Sections, about 1,200 members. Pat Seyd and Paul Whiteley, *Labour's Grassroots*, p. 229. The NEC officially accepted the establishment of Black Socialist Societies in July 1991. *NEC Report* (London, Labour Party, 1991).

6 In 1990 according to official records the Labour Party had 311,152 individual party members. *NEC Report* (London, Labour Party, 1990).

7 Branches are allowed one delegate per ten members. Each trade union affiliate can send up to five delegates.

8 This includes the constituency chair, two vice-chairs, the treasurer, the constituency women's officer, and the constituency youth officer.

9 'The cheap cards ... currently for pensioners and the unemployed are open to abuse. There are people who pay for dozens of cards to ensure their own selection, and that's corrupt and it ought to be put a stop to. I think I've heard ... that the same handwriting has been on a dozen applications. Well that should be discounted at once.' Interview No. 16.

10 It should be noted that some candidates who were eventually sponsored by unions were not included in the 'A' list, since sponsorship was sought after selection.

11 Interview No. 33.

12 Interview No. 34.

13 Derek Bird, Mark Beatson and Shaun Butcher, 'Membership of Trade Unions', *Employment Gazette* (May 1993), pp. 189–94.

14 Interview No. 34.

15 In 1970 the practice was ended of excluding nominees from the 'B' list on political grounds. See Eric Shaw, *Discipline and Discord in the Labour Party* (Manchester, Manchester University Press, 1988), p. 105.

16 Interview No. 2.

17 Interview No. 29.

18 Interview No. 2.

19 Interview No. 15.

20 See Eric Shaw, *Discipline and Discord*, p. 104.

21 Interview No. 9.

22 Interview No. 2.

23 Seyd and Whiteley's survey found that 5.5 per cent of party members belong to the Cooperative Party. Pat Seyd and Paul Whiteley, *Labour's Grass Roots*, p. 229.

24 Interview No. 36.

25 Interview No. 33.

26 Interview No. 5.

27 Interview No. 11.

28 Interview No. 17.

29 Interview No. 28.

30 This is based on estimates provided by MPs, candidates and list applicants in the *British Candidate Study*.

31 Interview No. 32.

32 Interview No. 33.

33 Interview No. 9

34 Interview No. 33.

35 Interview No. 9.

36 Interview No. 32.

37 There is a single exception since the Executive has the right to make one nomination.

38 Interview No. 9.

39 Interview No. 33.

40 Interview No. 33.

41 The number on the shortlist was fairly similar in inheritor and challenger seats. There were about 4.2 names on the shortlists in inheritor seats, compared with 4.1 in strong challenger seats and 3.6 in weak challenger seats.

42 The rule book states that each affiliated union branch may have up to five General

Committee delegates. To be eligible as an elector a union delegate must be a party member of at least twelve months standing, and have attended at least one General Meeting in the twelve months prior to the 'freeze date'. This rule is clearly intended to ensure that union electors have some attachment to constituency politics.

43 Iain McLean, 'Party Organisation', in Chris Cook and Ian Taylor, *The Labour Party* (London, Longman, 1980), pp. 32–49.

44 Michael Rush, *The Selection of Parliamentary Candidates*, pp. 228–32.

45 Eric Shaw, *Discipline and Discord*, pp. 185–200; D. Kogan and M. Kogan, *The Battle for the Labour Party* (Glasgow, Fontana, 1982); Robert McKenzie, 'Power in the Labour Party: The Issue of "Intra-Party Democracy"', in Dennis Kavanagh (ed.), *The Politics of the Labour Party* (London, Allen and Unwin, 1982), pp. 191–201; Iain Mclean, 'Party Organisation', in Chris Cook and Ian Taylor (eds.), *The Labour Party* (Longman, London, 1980), pp. 42–3.

46 Patrick Seyd, *The Rise and Fall of the Labour Left* (New York, St Martin's Press, 1987), pp. 103–36.

47 For the argument in favour of mandatory reselection see Hohn B. Burnell, *Democracy and Accountability in the Labour Party* (Nottingham, Spokesman for the Institute of Worker's Control, 1980), pp. 22–5.

48 See Criddle, 'Candidates' (1988, 1993); David Denver, 'Britain'; Eric Shaw, *Discipline and Discord*, pp. 185–200.

49 It should be noted that in addition in 1992 two other Labour MPs were deselected by the NEC, namely Terry Fields (Liverpool Broadgreen) and Dave Nellist (Coventry SE).

50 Interview No. 17.

51 Interviews No. 12 and No. 17.

52 Peter Paterson, *The Selectorate*.

53 Dennis Kavanagh, *The Politics of the Labour Party*.

54 For a discussion of these issues see Kavanagh, *ibid.*; Cook and Taylor, *The Labour Party*; Paul Whiteley, *The Labour Party in Crisis* (Methuen, London, 1981); Shaw, *Discipline and Discord*; Seyd, *The Rise and Fall of the Labour Left*; Pat Seyd and Paul Whiteley, *Labour's Grassroots*.

55 Interview No. 17.

56 Interview No. 13.

57 Interview No. 9.

58 Interview No. 36.

59 After the 'freeze date' party officials count which General Committee delegates are from party organisations, such as branches, young socialist groups and women's sections, and which are from affiliates such as trade union branches and the Co-operative party. The proportionate division determines the weighting of the different categories of vote.

60 This practice does not reduce the individual rights of the members of affiliated organisations, who are also entitled to be individual members of the party on the normal basis.

61 Interview No. 28.

62 Roy Hattersley, speaking in a BBC television interview *On the Record*, 21 November 1993.

63 Interview No. 28.

5. MINOR PARTY RECRUITMENT

1 The only exceptions were three seats fought by two contestants in 1979.
2 *Introduction to Assessment*, 2nd edn (London, Liberal Democrats, 1993).
3 'Article 11.3: Parliamentary Candidates', *Federal Constitution* (London, Liberal Democrats, 1991).
4 In some 'derelict' local parties, with less than fifty members, the regional party will be responsible for appointing a candidate following the usual procedures.
5 Austin Ranney, *Pathways to Parliament*, pp. 248–68.
6 *Ibid.* p. 255.
7 See Pippa Norris, *British By-elections*; C. H. Williams, *National Separatism* (Cardiff, University of Wales Press, 1982); Dennis Balsom, 'Plaid Cymru', in H. M. Drucker (ed.), *Multi-Party Britain* (London, Macmillan, 1979).
8 For details see *Procedure for Selection of Parliamentary Candidates* (Cardiff, Plaid Cymru, 1991).
9 See Pippa Norris, *British Byelections*; James Kellas, *The Scottish Political System* (Cambridge, Cambridge University Press, 1984); Jack Brand, *The Nationalist Movement in Scotland* (London, Routledge and Kegan Paul, 1978).
10 For details see the *Constituency Association Selection Meetings – Notes for Guidance* (Edinburgh, Scottish National Party, 1991).
11 Chris Rose, *Contesting the General Election* (London, Green Party General Election Working Group, 1990).
12 For example, the UK Elections Coordinator circulated a 'feedback form' asking local parties to send him the names and addresses if they had selected a prospective parliamentary candidate without informing him earlier. See Rose, *Contesting the General Election*.
13 Responses to open-ended questions in the survey.
14 Responses to open-ended question in the survey.
15 Responses to open-ended question in the survey.
16 Wolfgang Rudig, Lyn G. Bennie and Mark N. Franklin, *Green Party Members: A Profile* (Glasgow, Delta Publications, 1991), ch 3.; for comparative evidence see E. Gene Frankland and Donald Schoomaker, *Between Protest and Power: The Green Party in Germany* (Boulder CO; Westview Press, 1992); Ferdinand Muller-Rommel, 'New Political Movements and New Politics Parties', in Russell Dalton and Manfred Kuechler, *Challenging the Political Order* (Oxford, Polity Press, 1990).
17 Richard Rose, *The Problem of Party Government* (Macmillan, London, 1974), p. 148.

6. SUPPLY AND DEMAND EXPLANATIONS

1 For a discussion of this concept see A. H. Birch, *Representation* (London, Macmillan, 1978); A. H. Birch, *Representative and Responsible Government* (London, Allen and Unwin, 1964); A. H. Birch, *The Concepts and Theories of Modern Democracy* (London, Routledge, 1993); Iain McLean, 'Forms of Representation and Systems of Voting', in David Held (ed.), *Political Theory Today* (Palo Alto CA, Stanford University Press, 1991), pp. 172–96; Hanna Pitkin, *The Concept of Representation* (Berkeley CA, University of California Press, 1967);

J. R. Pennock and J. W. Chapman (eds.), *Nomos X, Representation* (New York, Atherton Press, 1968); Heinz Euleau and John C. Wahlke, *The Politics of Representation* (London, Sage Publications, 1978).
2 John Adams, quoted in McLean, 'Forms of Representation', p. 173.
3 See McLean, 'Forms of Representation', p. 173.
4 A. H. Birch, *Representation*, p. 20.
5 Anne Phillips, 'Political Inclusion and Political Presence. Or, Why Should it Matter Who our Representatives Are?' Paper presented at the Joint Sessions of the European Consortium on Political Research, Leiden, 1993.
6 Other countries with reserved seats include Singapore (for Malay, Indian and other ethnic communities), Croatia (for ethnic minorities), Ireland (for universities), Bhutan (for ecclesiastical bodies), Indonesia (for members of the army), Morocco (for professional bodies and employees organisations), Slovenia (for employer and employee representatives), Belarus (for war veterans, labour representatives and the disabled), and Tanzania (for women). See *Electoral Systems: A World-wide Comparative Study* (Geneva, Inter-Parliamentary Union, 1993).
7 R. D. Putnam, *The Comparative Study of Political Elites*; G. Loewenberg and S. C. Patterson, *Comparing Legislatures*, pp. 68–116; J. D. Aberbach, R. D. Putnam and B. A. Rockman, *Bureaucrats and Politicians in Western Democracies*, pp. 40–83.
8 See Martin Burch and Michael Moran, 'The Changing Political Elite'; Dennis Kavanagh, 'The Political Class and Its Culture', *Parliamentary Affairs*, 45, 1 (January 1992), pp. 18–32; Peter Richards, *The Backbenchers*, pp. 11–23; Byron Criddle, 'MPs and Candidates'. See also previous chapters in Nuffield series by David Butler et al. *The British General Election*.
9 For the earliest use of relative criteria see J. F. S. Ross, *Parliamentary Representation* (New Haven CT, Yale University Press, 1944). It should be noted that the composition of the elite could be compared against alternative baselines, for example the proportion of any group in the population. It seems preferable to adopt the electorate as the base, since citizenship defines the group eligible to stand for elected office.
10 It should be noted that there are a number of problems associated with the classification of members' prior occupational background, including lack of detailed information, and problems of consistent categorisation in different time series. For the time series data this study uses the standard sources, as referenced.
11 Robert McKenzie, *British Political Parties*, pp. 456–7.
12 F. F. S. Ross, *Parliamentary Representation*, table 19 and table 20, pp. 60–1.
13 Robert Price and George Sayers Bain, 'The Labour Force', in A. H. Halsey, *British Social Trends since 1900* (London, Macmillan, 1988), table 4.1(b), p. 164.
14 See David Butler, 'Electors and Elected', in A. H. Halsey, *British Social Trends since 1900*, table 8.6, 8.7, pp. 316–17. This is based on the Nuffield series of British General Election Studies. It should be noted that Burch and Moran, using a different classificatory scheme, estimate that the proportion of working class MPs is significantly lower. See Martin Burch and Michael Moran, 'The Changing Political Elite'. The Butler series is used in this study since it provides a longer time-span.
15 J. A. Thomas, *The House of Commons, 1832–1901* (Cardiff, University of Wales Press, 1939).

16 W. L. Guttsman, *The British Political Elites.*

17 John Greenwood, 'Promoting Working-Class Candidature in the Conservative Party: The Limits of Central Office Power', *Parliamentary Affairs*, 41 (October 1988), pp. 456–68.

18 *Ibid.*, p. 465.

19 On this development see Peter Riddell, *Honest Opportunism* (London, Hamish Hamilton, 1993).

20 According to Collin Mellors' classification of MPs' occupational backgrounds the first Labour social worker entered in 1966. Mellors, *The British MP.*

21 Robert Price and George Sayers Bain, 'The Labour Force', p. 163; *1991 Census Report for Great Britain* (Part 2), table 86 (London, OPCS, HMSO, 1993).

22 From 1945 to 1992 the proportion of all Conservative MPs attending Oxbridge declined from 53 to 45 per cent, and the proportion who attended other universities rose from 11 to 28 per cent.

23 A. H. Halsey, 'Higher Education', in A. H. Halsey (ed.), *British Social Trends since 1990* (London, Macmillan, 1988).

24 *1991 Census Report for Great Britain*, Part 2 table 84, p. 309.

25 Norris.

26 On turnout figures see Pippa Norris, 'Gender Differences in Political Participation in Britain: Traditional, Radical and Revisionist Models', *Government and Opposition*, 26 1, (Winter 1991), pp. 56–74.

27 Due to the 1991 Langbaurgh by-election they were joined on the Labour backbenches by Ashok Kumar, but Kumar failed to hold this seat in the subsequent general election.

28 For details see chapter 12.

29 Anthony Heath et al., *Understanding Political Change* (Oxford, Pergamon Press, 1991), pp. 112–13.

30 *1991 Census Report for Great Britain*, Part I; Andy Teague, 'Ethnic Group: First Results from the 1991 Census', *Population Trends*, 72 (Summer 1993), pp. 12–17.

31 It is difficult to generalise about the process of getting on the union 'A' list since different unions use different procedures. Labour party rules do not control or standardise this process, leaving it to the discretion of the unions concerned.

32 See, however, Joni Lovenduski and Pippa Norris, 'Party Rules and Women's Representation: Reforming the British Labour Party', in Ivor Crewe et al. *British Elections and Parties Yearbook, 1991*; Pippa Norris, 'Comparing Legislative Recruitment'.

33 See Mellors, *The British MP*; Burch and Moran, 'The Changing Political Elite'.

34 Austin Ranney, *Pathways to Parliament*, p. 119; W. L. Guttsman, *The British Political Elite*, p. 27.

35 John Bochel and David Denver, 'Candidate Selection in the Labour Party: What the Selectors Seek', *British Journal of Political Science*, 13 (1983), pp. 56.

36 John Greenwood, 'Promoting Working-class Candidature in the Conservative Party'.

37 Ranney, *Pathways to Parliament*, p. 4.

38 H. Jacob, 'The Initial Recruitment of Elected Officials in the US – A Model', *Journal of Politics*, 24 (1962).

39 One Conservative candidate reported being fired by an unsympathetic employer

for requesting leave of absence to fight the campaign: 'They said to me they wanted me gone as soon as the election was called. So I had to face that election with absolutely nothing. It was terrible when you've got that at the back of your mind. You've got all the excitement of the campaign but I knew there was no job at the end of that.'

40 Interview No. 15.
41 Interview No. 20.
42 Interview No. 21.
43 Interview No. 7
44 See Peter Riddell, *Honest Opportunity: The Rise of the Career Poltician* (London, Hamish Hamilton, 1993).
45 Ranney, *Pathways to Parliament.*
46 Michael Rush, *The Selection of Parliamentary Candidates*, p. 83.
47 Personal interview with Conservative MP No. 10.
48 Martin Holland, *Candidates for Europe* (Hants, Gower, 1986), pp. 193–8; Martin Holland, 'The Selection of Parliamentary Candidates'.
49 See S. Verba, N. Nie and J. Kim, *Participation and Political Equality: A Seven Nation Comparison* (Cambridge, Cambridge University Press, 1978), pp. 71–2; L. Milbrath and M. Goel, *Political Participation* (Chicago, Rand McNally, 1977), pp. 98–102; Geraint Parry, George Moyser and Neil Day, *Political Participation and Democracy in Britain* (Cambridge, Cambridge University Press, 1992), 68–76.
50 In parenthesis, it is worth noting that at the grassroots level, the rise of the Labour polytocracy, combined with the age and gender profile of the Conservatives, means that ironically the workers party is now the better educated.
51 Elizabeth Vallance, *Women in the House: A Study of Women Members of Parliament* (London, The Athlone Press, 1979); Elizabeth Vallance and Elizabeth Davies, *Women of Europe: Women MEPs and Equality Policy* (Cambridge, Cambridge University Press, 1986); Lisanne Radice, Elizabeth Vallance and Virginia Willis, *Member of Parliament: The Job of a Backbencher* (New York, St Martin's Press, 1987).
52 See Elizabeth Vallance, 'Women Candidates in the 1983 General Election', *Parliamentary Affairs* 37 (1984), pp. 301–9; Jorgen Rasmussen, 'The Electoral Costs of Being a Woman in the 1979 British General Election', *Comparative Politics*, 15 (July 1983), pp. 461–75; C. Martlew, C. Forester and G. Buchanan, 'Activism and Office: Women and Local Government in Scotland', *Local Government Studies* (March/April 1985), pp. 47–65.
53 Austin Mitchell, *Getting There* (London, Thames Methuen, 1982), p. 30.
54 Interview with a Conservative woman MP No. 31.
55 Interview with a Conservative woman MP No. 37.
56 John Bochel and David Denver, 'Candidate Selection in the Labour Party'.
57 Stephen Bristow, 'Women Councillors – An Explanation of the Under-representation of Women in Local Government', *Local Government Studies*, 6, 3 (1980), pp. 73–90; see also Jill Hills, 'Women Local Councillors: A Reply to Bristow' *Local Government Studies*, 8, 1 (1982), pp. 61–72.
58 Jill Hills, 'Life-styles Constraints on Formal Political Participation – Why so Few Women Local Councillors in Britain?' *Electoral Studies*, 2, 1 (1983), pp. 39–52.
59 Rush, *The Selection of Parliamentary Candidates*, p. 63.

60 Personal interview with a woman Labour applicant No. 29.

61 Rush, *The Selection of Parliamentary Candidates*, p. 65–6.

62 Interview with Conservative MP No. 31.

63 Personal interview with Conservative applicant No. 7.

64 See *Population Trends*, 72 (London, OPCS HMSO, 1993).

65 See Pippa Norris, Andrew Geddes and Joni Lovenduski, 'Race and Parliamentary Representation'.

66 Zig Layton Henry and Donley Studlar, 'The Electoral Participation of Black and Asian Britons: Integration or Alienation?' *Parliamentary Affairs*, 38, 3 (1985), pp. 307–18; Bochel and Denver, 'Candidate Selection', p. 56.

67 Personal interview with Asian Labour applicant.

68 Ivor Crewe, 'Representation and the Ethnic Minorities in Britain', in Nathan Glazer and Ken Young (eds.), *Ethnic Pluralism and Public Policy* (London, Heinemann Educational Books, 1983), p. 277–8.

69 Muhammad Anwar, *Race and Politics*.

70 See Norris, Geddes and Lovenduski, 'Race and Parliamentary Representation' for more details.

71 One interviewee (No. 7), aged over 45, was told in her initial interview by Central Office: 'Hmmm, well I suppose you're just about in the age bracket – another few months and you'd be what we would consider past it.' Another Conservative MP (No. 21) noted: 'There was a cut-off point at fifty. I mean, it was a tacit cut-off point. We all knew about it through it wasn't written down.'

72 It should be noted that the model was tested with social class (defined as manual/ non-manual) instead of occupation, but this proved statistically insignificant. Brokerage occupations are defined for this analysis as those which are professional or managerial (I and II), with a high level of income, career security, and flexibility over time. Therefore lower middle-class occupations (IIIN), such as secretaries, shop assistants and clerks, are categorised as non-brokerage occupations along with the skilled (IIIM) and unskilled (IV) manual workers. Class and occupation could not be entered into the final model due to problems of multi-collinearity.

7. GATEKEEPER ATTITUDES

1 For a recent statement of this assumption see Andrew Adonis: 'By and large, the selectorate, itself a predominantly middle class cohort, discriminates against men without a professional, political or managerial background and – at least until recently – against women of all kinds.' *Parliament Today* (Manchester, Manchester University Press, 1990), 36.

2 Jorgen Rasmussen, 'The Electoral Costs of Being a Woman in the 1979 General Election', p. 473; see also Elizabeth Vallance, 'Women Candidates in the 1983 General Election', pp. 301–9; Elizabeth Vallance, *Women in the House*; Austin Mitchell, *Getting There*, p. 30.

3 John Greenwood, 'Promoting Working Class Candidature in the Conservative Party'.

4 Les Back and John Solomos, 'Who Represents Us? Racialised Politics and Candidate Selection', Research Paper No 3, Department of Politics and Sociology (May 1992).

5 John Bochel and David Denver, 'Candidate Selection in the Labour Party'.
6 Quoted in Austin Ranney, *Pathways to Parliament*, pp. 60–1.
7 Interview No. 31.
8 Interview No. 21.
9 Interview No. 7.
10 Interview No. 17.
11 Interview No. 5.
12 Interview No. 34.
13 Interview No. 27.
14 Interview No. 38.
15 Interview No. 19.
16 Interview No. 19.
17 Interview No. 13.
18 Interview No. 26.
19 Interview No. 21.
20 Interview No. 26.
21 Interview No. 22.
22 Interview No. 22.
23 Interview No. 14.
24 Ranney, *Pathways to Parliament*, p. 96.
25 Interview No. 22.
26 Interview No. 37.
27 Interview No. 36.
28 Interview No. 36.
29 Interview No. 37.
30 Interview No. 36.
31 Interview No. 39.
32 'Our party [Labour] has become an extremely middle class party and middle class people are, by and large, ... reasonably well educated, can articulate an argument, and I've seen positions arise where the working class person, whether that be a man or woman, has great difficulty getting around the country for interviews. It's a long process, it's a costly process. So you've got to have some resources and you've got to have a good employer ... ordinary working class are at a disadvantage in the Labour party, there's no doubt about it.' Interview No. 5.
33 Interview No. 17
34 See John Bochel and David Denver, 'Candidate Selection in the Labour Party'.
35 Interview with regional officer.
36 Interview with Conservative Regional Officer.
37 In the 24 Labour and Conservative selection meetings there were, in total, 101 applicants being interviewed (on average 4.2 per meeting). It should be noted that it was intended to test the impact of the applicants' gender, occupational class, race and age through this method. Unfortunately the number of working class and black applicants being interviewed was too small, and there was too little variance in age, for reliable analysis. Accordingly only the effects of the gender of applicants were tested in this analysis.

8. CANDIDATE RESOURCES

1 See Geraint Parry, George Moyser and Neil Day, *Political Participation*, pp. 63–119.
2 For example, with union sponsorship, members and applicants cannot be compared since, by definition, only applicants on Labour's 'A' list have such support.
3 See Michael Pinto-Duschinsky, *British Political Finance 1830–1980* (Washington DC, AEI, 1981), pp. 129–30, 159. Austin Ranney, *Pathways to Parliament*, pp. 51–5.
4 See, for example, Frank Sorauf, *Inside Campaign Finance* (New Haven CT, Yale University Press, 1992); Herbert Alexander, *Financing Politics* 4th edn (Washington DC: Congressional Quarterly Press, 1992).
5 Interview with Conservative woman candidate from the north No. 5.
6 *Parliamentary Election Manual*, 16th Edition (London, Conservative and Unionist Central Office, 1991), p. 14.
7 Interview No. 9.
8 Interview No. 2
9 Interview No. 7.
10 Interview No. 12.
11 Interview No. 10.
12 Interview No. 19.
13 Interview No. 19.
14 *Report of the Review Body on Top Salaries* (London, HMSO, July 1992).
15 The House of Commons, *Information Office*; J. A. G. Griffith and Michael Ryle, *Parliament: Functions, Practice and Procedures* (London, Sweet and Maxwell, 1989), p. 75.
16 See Anthony King, 'The Rise of the Career Politician'.
17 Griffith and Ryle, *Parliament*, pp. 57–8.
18 Barker and Rush, *The Member of Parliament and his Information*.
19 Norman J. Ornstein, Thomas E. Mann and Michael J. Malbin, *Vital Statistics on Congress, 1987–1988* (Washington DC, AEI/CQ Press, 1987).
20 Martin Harrison, *Trade Unions and the Labour Party* (London, Allen and Unwin, 1960).
21 It should be noted that unions set their own rules for determining who should be sponsored. Some unions like the TGWU retrospectively sponsor any member who gets adopted by a constituency, while others only sponsor those who get a place in advance on their list of nominees. The method of selection also varies between unions, with some using rigorous tests, as outlined in chapter 4.
22 Interview No. 29.
23 Interview No. 2.
24 Interview No. 32.
25 Interview No. 11.
26 Interniew No. 2.
27 Interview No. 37.
28 Interview No. 5.
29 Interview No. 29.
30 Interview No. 33.
31 Interview No. 27.

32 Ranney, *Pathways to Parliament*, p. 235; Rush, p. 181.
33 Rush *op. cit.* table 6, 8, p. 181.
34 See D. Butler and G. Butler, *British Political Facts.*
35 Interview No. 5.
36 ASLEF's head office is based in Glenda Jackson's constituency of Hampstead and Highgate.
37 Ranney, *Pathways to Parliament*, p. 236.
38 *Ibid.*, pp. 237–8.
39 Ranney, *Pathways to Parliament*, p. 78.
40 Interview No. 39.
41 Interview No. 6.
42 Interview No. 29.
43 Interview No. 6.
44 Estimated from the British Candidate Study Q30 for MPs: 'Roughly how many hours do you think you usually devote to the following activities in the average month when the house is sitting?'
45 In May 1983 the Review Body on Top Salaries sent a questionnaire to members, and found that members spent, on average, over 62 hours per week on all forms of Parliamentary work, averaging 69 hours when the house was sitting and 42 hours during recess. See Griffith and Ryle, *Parliament*, p. 74.
46 *Report of the Review on Top Salaries.*
47 Jill Hills, 'Lifestyle Constraints', p. 46.
48 Interview No. XX.
49 It should be noted that this data is unavailable at present for Conservative members.
50 Interview No. 31.
51 Personal interview with prospective Conservative candidate.
52 Ranney, *Pathways to Parliament.*
53 Interview No. 19.
54 Interview No. 27.
55 Interview No. 29.
56 Interview No. 15.
57 Interview No. 12.
58 Interview No. 36.
59 Interview No. 20.
60 Interview No. 19.

9. CANDIDATE MOTIVATION

1 Interview No. 21.
2 Jim Chandler, *Local Government Today* (Manchester, Manchester University Press, 1991).
3 Moshe M. Czudnowski, 'Political Recruitment', p. 211.
4 For recent popular, personal and autobiographical accounts of Westminster life see: John Biffen, *Inside the House of Commons: Behind the Scenes at Westminster* (London, Grafton Books, 1989); Paul Rose, *Backbench Dilemma* (London, Frederick Muller Ltd, 1981), ch. 14; Woodrow Wyatt, *Turn Again Westminster* (London, Andrew Deutsch, 1973); John Grant, *Member of Parliament* (London,

Michael Joseph 1974); Fred Willey, *The Honourable Member* (London, Sheldon Press, 1974; Austin Mitchell, *Westminster Man* (London, Thames Methuen, 1982); Nesta Wyn Ellis, *Dear Elector: The Truth about MPs* (London, Coronet, 1974); Dennis Healey, *The Time of my Life* (London, Michael Joseph, 1989); Richard Needham, *Honourable Member: An Inside Look at the House of Commons* (London, Patrick Stephens, 1983).

 5 Anthony King, *British Members of Parliament: A Self-Portrait* (London, Macmillan/Grenada TV, 1974); Anthony King and Anne Sloman, *Westminster and Beyond* (London, Macmillan, 1973); Lisanne Radice, Elizabeth Vallance and Virginia Willis, *Members of Parliament* (New York, St Martin's Press, 1987); Peter Riddell, *Honest Opportunism*.

 6 See, for example, Peter Riddell, *Honest Opportunism*, chapters 2 and 3.

 7 Harold Lasswell, *Psychopathology and Politics* (New York, Viking, 1960).

 8 See for example James David Barber, *The Presidential Character: Predicting Performance in the White House* (Englewood Cliffs NJ, Prentice Hall, 1972); Doris Kearns, *Lyndon B. Johnson and the American Dream* (New York, Harper Collins, 1975). For a British example in this tradition see a psychobiography studying the motivation of prime ministers by Lucille Iremonger, *The Fiery Chariot: A Study of British Prime Ministers and the Search for Love* (London, Secker and Warburg, 1970).

 9 James David Barber, *The Law-makers* (New Haven CT: Yale University Press, 1965).

10 James David Barber, *The Presidential Character*.

11 See Oliver Woshinsky, *The French Deputies* (Lexington, MA, Lexington Books, 1973).

12 Linda Fowler, *Candidates, Congress and the American Democracy* (Ann Arbor, Michigan, University of Michigan Press, 1993).

13 Anthony King, 'The Rise of the Career Politician.

14 See Matthews, 'Legislative Recruitment and Legislative Careers'.

15 For example Ranney and Rush do not refer to this.

16 Joseph Schlesinger, *Political Parties and the Winning of Office* (Ann Arbor MI, University of Michigan Press, 1991).

17 Interview No. 29.

18 Interview No. 32.

19 Interview No. 15.

20 Interview No. 19.

21 Interview No. 30.

22 Interview No. 6.

23 Interview No. 6.

24 Interview No. 3.

25 Interview No. 10.

26 Interview No. 20.

27 As before high prospect challengers are defined as candidates whose party was in second place in marginal seats (where the vote difference between the party in first and second place was less than 10% in the 1987 election). Low prospect challengers are all other candidates. List applicants are those on the national list who failed to be adopted in 1992.

28 p. 70.

29 p. 69.

30 p. 1.
31 Interview No. 11.
32 Interview No. 5.
33 Response in the candidate survey.
34 Interview No. 21.
35 Interview No. 38.
36 Interview No. 14.
37 Interview No. 11.
38 Interview No. 12.

10. COMPARATIVE CANDIDATE RECRUITMENT

 1 It should be noted that much of the empirical data on party recruitment
    procedures is derived from three main sources: Joni Lovenduski and Pippa
    Norris (eds.), *Gender and Party Politics*; Richard Katz and Peter Mair, *Party
    Organisations*; Michael Gallagher and Michael Marsh (eds.), *Candidate Selection
    in Comparative Perspective*.
 2 See Gerhard Loewenberg and Samuel C. Patterson, *Comparing Legislatures*,
    pp. 69–75; Robert Putnam, *The Comparative Study of Political Elites*, ch. 2;
    Michael Mezey, *Comparative Legislatures*, ch 11.
 3 See Leon D. Epstein, *Political Parties in Western Democracies*, ch. 7.
 4 Gerhard Loewenberg and Samuel C. Patterson, *Comparing Legislatures*, p. 72;
    Epstein, *Political Parties*, pp. 181–8; Mezey, *Comparative Legislatures*, table
    11.1, pp. 240–51.
 5 *The Guardian*, 23 November 1993.
 6 Ronald Inglehart, *Culture Shift* (Ann Arbor MI, University of Michigan Press,
    1991); *The Silent Revolution* (Princeton, Princeton University Press, 1977).
 7 Inter-Parliamentary Union, *Parliaments of the World: A Comparative Reference
    Compendium*, (Hants, Gower, 1986 2nd edn), p. 65.
 8 *Ibid*, p. 66.
 9 For details see Inter-Parliamentary Union, *Parliaments of the World*, table 2,
    pp. 70–101. Interestingly in the Republic of Korea teachers and journalists are
    banned from the National Assembly, a regulation which would decimate parlia-
    ments if adopted in some other counties.
10 There are certain variations. Some states like Michigan continue to employ
    conventions of party delegates for some state offices, and sometimes (as in
    Connecticut) conventions are used as a preliminary step to endorse candidates
    before primaries. Other variations include runoff majoritarian (second ballot)
    primary elections in Louisiana, Georgia and South Dakota. For details on a
    state-by-state basis see Richard G. Smolka, 'Election Legislation 1900–91', table
    5.3; *The Book of the States*, 1992–93 edition, volume 29 (Lexington, Kentucky,
    The Council of State Governments, 1992).
11 See Eva Kolinsky, 'Germany' in Joni Lovenduski and Pippa Norris (eds.),
    Gender and Party Politics.
12 Henry Valen, 'Norway: Decentralisation and Group Representation', in M. Gal-
    lagher and M. Marsh (eds.), *Candidate Selection in Comparative Perspective*;
    Hege Skjeie, 'Norway', in Joni Lovenduski and Pippa Norris (eds.), *Gender and
    Party Politics*.

13 Austin Ranney, *Pathways to Parliament*.

14 *Women and Political Power*, Inter-Parliamentary Union Reports and Documents No. 19 (Geneva, IPU, 1992), p. 97.

15 Lynda Erickson, 'Canada', in Joni Lovenduski and Pippa Norris (eds.), *Gender and Party Politics*; Michael Marsh, 'Ireland', in Gallagher and Marsh, *Candidate Selection*; Yvonne Galligan, 'Ireland', in Joni Lovenduski and Pippa Norris (eds.), *Gender and Party Politics*.

16 D. Jaensch, *The Australian Party System* (Sydney, Allen and Unwin, 1983).

17 From 1958 to the early 1980s Germany used to be seen as a classic 'two-and-a-half' party system, with catch-all middle-of-the-road parties. From 1983 to 1990 the growth of the Greens produced a four-party system. Since unification, support for the PDS (the reformed communist party) in eastern Germany, coupled with the resurgence of far right parties (the Republicans and German People's Union (DVU List-D)), with sporadic success in some Lander elections, indicates Germany has become a more fragmented and ideologically polarised multi-party system. See Klaus von Beyme, 'Electoral Unification: The First German Elections in Dec. 1990', *Government and Opposition*, 26, 2 (1991); Ronnie Irving, and W. E. Paterson, 'The 1990 German Election', *Parliamentary Affairs*, 44, 3 (1991), pp. 353–72; Peter Pulzer, 'The German Federal Election of 1990', *Electoral Studies*, 10, 2 (1991), pp. 145–54; Geoffrey Roberts, 'The Growth of the Far Right', *Parliamentary Affairs* (July 1992).

18 Czudnowski, 'Political Recruitment', p. 221.

19 Michael Gallagher, *Candidate Selection*, p. 258.

20 Wilma Rule and Joseph Zimmerman (eds.), *U.S. Electoral Systems: Their Impact on Minorities and Women* (Westport CT: Greenwood Press, 1992); Rule, 'Why Women Don't Run'; Rule, 'Electoral Systems, Contextual Factors and Women's Opportunity for Election to Parliament in Twenty-Three Democracies', *Western Political Quarterly*, 40 (19XX), pp. 477–86; Pippa Norris, 'Women's Legislative Participation in Western Europe', *West European Politics*, 8, 4 (1985), pp. 90–101.

21 See Wilma Rule and Joseph Zimmerman (eds.), *Electoral Systems*; Richard Niemi, *Minority Representation and the Quest for Voting Equality* (Cambridge, Cambridge University Press, 1992).

22 For a review see Vernon Bogdanor and David Butler, *Democracy and Elections* (Cambridge, Cambridge University Press, 1983).

23 Between 1945 and 1956, and again in 1986, the French used proportional representation with department party lists without preference voting in the National Assembly. Although proportional the system used in France in 1986 employed few seats per department, resulted in a relatively high level of district magnitude. In contrast in the national elections from 1958 to 1981, and again in 1988, the system was changed so that candidates were elected by a single-member first ballot majority system, with a second runoff plurality ballot. As a result more women were elected each term to the National Assembly by proportional representation than to any Assembly using the majoritarian system, with the exceptions of elections in 1981 and 1988.

24 See Joseph Schlesinger, *Political Ambition*; Michael Mezey, *Comparative Legislatures*, ch 11.

25 See Loewenberg and Patterson, *Comparing Legislatures*, pp. 106–8; Mezey, *Comparative Legislatures*, pp. 224–35.

26 Mezey, *Comparative Legislatures*, p. 227.
27 Inter-Parliamentary Union, *Chronicle of Elections* (Geneva, IPU, quarterly series, to 1992).
28 Pippa Norris, Elizabeth Vallance and Joni Lovenduski, 'Do Candidates Make a Difference?' *Parliamentary Affairs*, 45, 4 (1992), pp. 496–517.
29 Richard Matland, personal communication with author.
30 In Britain Ministers may also be drawn from the House of Lords so an elected seat is not necessary for government office, though it is usual.
31 Austin Ranney, 'Candidate Selection', table 5.1; Michael Gallagher, Michael Laver, and Peter Mair, *Representative Government in Western Europe*, table 5.2.
32 For a summary of the rules and party agencies controlling candidate selection in twelve Western democracies see Richard Katz and Peter Mair, *Party Organizations*.
33 Constituency (that is, district, riding or branch) meetings may be called selection conferences or conventions.
34 See Michael Gallagher and Michael Marsh, *Candidate Selection*, pp. 12–15, 236–65.
35 See Marila Guadagnini, 'Italy', in Joni Lovenduski and Pippa Norris (eds.), *Gender and Party Politics*; Douglas Wertman, 'Italy', in Gallagher and Marsh, *Candidate Selection*, pp. 145–68.
36 It remains to be seen how the move towards single-member plurality constituencies under the new electoral system will change the selection process within Italian parties.
37 Jean-Louis Thiebault, 'France, the Impact of Electoral System Change', in Michael Gallagher and Michael Marsh (eds.), *Candidate Selection in Comparative Perspective* (London: Sage, 1988), pp. 72–93.
38 Andrew Appleton and Amy Mazur, 'France', in Joni Lovenduski and Pippa Norris (eds.), *Gender and Party Politics*.
39 Lynda Erickson, 'Canada', in Joni Lovenduski and Pippa Norris (eds.), *Gender and Party Politics*; Robert J. Williams, 'Candidate Selection', in H. R. Penniman, *Canada at the Polls, 1979 and 1980* (Washington DC, AEI Press, 1981), pp. 104–5.
40 For the use of voter primaries see Gallagher and Marsh, *Candidate Selection*, pp. 238–9. It should be noted that other political systems, such as Norway, Canada and Israel, use 'primaries' but these are elections where party members are enfranchised. These will be referred to as membership primaries. In the United States party 'membership' is a much looser concept, and 'open' primaries allow any voter to participate, irrespective of party affiliation.
41 Barbara Burrell, 'The USA', in Joni Lovenduski and Pippa Norris (eds.), *Gender and Party Politics*.
42 Lynda Erickson, 'Canada'.
43 *Ibid.*
44 See Diane Sainsbury, 'Sweden', in Joni Lovenduski and Pippa Norris (eds.), *Gender and Party Politics*.
45 See Yvonne Galligan, 'Ireland', in Joni Lovenduski and Pippa Norris (eds.), *Gender and Party Politics*.
46 Eva Kolinsky, 'Germany'.
47 Marila Guadagnini, 'Italy'.
48 Gallagher and Marsh, *Candidate Selection*, pp. 243–5.

49 Joni Lovenduski, 'Introduction', to *Gender and Party Politics*.
50 Diane Sainsbury, 'Sweden'.
51 Hege Skjeie, 'Norway', in Joni Lovenduski and Pippa Norris (eds.), *Gender and Party Politics*.

11. THE VALUES, PRIORITIES AND ROLES OF MPs

1 Alexander Hamilton, *The Federalist*, No. 35.
2 For general reviews of the literature on gender representation in British politics see Vicky Randall, *Women and Politics*; Joni Lovenduski and Vicky Randall, *Contemporary Feminist Politics* (Oxford, Oxford University Press, 1993); for work on racial representation in British politics see Zig Layton-Henry, 'The Party and Race Relations', in Anthony Seldon and David Butler (eds.), *The Conservative Party Since 1900* (Oxford, Oxford University Press, forthcoming); Zig Layton-Henry, *The Politics of Race in Britain* (London, Allen and Unwin, 1984); I. Crewe, 'Representation and the Ethnic Minorities in Britain', in N. Glazer and K. Young, *Ethnic Pluralism and Public Policy*; A. Messina, *Race and Party Competition in Britain* (Oxford, Clarendon, 1989); John Solomos, *Race and Racism in Contemporary Britain* (London, Macmillan, 1990); M. Anwar, *Race and Politics* (London, Tavistock, 1986); Zig Layton-Henry and Paul Rich (eds.), *Race, Government and Politics in Britain*.
3 See Donald Matthews, 'Legislative Recruitment and Legislative Careers', in Gerhard Loewenberg, Samuel Patterson and Malcolm Jewell (eds.), *Handbook of Legislative Research*, p. 25.
4 Colin Mellors, *The British MP*, p. 3; see also L. J. Edinger and D. Searing, 'Social Background in Elite Analysis: A Methodological Inquiry', *American Political Science Review* (1967); David Butler and Michael Pinto-Duschinsky, 'The Conservative Elite 1918–78: Does Unrepresentativeness Matter?', in Zig Layton-Henry, *Conservative Party Politics* (London, Macmillan, 1980).
5 Dennis Kavanagh, 'The Political Class and its Culture'; see also Dennis Kavanagh, 'Social Change in Elite Recruitment', pp. 95–110.
6 For example Irene Diamond suggests that in the mid-1970s American women in state politics were divided amongst themselves into different types, with some sympathetic to the concerns of the women's movement while an older generation more closely follows the model of a traditional civic worker. See Irene Diamond, *Sex Roles and the State House* (New Haven CT, Yale University Press, 1977).
7 Moshe M. Czudnowski, 'Political Recruitment'.
8 Barry Hindess, *The Decline of Working class Politics* (London, McGibbon and Kee, 1971); see also Jean Blondel for an earlier version of this argument, *Voters, Parties and Leaders* (Harmondsworth, Penguin, 1963) pp. 145–6.
9 Hugh Berrington, 'The Labour Left in Parliament: Maintenance, Erosion and Renewal', in Dennis Kavanagh (ed.), *The Politics of the Labour Party* (London, Allen and Unwin, 1982) pp. 69–94; S. E. Finer, H. B. Berrington and D. J. Bartholomew, *Backbench Opinion in the House of Commons, 1955–59*; Hugh Berrington, *Backbench Opinion in the House of Commons 1945–55*.
10 Frank Parkin, *Middle Class Radicals* (Manchester, Manchester University Press, 1968).
11 Patrick Seyd and Paul Whiteley, *Labour's Grass Roots*, p. 137.

12 Anthony Heath and Geoff Evans, 'Working Class Conservatives and Middle Class Socialists', in Roger Jowell (ed.), *British Social Attitudes, the 5th Report* (SCPR/Dartmouth, 1989), pp. 53–66.
13 Elizabeth Vallance and E. Davies, *Women of Europe: Women MEPs and Equality Policy* (Cambridge, Cambridge University Press, 1986).
14 See Drude Dahlerup, 'From a Small to a Large Minority: Women in Scandinavian Politics' *Scandinavian Political Studies* 11, 4 (1988), pp. 275–98; Torild Skard and Elina Haavio-Mannila, 'Women in Politics', in Drude Dahlerup, *Unfinished Democracy* (Oxford, Pergamon Press, 1985), pp. 51–80.
15 See Susan Welch, 'Are Women More Liberal than Men'; Sue Thomas and Susan Welch, 'The Impact of Gender on Activities and Priorities of State Legislators', *Western Political Quarterly* 44, 2 (1991), pp. 445–56; Frieda Gehlen, 'Women Members of Congress: A Distinctive Role?' in Marianne Githens and Jewel Prestage (eds.), *A Portrait of Marginality* (New York, McKay, 1977); M. St. Germain 'Does their Difference make a Difference? The Impact of Women on Public Policy in the Arizona State Legislature', *Social Science Quarterly*, 70 (1989), pp. 956–68; Susan Thomas, 'Voting Patterns in the California Assembly: The Role of Gender' *Women and Politics*, 9 (1989), pp. 43–56; Kathlene Lyn, Susan Clarke and Barbara A. Fox, 'Ways Women Politicians are Making a Difference' in Debra L. Dodson (ed.), *Gender and Policymaking: Studies of Women in Office* (New Brunswick NJ, Center for the American Woman and Politics, 1991), pp. 31–8; Sue Thomas, 'The Impact of Women on State Legislative Policies', *The Journal of Politics*, 53 (1991), pp. 958–76; Sue Thomas, *When Women Legislate* (forthcoming); Sue Thomas, 'Women Officeholders: Role Conflict and Mixed Motivations', Paper delivered at the Annual Meeting of the American Political Science Association, Chicago, 1992. For the problems of crosscultural comparisons see Iva Ellen Deutchman and Mark Considine who found women were not more likely to put forward legislation on women's issues in Australia, possibly due to the greater strength of party discipline. See 'Sex and Representation: A Comparison of American and Australian State Legislators', Paper presented at the Annual Meeting of the American Political Science Association, 1992, Chicago.
16 Jean Bethke Elshstain, 'The Power and Powerlessness of Women' in G. Bock and S. James (eds.), *Beyond Equality and Difference* (London, Routledge, 1992).
17 There is an extensive literature on racial representation in America. For a recent study of the impact of race in the United States Congress see Carol Swain, *Black Faces, Black Interests* (Cambridge MA, Harvard University Press, 1993). Nevertheless it is not necessarily appropriate to generalise from Congress to the British Parliament.
18 Legislative votes are among the most important dimensions of behaviour, but roll call analysis is not employed in this chapter given the constraints of party discipline in the British parliament.
19 For further details of this see Pippa Norris, 'Has Labour Become a 'Catch-all' Party?' Paper delivered at the 1992 British General Election Study Conference, Nuffield College, April 1993. Revised version in Anthony Heath et al. (eds.), *Labour, Last Chance?* (Dartmouth Press, 1994).
20 It should also be noted that the effects of occupational class were tested using different measures. In the final model the respondent's standard occupational

classification (SOC 1991) was recoded into 17 socio-economic groups, and these were then collapsed into middle (1.1 thru 7,16) and working (8 thru 11). The class of MPs was defined by the last occupation and employer immediately prior to being elected.

21 It should be noted that the effects of region, housing tenure and public school education were also tested, but dropped from the analysis on the grounds of parsimony, since they were not found to be significant.

22 For the 'socialist-laissez faire' scale Cronbach's alpha was .78, the kurtosis was .392 and the skew .036. For the 'libertarian-authoritarian' scale Cronbach's Alpha was .82, the kurtosis was .314 and the skew .093.

23 Berrington, 'The Labour Left'.

24 See Pippa Norris, 'The Gender-Generation Gap in British Elections', in David Denver et al. (eds.), *British Parties and Elections Yearbook, 1993* (Hemel Hempstead, Harvester Wheatsheaf, 1993).

25 It should be noted that this remained true when tested with separate regression analysis within each party.

26 Heath, for example, found a significant association betwen education, non-establishment religion, and the liberal-authoritarian attitudes in the 1987 election. Anthony Heath, *Understanding Political Change* (Oxford, Pergamon Press, 1991), p. 175, table 11.2. See also Anthony Heath and Geoff Evans, 'Working-class Conservatism.'

27 See Berrington, 'The Labour Left'.

28 For more details about party positions on these scales see Pippa Norris, 'Has Labour Become a "Catch-all" Party?'

29 See, for example, Ronald Inglehart, *Culture Shift*.

30 It should be noted that this pattern was confirmed by comparing the mean proportion of post-materialists within each party by these variables. For example, in the Green party slightly more men (87 per cent) than women (70 per cent) candidates proved post-materialist.

31 See Clyde Wilcox, 'The Causes and Consequences of Feminist Consciousness among Western European Women', *Comparative Political Studies*, 23, 4 (1991), pp. 519–45.

32 For a review see Torild Skard and Elina Haavio-Mannila, 'Women in Parliament'.

33 It should be noted that there were obvious party differences within each major category, for example within the 'economic' category Labour were more likely to prioritise unemployment while Conservatives mentioned business confidence or inflation more frequently.

34 See Donald D. Searing, 'New Roles for Postwar British Politics: Ideologues, Generalists, Specialists and the Progress of Professionalisation of Parliament', *Comparative Politics*, 19, 4 (1987), pp. 431–53; Donald Searing, 'The Role of the Good Constituency Member and the Practice of Representation in Great Britain', *Journal of Politics*, 47 (1985), pp. 348–81; J. Vincent Buck and Bruce E. Cain, 'British MPs in Their Constituencies', *Legislative Studies Quarterly*, 15 (1990), pp. 127–43; Bruce E. Cain, John A. Ferejohn and Morris P. Fiorina, *The Personal Vote: Constituency Service and Electoral Independence*, (Cambridge MA, Harvard University Press, 1987); Philip Norton and David Wood, 'Constituency Service'.

35 Donald Searing, 'New Roles for Postwar British Politics'; Donald Searing, 'The Role of the Good Constituency Member', p. 47; Donald Searing, 'Measuring Politicians' Values: Administration and Assessment of a Ranking Technique in the British House of Commons', *American Political Science Review*, 72 (1978), pp. 65–79. The Searing study was based on a range of personal interviews and self-completed questionnaires with MPs (N = 338).

36 Searing (*ibid.*) classified members' roles into four major categories: 'ministerial aspirants' (25 per cent of backbenchers) sought to gain front-bench status; 'parliamentary men' (9 per cent) wanted to maintain the status and privileges of the institution; 'constituency members' (25 per cent) saw themselves as welfare officers and protectors of local interests; while the largest group were 'policy advocates' (40 per cent) who viewed the job as influencing legislation.

37 Q26: 'In your view how important are the following parts of an MPs job?' Very, quite, not very, not at all important . . .

38 Factor analysis was based on principal component analysis transformed with varimax rotations. Factors with eigenvalues less than 1.5 were excluded, which required dropping one item which did not prove significantly related to any factor. Thirteen items with factor loadings greater than 0.5 were used for the final analysis.

39 Interview No. 21.
40 Interview No. 39.
41 Interview No. 20.
42 Interview No. 29.
43 Interview No. 10.
44 Interview No. 21
45 Interview No. 7.
46 Interview No. 29.
47 Interview No. 21.
48 Interview No. 33.
49 Interview No. 11.
50 Interview No. 17.

51 It should be noted that a regression analysis was tested using the same model, with the number of hours spent by MPs on constituency work, party work and parliamentary activities as the dependent variables. The results are not reported here because the model failed to explain any significant proportion of variance in the time spent on different tasks. It seems probable that other factors need to be brought into the analysis to explain legislative workloads, such as front-bench roles, length of incumbency, and type of seat.

12. THE PERSONAL VOTE

1 Byron Criddle, 'Candidates', p. 191.

2 See Bruce Cain, John Ferejohn and Morris Fiorina, *The Personal Vote*, chapter 3; also Bruce Cain, John Ferejohn and Morris Fiorina, 'The Constituency Component: A Comparison of Service in Great Britain and the United States', *Comparative Political Studies*, 16, 1 (1983), pp. 67–91.

3 These figures are remarkably close to earlier estimates by Phillip Williams, based on the electoral performance of members in marginal seats from 1950 to 1966. Phillip Williams 'The MP's Personal Vote'.

4 John Curtice and Michael Steed, Appendix 2, in David Butler and Dennis Kavanagh, *The British General Election of 1992* (London, Macmillan, 1992), pp. 333–5. (See also previous volumes 1979–87).

5 Philip Norton and David Wood, 'Constituency Service by Members of Parliament'; see also David Wood and Philip Norton, 'Do Candidates Matter?' pp. 227–38.

6 Interview with a Conservative woman MP.

7 Length of parliamentary career was measured from the year in which an MP was first elected to the constituency, or an adjacent constituency where there had been a boundary change, irrespective of interruptions in their political career.

An alternative measure was tested, namely the year in which an MP had been elected with uninterrupted service in the same constituency. There was no significant difference to the results using these measures and, on balance, the first was judged preferable.

8 *Review Body on Top Salaries*, pp. 140–1. This estimated over one year MPs spent, on average, just over 62 hours each week on all forms of parliamentary work, averaging 69 hours when the house was sitting and 42 hours during recess.

9 Philip Norton and David Wood, 'Constituency Service by Members of Parliament'; see also David Wood and Philip Norton, 'Do Candidates Matter?'.

10 See James Payne, 'The Personal Electoral Advantage of House Incumbents, 1936–76', *American Politics Quarterly*, 8, 4 (1980), pp. 465–82; D. R. Mayhew, 'Congressional Elections: The Case of the Vanishing Marginals', *Polity*, 6 (1974), pp. 295–317.

11 The 'retirement slump' was far stronger in some Labour seats. For example, in 'mixed urban-rural' Scottish seats the mean fall in the Labour vote was 2.9 percent but in Falkirk East, where Harry Ewing retired after 18 years, it dropped by 8.1 points and the majority was halved from 14,023 to 7,969. The majority fell from 16,633 to 10,680 in Cunningham North which Brian Donohue, a NALGO trade union official, inherited after 22 years service by David Lambie.

12 Some Labour second-timers did particularly well, compared with neighbouring constituencies. In the East Midlands the mean rise in the Labour vote was 7.4 per cent but in Mansfield Alan Meale increased his vote by 16.9 percentage points (and his majority from 56 to 11,724) with the largest pro-Labour swing in the country (10.6 per cent). In Bristol South Dawn Primarolo's vote rose by 9.3 per cent, and her majority from 1,404 to 8,919, on a swing of 7.5 per cent; in the other four Bristol seats the mean swing was 5.5 per cent. And, as discussed later, three of the four black Labour second-time incumbents experienced substantial swings in their favour.

Some Conservative second-timers also did remarkably well: John Bowis consolidated his 1987 gain of Battersea, with a 3.7 per cent swing from Labour, while Graham Riddick increased his majority in the formerly Liberal Colne Valley from 1,677 to 7,225 on a 3.2 per cent swing; in the surrounding West Yorkshire seats the mean swing was 0.6 per cent to the Conservatives.

13 The model controls for factors which produce significant variations in constituency results, including the regional swing, the tactical battleground, and by-election interventions.

The swing to Labour was above average in the Midlands, East Anglia and

London, and below average in Scotland, the North, and Yorkshire and Humberside. Tactical voting was evident since Labour achieved a 4 per cent swing in Conservative–Labour seats, compared with a 2 per cent national swing. Lastly the Conservatives regained all their by-election losses during the previous Parliament, but their support remained depressed in these seats.

Accordingly to control for these factors the model enters region, (coded into North/South), the type of tactical battleground classified by the party in first and second place; and excludes 23 seats with a by-election in the last parliament. The battleground contest was classified as a dummy variable in Conservative seats as Labour (0) or Other (1), and in Labour seats as Conservative (0) or other (1).

For details of the 1992 results see Ivor Crewe, Pippa Norris and Robert Waller, 'The 1992 Election: Conservative Hegemony or Labour Recovery?' in Pippa Norris, Ivor Crewe, David Denver and David Broughton (eds). *British Elections and parties Yearbook, 1992* (Hemel Hempstead, Harvester Wheatsheaf, 1992).

14 See Bruce Cain, John Ferejohn and Morris Fiorina, *The Personal Vote*, chapter 3; also Bruce Cain, John Ferejohn and Morris Fiorina, 'The Constituency Component.'

15 Elizabeth Vallance concluded that gender had a negligible impact on the 1983 and 1987 results. See Elizabeth Vallance, 'Women Candidates in the 1983 General Election' *Parliamentary Affairs*, 37, (1984), pp. 301–9; Elizabeth Vallance, 'Two Cheers for Equality', *Parliamentary Affairs*, 41, 1 (1988), pp. 86–91.

Welch and Studlar found women and men candidates won almost identical votes in local council offices, controlling for incumbency and the number of opponents. See Donley Studlar and Susan Welch, 'Understanding the Iron Law of Andrarchy: Effect of Candidate Gender on Voting in Scotland', *Comparative Political Studies*, 20, 2 (1987), pp. 174–91; Susan Welch and Donley Studlar, 'The Effects of Candidate Gender on Voting for Local Office in England', *British Journal of Political Science*, 18 (1988), pp. 273–81.

See also Jorgen Rasmussen, 'The Electoral Costs of Being a Woman in the 1979 British General Elections'; 'Female Political Career Patterns and Leadership Disabilities in Britain: The Crucial Role of Gatekeepers in Regulating Entry to the Political Elite' *Polity*, 13 (1981), pp. 600–20; Donley Studlar, Ian McAllister and Alvaro Ascui, 'Electing Women to the British Commons: Breakout from the Beleaguered Beachhead?' *Legislative Studies Quarterly*, 13, 4 (1988), pp. 515–28.

16 Graham Upton analysed voting change in England between the 1983 and 1987 elections where a female candidate replaced a male, and vica versa. He found that women suffered a slight electoral penalty, which was very small – amounting to the loss of about 250 votes – but which could be sufficient to tip the balance in highly marginal constituencies. See Graham Upton, 'The Components of Voting Change in England 1983–1987', *Electoral Studies*, 8, 1 (1989), pp. 70–2.

13. REFORMING RECRUITMENT

1 J. Webb and S. Liff, 'Play the White Man: The Social Construction of Fairness and Competition in Equal Opportunities Polices', *Sociological Review*, 36, 3 (August 1988).

2 For the older debate see Bernard Crick, *The Reform of Parliament*, 2nd edn

(London, Weidenfeld and Nicolson, 1970); Philip Norton, *The Commons in Perspective* (Oxford, Martin Robertson, 1981); David Judge (ed.), *The Politics of Parliamentary Reform* (London, Heinemann, 1983); S. Walkland and M. Ryle (eds.), *The Commons Today* (London, Fontana, 1981).

3 J. S. Mill, *Representative Government* (London, Dent, 1964), p. 239.

Select bibliography

Aaronovitch, S. *The Ruling Class* (London, Lawrence and Wishart, 1961).

Aberbach, J. D., Putnam, R. D. and Rockman, B. A. *Bureaucrats and Politicians in Western Democracies* (Cambridge MA, Harvard University Press, 1981).

Adonis, Andrew, *Parliament Today* (Manchester, Manchester University Press, 1990).

Anwar, Muhammad. *Ethnic Minorities and the 1983 General Election* (London, Comission for Racial Equality, 1984).

Race and Politics (London, Tavistock, 1986).

Back, Les and Solomos, John. 'Who Represents Us?: Racialised Politics and Candidate Selection', *Research Papers*, No. 2 London, Department of Politics and Sociology, Birkbeck College, 1992)

Ball, Alan R. *British Political Parties: The Emergence of a Modern Party System* (London, Macmillan, 1981).

Barber, James. *The Lawmakers* (New Haven CT, Yale University Press, 1965).

The Presidential Character: Predicting Performance in the White House (Englewood Cliffs NJ, Prentice Hall, 1972).

Barker, Anthony and Rush, Michael, *The Member of Parliament and his Information* (London, Allen and Unwin, 1970).

Barron, Jacqueline, Crawley, Gerald and Wood, Tony. *Councillors in Crisis: The Public and Private Worlds of Local Councillors* (London, Macmillan, 1990).

Beer, Samuel H. *Modern British Parties* (London, Faber and Faber, 1982).

Berrington, Hugh. *Backbench Opinion in the House of Commons, 1945–55* (Oxford, Pergamon Press, 1973).

Biffen, John. *Inside the House of Commons: Behind the Scenes at Westminster* (London, Grafton Books, 1989).

Birch, A. H. *Representative and Responsible Government* (London, Allen and Unwin, 1964).

Representation (Macmillan, London, 1971).

The Concepts and Theories of Modern Democracy (London, Routledge, 1993).

Blondel, Jean *Votes, Parties and Leaders* (London, Penguin, 1963).

Bochel, John and Denver, David 'Candidate Selection in the Labour Party: What the Selectors Seek' *British Journal of Political Science* 13, pp.45–69.

Bogdanor, Vernon and Butler, David. *Democracy and Elections* (Cambridge, Cambridge University Press, 1983).

Bogdanor, Vernon (ed) *Liberal Party Politics* (Oxford, Oxford University Press, 1983).

Representatives of the People? Parliamentarians and Constituents in Western Democracies (Hants, Gower, 1985).

Bottomore, Tom. *Elites and Society* (London, Watts, 1964).

Brooks, Rachel, Eagle, Angela and Short, Clare. *Quotas Now: Women in the Labour Party* (London, Fabian Society Tract 541, 1990).

Buck, J. Vincent and Cain, Bruce E. 'British MPs in Their Constituencies', *Legislative Studies Quarterly*, 15, 1 (February 1990), pp. 127–143.

Buck, P. W. *Amateurs and Professionals in British Politics 1918–59* (Chicago, University of Chicago Press, 1963).

Burch, M. and Moran, M. 'The Changing Political Elite', *Parliamentary Affairs*, 38 (1985), pp. 1–15.

Butcher, Bob and Dodd, Patricia. 'The Electoral Register – Two Surveys', *OPCS Population Trends*, 31 (Spring 1983), pp. 15–19.

Butler, David *The British General Election of 1951* (London, Macmillan, 1952).

Butler, David *The British General Election of 1955* (London, Macmillan, 1955).

Butler, David. 'The Renomination of MPs', *Parliamentary Affairs* vol. 5 (Spring 1978).

Butler, David. 'Electors and Elected', in A. H. Halsey (ed.), *British Social Trends Since 1900* (London, Macmillan, 1988).

Butler, David and Butler, Gareth. *British Political Facts, 1900–1985* (London, Macmillan, 1986).

Butler, David and Kavanagh, Dennis. *The British General Election of February 1974* (London, Macmillan, 1974).

Butler, David and Kavanagh, Dennis. *The British General Election of October 1974* (London, Macmillan, 1975).

Butler, David and Kavanagh, Dennis. *The British General Election of 1979* (London, Macmillan, 1979).

Butler, David and Kavanagh, Dennis. *The British General Election of 1983* (London, Macmillan, 1984).

Butler, David and Kavanagh, Dennis. *The British General Election of 1987* (London, Macmillan, 1988).

Butler, David and Kavanagh, Dennis. *The British General Election of 1992* (London, Macmillan, 1992).

Butler, David and King, Anthony. *The British General Election of 1964* (London, Macmillan, 1964).

Butler, David and King, Anthony. *The British General Election of 1966* (London, Macmillan, 1966).

Butler, David and Pinto-Duschinsky, Michael. *The British General Election of 1970* (London, Macmillan, 1970).

Butler, David and Pinto-Duschinsky, Michael. 'The Conservative Elite 1918–78: Does Unrepresentativeness Matter?' in Zig Layton Henry (ed.), *Conservative Party Politics* (London, Macmillan, 1980) pp. 186–204.

Butler, David and Rose, Richard *The British General Election of 1959* (London, Macmillan, 1959).

Byrne, Tony. 'The Councillors', vol. 5 *Local Government in Britain* (Harmondsworth, Penguin, 1986).

Cain, Bruce, Ferejohn, John and Fiorina, Morris. *The Personal Vote: Constituency Service and Electoral Independence* (Cambridge MA, Harvard University Press, 1987).

Chandler, J. A. *Local Government Today* (Manchester, Manchester University Press, 1991).

Chandler, J. A. and Morris, D. 'The Selection of Local Candidates', in S. Bristow, D. Kermode and M. Manning (eds.) *The Redundant Counties?* (Ormskirk, Hesketh Press, 1983).

Chapman, Jenny. *Politics, Feminism and the Reformation of Gender* (London, Routledge, 1993).

Coates, David, Johnston, Gordon and Bush, Ray. *A Socialist Anatomy of Britain* (Oxford, Polity Press, 1985).

Conservative Party. *Notes on Procedure for the Adoption of Conservative Parliamentary Candidates in England, Wales and Northern Ireland* (London, Conservative and Unionist Central Office, 1990).

Conservative Party, *Rules and Standing Orders of the National Union of Conservative and Unionist Associations* (London, Conservative Central Office, 1990).

Conservative Party, *Parliamentary Election Manual*, 16th edn (London, Conservative and Unionist Central Office, 1991).

Cook, Chris. *A Short History of the Liberal Party, 1900–92*, 4th edn (London, Macmillan, 1993).

Cook, Chris and Taylor, Ian. *The Labour Party* (London, Longman, 1980).

Craig, F. W. S. *British Electoral Facts, 1832–1987* (Dartmouth, Parliamentary Research Services, 1989).

Crewe, Ivor. 'Representation and the Ethnic Minorities in Britain', in Nathan Glazer and Ken Young (eds.), *Ethnic Pluralism and Public Policy* (London, Heinemann Educational Books, 1983).

Crewe, Ivor. 'MPs and their Constituents in Britain: How Strong are the Links?', in Vernon Bogdanor (ed.), *Representatives of the People?* (Hants, Gower, 1985).

Crewe, Ivor and Fox, Anthony. *British Parliamentary Constituencies* (London, Faber, 1984).

Crick, Bernard. *The Reform of Parliament*, 2nd edn (London, Weidenfeld and Nicolson, 1970).

Criddle, Byron. 'MPs and Candidates', in David Butler and Dennis Kavanagh (eds.), *The British General Election of 1992* (London, Macmillan, 1992).

Curtice, John, Rudig, Wolfgang and Bennie, Lynn. *Liberal Democrats Reveal All* (Strathclyde, Strathclyde Papers No. 96, 1993).

Czudnowski, Moshe M. 'Political Recruitment', in Fred Greenstein and Nelson W. Polsby (eds.), *Handbook of Political Science*, Vol 2, *Micropolitical Theory* (Reading MA, Addison-Wesley, 1975), pp. 155–242.

Dahlerup, Drude. *Unfinished Democracy* (Oxford, Pergamon Press, 1985).

'From a Small to a Large Minority: Women in Scandinavian Politics' *Scandinavian Political Studies*, 11, 4, (1988), pp. 275–298.

Denver, David. 'Britain: Centralised Parties with Decentralised Selection', in M. Gallagher and M. Marsh (eds.), *Candidate Selection in Comparative Perspective* (London, Sage, 1988).

Diamond, Irene. *Sex Roles in the State House* (New Haven CT, Yale University Press, 1977).

Dowse, Robert E. 'The M.P. and His Surgery', *Political Studies* (October 1963), pp. 333–341.

Drucker, H. M. *Multi-Party Britain* (London, Macmillan, 1979).

Dunleavy, Pat and Husbands, Chris. *British Democracy at the Crossroads* (London, Allen and Unwin, 1985).

Ehrenhalt, Alan. *The United States of Ambition* (New York, Times Books, 1992).

Ellis, Nesta Wyn. *Dear Elector: The Truth about MPs* (London, Coronet, 1974).

Epstein, Leon. *Political Parties in Western Democracies* (New Brunswick NJ, Transaction Books, 1980).

Euleau, Heinz and Wahlke, Jon C. *The Politics of Representation* (London, Sage Publications, 1978).

Finer, S. *The Changing British Party System, 1945–79* (Washington DC, American Enterprise Institute, 1980).

Finer, S., Berrington, H. B. and Bartholemew, D. J. *Backbench Opinion in the House of Commons, 1955–59* (Oxford, Pergamon Press, 1961).

Fitzgerald, Marian. 'The Parties and the Black Vote', in Ivor Crewe and Martin Harrop (eds.), *Political Communications: The General Election Campaign of 1983* (Cambridge, Cambridge University Press, 1986).

Fitzgerald, Marian. 'Black Sheep? Race in the 1987 Election Campaign', in Ivor Crewe and Martin Harrop (eds.), *Political Communications: The General Election Campaign of 1987* (Cambridge, Cambridge University Press, 1989).

Fowler, Linda. *Candidates, Congress and the American Democracy* (Ann Arbor MI, University of Michigan Press, 1993).

Fowler, Linda and McClure, Robert D. *Political Ambition: Who Decides to Run for Congress* (New Haven CT, Yale University Press, 1989).

Gallagher, M., Laver, M. and Mair, P. *Representative Government in Western Europe* (New York, McGraw Hill, 1992).

Gallagher, M. and Marsh, M. (eds.). *Candidate Selection in Comparative Perspective* (London, Sage, 1988).

Garner, Robert and Kelly, Richard. *British Political Parties Today* (Manchester, Manchester University Press, 1993).

Geddes, Andrew, Lovenduski, Joni and Norris, Pippa. 'Candidate Selection: Reform in Britain', *Contemporary Record* 4 (April 1991), pp. 19–22.

Grant, John. *Member of Parliament* (London, Michael Joseph, 1974).

Greenwood, John. 'Promoting Working-Class Canditatures in the Conservative Party: The Limits of Central Office Power', *Parliamentary Affairs*, 41, 4, (October 1988), pp. 456–68.

Griffith, J. A. G. and Ryle, M. *Parliament: Functions, Practice and Procedures* (London, Sweet and Maxwell, 1989).

Guttsman, W. L. *The British Political Elite* (London, MacGibbon and Kee, 1968).

Haavio-Mannila, Elina, et al. *Unfinished Democracy: Women in Nordic Politics* (New York, Pergamon, 1985).

Hanham, H. J. *Elections and Party Management: Politics in the Time of Disraeli and Gladstone* (London, Harvester Press, 1978).

Harrison, Martin. *Trade Unions and the Labour Party* (London, Allen and Unwin, 1960).

Healey, Dennis. *The Time of my Life* (London, Michael Joseph, 1989).

Heath, Anthony, et al. *Understanding Political Change* (Oxford, Pergamon Press, 1991).

Heath, Anthony and Evans, Geoff. 'Working Class Conservatives and Middle Class Socialists' in Roger Jowell et al. (eds), *British Social Attitudes, the 5th Report* (Hants, SCPR/Gower, 1989) 53–66.

Hewitt, Patricia and Mattinson, Deborah. *Women's Votes: The Key to Winning* (London, Fabian Society Research Series 353, 1989).

Hills, Jill. 'Candidates, the Impact of Gender', *Parliamentary Affairs*, 34 (1981), pp. 221–8.

Hindess, Barry. *The Decline of Working Class Politics* (London, McGibbon and Kee, 1971).

Holland, Martin. *Candidates for Europe* (Farnborough, Hants, Gower, 1986).

Holland, Martin. 'The Selection of Parliamentary Candidates: Contemporary Developments and the Impact of the European Elections', *Parliamentary Affairs*, 34, 2, (1987), pp. 28–46.

Houghton, Lord. *Report of the Committee on Financial Aid to Political Parties* (London, HMSO, 1976).

Ingle, Steve. *The British Party System* (Oxford, Basil Blackwell, 1987).

Inglehart, Ronald. *Culture Shift* (Ann Arbor MI, University of Michigan Press, 1991).

Silent Revolution (Ann Arbor MI, University of Michigan Press, 1977).

Inter-Parliamentary Union. *Parliaments of the World: A Comparative Reference Compendium*, 2nd edn (Hants, Gower, 1986).

Inter-Parliamentary Union. *Women and Political Power*, Reports and Documents No.19 (Geneva, Interparliamentary Union, 1992).

Inter-Parliamentary Union. *Chronicle of Elections* (Geneva, Inter-parliamentary Union, quarterly series to 1992).

Inter-Parliamentary Union. *Electoral Systems* (Geneva, Inter-Parliamentary Union, 1993).

Iremonger, Lucille. *The Fiery Chariot: A Study of British Prime Ministers and the Search for Love* (London, Secker and Warburg, 1970).

Janosik, Edward G. *Constituency Labour Parties in Britain* (London, Pall Mall Press, 1968).

Jewell, Malcolm E. 'Legislators and Constituents in the Representative Process', in Gerhard Loewenberg, Samuel C. Patterson and Malcolm E. Jewell (eds.), *Handbook of Legislative Research* (Cambridge MA, Harvard University Press, 1985), pp. 97–131.

Judge, David (ed.). *The Politics of Parliamentary Reform* (London, Heinemann, 1983).

The Parliamentary State (London, Sage, 1993).

Katz, Richard and Mair, Peter. *Party Organisations: A Data Handbook on Party Organizations in Western Democracies, 1960–90* (London, Sage, 1992).

Kavanagh, Dennis (ed.). *The Politics of the Labour Party* (London, George Allen and Unwin, 1982).

Kavanagh, Dennis. 'The Political Class and its Culture', *Parliamentary Affairs*, 45 (1992), pp. 18–32.

King, Anthony. *British Members of Parliament: A Self-Portrait* (London, Macmillan, 1974).

King, Anthony. 'The Rise of the Career Politician in Britain – And Its Consequences', *British Journal of Political Science* vol. 11 (July 1981), pp. 249–263.

King, Anthony. *Britain at the Polls, 1992* (Chatham NJ, Chatham House, 1992).

King, Anthony and Sloman, Anne. *Westminster and Beyond* (London, Macmillan, 1974).

Kilroy-Silk, Robert. *Hard Labour* (London, Chatto and Windus, 1986)

Kogan, D. and Kogan, M. *The Battle for the Labour Party* (London, Fontana, 1982).

Labour Party. *Selection of Parliamentary Candidates: Report of the NEC Consultation* (London, Labour Party, 1990)

Labour Party. *Representation of Women in the Labour Party: Statement by the National Executive Committee* (London, Labour Party, 1990).

Labour Party. *NEC Report* (London, Labour Party, 1990).

Labour Party. *Selection and Reselection of Parliamentary Candidates* (London, Labour Party, 1991).

Labour Party. *Rule Book, 1991–2* (London, The Labour Party, 1992).

Lasswell, Harold, Lerner, David and Rothwell, C. Easton. *The Comparative Study of Political Elites* (Stanford CA, Stanford University Press, 1952).

Lassell, Harold. *Psychopathology and Politics* (New York, Viking, 1960).

Layton-Henry, Zig. *The Politics of Race in Britain* (London, Allen and Unwin, 1984).

Layton-Henry, Zig. 'Black Participation in the General Election of 1987', *Talking Politics*, 1, 1 (Autumn 1988) pp. 20–24.

Layton-Henry, Zig and Studlar, Donley. 'The Electoral Participation of Black and Asian Britains: Integration or Alienation?' *Parliamentary Affairs*, 38, 3 (Summer 1985), pp. 307–18.

Lees, J. D. and Kimber, R. *Political Parties in Modern Britain* (London, Routledge, 1972).

Le Lohe, Michael. 'The Performance of Asian and Black Candidates in the British General Election of 1987', *New Community*, 15, 2 (1989) pp. 159–170.

Leonard, Dick. *Elections in Britain Today* (New York, St Martin's Press, 1991).

Liberal Democrats. *Federal Constitution* (London, Liberal Democrats, 1991).

Lindsay, T. F. and Harrington, M. *The Conservative Party, 1918–1979*, 2nd edn (London, Macmilan, 1979).

Loewenberg, Gerhard and Patterson, Samuel C. *Comparing Legislatures* (Boston, Little, Brown and Company, 1979).

Loewenberg, Gerhard, Patterson, Samuel C. and Jewell, Malcolm (eds.). *Handbook of Legislative Research* (Cambridge MA, Harvard University Press, 1985).

Lovenduski, Joni, 'Will Quatos Make Labour more Women-friendly?' *Renewal* 2, 1 (1994).

Lovenduski, Joni and Norris, Pippa. 'Selecting Women Candidates: Obstacles to the Feminisation of the House of Commons', *European Journal of Political Research*, 17 (Autumn 1989), pp. 533–62.

Lovenduski, Joni, Norris, Pippa and Burgess, Catriona. 'The Party and Women', in Anthony Seldon and Stuart Ball (eds.), *The Conservative Party Since 1900* (Oxford, Oxford University Press, 1994).

Lovenduski, Joni and Norris, Pippa. 'Political Recruitment: Gender, Class and Ethnicity', in Lynton Robbins, Hilary Blackmore and Robert Pyper (eds.), *Britain's Changing Party System* (Leicester, Leicester University Press, 1994) pp. 125–46.

Lovenduski, Joni and Norris, Pippa. 'Party Rules and Women's Representation: Reforming the British Labour Party', in Ivor Crewe et al. (eds.), *British Elections and Parties Yearbook, 1991* (Hemel Hempstead, Harvester Wheatsheaf Press, 1991), pp. 189–206.

Lovenduski, Joni and Norris, Pippa (eds.). *Gender and Party Politics* (London, Sage, 1993).

Lovenduski, Joni and Randall, Vicky. *Contemporary Feminist Politics* (Oxford, Oxford University Press, 1993).

Lovenduski, Joni and Norris, Pippa. 'Labour and the Unions: *Government and Opposition*, 29, 2 (1994), pp. 201–217.

Matthews, Donald R. 'Legislative Recruitment and Legislative Careers', in Gerhard Loewenberg, Samuel C. Patterson and Malcolm E. Jewell (eds.), *Handbook of Legislative Research* (Cambridge MA, Harvard University Press, 1985), pp. 17–55.

McKenzie, R.T. *British Political Parties* (London, Heinemann, 1955)

McLean, Iain. 'Forms of Representation and Systems of Voting', in David Held (ed.), *Political Theory Today* (Paolo Alto CA, Stanford University Press, 1991).

Maud Committee Report. *Report of the Committee on the Management of Local Government*, vol 2, *The Local Government Councillor* (London, HMSO, 1967).

Mellors, Colin. *The British MP: A Socio-Economic Study of the House of Commons* (Farnborough, Hants, Saxon House, 1978).

Messina, Anthony. *Race and Party Competition in Britain*, (Oxford, Clarendon Press, 1989).

Mezey, Michael L. *Comparative Legislatures* (Durham NC, Duke University Press, 1979).

Miliband, Ralph. *The State in Capitalist Society* (London, Weidenfeld and Nicolson, 1969).

Miliband, Ralph. *Capitalist Democracy in Britain* (Oxford, Oxford University Press, 1982).

Mills, C. Wright. *The Power Elite* (Oxford, Oxford University Press, 1956).

Minkin, Louis. *The Contentious Alliance* (Edinburgh, Edinburgh University Press, 1992).

Mitchell, Austin. *Westminster Man* (London, Methuen, 1982).

Needham, Richard. *Honourable Member: An Inside Look at the House of Commons* (London, Patrick Stephens, 1983).

Norris, Pippa. 'Women's Legislative Participation in Western Europe', *West European Politics*, 8, 4 (1985), pp. 90–101.

Norris, Pippa. 'Labour Party Quotas for Women', in David Denver et al. (eds.), *British Elections and Parties Yearbook, 1994* (London, Frank Case, 1994).

Norris, Pippa. 'Party Leaders, members and vote's: May's Law of Curvalinear Disparity Revisited', in *Party Politics*, 1994.

Norris, Pippa and Lovenduski, Joni. 'Pathways to Parliament', *Talking Politics*, 1, 3 (Summer 1989), pp. 90–94.

Norris, Pippa. *British By-elections: The Volatile Electorate* (Oxford, Clarendon Press, 1991).

Norris, Pippa. 'The Gender generation gap in British Elections', in David Denver et al. (eds.), *British Parties and Elections Yearbook, 1993* (Hemel Hempstead, Harvester Wheatsheaf, 1993).

Norris, Pippa. 'Labour Party Factionalism and Extremism: Changing the Party and 'Hanging the Image' in Anthony Heath et al. (eds.), *Labour's Last Chance?* (Hants, Dartmouth Press, 1994).

Norris, Pippa, Carty, R. K., Erickson, Lynda, Lovenduski, Joni and Simms, Marian. 'Party Selectorates in Australia, Britain and Canada: Prolegomena for Research in the 1990s', *The Journal of Commonwealth and Comparative Politics*, 28, 2 (July 1990), pp. 219–245.

Norris, Pippa and Crewe, Ivor. 'Did the British Marginals Vanish? Proportionality and Exaggeration in the British Electoral System Revisited', *Electoral Studies* (June 1994).

Norris, Pippa, Geddes, Andrew and Lovenduski, Joni. 'Race and Parliamentary Representation', in Pippa Norris, et al. (eds.), *British Parties and Elections Yearbook 1992* (Hemel Hempstead, Harvester Wheatsheaf, 1992)

Norris, Pippa and Lovenduski, Joni. 'Women Candidates for Parliament: Transforming the Agenda?', *British Journal of Political Science*, 19, 1 (January 1989), pp. 106–115.

Norris, Pippa and Lovenduski, Joni. 'Gender and Party Politics in Britain', in Joni Lovenduski and Pippa Norris (eds.), *Gender and Party Politics* (London, Sage, 1993).

Norris, Pippa and Lovenduski, Joni. '"If Only More Candidates Came Forward": Supply-side Explanations of Candidate Selection in Britain', *British Journal of Political Science*, 23 (June 1993), pp. 373–408.

Norris, Pippa, Vallance, Elizabeth and Lovenduski, Joni. 'Do Candidates Make a Difference?: Gender, Race, Ideology and Incumbency', *Parliamentary Affairs*, 45, 4 (October 1992), pp. 496–517.

Norton, Philip. *Conservative Dissidents* (London, Temple Smith, 1978).

Norton, Philip. *Dissension in the House of Commons, 1945–1979* (Oxford, Clarendon Press, 1980)

Norton, Philip. *The Commons in Perspective* (Oxford, Martin Robertson, 1981).

Norton, Philip. 'The House of Commons: Behavioural Changes', in Philip Norton (eds.), *Parliament in the 1980s* (Oxford, Basil Blackwell, 1985).

Norton, Philip and Aughey, Arthur. *Conservatives and Conservatism* (London, Temple Smith, 1981).

Norton, Philip and Wood, David. 'Constituency Service by Members of Parliament: Does it Contribute to a Personal Vote?' *Parliamentary Affairs*, 43, 2 (April 1990), pp. 196–208.

Ostrogorski, M. *Democracy and the Organisation of Political Parties* (London, 1902).

Pannebianco, A. *Political Parties: Organisation and Power* (Cambridge, Cambridge University Press, 1988).

Parry, Geraint. *Political Elites* (London, Allen and Unwin, 1969).

Parkin, Frank. *Middle Class Radicals* (Manchester, Manchester University Press, 1968).

Parkinson, M. 'Central-Local Relations in British Parties: A Local View', *Political Studies*, 19, 4 (1982), pp. 440–6.

Parry, Geraint, Moyser, George and Day, Neil. *Political Participation and Democracy in Britain* (Cambridge, Cambridge University Press, 1992).

Patterson, Peter. *The Selectorate* (London, Macmillan, 1966).

Pennock, J.R. and Chapman, J.W. (eds.). *Nomos X, Representation* (New York, Atherton Press, 1968).

Pinto-Duschinsky, Michael. 'Central Office and "Power" in the Conservative Party', *Political Studies*, 20, 1 (19   ), pp. 1–16.

Pinto-Duschinsky, Michael. *British Political Finance, 1830–1980* (Washington DC, AEI, 1981).

Pimlott, Ben and Cook, Chris. *Trade Unions in British Politics: The First 250 Years* (London, Longman, 1991).

Pitkin, Hanna. *The Concept of Representation* (Berkeley CA, University of California Press, 1967).

Plaid Cymru. *Procedure for Selection of Parliamentary Candidates* (Cardiff, Plaid Cymru, 1991).

Putnam, R.D. *The Comparative Study of Political Elites* (Englewood Cliffs NJ, Prentice Hall, 1976).

Radile, Lisanne, Vallance, Elizabeth and Willis, Virginia. *Members of Parliament* (New York, St. Martin's Press, 1987).

Ragsdale, Lyn. 'Legislative Elections', in Gerhard Loewenberg, Samuel C. Patterson and Malcolm E. Jewell (eds.), *Handbook of Legislative Research* (Cambridge MA, Harvard University Press, 1985) pp. 57–96.

Randall, Vicky. *Women and Politics*, 2nd edn (London, Macmillan, 1987).

Ranney, Austin. *Pathways to Parliament: Candidate Selection in Britain* (London, Macmillan, 1965).

Ranney, Austin. 'Candidate Selection and Party Cohesion in Britain and the United States', in William J.Crotty (ed.), *Approaches to the Study of Party Organisation* (Boston MA, Allyn and Bacon, 1968)

Ranney, Austin. 'Candidate Selection', in D. Butler, H. Penniman and A. Ranney (eds.), *Democracy at the Polls* (Washington DC, AEI, 1981), pp. 75–106.

Ranney, Austin. 'Inter-Constituency Movement of British Parliamentary Candidates, 1951–1959', *American Political Science Review* (1965).

Rasmussen, Jorgen. 'The Electoral Costs of Being a Woman in the 1979 British General Election', *Comparative Politics* 18 (July 1983), pp. 460–475.

Richards, Peter. *Honourable Members* (London, Faber and Faber, 1964).

Richards, Peter. *The Backbenchers* (London, Faber and Faber, 1972).

Riddell, Peter. *Honest Opportunism: The Rise of the Career Politician* (London, Hamish Hamilton, 1993).

Rose, Paul. *Backbench Dilemma* (London, Frederick Muller, 1981).

Rose, Richard. 'The Policy Ideas of English Party Activists', *American Political Science Review*, 56, 2 (1962), pp. 360–71.

Rose, Richard. *Studies in British Politics* (London, Macmillan, 1969).

Rose, Richard. *The Problem of Party Government* (New York, The Free Press, 1974).

Ross, J. F. S. *Parliamentary Representation* (New Haven CT, Yale University Press, 1944).

Ross, J. F. S. *Elections and Electors* (London, Eyre and Spottiswoode, 1955).

Rudig, Wolfgang, Bennie, Lynn and Franklin, Mark N. *Green Party Members: A Profile* (Glasgow, Delta Publications, 1991).

Rule, Wilma. 'Why Women Don't Run: The Critical Contextual Factors in Women's Legislative Recruitment', *Western Political Quarterly*, 34 (1981), pp. 60–77.

Rule, Wilma. (1987) 'Electoral Systems, Contextual Factors and Women's Opportunity for Election to Parliament in Twenty-Three Democracies', *Western Political Quarterly*, 40 (1987), pp. 477–98.

Rule, Wilma and Zimmerman, Joseph F. (eds.). *U.S. Electoral Systems: Their Impact on Minorities and Women* (Westport CT, Greenwood Press, 1992).

Rush, Michael. *The Selection of Parliamentary Candidates* (London, Nelson, 1969).

Rush, Michael, 'The Members of Parliament', in S. A. Walkland (ed.), *The House of Commons in the Twentieth Century* (Oxford, Clarendon Press, 1979), pp. 69–123.

Rush, Michael. 'The Selectorate Revisited', *Teaching Politics*, 15, 1 (1986).

Rush, Michael. *The Professionalisation of the British Member of Parliament*. Papers in Political Science: 1 (Exeter, Department of Politics, 1989).

Rush, Michael, *Political Society: An Introduction to Political Sociology* (Hants, Harvester Wheatsheaf, 1992), pp. 128–48.

Sampson, Anthony. *The Changing Anatomy of Britain* (London, Hodder and Stoughton, 1982).

Schlesinger, Joseph. *Ambition and Politics: Political Careers in the United States* (Chicago, Rand McNally and Co, 1966).

Schlesinger, Joseph. *Political Parties and the Winning of Office* (Ann Arbor MI, University of Michigan Press, 1991).

Schnatterschneider, E. E. *Party Government* (New York, Holt, Rinehart and Winston, 1942).

Scott, John. *Who Rules Britain?* (Oxford, Polity Press, 1991).

Scott, John. *The Upper Classes* (London, Macmillan, 1982).

Scott, John. *Corporations, Classes and Capitalism*, 2nd edn (London, Hutchinson, 1985).

Scottish National Party. *Constituency Association Selection Meetings – Notes for Guidance* (Edinburgh, Scottish National Party, 1991).

Searing, Donald. 'Measuring Politicians' Values: Administration and Assessment of a Ranking Technique in the British House of Commons', *American Political Science Review*, 72 (March 1978), pp. 65–79.

Searing, Donald D. 'The Role of the Good Constituency Member and the Practice of Representation in Great Britain', *Journal of Politics*, 47 (May 1985), pp. 348–81.

Searing, Donald D. 'New Roles for Postwar British Politics', *Comparative Politics*, 19, 4 (July 1987), pp. 431–2.

Seldon, Anthony and Ball Stuart, (eds.). *The Conservative Party Since 1900* (Oxford, Clarendon Press, 1994).

Seyd, Patrick. *The Rise and Fall of the Labour Left*, (London, Macmillan, 1987).

Seyd, Patrick and Whiteley, Paul. *Labour's Grassroots: The Politics of Party Membership* (Oxford, Oxford University Press, 1992).

Seyd, Patrick, Whiteley, Paul and Richardson, Jeremy. 'Who are the True Blues? The Conservative Party Members', Unpublished paper at the Annual Meeting of the Political Studies Association, Leicester, April 1993.

Shaw, Eric. *Discipline and Discord in the Labour Party* (Manchester, Manchester University Press, 1988).

Smith, Martin J. and Spear, Joanna (eds.). *The Changing Labour Party* (London, Routledge, 1992).

Smith, Susan J. *The Politics of 'Race' and Residence* (Oxford, Polity Press, 1989).

Solomos, John. *Race and Racism in Contemporary Britain* (London, Macmillan, 1980).

Sorauf, Frank. *Inside Campaign Finance* (New Haven CT, Yale University Press, 1992).

Stanyer, Jeff. *Understanding Local Government* (London, Martin Robertson/Fontana, 1976)

Stevenson, John. *Third Party Politics Since 1945* (Oxford, Basil Blackwell, 1993).

Stewart, Robert. *The Foundation of the Conservative Party* (London, Longman, 1978)

Studlar, Donley, McAllister, Ian, and Ascui, Alvaro. 'Electing Women to the British Commons: Breakout from the Beleaguered Beachhead' *Legislative Studies Quarterly*, 13, 4 (November 1988), pp. 515–528.

Studlar, Donley and Welch, Susan. 'Understanding the Iron Law of Andrarchy: The Effect of Candidate Gender on Voting in Scotland', *Comparative Political Studies*, 20, 2 (July 1987), pp. 174–91.

Swain, Carol. *Black Faces, Black Interests* (Cambridge MA, Harvard University Press, 1993).

Tether, Philip. 'Recruiting Conservative Party Members: A Changing Role for Central Office', *Parliamentary Affairs*, 44, 1 (January 1991), pp. 20–29.

Thomas, J. A. *The House of Commons, 1832–1901: A Study of its Economic and Functional Character* (Cardiff, University of Wales Press, 1939).

The Times Guide to the House of Commons (London, Times Books, 1945–92).

Urry, John and Wakeford, John. *Power in Britain* (London, Heinemann, 1973).

Vallance, Elizabeth. *Women in the House: A Study of Women Members of Parliament* (London, Athlone Press, 1979).

Vallance, Elizabeth. 'Women Candidates in the 1983 General Election', *Parliamentary Affairs*, 37 (1984), pp. 301–9.

Vallance, Elizabeth and Davies, Elizabeth *Women of Europe: Women MEPs and Equality Policy* (Cambridge, Cambridge University Press, 1986).

Verba, S. , Nie, N. and Kim, J. *Participation and Political Equality: A Seven Nation Comparison* (Cambridge, Cambridge University Press, 1978).

Walkland, S.A. and Ryle, M. (eds.). *The Commons Today* (London, Fontana, 1981).

Warner, Gerald. *The Scottish Tory Party: A History* (London, Weidenfeld and Nicolson, 1988).

Welch, Susan. 'Are Women more Liberal than Men in the US Congress?' *Legislative Studies Quarterly*, 10. 1 (February 1985), pp. 125–134.

Welch, Susan and Studlar, Donley. 'The Effects of Candidate Gender on Voting for Local Office in England', *British Journal of Political Science*, 18 (1988), pp. 273–281.

Whiteley, Paul, Seyd, Pat and Richardson, Jeremy. *True Blues: The Politics of Conservative Party Members* (Oxford, Oxford University Press, 1994).

Widdicombe, D. *The Widdicombe Report: Conduct of Local Authority Business* (London, HMSO, 1986).

Willey, Fred. *The Honourable Member* (London, Sheldon Press, 1974).

Williams, Philip. 'The MP's Personal Vote', *Parliamentary Affairs*, 20 (1966), pp. 23–30.

Williams, Robert J. 'Candidate Selection', in H. R. Penniman *Canada at the Polls, 1979, 1980* (Washington DC, AEI, 1981).

Williams, Shirley and Lascher, Edward L. *Ambition and Beyond: Career Paths of American Politicians* (Berkeley CA: University of California Press, 1993).

Wyatt, Woodrow. *Turn Again Westminster* (London, Andre Deutsch, 1973).

Young, Alison. *The Reselection of MPs* (London, Heinemann, London, 1983).

Index